D1736176

PARADOXES OF TRADITIONAL CHINESE LITERATURE

Paradoxes of Traditional Chinese Literature

Edited by
Eva Hung

With an introduction by
Robert E. Hegel

The Chinese University Press

ISBN 962–201–594–8

THE CHINESE UNIVERSITY PRESS
The Chinese University of Hong Kong
SHATIN, N.T., HONG KONG

Printed in Hong Kong by Nam Fung Printing Co. Ltd.

Contents

Acknowledgements

This volume of articles has as its origin a conference entitled "Paradox of Virtue: An Investigation of Chinese Morality as Reflected in Traditional Literature" convened by Joseph S. M. Lau and Eva Hung in April 1989 under the sponsorship of the Institute of Chinese Studies, The Chinese University of Hong Kong.

The idea for the conference was first raised by Professor Joseph Lau who, because of his commitment to various other projects, found it impossible to be involved more actively in the editing of this volume. On behalf of all those who participated in the conference, the editor would like to give a vote of thanks to Professor Lau.

The Editor would also like to express her gratitude to all the contributors for their help in the preparation of this volume, and to Professors Leo Ou-fan Lee and Wang Ch'iu-kuei, whose role as commentators at the conference was much appreciated by all the particpants. To Professor Robert Hegel, who has provided a truly stimulating introduction, the editor is deeply grateful. Thanks is also due to Mrs Franciose Parkin for her expert preparation of the index.

E.H.
Research Centre for Translation,
The Chinese University of Hong Kong,
August 1993.

Contributors

GLEN DUDBRIDGE received his B.A. degree in Chinese from Cambridge University in 1962 and his Ph.D. from Oxford University, where he is now Professor of Chinese. He is the author of *The Hsi-yu Chi: A Study of Antecedents of the Sixteenth Century Novel, The Tale of Li Wa: Study and Critical Edition of a Chinese Story from the Ninth Century,* and *The Legend of Miao-shan.*

ROBERT E. HEGEL is Professor of Chinese at the University of Washington. His works include *Expressions of Self in Chinese Literature* and *The Novel in Seventeenth Century China.*

WILT L. IDEMA is Professor of Chinese Literature at Leiden University. He is the author of *Chinese Vernacular Fiction, the Formative Period, The Dramatic Oeuvre of Chu Yu-tun (1379–1439),* and co-editor and co-translator (with Stephen West) of *The Moon and the Zither: The Story of the Western Wing.*

KARL S. Y. KAO received his Ph.D. in Comparative Literature from the University of Wisconsin, Madison. He now teaches in the Department of Comparative Literature and Film Studies and the Department of East Asian Languages and Literatures, University of Alberta, Canada.

WILLIAM H. NIENHAUSER, Jr. is Professor of Chinese Literature at the University of Wisconsin. His publications include several books on Tang Dynasty literature and *The Indiana Companion to Traditional Chinese Literature.* Currently he is directing a team translating and annotating Sima Qian's *Shi ji.*

ANDREW H. PLAKS received his Ph.D. from Princeton University and is presently Professor of East Asian Studies at Princeton University. His many publications in the field of traditional Chinese fiction include *Archetype and Allegory in the Dream of the Red Chamber* and *The Four*

Masterworks of the Ming Novel. He is also the editor of *Chinese Narrative: Critical and Theoretical Essays* and a contributor to *How to Read the Chinese Novel* (edited by David L. Rolston). He is currently engaged in work on a compilation of traditional criticism on the *Dream of the Red Chamber.*

DAVID D. W. WANG is Associate Professor of Chinese at Columbia University. He is co-author (with Ellen Widmer) of *From May Fourth to June Fourth: Fiction and Film in Twentieth Century China*, and (with Jeanne Tai) of *Running Wild: China's New Writers.*

STEPHEN H. WEST is Professor of East Asian Languages at the University of California, Berkeley. He is currently Director of the University of California Centre in China, Peking University, Beijing. His recent works include, in collaboration with Wilt Idema, *The Moon and the Zither: The Story of the Western Wing.*

ELLEN WIDMER teaches Chinese Literature at Weslyan University. She is the author of *The Margins of Utopia: Shui-hu hou-chuan and the Literature of Ming Loyalism* and co-editor (with David Wang) of *From May Fourth to June Fourth: Fiction and Film in Twentieth Century China.*

HENRY Y. H. ZHAO is senior lecturer in Modern Chinese Literature at the School of Oriental and African Studies, University of London. He has published extensively on Chinese literature while writing fiction and poetry in Chinese himself. His recent book on the history of Chinese fiction is being published by the Oxford University Press.

Introduction

Robert E. Hegel

Paradoxes and Chinese Literature: General Observations

Paradoxes are hardly limited to cases such as the Cretan who declared that all natives of his island were incapable of telling the truth; incongruities and apparently mutually contradictory propositions are endemic throughout the spectrum of human knowledge. Light behaves as both particles and waves; this logically impossible duality has long been accepted in the physical sciences. One senior science writer describes the inescapable paradoxes inherent in quantum physics as follows:

> Photons, neutrons and even whole atoms act sometimes like waves, sometimes like particles, but they actually have no definite form until they are measured. Measurements, once made, can also be erased, altering the outcome of an experiment that has already occurred. A measurement of one quantum entity can instantaneously influence another far away.[1]

Physicists are thus confronted with a considerable challenge: how can they measure, thus understand, phenomena without drawing irrevocably distorted conclusions?

Another set of paradoxes confronts social scientists. The controversy surrounding the classic cultural studies by Margaret Mead are a case in point. Long heralded as a pioneer in anthropological field research, certain of her conclusions have not been substantiated by later investigators. Her inaccuracies apparently stem from the questions she asked of her subjects — questions that were relevant to *her* culture but not to *theirs*. Some of the reasons behind the answers they gave her are perhaps obvious, others undoubtedly not so to people from other cultures. That the ethnographer must not record her own values is equally obvious, but it involves a paradoxical situation: just by her *presence* — even before she begins her interviews — the anthropologist modifies the behaviour, hence the apparent values and practices, of the people she studies. A further conundrum arises in the *recording* of the data the researcher observes. James Clifford explains persuasively how the interpretive ethnographer necessarily "fashions" or even "makes up" the culture she describes, introducing a "degree of falsehood" by privileging certain voices and silencing others, particularly when deciding — necessarily — that some data are irrelevant.[2]

Moreover, paradoxes abound in less specialized areas of human inquiry. Seemingly impossible or mutually exclusive propositions and actions confront us in the public realms of politics, art, and religion in addition to the more private domain of personal behaviour. How often can we find examples of nations that negotiate for peace while preparing constantly for war, religions that preach brotherhood and practise intolerance, art that deceives the eye as well as the mind — and at least in the latter case, we humans take delight in these contradictions. Certainly there is no human artifact more fraught with elements that contrast sharply with common sense and expectations than literature. The extremes of heroism, of villainy, of seductiveness, or of strength, the heights of inspiration that utterly elude the bulk of our species — all of these common features are taken for granted in literature with the "willing suspension of disbelief" and conventions of reading that celebrate artifice and lay logical niceties quietly aside.

Paradoxes exist in art; their appearance in daily life is hardly more troubling. Humanity has always been able to ignore them or to fabricate a theoretical explanation for them. However, many of the "paradoxes" of one age — such as the perceived retrograde motion of the planets — are easily understood when new information is supplied to explain why *apparently* contradictory phenomena are in fact not so. Probably no area of human activity is so fraught with conclusions that seem to contradict each other than literary research and criticism: scholars must necessarily deal in paradoxology as they uncover new information, new insights that conflict with received wisdom about their subjects. Without a regular supply of "paradoxes" to spur further reading, literary study might hold little charm. In fact, the number and profundity of unexpected observations they accumulate are one basis on which junior members of the academic profession are adjudged qualified for promotion or permanent employment in many institutions of higher learning; one may not have run the gauntlet successfully unless one has exposed paradoxes and has contradicted generally held propositions about the field or of certain works within it.

Students of Chinese literature regularly deal with a body of writing so vast that no one can ever really claim competence in all of its periods and forms: any human life that also encompasses raising a family, earning a living, sleeping, political activity, and otherwise behaving as a social being can scarcely accommodate reading more than a fraction of the whole. Generalizations thus must necessarily be made only on the portion that an individual has read or with which one is familiar. The study of Chinese writing is fraught with paradoxicality as a consequence: as it becomes ever more thoroughly investigated, this literature will inevitably yield ever new insights into its methods and its meaning, engendering conclusions that are contradictory to commonly accepted opinions about how to read it and what it means.

Students of Chinese literature are no more paradoxicians than scholars of other fields; we live in an era of scholarly activity so intense that libraries are swamped with material in virtually every subject area currently known to humankind. (Of course new fields, in the sciences in particular, are being developed constantly.) The international group of scholars who gathered at The Chinese University of Hong Kong in April of 1989 were invited to present papers on paradoxes in Chinese literature, and without exception, all participants proved to be paradoxigraphical in inclination. The organizers of this small conference, Professor Joseph S. M. Lau of the University of Wisconsin in the United States and Dr. Eva Hung of the Research Centre for Translation at The Chinese University of Hong Kong, specifically asked that we address situations in Chinese literature when virtue does not bring appropriate rewards or when vice goes unpunished. While the conveners did not phrase it so bluntly, they apparently sought, among other topics, the participants' observations on fictional situations that most closely approximate the inequities of real life and human history. (The conference concluded just before the death of the reformist Chinese leader Hu Yaobang, memorial services for whom led to the widespread but unanticipated demonstrations so violently terminated on June Fourth of that year.)

What this group of scholars addressed on that occasion and in the papers that follow was a very broad range of paradoxes, advancing conclusions that answer a variety of perplexing questions and others that seemingly contradict certain commonly accepted views of Chinese literature. If one were to make a single comment about all of these presentations, it would be that their readings are more complicated than those of earlier scholarship; thus these papers advance our field as surely as do research reports in the sciences that propose new analytical methods or announce new materials to be studied.

It is hardly paradoxical that the conference was successful in this regard. Armed with the methodologies of other disciplines or of the study of other literatures — or through new comparisons and broader fields of concern, expanding the literary and cultural contexts for the works under scrutiny — panelists broke new ground in areas of Chinese fiction and drama considered already well studied. They utilized a variety of analytical paradigms. Their papers offer insightful new findings concerning literary conventions of both writing and reading, literary relations, both inter–textual and between different artistic forms and social classes, and of literary values, whether implicit or manifest in individual works of art. All of these essays deal with narratives, either fiction or drama or both. Their temporal range is more than a millennium, from the middle of the Tang through the end of the Qing period. All assume that literary works are polysemous; they posit questions that entail unexpected conclusions. For example: What is the meaning of the rampant sexuality of certain Tang period female characters? What were the motivations of the famous Ying-ying 鶯鶯 ? To what extent does literati writing draw upon popular narra-tives for its material? What is the nature of the relationships between major Chinese novels? Why do their protagonists sometimes behave in ways that display mutually contradictory values? Not surprisingly, many of these scholars are concerned with issues of gender, status, and personal integrity as revealed in Chinese narratives; most also confront our still sketchy knowledge of conventional practice and the implicit values that might well have been obvious to the intended readers of these texts. Many pose questions never raised before: comparative study, particularly of works from different periods or of contrastive literary forms within the spectrum of Chinese literature, allows new and intriguing possibilities for explica-tion.

To use the analogy of quantum physics one last time, Princeton scien-tist John A. Wheeler suggests that certain phenomena may be neither particles nor waves but are "intrinsically undefined until the moment they are measured". He further proposes that reality may be "defined by the questions we put to it".[3] This observation can hardly be less true of the study of literature; the questions we ask distinguish, if not designate, the object of our endeavour. Many paradoxes in Chinese literature must be defined before they can be observed; in fact, the scholar must, to at least some degree, *create* the question through one's interaction with the chosen texts. But the obvious fact that all readings are contingent in no way lessens the value of essays that are perceptive and persuasive, that reveal ever more art in the writings we study. These readings carry the imprint of late twentieth-century humanistic scholarship in breadth, depth and degree of critical acumen — with its own set of inherent paradoxes. A brief introduction to each of these papers follows.

Readers' Expectations and Contradictory Evidence

In "Female Sexuality and the Double Standard in Tang Narratives", William H. Nienhauser, Jr. takes up the surprising presentation of female sexuality in several Tang period prose narratives. A chaste wife, once seduced, becomes insatiable in her sexual desire and a poetic young man becomes so deranged that he confuses apparent opposites with each other, specifically the pleasures of life with physical corruption; overwhelming desire figures prominently in the second story as well. But by contrasting these tales with the better known *Li Wa zhuan* 李娃傳, *Yingying zhuan* 鶯鶯傳, and *Youxian ku* 遊仙窟, Nienhauser demonstrates what should have been obvious but was not: these stories project in various guises the same set of male values concerning women. All present strategies for the containment of female sexuality, which is seen as a threat to the men who wrote and read these tales.

Stephen H. West and Wilt L. Idema take up the enigmatic character of Yingying in the earliest extant version of the *Xixiang ji* 西廂記 plays. In this fullest (and most fully illustrated) rendition of the Tang *chuanqi* story, the heroine is at her most contradictory: she is filial, chaste, and shy while, at least at key moments, she also abandons herself in reckless pursuit of gratification for her romantic feelings. West and Idema find explanations for these mutually contradictory traits both in the received character and in the stage conventions which she is adapted to fit. Recognizing in this portrayal male fears of the intoxicating and dangerous female sexuality identified by Nienhauser, the two authors note that Yingying is portrayed in a *huadan* 花旦 or coquette role category in the play. Likewise, the relationship between Yingying, her lover Zhang 張生, and her mother parallels the conventional combination of courtesan, student, and madam; elements suggestive of earlier stories based on this triangle are to be found here, including the seductiveness of the young woman and the "transactional" nature of the exchanges between Yingying and her mother. Yet the

Xixiang ji seductress is just emerging from adolescence. Her diffidence and passion seemingly reflect the duality within this character, the awareness of transition from maidenhood to maturity during which both stages paradoxically coexist.

The Tang tale of Liu Yi 柳毅 and the Dragon King's daughter, Glen Dudbridge demonstrates, has a complex history through which the elements of the story have separate careers and distinguishable meanings. Its layers of narrative material each carry moral or ethical value; in their earlier appearances they demonstrated conventional understandings of *bao* 報 (reciprocity), *xin* 信 (trustworthiness), and the like. But in Li Chaowei's 李朝威 redaction, the original balance between good deeds and appropriate recompense has been thrown askew; some acts and responses even stand in contradictory relation to each other when contrasted with their original manifestations. Dudbridge concludes that these variations relate to the aim of clarifying higher ethical standards, particularly the role of individual conscience, here of Liu Yi, in the face of pressures and attractions from others. Undoubtedly these new twists on old themes would amuse sophisticated Tang period readers well practised in discerning intertextual references and who would appreciate its paradoxical distortions of traditional story elements.

Y. H. Zhao spread his net even more widely, to bring in three diverging adaptations of the "White Rabbit" tale, a portion of the life of the tenth-century founder of the Later Han dynasty Liu Zhiyuan 劉智遠. His versions date from the 1470s, the 1590s and the 1630s; they are intended for quite different audiences and reflect yet older redactions that are no longer extant. Unexpectedly, all three reflect their common origins in what Zhao terms "subcultural" texts, stories that circulated among China's masses who were innocent of the high "culture" of China's literati. Zhao concludes, as others had earlier through less sophisticated methodology,[4] that the culturally less complex texts are informed most fully by those conventional moral values nominally identified with the ruling class. He also demonstrates, unexpectedly, that certain elite texts are simplified from received popular materials in order to delete the morally irrelevant or disruptive elements typical of mass entertainments, thus imparting a greater degree of ethical — and thematic — coherence. By contrast, later anthologies of selected segments for literati readers generally expand these popular versions while implicitly referring to the ethical context supplied by the broad reading in literature and history of their intended audience.

While comparisons of the great Ming novel *Jin Ping Mei* 金瓶梅 with the greatest of Qing novels *Honglou meng* 紅樓夢 are becoming ever more common and productive, Andrew H. Plaks has found a startling angle from which to compare the two. He has taken up the theme of incest, itself an infrequent subject for Chinese writers. In the earlier novel, incest functions symbolically as one example of the general social chaos that it portrays so graphically. But it is the central male figures of the two novels that have the most in common: both Ximen Qing 西門慶 and Jia Baoyu 賈寶玉 embody the morally dubious illusion of self-containment. In an era during which the mutually contradictory statements of the canonical *Daxue* 大學 concerning self-involvement and engagement with society were officially espoused by the Neo-Confucian state, self-love, self-satisfaction, even self-concern were potentially if not actually socially destructive. Such concerns with self are cloaked with the language of incest and symbolically equated with that most deadly of sins in both novels as a means to suggest the magnitude of the dangers presented by personal involution. By pursuing this anomalous parallel between the two classic novels, Plaks has brought into existence an aspect of *Honglou meng* that may have lain undetected because it was potentially so threatening to its intended readers.

In my own paper for this volume I address the internal contradictions and disjunctions in several Ming and Qing novels that have puzzled earlier analysts. In particular, how can such noble characters as Qin Shubao 秦叔寶 from *Sui shi yiwen* 隋史遺文 change so dramatically from being fools to resourceful leaders of men? How can Qin Keqing 秦可卿 in *Honglou meng* shift roles from house-wrecker to a wellspring of domestic good advice? Why is *Honglou meng* filled with so many internal inconsistencies? To answer these questions I review conventions of writing in extended narratives and discover deliberate attempts to subvert those conventions in innovative ways that expand the scope and depth of meaning in literati fiction.

In her essay "Tragedy or Travesty?" Ellen Widmer compares stories in the seventeenth-century collection of short fiction *Shi dian tou* 石點頭 with stories in the *Sanyan* 三言 collections that can be identified with the author known as Langxian 浪仙 . She begins with a story that brings only a hollow victory, deification, for a woman who boldly sacrifices herself for the benefit of her husband and his mother. The story is disturbing at first reading, but Widmer sensitively explores its implicit values to discover, when she investigates the entire corpus of Langxian stories, that these are distinctive. When compared with the conventions in others of that period and with contemporary social attitudes, Langxian stories focus on self-mutilation and strong-willed women in particular. Not surprisingly, Widmer unravels initially incongruous elements in this fiction to reveal male attitudes toward females suggestive of continuities from the male apprehensions William Nienhauser discovered in narratives of the Tang.

Karl Kao begins his study by observing that the very existence of *Liaozhai zhiyi* 聊齋誌異 is surprising: it represents the revival of narrative forms from the Six Dynasties and Tang periods that had fallen out of favour with China's writers long before the Qing. But Pu Songling's 蒲松齡 collection is not simply a continuation of earlier genres: his writings involve a "new kind of strangeness aesthetics" in which the author manipulates the mental associations of the images and situations he writes about. However, Pu also indulged in "literary wit and male fantasies", paradoxical elements that demand a more complicated reading than his predecessors of the Tang or before. What Kao uncovers in *Liaozhai* narratives is a very self-conscious use of irony in the manipulation of conventions, both of fiction and of history. Moreover, his use of "authorial" commentaries at the end of stories (attributed to Yishi shi 異史氏, a pen-name that suggests he was a historian) do allow the author a second voice with which to discuss his material. Yet the interpretations so provided are only partial, tending toward simplistic moralistic readings, Kao observes; in effect they are subversive of current conventions of reading. Other examples of Pu Songling's sophisticated literary play are to be found throughout the collection when his stories are recognized as art rather than merely the social commentary earlier critics frequently have discerned.

David Wang's study of three late Qing period novels devoted to courtesans and other "female" entertainers provides new entries for reading and decoding their conventions. The anomalous situation in the 1852 novel *Pinhua baojian* 品花寶鑑 of having opera singers (female impersonators) cast in the role of "beauties" for its "scholars" is a product of women's real social position in the formation of romantic conventions, Wang points out: the homosexual lovers simply exemplify the clichéd attributes of the ideal female in the eyes of the novel's male readers — and that are embodied in the conventional female heroines of other love stories. Thus characterization in this novel is not ironic as one might expect. Wang compares it with *Haishang hua* 海上花 which self-consciously demolishes the conventions of courtesan fiction: all of these later characters know that they are playing roles. (One is reminded of Li Yu's story of the "male Mencius' mother" in this regard.[5]) In fact, *Haishang hua* pointedly exposes the myths inherent in conventions of reading at that time. *Niehai hua* 孽海花 to an even greater extent problematizes all social and literary assumptions concerning virtue and heroism by presenting a morally corrupt woman as the heroine of her new age, thus demanding a more complicated reading than any usual courtesan tale might warrant.

The sum of these readings is hardly paradoxical: one might hope and expect to have a new or refreshed understanding of Chinese literature from such a far-ranging group of essays. This is precisely their effect. Ellen Widmer proves the importance of reading very broadly, both the collected works and the works of contemporaries, before one draws conclusions about a writer; Glen Dudbridge similarly establishes the necessity of reading the historical antecedents for a piece of writing, an approach he utilized to great advantage in his previous studies of *Xiyou ji* 西遊記 and the story of Li Wa. Y. H. Zhao exposes the predilections of literati writers by contrasting their concern with logical and ethical structures in narrative against the seeming anarchy of characterization and theme in more popular texts. The self-conscious artistry inherent in literati authors' experimentation with conventions, their deliberate use of irony and parody, the imaginative literary games they played with received materials and practices are explored in papers by Karl Kao and David Wang. The fact that all writers examined here were men and thus bore the baggage of male attitudes toward women has been explored with sensitivity by West and Idema, by Nienhauser, by Widmer, and by Wang. Apparent discontinuities and conflicting values have been identified and explained through these nuanced readings. Andrew Plaks' courageous investigation of the theme of incest in many ways typifies this collection of essays and of innovative humanistic scholarship in general. On the basis of extensive and careful reading of the literary, intellectual, cultural, and social contexts for two of China's major novels, he has accomplished what he himself has considered a paradoxical feat.[6] Although an "outsider" to Chinese tradition whose readings are contingent on values and experiences quite alien to the novels' original readers, he has asked a new and yet obvious question about the implications of Baoyu's self-absorption. And by redefining Baoyu's relationship to himself, Plaks has once again complicated our reading of *Honglou meng*. Surely his paper, and the others in this volume, will encourage further attempts to fathom the masterworks — and the lesser writings — of Chinese tradition whose intrinsic complexities will ever invite and yet evade the precise, rational analyses espoused by the physical sciences. Like the effect of the magnifying lenses on human knowledge of the nature of matter and our environment, ever closer, ever more focussed

— and ever broader, ever more thorough — readings of China's literary texts will continue to yield degrees and types of understanding undreamed of before some of these paradoxes were proposed.

Notes

1. John Horgan, "Quantum Philosophy", *Scientific American,* Vol. 267, No. 1 (July 1992), p. 96.
2. James Clifford, "Introduction: Partial Truths", *Writing Culture: The Poetics and Politics of Ethnography*, edited by James Clifford and George E. Marcus (Berkeley: University of California Press, 1986), p. 6. Clifford provides a pointed survey of attitudes toward recent self-criticisms in the field here, including the relative empowerment of the "indigenous enthnographer"; compare Andrew Plaks' apologia cited in note 6 below.
3. Horgan, pp. 97, 101.
4. See, for example, my "Distinguishing Levels of Audiences for Ming-Ch'ing Vernacular Literature: A Case Study", *Popular Culture in Late Imperial China*, edited by David Johnson, Andrew J. Nathan and Evelyn S. Rawski (Berkeley: University of California Press, 1985), pp. 112–142. Zhao cites a number of studies of English cultural history for parallels, but one would need to look no further than the extensive campaigns in Yan'an and during subsequent periods of Chinese Communist Party control to rid popular theatrical and art forms of the pernicious traditional values they so thoroughly embodied.
5. See the sixth story in Li Yu's (1610–1680) *Wusheng xi* collection, "Nan Mengmu jiaohe sanqian", translated by Gopal Sukhu and Patrick Hanan in *Silent Operas*, edited by Patrick Hanan (Hong Kong: Renditions Paperbacks, 1990), pp. 97–134.
6. See Andrew H. Plaks, *The Four Masterworks of the Ming Novel: Ssu ta ch'i-shu* (Princeton: Princeton University Press, 1987), p. xi.

1

Female Sexuality and the Double Standard in Tang Narratives: A Preliminary Survey

William H. Nienhauser, Jr.

Prologue: The Exceptions

I would like to begin with a story:

> Hejian was a lewd woman. I don't want to disclose her identity, so I've called her after her district. In the beginning, she lived in Relatives' Village[1] and was very virtuous. Even before she married, she abhorred the disorderly behaviour of her relatives and deemed it a disgrace to be associated with them. She remained discreetly in her quarters and attended to her dress designs, spinning, weaving and knitting.
>
> When she married, her father-in-law was already dead, so she served her mother-in-law most respectfully. She never talked about anything that happened outside her house. She was properly reverential to her husband, and they treated one another like host and guest, sharing each other's very thoughts.
>
> Those of her relatives who were up to no good got together and plotted against her, asking, "What can we do about Hejian?" The worst amongst them said, "We must try to corrupt her." They agreed on a plan, after which they took a carriage, and as a group called on her. They invited her to go out and enjoy herself with them, flattering her: "Since you came here, the people of Relatives' Village have all been encouraged to cultivate and restrain themselves day and night. When they have committed even a slight misdemeanour they are afraid of people hearing of it. Now we want to improve on our former behaviour by emulating your propriety. We want to observe your proper bearing so that morning and night we may be watchful of our own."
>
> Hejian firmly declined the offer, but her mother-in-law said angrily, "They have come with compliments to have you become their teacher. Why did you reject them so strongly?" "I have heard," Hejian replied, "that the

way a woman should behave is to be pure, obedient, quiet, and loyal. To show off fancy carriages, exhibit costumes and jewellery, and go out in a group to make merry, to eat, drink and gad about are not proper for a woman." Her mother-in-law urged her, and she finally consented and went with the group.

As they passed the market, someone said: "A little south of here, we'll enter a Buddhist temple. There Old Wu, a painter known throughout the nation, has just painted the southeastern wall. These paintings are very uncanny.[2] We can have the groom clear the way so we can go in to look at them." After they had finished viewing, Hejian was invited to take the seat of honour, and food was spread out beside a curtained bed. Suddenly, she heard a man's cough. She was so frightened that she ran out without her shoes. Thereupon, she ordered an attendant to take her home post-haste in a carriage. She wept for several days, and thereafter she confined herself even more to her own house, refusing to have anything to do with her relatives.

Then they came to offer their apologies, saying, "Why were you so rash? Are you blaming us, because of our previous behaviour? The man who coughed that day was only a kitchen hand."

"But why did several people laugh near the door?" she asked. Upon hearing this, the relatives withdrew.

It was not until a whole year later that the relatives dared call on Hejian's mother-in-law again to invite Hejian out through her, knowing she would be sure to make her go with them. Then they went to a place between two ponds in a temple at Feng River.[3] They knocked at the animal pen, and fish and turtles were brought out to feed.[4] Hejian smiled, and her companions were pleased. She was soon led to a dining-room without any curtains where the corridors were open and spacious. Hejian consented to enter this room. Earlier, a number of wicked youths had been secreted in the wall under the northern window.[5] Then the curtain was let down and some girls were ordered to play Qin music.[6] Hejian and the others squatted down to watch them.

Shortly afterward, from among those secreted in the wall, one pre-selected because of his good looks and large organ emerged to take care of Hejian.[7] Then he embraced her. She screamed and cried and female servants held her between them, trying to get her to see the benefits it would bring her or scolding and making fun of her. Hejian stole a glance at the man who had her in his arms and found him very handsome. Those around her indulging in wicked behaviour were enjoying themselves more and more, breathing heavily, so that she could not avoid being aroused, and, as she relaxed her resistance a little, her adversary had his way with her. Then he led her off to a separate room. Hejian stopped crying and began to feel very good, congratulating herself on what she had never experienced before.

When dinner was being served toward evening and she was called to partake of it, she said, "I'm not going to eat." Later, as the carriage was harnessed they warned her they were going back, but Hejian said, "I am not going back. I won't be parted from this man until I die." Her relatives were at a great loss and they had no alternative but to stay there overnight.

Hejian's husband came to fetch her home, but he did not get to see her. The next day when those about her insisted, she consented to go home. As she left she grabbed that dissolute man and cried bitterly. She swore eternal loyalty and bit his arm.[8] On her arrival home, she could not bear to look at her husband. Keeping her eyes closed, she said, "I am sick." He gave her all kinds of food, but she refused to eat. He fed her good medicine, but she waved it away. She was as tense as a string on a lute. Whenever her husband came near her, she scolded him severely. She never opened her eyes, and became more and more resentful of him. The distress was more than the husband could stand. "I am so sick that I shall soon die!" she said several days later. "I cannot possibly be cured by medicine; summon a spirit to get me released from this condition, but it must be by night."

Since Hejian had become sick, she raved like a lunatic and her husband racked his brains to find a way to please her. She reckoned that he was prepared to go to any lengths. At that time the Emperor abhorred the practice of praying to spirits at night, but the husband was prepared to try it. When the utensils were all arranged for the ceremony, Hejian ordered the local officials to accuse her husband of attempting to summon spirits to bring evil to others. Officials of various ranks looked into the matter and the husband was beaten with the bamboo until he died. Even when he was on the point of death, he cried, "I have failed my wife! I have failed my wife!"

Hejian was greatly pleased and did not mourn for her husband. She opened her door and sent for the man with whom she had acted lasciviously. Chasing about naked, they lost themselves in drinking and sex. But, after the lapse of a year, the man showed signs of flagging. She became bored with him, and drove him out.

Then she called together a group of good-for-nothings from Chang'an, and they engaged in orgies day and night in her home. Still not satisfied, she set up a wine shop at the southwestern corner of the house and stayed upstairs herself to spy on customers. She had a small door cut and sought to attract passers-by, using young servant girls as bait. Of the men who went in to drink, she chose only those with big noses, the robust, the young and the handsome, and those most frolicsome during wine games, to be taken upstairs to give her satisfaction. As they coupled, she would keep an eye to the door, lest she miss even one man. And yet daily she sighed dreamily, thereby showing her appetites to be still unsatiated.

After more than a decade of dissipation, she was exhausted; her bones began to dry up,[9] and she soon died. Thereafter, even those in Relatives'

Village who led an immoral life would wince whenever the name of Hejian was mentioned. No one cared to talk about her.

Mr. Liu comments: "Of the scholars of the world, who can compare in virtue and purity with Hejian when she first became a wife? Of friends who are said to have admired one another, is there any who can be as close as Hejian was to her husband? Once she succumbed to force, she became convinced of the pleasure, and returned home even to oppose her husband, treating him like a robber and an enemy. She could not bear to see his face and finally plotted his death, not grieving for him for a moment. Can those, then, who are joined together by affection and love be free from the evil influence of self-interest? Indeed, enough for us to know that mutual affection is something difficult to rely upon. Since this is certainly true of friends, is it not even more terrifying in the relationships between a ruler and his subjects? I have therefore taken the liberty to enumerate these events."[10]

This tale may seem to some to be a variation of a modern movie script, but it is actually from the pen of Liu Zongyuan 柳宗元 (773–819), entitled *Hejian zhuan* 河間傳 (An Account of Hejian). Although the basic story commands our attention, in his commentary Liu points us to a metaphoric understanding of the text. If the love of husband and wife, one of the basic relations of Chinese society, can be so tenuous, is not the relationship between ruler and subject even more precarious? Traditional commentators have followed Liu's lead to read this work into the context of his involvement with the Wang Shuwen 王叔文 (753–805) clique and his resultant alienation from Emperor Xian Zong 憲宗 (r. 806–820).[11] Such a topical reading, however, threatens to break down under the excessive detail of the story at the literal level. Moreover, the lurid and lengthy account of Hejian's sexual excesses recall our attention to the basic story line.

Indeed, for an allegorical attack a single instance of infidelity would have sufficed. But Liu Zongyuan leads us further in a description of the pleasure Hejian derives from the seduction:

> Hejian stopped crying and began to feel very good, congratulating herself on what she had never experienced before.

This is certainly enough to shock any Tang reader. But Liu was not yet satisfied. Subsequently he catalogues Hejian's murderous plot and unlicensed sexual voracity, perhaps best summarized in her "keep[ing] an eye to the door" while she was copulating upstairs, "lest she miss even one man" below in the wineshop.

Although we must admit the possibility of a topical, allegorical reference, it is of little significance to the modern reader. After all, we know from other texts that Liu felt betrayed by Wang Shuwen and his colleagues in the clique. The significance of this text for us is, therefore, the obsessive intensity of the passion with which Liu condemns Hejian, whomever she may represent. And of especial interest for this study is his decision to adopt female sexuality as the vehicle for this assault.

"The Account of Hejian" is not, however, Liu Zongyuan's only attempt to portray the power of female sexuality. His *Li Chi zhuan* 李赤傳 (An Account of Red Li), to which we now turn, is another example:

Red Li was one who wandered the lakes and rivers.[12] He once said, "I am good at writing poetry comparable to that of Li Bai ['White' Li]." Therefore, he gave himself the name "Red" Li.

He paid a visit to Xuanzhou where the local people gave him lodgings. One of those who was travelling with him had an in-law there. After several days he came to join Red at his lodgings. Red was just then speaking to a woman and his friend teased him about this. Red replied, "She proposed to me — I am going to marry her." The friend was astonished and said, "You, sir, have a wife in good health and your own mother is still alive.[13] How could this take place? Can it be that you are deranged or deluded?"

The friend then took some "crimson snow"[14] to feed him, but Red refused to take it. Presently the woman came back and spoke with Red. Then she took a scarf and began to strangle him. Red himself helped her, using both hands, until his tongue hung completely out. His friend called out and saved him. The woman let the scarf loose and ran off. "Why did you do that?!" Red said to his friend angrily. "I was going to be with my wife. How could you?"

He then went to the window, wrote a letter, rolled it up, and sealed it. He wrote another letter and sealed it in the regular manner.[15] When he finished, he went to the privy, and stayed there a long time. His friend followed him and saw Red leaning into the privy embracing the opening.[16] He was chuckling weirdly and, looking to the side, was about to descend into it. The friend entered and dragged him out upside down. Again Red reacted in great furore, "I had already entered the hall and faced my wife. Her appearance can't be matched anywhere in the world. The decorations of her hall are grand, ornate, and richly beautiful, and an air of pepper and orchids arises there profusely.[17] Looking back at your world it is like a privy to me, while the residence of my wife can't be distinguished from the Heavenly Emperor's in the Celestial City. Why then do you keep causing me to suffer so?"

Only then did his friend know that what Red had encountered was none other than the privy ghost. He gathered the servants and they agreed on a plan:

they must immediately get away from this privy. They travelled ten miles away to spend the night. During the night Red again went to the privy. After some time, they followed him and found that he had gone in again. They lifted him out, washing off the filth, and kept watch around him until dawn. Then they left for another county. The county officials were in the midst of a banquet when they arrived. Red paid his respects to them, showing no sign of his previous strange behaviour. Wine was passed around and before his friend could say anything they all drank a toast, then he looked for Red, but he had already gone. He ran after him. Red had entered the privy and raised up a bench to block the door so that no one else could get in. His friend called out and told the others the situation. They dismantled the walls and entered. Half of Red's face had already sunk into the excrement. Again they brought him out and washed him.

The county officials then summoned a shaman who was skilled in charms to watch Red. Red's appearance was normal. Midway through the night those who were watching him tired and fell asleep. When they awoke, they called to him and went to look for him. They saw his feet outside the privy. Red had been dead for some time. They could only take his corpse and return it to his home. When they read the letters he had written, they found that they were farewells to his mother and wife. His words were like those of a normal person.

Mr. Liu comments: "The Account of Red Li" is no falsehood. Was it his sick psyche which caused this, or was there indeed a privy ghost? Red's reputation is known throughout the rivers and lakes. In the beginning he was a scholar, no different from any other man. Once deluded by the uncanny, he became like this, rejecting the world as a cesspool and seeing in a cesspool the Celestial City of the Heavenly Emperor. The significance of this is clear. We of the present generation know only to laugh at Red's delusion. But when we reach the point when we must decide what is right and what is wrong, what to take and what to give, what to face and what to turn our backs on, there are few who would not be like Red. It would be fortunate indeed to discipline oneself so that one's mind will not be changed by fondness for the loathsome or by desire for profit! How can people find the time to laugh at Red?[18]

There is an analogue to this tale which was collected in the late ninth-century *Duyi zhi* 獨異志 (Records of the Uniquely Unusual),[19] which may also have been Liu's source.[20] In it the story is told more simply in about a third of the six-hundred characters Liu used. Thus although the sexuality of the privy goddess — an adaptation of Zigu 紫姑 (Miss Purple) — is not as great as that of Hejian, we can see through a comparison of the *Duyi zhi* version with that of Liu that this sexuality has been added by Liu Zong-yuan. The attempted strangulation is the most overt expression of the goddess' urges, but we can see suggestions of it in the intimate conversation she has with Red during which she proposes to him, in Red's detailed description of her private quarters, and in his generally deluded behaviour in an attempt to join her in the privy world. The key word in the passage is *huo* 惑 , "to delude". Red's friend first asks him, "Can it be that you are deranged or deluded?" (豈狂易病惑耶 ?) And Liu Zongyuan in his commentary echoes this: "Once deluded by the uncanny, he became like this, rejecting the world as a cesspool and seeing in a cesspool the Celestial City of the Heavenly Emperor" (一惑於怪，而所爲若是，及反以爲溷，溷爲帝居清都).

Further support for this interpretation of the story focussing on an inordinate, even diseased desire, can be found in the scholar Lin Shu's 林紓 (1852–1924) allegorical interpretation of this story:

> In the story of Red Li ... I venture to say that Wang Shuwen is the privy ghost, Liu Zongyuan is Red Li; when he had already fallen into the toilet, it was too late for regret.[21]

Although the reader is intended to see Liu's errors in joining Wang Shuwen's clique of over-zealous reformers as a kind of delusion, the wild actions of the privy goddess and Red Li further indicate the power female sexuality was accorded during the Tang.

Establishing the Norm

Given the sexuality expressed in the two texts examined above, and the great number of Tang narratives which focus on love affairs between young scholars and courtesans, one would expect to find numerous explicit depictions of female sexuality in these texts.

With this expectation in mind, let us turn to one of the earlier Tang narratives, the seventh-century *Youxian ku* 遊仙窟 (The Grotto of Playful Transcendents) by Zhang Zhuo 張鷟 (657–730). The tale relates how a young scholar-official travelling late in the day through a remote, mountainous region in northwest China stumbles across the home (likely in a cave) of "immortals". Encountering a maid servant washing clothes by a stream, he solicits an invitation to stay the night. When he inquires about his host, he learns that she is a woman, Ms. Cui 崔氏 . The maid then describes her mistress in shocking detail:

Her fair looks are captivating and without an equal in Heaven above. Her jade body is lithesome, and seldom matched among mortals. Her shining countenance is so fine and soft that one fears one might penetrate the skin with the merest touch. Her willowy waist flickers so that one suspects it might break in two if clasped in fond embrace.[22]

Yet the text does not immediately descend into a seamy depiction of the young man's triumphs. After he finally meets Cui Shiniang 崔十娘 (Tenth Maiden), he learns she is a widow:

The Tenth Maiden replied, "I am the last descendant of Duke Cui of Qinghe. I married the eldest son of Lord Yang of Hongnong.... My elder brother and my husband threw away their writing brushes and went forth into battle. They lost their lives on enemy fields, and their lonely souls never returned. This happened when I was seventeen; I have firmly guarded my chastity ever since. Elder Brother's wife, who was then nineteen, vowed that she would never again wed."[23]

Thus superficially at least the young man is faced with chaste widows. The widows, however, soon prove themselves more inclined to reconsider their commitments, and Elder Brother's wife subsequently offers to act as a matchmaker for the forthcoming "marriage" between the young man and Tenth Maiden. Yet prolonged flirtatious banter, the exchange of suggestive poems, and drinking and gaming, precede the night of love finally accorded the two. Here the relationship seems to be one of a courtesan and her "mother" to a customer. Once, when impatient for Tenth Maiden to reappear, the young man asks her sister, "Where has Tenth Maiden gone? Does she have an engagement with another?" (十娘何處 去，應有別人邀？)[24] as if they were all in a bordello. Moreover, the description of sexual arousal is decidedly one-sided, portraying only the young man's emotions (again such as might be expected in lovemaking with a courtesan):

By then night had long been with us and the hour was late. My love feelings became urgent, and I was filled with passion.... A flowered countenance filled my eyes; a fragrant breeze rent my nostrils. My heart departed uncontrollably and my love feelings came in irrepressibly.... One bite, and my thoughts rejoiced, one embrace, and my heart felt pained. There was a tingling ache in my nostrils and a tight constriction in my breast. My eyes soon became dazzled, my ears felt feverish, my veins filled, and my muscles slackened.[25]

Here we have only the young man's reaction to their passion. Of Tenth

Maiden's ecstasy we see nothing. In fact, Tenth Maiden is made to seem more licentious in her repartee and versifying than in her lovemaking.

A number of narratives which avoid description of the sexuality of their heroines similar to what we have seen in "The Grotto of Playful Transcendents" could be cited: the anonymous *Baiyuan zhuan* 白猿傳 (Tale of the White Monkey), Shen Jiji's 沈既濟 (c. 740–c. 800) *Renshi zhuan* 任氏傳 (Tale of Ms. Ren), Bai Xingjian's 白行間 (c. 776–c. 826) *Li Wa zhuan* 李娃傳 (Tale of Li Wa), Huangfu Mei's 皇甫枚 *Bu Feiyan* 步飛煙 and Huang Pu's 黃璞 (ninth century) *Ouyang Xingzhou zhuan* 歐陽行周傳 (An Account of Ouyang Zhan).[26] Each contains a love affair fraught with problems. And in each one of two means is used to resolve these problems, problems which can be seen as closely related to the heroine's sexuality. In the first type of resolution, where the heroine's desires continue unabated, as in *Yingying zhuan* 鶯鶯傳, *Bu Feiyan*, or *Ouyang Xingzhou zhuan*, tragedy results.[27] In the second type the heroine assumes a virtually asexual role as a dutiful wife, resolving the sexual tension. (Here I am thinking of Li Wa's transformation from courtesan to mentor or Ren Shi's conversion from seductress of Zheng Liu to a virtuous "wife" who fights off Wei Yin and advises Zheng on a number of matters.)[28]

In the cases where the sexual relations result in tragedy the woman's power to delude (*huo*) her lover is always emphasized. *Yingying zhuan* will serve as an example of this type of tale. The story depicts the relationship between a young scholar named Zhang, who has sometimes been identified with the author, Yuan Zhen 元稹 (779–831), and Yingying, the daughter of a widowed Mrs. Cui 崔氏. Zhang is an innocent, untutored in the ways of women —年二十三，未嘗近女色— who claims that he is nevertheless a "true lover":

> Dengtu Zi was no lover, but a lecher. I am the true lover — I just never happened to meet the right girl. How do I know that? It's because all things of outstanding beauty [or "all outstanding beauties"] never fail to make a permanent impression on me. That shows I am not without feelings.[29]

Yet in his search for "things of outstanding beauty" (物之尤者) the reader is forewarned of the probable appearance of a *youwu* 尤物 (outstanding creature) or *femme fatale*. Zhang falls prey to such a woman in Cui Yingying, after first meeting her at a dinner set to repay his protection of Yingying and her mother during a local mutiny:

> After a while she appeared, wearing an everyday dress and no makeup on her

smooth face, except for a remaining spot of rouge. Her hair coils straggled down to touch her eyebrows. Her beauty was extraordinary, so radiant it took the breath away. Startled, Zhang made her a deep bow as she sat down beside her mother. Because she had been forced to come out against her will, she looked angrily straight ahead, as though unable to endure the company. Zhang asked her age. Mrs. Cui said, "From the seventh month of the fifth year of the reigning emperor to the present twenty-first year, it is just sixteen years."

Zhang tried to make conversation with her, but she would not respond, and he had to leave after the meal was over. From this time on Zhang was deluded but had no way to make his feelings known to her.[30]

Again the heroine produces shock and "delusion" (*huo*) in her suitor. Yingying, however, at first resists Zhang's advances. Finally, Zhang's persistence wins her over:

Zhang sat up straight and rubbed his eyes. For some time it seemed as though he were still dreaming, but nonetheless he waited dutifully. Then there was Hongniang again, with Miss Cui leaning on her arm. She was shy and yielding, and appeared almost not to have the strength to move her limbs. The contrast with her stiff formality at their last encounter was complete.

This evening was the night of the eighteenth, and the slanting rays of the moon cast a soft light over half the bed. Zhang felt a kind of floating lightness and wondered whether this was an immortal who visited him, not someone from the world of men. After a while the temple bell sounded. Daybreak was near. As Hongniang urged her to leave, she wept softly and clung to him. Hongniang helped her up, and they left. The whole time she had not spoken a single word. With the first light of dawn Zhang got up, wondering whether it was a dream. But the perfume still lingered, and as it got lighter he could see on his arm traces of her makeup and the teardrops sparkling still on the mat.[31]

Again here, despite the captivating effect Yingying had on Zhang, she seems a passive lover — "the whole time she had not spoken a single word".

Yet their affair ends tragically. Zhang goes off to succeed in the examinations and — despite assurances to the contrary — abandons Yingying. His rationalization focuses on the belief that beautiful women can be dangerous.[32]

He [Zhang] said, "It is a general rule that those women endowed by Heaven with great beauty invariably either destroy themselves or destroy someone else. If this Cui woman were to meet someone with wealth and position, she would use the favour her charms gain her to be cloud and rain or dragon or monster — I can't imagine what she might turn into.... I have no inner strength to withstand this evil influence. That is why I have resolutely suppressed my love."[33]

Here again the supernatural power of extreme beauty is stressed. *Yao* 妖, which Hightower renders as "destroy", might better be understood as "bewitch". Yet the powers of this beauty to transform its own person or others is made clear. Indeed, although it may seem difficult for the modern reader to condone Zhang's cowardice, contemporary observers understood:

His contemporaries for the most part conceded that Zhang had done well to rectify his mistake. I have often mentioned it among friends so that, forewarned, they might avoid doing such a thing, or if they did, that they might not be deluded by it.[34]

Delusion (*huo*) lies at the basis of this relationship, too.

Challenging the Norm

Having seen that normally the depiction of physical love in Tang narratives avoids female sexuality, let us look at several texts which challenge this norm.

The first, *Feng Yan zhuan* 馮燕傳 (The Story of Feng Yan) by Shen Yazhi 沈亞之 (c. 770–c. 830), has been called a knight-errant tale,[35] but it is also a story of adultery and its dangers. Feng Yan was a heroic type in the mold of the typical *xia* 俠. The plot is set in motion by lovers spying one another through an open doorway:

When Feng was out for a stroll in the neighbourhood one day, he saw a woman in a doorway, watching him even as she veiled herself with her sleeve.[36] Her appearance was so seductive that her intentions were not to be missed, so Feng took her as a "wife". Her [actual] husband, Zhang Ying, was the garrison commander of Hua. When he heard of the affair, he beat his wife repeatedly:[37]

Nevertheless, Feng Yan returns again:

Once when Zhang had gone to drink with companions, Feng seized the opportunity to again lie in his bedchamber, blocking the door. On Zhang's return, his wife opened the door to let him in, at the same time concealing Feng behind her skirt. Feng then crouched low and tiptoed to cover. As he was turning around to hide behind the door, his kerchief fell to the pillow near Zhang's sword. Zhang was drunk and had fallen asleep. Feng pointed to the kerchief, asking the woman to get it, but she handed him the sword instead. Feng looked at her for a long time, then slit her throat, put on his kerchief and left.[38]

The woman's immorality shown in her invitation to Feng Yan by brazenly staring at him through the doorway — in a Chinese household women were expected to remain in the innermost rooms — suggests her total moral debility. When Feng intends to leave quietly, she urges him to kill her husband. The "morality" that informs Feng's act escapes many modern readers, resulting in E. D. Edwards misinterpreting the storyteller's coda as a condemnation of Feng Yan:

> "Such," concludes the author, "is the story as narrated for me to record. Would that I were writing of wholesome things! That Feng! Killing at random, and never having to pay the penalty! A bully of the old type indeed! Alas! Is not a dissolute heart more to be feared than fire and flood?"[39]

The "dissolute heart" actually belongs to Zhang Ying's wife as the following emended translation reveals:

> "I esteem the words of the Grand Historian and I am also fond of relating events in which justice and righteousness are upheld.... *Alas! A licentious, deluding mind is worse than flood or fire and certainly to be dreaded. But Feng's killing an unjust person, his exonerating an innocent man — these are truly the ways of the heroes of old!*"[40]

The offending "licentious, deluding" mind is a *yinhuo zhi xin* 淫惑之心 and here we have the strongest judgement — and sentence — for this type of woman.

Finally, let us turn to two accounts of virtuous women (*lienü* 烈女) in the dynastic histories of the Tang. The first occurs in the *Xin Tang shu* 新唐書 :[41]

> When Li the "Firmly True and Chaste Wife" was seventeen she was married to Zheng Lian. Less than a year thereafter Zheng died, and she always wore plain clothing and ate no meat. One night suddenly she dreamed that a man was seeking her hand in marriage. At first she didn't consent — later she dreamed of him many times.
>
> She began to wonder whether the dream came about because her beauty had not yet faded, so she cut off her hair, wore hempen clothing, didn't perfume or ornament herself, soiled her face and skin, and from that time on she didn't have this dream.

The prefect Bo Dawei admired her restraint, and titled her the Firmly True and Chaste Wife, displaying a pennant above their outer gate,[42] and naming the village where she lived "Chaste-wife Hamlet".

That the suppressed sexuality of a young woman married less than a year resulted in sexual dreams — for that is how we understand her plight (cf. "at first she didn't consent — later she dreamed of him many times") — is not surprising. Edward H. Schafer observes that beginning in the Tang one finds records of medical prescriptions for such nocturnal sexual fantasies.[43] Michael Strickmann cites a Taoist text, the *Yufang mijue* 玉房秘訣 (The Secret Formulae from the Jade Alcove), which seems relevant here:

> The ailment of demonic sexual relations comes about when a woman's sexual desire is so great as to cause demons and phantoms to take on human form and couple with her. They say that it is greatly superior to having intercourse with ordinary men. If it goes on for a long time, the woman becomes deluded, keeps it secret, and is unwilling to tell anyone what is happening, so wonderful does she find it. Thus she may die, all alone, and no one ever comes to know of it.[44]

Demons or dreams, these texts argue for a latent female potency which threatened a basic tenet of Confucian social order.

The final text is that taken from the *Lienü zhuan* 烈女傳 (Virtuous Women) collective biography of the *Jiu Tang shu* 舊唐書. It treats the abduction of a married woman by Fang Qidi 房企地 (also known as Pang Qidi 旁企地), a hearty of the Jiang 羌 tribe and one of the original group of rebels assembled around Xue Rengao's 薛仁杲 (d. 618) father, Xue Ju 薛舉 (d. 618). Both his father and then Rengao threatened the new Tang government in Chang'an from their Gansu base for most of 618 A.D. The events described below probably took place not long after 618 after Fang had apparently moved south (Liangzhou is about 125 miles southwest of Chang'an) towards his native area:

> Wei Heng's wife née Wang was from Qi County in Zi Prefecture [modern Sichuan]. At the beginning of the Wude reign period [618–627] one of the old lieutenants of Xue Rengao [i.e., one who served his father], Fang Qidi, sacked Liang Prefecture where he captured Ms. Wang and forced her to marry him. Later when Fang grew in strength, Wei Heng planned to join his city to the rebels. Fang led his army toward Liang Prefecture, but still at some considerable distance (literally "several tens of *li*") short of the city he drank and fell into a stupor. Ms. Wang took his dagger, cut off his head, and carried it into the city. The rebel host dispersed.

> Emperor Gaozu was greatly pleased. He enfeoffed her as the Exalted
> Dutiful Lady and pardoned Wei Heng's traitorous association with the
> rebels.[45]

The story recalls the apocryphal tale of Judith and Holofernes. But in the
Chinese context there is another significance. When Fang Qidi took Ms.
Wang captive she was expected to resist his advances even if it meant her
death.[46] Other accounts in the *Lienü zhuan* are filled with comparable
situations in which all the other women distinguished themselves by steadfast resistance to rebels or bandits resulting in their deaths (see, for example, the events surrounding the death of Fu Feng's wife cited in the
section on "Widows" which follows).[47] The sexuality here is all implicit.
Ms. Wang's forced "marriage" to a non-Chinese for a considerable period
of time ("later when Qidi grew in strength") and more specifically the
scene which comes to mind as Fang drank himself unconscious with Ms.
Wang in attendance, were apparently offensive to Confucian sensibilities,
since this story is one of very few which were included in the *Jiu Tang shu*
but rejected by the *Xin Tang shu* editors. Ms. Wang may have been "dutiful", but she was not chaste.[48]

Towards a Conclusion

What do the three groups of texts we have examined have in common?
They share the belief that female sexuality is fraught with inherent
dangers. They thereby reflect the parameters of paradox in traditional
Chinese views of that sexuality. While recognizing the nearly unlimited
potential of the female in *ars amorata*, they realize that this sexuality in
China, as in most traditional cultures, must be suppressed. Here Gerda
Lerner's comments on the origin of the double standard in early Western
society are of relevance:

> Surpluses from herding were appropriated by men and became private proper-
> ty. Once having acquired such private property, men sought to secure it to
> themselves and their heirs; they did so by instituting the monogamous family.
> By controlling women's sexuality through the requirement of prenuptial chas-
> tity and by the establishment of the sexual double standard in marriage, men
> assured themselves of the legitimacy of their offspring and thus secured their
> property interest.[49]

Chinese ritual texts (here the *Liji* 禮記) lend support to Lerner's claim:

> The ceremony of marriage was intended to be a bond of amity between two [families of different] surnames, among the upper classes to secure the services in the ancestral temple, and among the lower to secure the continuance of the family line.[50]

From this basic role provided a wife early in the development of civilizations, it was not a great step to the Confucian principles of marriage:[51]

(1) sexual inequality with male dominance;
(2) family welfare before the individual's interests;
(3) monogamy.

Although there are a number of classical Chinese works which teach submissiveness and loyalty as the basic feminine virtues (on the history of women's education in China, as well as the major texts of this tradition)[52] the following passages from the *Liji* are representative:

> A girl at the age of ten ceased to go out [from the women's quarters]. Her governess taught her [the arts of] pleasing speech and manners, to be docile and obedient, to handle the hempen fibres....[53]

and again:

> Faithfulness is requisite in all service of others, and is [specially] the virtue of a wife. Once mated with her husband, all her life she will not change [her feeling of duty to him], and hence, when the husband dies she will not marry [again].[54]

Woman's passiveness and duty to her husband was carried over even into Chinese sexology, where the female was primarily a vessel to increase male potency:

> Sexual intercourse was considered to have a two-fold aim. Primarily, the sex act was to achieve the woman's conceiving so that she would give birth to sons to continue the family. Not only did a man thus fulfill his assigned role in the order of the universe, but it was also the sacred duty to his ancestors. The peace of the dead could only be assured by regular sacrifices made by their descendants on earth. Secondly, the sexual act was to strengthen the man's vitality by making him absorb the woman's *yin* essence, while at the same time the woman would derive physical benefit from the stirring of her latent *yin* nature.[55]

And there are also different sexual roles to be played by women — as widows, wives, concubines, courtesans, prostitutes and lovers. An old Chinese saying about the quality of sex along such a hierarchy perhaps expresses these distinctions best, at least from a man's point-of-view:

[Sexual relations] with a wife is not as good as with a concubine, with a concubine not as good as with a maid servant, with a maid servant not as good as with a prostitute, with a prostitute not as good as with an adulteress, with an adulteress not as good as lusting for it.

The problem here is that traditional sexology as expressed in handbooks authored by men contained the same contradictions as society itself. Faced with the vast powers of *yin* 淫 , they provide at best prescriptive descriptions which, like traditional ritual, were intended to keep this female threat in check.

Thus the avoidance of depictions of female sexuality in works which are typical, such as *Yingying zhuan*, cannot be attributed solely to their male authorship, since we have seen males quite capable of limning the most outrageous sexuality in Hejian, but rather to a part of the social code, reflecting again a passage from the *Liji*:

The things which men greatly desire are comprehended in meat and drink and sexual pleasure; those which they greatly dislike are comprehended in death, exile, poverty, and suffering. Thus liking and disliking are the great elements in men's minds. But men keep them hidden in their minds, where they cannot be fathomed or measured. The good and the bad of them being in their minds, and no outward manifestation of them being visible, if it be wished to determine these qualities in one uniform way, how can it be done without the use of rules of propriety?[56]

What we find in texts as widely varied as *Yingying zhuan* and *Hejian zhuan* are not depictions of female sexuality, but rather male conceptions of that sexuality, essentially creating a literary double standard to conform with that which existed in society. Therefore, there can be no sexual gratification for these Tang heroines — not even for the unrestrained Hejian — since their sexuality is never really the subject at hand. Heroines either learn to eliminate their sexuality (like Li Wa), or they bring disaster on themselves (like Hejian). Often, their powers to *huo* or "delude" bring down male heroes as well (Ouyang Zhan). For a woman who continues to express natural desires, such as Yingying, there can be only contempt.

Thus the basic principles of Chinese sexuality apply also to these Tang narratives, namely that Chinese *erotics* are concerned with extra-marital relations and are reserved almost exclusively for males, while for women there was only an *ethics* centred upon chastity and loyalty.

Notes

1. Maeno Naoaki 前野直彬 Tōdai denki shū 唐代伝記集 (Tokyo: Heibonsha, 1963), Vol. 1, p. 83, note 2, points out that a Qili 戚里 (Relatives' Village) was the residence of imperial relations during the Han; he believes that here it indicates that Hejian was a member of the Tang aristocracy.

2. "Old Wu" refers to Wu Daozi 吳道子. On the origin of his predilections for and skill at painting scenes of hell, see Victor H. Mair, "Records of Transformation Tableaux", TP, LXXII (1986), p. 32, note 202, p. 33, and p. 40. Cf. also Youyang zazu 酉陽雜俎 (1983), sections 147 (p. 247), 172 (p. 252), and 204 (pp. 261–262). See also Religios Malerei aus Taiwan, translated by Jorinde Ebert and Barbara Kaulbach (Marburg: Religionskundliche Sammlung der Philips-Universität Marburg, 1981).

3. I have not been able to locate Fengkai zhou 豐隑州; Maeno (Tōdai denki shū, p. 83, note 3) believes it is an error for Feng Shui 灃水, a stream which flowed through the southwestern part of Chang'an.

4. These animals were presumably held to be "released from captivity" (fangsheng 放生), as is the Buddhist custom.

5. Beiyou 北牖 (the northern window) indicates in a number of classical texts a place for sleeping — thus there must have been beds nearby. It was under the northern window in another Buddhist temple that Qunyu Fen 淳于棼 is supposed to have dallied with the woman who attends on him just before his wedding in the tale "Nanke Taishou zhuan" 南柯太守傳 (An Account of the Governor of the Southern Branch), Tangren xiaoshuo 唐人小説, compiled by Wang Bijang 汪辟疆 (Shanghai: Guji chubanshe, 1978), p. 86.

6. One of the traditional types of music considered licentious.

7. On monks (often foreign) known for their ample endowment, see Robert H. van Gulik, Erotic Colour Prints of the Ming Period, Essay on Chinese Sexual Life from the Han to the Ching Dynasty, B.C. 206– A.D. 1644, 3 vols. (Taipei: Tanching, 1986), reprint of privately published edition, first published in Tokyo, 1951, pp. 93–94.

8. This was originally a custom from Yue 越 which gradually developed into a manner of expressing a lover's vow, cf. Zhongwen dacidian 中文大辭典, entry 49657. 20–21, p. 17175.

9. In traditional Chinese medicine sexual dissipation — the expulsion of too much "sexual fluid" — was thought to result in the drying up of all the body's fluids, including bone marrow.

10. Liu Zongyuan ji 柳宗元集, edited by Wu Wenzhi 吳文治 et al. (Beijing: Zhonghua shuju, 1979), Vol. 4, "Waiji (shang)" 外集, pp. 1341–1345. Although there is a translation by Shih Shun Liu, Classical Chinese Prose, the Eight Masters of the Tang Sung Period (Hong Kong: The Chinese University

Press, 1979), pp. 120–127, this and other renditions are by the author unless otherwise noted.

11. There are several theories concerning the meaning of this piece (three of them are cited by Matsuzaki Haruyuki 松崎治之, "Tōdai denki ni mieru itan no joseizo — 'Kaken den' ni tsuite no ikkosatsu"唐代伝奇に見える異端の女性像——「河間伝」についての一考察, *Tsukushi Jogakuen Tankidaigaku kiyo* 筑紫女学園短期大学紀要, 18(1984), pp. 49–50. Some commentators claim Hejian refers to Wang Shuwen himself, but it seems more likely that Liu Zongyuan means for her to represent Wang's mother (in the tradition of Chinese insults), *née* Liu 劉, who was descended from Prince Xian of Hejian 河間獻王, Liu De 劉德 (d. 130 B.C.) — cf. Liu's memorial text for Ms. Liu, *Liu Zongyuan ji*, Vol. 2, Juan 13, pp. 343–346; see also Matsuzaki's comments on Hejian as a place of immortality during the Six Dynasties (p. 34) and note 1 above.

12. Those who "wandered the lakes and rivers" lived outside of normal conventions and had usually rejected the world in some way.

13. Parents should be in charge of marriage arrangements. And, of course, such behaviour as this could hardly be considered filial.

14. A Taoist concoction which seems to have served as a medicine as well as a drug of immortality and an aphrodisiac. Maeno, *Tōdai denki shū*, p. 76, note 1 says this is a *fanhun dan* 返魂丹, "a soul-returning pill".

15. The meanings of *yuanfeng* 圓封 (here tentatively as "sealed it [rolled up]") and *bofeng* 博封 (here "in a regular manner" [i.e., flat]) remain obscure.

16. I have been unable to determine the exact arrangements of the privy and its accoutrements in Tang times.

17. The fragrance of pepper and orchids was considered an aphrodisiac, and was infused in various manners into the walls of the harem or the boudoir.

18. *Liu Zongyuan ji*, Vol. 2, Juan 17 [translation modified from that by William H. Nienhauser, Jr. in Karl S. Y. Kao (ed.), *Classical Chinese Tales of the Supernatural and the Fantastic* (Bloomington, Indiana: Indiana University Press, 1985), pp. 190–192].

19. Compiled by Li Yin 李冘; this passage was cited in the *Taiping guangji* 太平廣記 (Taipei: Wenshizhe, 1982), Vol. 4, Juan 341, pp. 2703–2704.

20. This tends to confirm the supposition by Wang Meng'ou, Glen Dudbridge and others that literati were familiar with such popular tales.

21. Zhang Shichao 章士釗, *Liuwen zhiyao* 柳文指要 (Beijing: Zhonghua shuju, 1973), Juan 17, p. 551.

22. Howard Levy (trans.), *The Dwelling of Playful Goddesses* (Tokyo: Dai Nippon, 1965), p. 12.

23. Levy, pp. 18–19; Original text from *Tangren xiaoshuo*, p. 21.

24. Modified from Levy, p. 30; *Tangren xiaoshuo*, p. 30.

25. Levy, pp. 49–50; *Tangren xiaoshuo*, p. 31.

26. *Li Wa zhuan* has been the subject of a recent monograph by Glen Dudbridge entitled *The Tale of Li Wa, Study and Critical Edition of a Chinese Story from the Ninth Century* (London: Ithaca Press, 1983). All but one of these texts can be found in *Tangren Xiaoshuo — Ouyang Xingzhou zhuan* is preserved in the *Taiping guangji*, Vol. 3, Juan 274, pp. 2161–2162.

27. There is a translation of *Bu Feiyan* [The Tragedy of Pu Fei-yen]. *Traditional Chinese Stories: Themes and Variations*, edited by Y. W. Ma and Joseph S. M. Lau (New York: Columbia University Press, 1978), pp. 172–176. "An Account of Ouyang Zhan" relates how Ouyang falls in love with a courtesan while visiting Taiyuan. On his return to Chang'an he promises to send for her, but does not — probably because of the social disparity between them. She pines away and on her deathbed sends him a plait or her hair and a poem. When he opens the package containing both his heart and spirit are broken, resulting in a short time in his own death.

28. See Ylva Monschein on the fox fairy during the Tang as an icon of the Tang courtesan: *Der Zauber der Fuchsfee, Entstehung and Wandel eines "Femme-fatale" — Motives in der Chinesischen Literatur* (Frankurt: Haag und Herchen, 1988).

29. Translation modifed slightly from James Robert Hightower, "Yüan Chen and 'The Story of Ying-ying'," *HJAS*, 33 (1973), p. 93; *Tangren xiaoshuo*, p. 135.

30. Ibid.

31. Hightower, p. 96; *Tangren xiaoshuo*, p. 137.

32. Hightower, p. 102, note 48 traces this concept to the *Zuo zhuan* 左傳 .

33. Hightower, p. 103.

34. Ibid.

35. Ma and Lau, p. ix.

36. Cf. *Liji Zhengzhu* 禮記鄭注 (*Sibu beiyao* ed., Juan 8, fol. 17a; *Li Chi, Book of Rites*, translated by James Legge, edited by Chu Chai and Winberg Chai, 2 vols. (New York: University Books, 1967), Vol. 1, p. 455: "When a woman goes out at the door, she must keep her face covered" (女子出門，必擁蔽其面).

37. Translation revised from Nienhauser in Ma and Lau, p. 50.

38. Ibid.

39. E. D. Edwards, *Chinese Prose Literature of the Tang Period*, 2 vols. (London: Probsthain, 1937–1938), Vol. 2, p. 46.

40. Translation revised from Nienhauser, p. 51; emphasis ours.

41. Ouyang Xiu 歐陽修 and Song Qi 宋祁 (eds.), *Xin Tang shu*, 20 vols. (Beijing: Zhonghua shuju, 1975), Juan 205, p. 5228.

42. *Menque* 門闕 normally means the palace gate, but here must refer to the village.

43. Edward H. Schafter, "Notes on T'ang Culture, II", *MS* 24, p. 138.

44. Michael Strickmann, "Dreamwork of Psycho-Sinologists: Doctors, Taoists, Monks", *A Conference Report: Dreamworks of Psycho-Sinology, the*

Universe of Dreams in Chinese Culture, edited by Carolyn T. Brown (Lanham, Maryland: University Press of America), p. 30. Strickmann does not provide an exact reference to the original text.

45. Liu Xun 劉昫 (ed.), *Jiu Tang shu*, 16 vols. (Beijing: Zhonghua shuju, 1975), Vol. 16, Juan 193, p. 5140.

46. T'ien Ju-k'ang in *Male Anxiety and Female Chastity, a Comparative Study of Chinese Ethical Values in Ming-Ch'ing Times* (Leiden: E. J. Brill, 1988) notes that rape by soldiers was generally accepted by society — i.e., the victims were not expected to take their own lives. But the *lienü* accounts for the Tang, and certainly post-Tang Neo-Confucian ethics, argue to the contrary.

47. On this cf. Foucault, *The Use of Pleasure, Volume 2 of the History of Sexuality*, translated by Robert Hurley (New York: Pantheon Books, 1985), p. 82: "The day would come when the paradigm most often used for illustrating sexual virtue would be that of the woman or girl, who defended herself from the assaults of a man who had every advantage over her; the safeguarding of purity and virginity, and faithfulness to commitments and vows, were to constitute the standard test of virtue."

48. Note the similarities of this case to that which Bai Juyi 白居易 (772–846) deliberated in which a woman had asked a man to take revenge on the bandits who had slain her husband. After he did, she married him (as a sort of repayment?). Bai condemns her, however, and allows no exceptions to the rules of remarriage by widows. Cf. *Bai Juyi ji* 白居易集 (Beijing: Zhonghua shuju, 1979), 4 vols., Vol. 4, Juan 66, pp. 1378–1379.

49. Gerda Lerner, *The Creation of Patriarchy; Women and History*, Vol. 1 (Oxford: Oxford University Press, 1986), p. 6.

50. *Li Chi, Book of Rites*, Vol. 2, p. 428.

51. Wong Sun-ming, "Confucian Ideal and Reality: The Transformation of the Institution of Marriage in T'ang China (A.D. 618–907)". Unpublished Ph. D dissertation, University of Washington, 1979, p. 22.

52. See Tienchi Martin-Liao, *Frauenerziehung im Alten China, Eine Analyse der Frauenbücher* (Bochum: Brockmeyer, 1984).

53. Legge, Vol. 1, p. 479.

54. Ibid., Vol. 2, p. 439.

55. van Gulik, pp. 6–7.

56. Legge, Vol. 1, p. 380.

2

Sexuality and Innocence: The Characterization of Oriole in the Hongzhi Edition of the *Xixiang ji*

Stephen H. West and Wilt L. Idema

Yingying 鶯鶯 (hereafter Oriole) has emerged as one of the more enigmatic personalities in classical and vernacular literature, and from her first appearance in the *Huizhen ji* 會真記 (Tale of Encountering a Realized One), also known as the *Yingying zhuan* 鶯鶯傳 (Legend of Oriole) to her complex portrayal in the Yuan drama, *Xixiang ji* 西廂記 (Story of the Western Wing), her character has remained a steady study in the conflict between desire and shame. This paper is a preliminary exploration of that latter characterization as a young woman just emerging from the torpor of adolescent longing and whose innocence and allure are a product both of psychological realism, but also of the convergence of literary and dramatic convention.[1]

Textual Choices

This discussion is based on the *Xixiang ji* as represented in the Hongzhi 弘治 edition of 1498. This text was unknown to the scholarly world until it was acquired in the late 1940s by Yanjing University, from where it passed into the holdings of Beijing University Library. This handsome edition was produced by a commercial publishing firm, the Yue — family of Jintai, Beijing.[2] The upper register of each page of the main text is graced by a continuous set of illustrations that occupy two-fifths of each plate. These illustrations are of a fine quality, especially when compared to other editions from the Ming, and by themselves provide a highly interesting interpretative commentary on the text. It is clear from the publisher's advertisements that the illustrations were meant to provide visual clues to famous scenes on stage, but it is also clear that they represent the story itself and not any single performance.

The play is printed in two large volumes, and in each volume the main text of the play is preceded by a variety of other materials, more or less (but sometimes not at all) related to the play and occasionally carrying their own illustrations. I have consistently compared this text to the edition prepared by the playwright and drama-critic Wang Jide 王冀德 (ca. 1560–1623) and published in 1614,[3] which itself contains a very detailed line by line comparison between the text of the play and of Wang Shifu's 王實甫 immediate source, Dong Jieyuan's 董解元 (fl.1190–1208) *Xixiang ji zhugongdiao* 西廂記諸宮調 (Story of the Western Wing in All Keys and Modes), a chantefable treatment of this famous love story.[4]

Another edition that appeared in 1622 and deserves separate mention is that issued by the playwright and novelist Ling Mengchu 凌濛初 (1580–1644). Ling claimed that his edition was based on an earlier one that had been published by Zhu Youdun 朱有燉. While this assertion may have been simply a sales pitch to assure buyers of a reliable and authentic text, the edition is indeed remarkable among other late Ming texts for its close similarity in parts to the Hongzhi edition, a text that, in turn, appears to imitate the editorial practices of Zhu Youdun's private printings of his own *zaju* 雜劇. It is quite conceivable that Ling Mengchu indeed based his recension on a copy of the Hongzhi edition — but one missing the vulnerable final leaf of the second volume that carries the publisher's colophon — and in good faith might have concluded that, based upon the similarities in editorial convention, that this edition was indeed one prepared by Zhu Youdun.[5]

Despite the many fine qualities of the Hongzhi and Ling Mengchu's editions, practically all scholarly discourse on the drama is based on Jin Shengtan's 金聖嘆 (1610–1661) printing of 1656. Jin Shengtan was a highly idiosyncratic literary critic who had the audacity to put the major works in the vernacular language on a par with the hallowed masterworks of the classical tradition. Earlier, in 1641, he had produced an edition of the famous novel *Shuihu zhuan* 水滸傳 (Water Margin), his recension of which was supposedly based on an ancient text (*guben* 古本) and was distinguished by an extensive critical commentary that included general introductory essays, individual essays accompanying each chapter, and a very detailed interlinear commentary. Jin Shengtan frequently rewrote the main text in order to make it fit with his own critical statements — even to the extent of completely cutting out the final one-third of the text.

However, because of the resulting literary quality of his abridged text, its manageable bulk, and the acumen and wit of his commentary, this edition of *Shuihu zhuan* became the standard version of the novel until well into the present century.[6]

Jin Shengtan's edition of the *Xixiang ji* basically adheres to the same format as his earlier venture into vernacular criticism. The main text is preceded by two prefaces and two general essays, each act is preceded by its own critical introduction, and the body of the text itself is accompanied by an extensive interlinear commentary. Again, the wording of the text occasionally has been changed to fit the commentary. If the metrical requirements kept most of the songs inviolate, the prose dialogue suffered all the more. One of Jin Shengtan's major concerns was to safeguard Oriole from any accusation of indecency. He attempted that by proving that she had remained chaste under all circumstances — even when she gave herself to the student Zhang Gong (in Jin's opinion she simply enacts the promise of marriage her mother had retracted). Accordingly many small changes were made throughout the text, supposedly once more on the authority of an otherwise unspecified "ancient edition". In the process the text was also thoroughly bowdlerized.[7] As in the case of his edition of the *Shuihu zhuan*, Jin Shengtan's textual changes may well have enhanced the readability of the text and increased its general acceptability by downplaying its morally offensive aspects. A seminal attraction remained in the bulk and wit of his commentary.

During the nearly three centuries of the Qing Dynasty, Jin Shengtan's recension of the play enjoyed equal popularity with his edition of *Shuihu zhuan*, and likewise nearly eclipsed all earlier editions.[8] Earlier Western language translations of the *Xixiang ji* have heretofore also all been based on the Jin Shengtan edition. Jin Shengtan firmly subscribed to the view that Wang Shifu only had authored the first four plays of the *Xixiang ji*, an opinion quite commonly held during the sixteenth century and later, and consequently he included the fifth play of the cycle only as a sequel. As a result, some of these earlier Western language renditions do not translate the fifth play at all.[9]

Whatever the merits of Jin's version, it is abundantly clear that his strong editorial hand had altered the face of the original text. To break with tradition is not easy, but in this instance, I will work from the earliest extant complete text. There is good precedent for this, as Zheng Qian 鄭騫 has pointed out elsewhere in regard to Zang Maoxun's 藏懋循 *Yuanqu xuan* 元曲選 , and we should not continue to be subject to the predilections of literati editors of the final decades of the Ming when evaluating or analyzing Yuan and Ming drama.

A Book That Teaches Lechery

In chapter 23 of the *Honglou meng* 紅樓夢 (Dream of the Red Chamber), Lin Daiyu 林黛玉 surprises Jia Baoyu賈寶玉 reading the *Xixiang ji*, he at first tries to hide the true nature of the title from her, but his attempts are unconvincing:

> "Don't try to fool me!" said Dai-yu. "You would have done much better to let me look at it in the first place, instead of hiding it so guiltily." "In your case, coz, I have nothing to be afraid of," said Bao-yu, "but if I do let you look, you must promise not to tell anyone. It's marvellous stuff. Once you start reading it, you'll even stop wanting to eat!" He handed the book to her, and Dai-yu put down her things and looked. The more she read, the more she liked it, and before long she had read several acts. She felt the power of the words and their lingering fragrance. Long after she had finished reading, when she had laid down the book and was sitting there rapt and silent, the lines continued to ring in her head. "Well," said Bao-yu, "is it good?" Dai-yu smiled and nodded.[10]

However, as soon as Baoyu starts to tease her with a quotation from the *Xixiang ji*, she calls it a "horrid play" and threatens to denounce him to his parents for reading it. On another occasion, when Jia Baoyu again offends her by a quotation from Wang's work, she even calls it a "crude, disgusting book". Nevertheless, she continues to compare herself to Oriole, and is caught quoting from it herself by Xue Baochai 薛寶釵 , who sternly berates her — but first confesses she herself had read plays while still at her grandfather's place.

> … My grandfather was a bibliophile, so the house we lived in was full of books. We were a big family in those days. All my boy cousins and girl cousins on my father's side lived with us in the same house. All of us younger people hated serious books but liked reading poetry and plays. The boys had got lots and lots of plays: *The Western Chamber* [i.e. *Xixiang ji*], The *Lute Player, A Hundred Yuan Plays* — just about everything you could think of. They used to read them behind our backs, and we girls used to read them behind theirs…. As for girls like you and me: spinning and weaving are our proper business. What do we need to be able to read for? But since we can read, let us confine ourselves to good, improving books; let us avoid like the

plague those pernicious works of fiction, which so undermine the character that in the end it is past reclaiming.[11]

At a later occasion Xue Baochai even feigns total ignorance of the contents of the *Xixiang ji* and another romantic play, to be berated in her turn as overly "stuffy" by yet another character in the novel:

> … There can't be a man, woman or child who isn't familiar with them [i.e. the places mentioned in those plays]. And even if one knows them from the books it can hardly be said that to have read a few lyrics from *The Western Chamber* or *The Soul's Return* is tantamount to reading pornography.[12]

If it was a matter of controversy whether or not the *Xixiang ji* was fit reading for impressionable adolescents, performances of scenes from the play in a later adaptation are presented in front of the collected household in other chapters of the novel.[13] These anecdotes are revealing precisely because they show the ambivalent attitude held toward the *Xixiang ji*. Certainly numberless adolescents saw themselves in the protagonists of the play and recognized in Oriole's and the student's dilemma their own plight in patriarchal Chinese society. This, coupled with the suggestiveness of an erotic language that borders on licentiousness, caused champions of Neo-Confucian morality to decry the play as "a book that instructs or incites one to lechery" (*huiyin zhi shu* 誨淫之書). Some even condemned the author to Hell, there to have his tongue ripped out — an opprobrium that probably further increased the appeal of the work among its juvenile audience.

At the centre of this comedy stands Oriole, a girl just emerging from the cocoon of adolescence into the world of sexuality, caught between innocence and shame on the one hand and desire and allure on the other, incapable of fathoming her own feelings or of being aware of their effects on others. In the drama, Oriole stands at the conjunction of dramatic convention and psychological realism, as a representation of celestial beauty and earthy delight. Her character unfolds along two distinct planes that roughly correspond to the celestial and the earthly sphere.

The single image that ties these two mirror worlds together is the Yellow River. In the second scene of the drama, Student Zhang introduces himself by a long aria that describes his hardships as a poor student. Almost as a non-sequitur, he suddenly switches to a direct lyric description of the Yellow River, which he must cross to reach East of Pu (Pudong 蒲東) and his eventual but as-yet-unknown destination of the Monastery of Universal Salvation. This switch has bothered critics for some time. Wang

Jide, for instance, noted that it was "extremely odd, but also based generally on the gist of Dong Jieyuan's text".[14] Geographically, of course, it is an
accurate description of the point at which Student Zhang will cross the
River, but it certainly sets as well the general mood of the story, and the
"wind-tossed billows" of the River foreshadow the difficulties that the
star-crossed lovers will face in the pursuit of fulfilment:

> Where are the wind-tossed billows of the Nine Bends most conspicuous?
> [(Student speaks:)] None of the waters of the world are as tricky as those of
> the Yellow River:
> [*Youhulu*] (Student sings:)
> ...
>
> Only this place is paramount.
> This River belts Qi and Liang,
> Divides Qin and Jin,
> Cuts off You and Yan.
> Snowcapped waves beat the long sky,
> At heaven's edge autumn clouds furl.[15]

The turmoil suggested in the final couplet above by the strong verb *pai* 拍 ,
to "beat against" or "slap" and the pun on "autumn", *qiu* 秋 and "sorrow",
chou 愁 — lends an emotional edge to two further puns in the middle
couplet. Qin and Jin were a pair of ancient states in the Zhou Dynasty that
were physically divided by the Yellow River and which intermarried as a
matter of state policy. In vernacular literature, including drama, the term
Qin and Jin became a common metaphor for "a good marriage". For
instance, in the scene where the monastery is surrounded by bandits seeking to take Oriole away by force, the young girl suggests that she be given
as a reward to whomever could drive them away:

> Whomsoever it may be,
> If he establish his meritorious service,
> And drive away those traitorous troops,
> And sweep away their malignant aura,
> Then let us give as dowry our family reputation,
> As, with that brave, I will gladly
> Unite in wedlock,
> As did the states of Qin and Jin.[16]

Thus, the line may also be interpreted as "our good marriage will be
thwarted". In the second line of that couplet, the place names *you* and *yan*
may also be read as an adjective-noun phrase, *youyan* 幽宴 , which means

a "secret feast" or "secret meeting". Hence, our young lovers seem to have nary a chance; authority, in the form of the old madam, will thwart their marriage chances and block their love trysts, and so hang the clouds of autumn, the gloom of sorrow, on a horizon of frustrated love.

Sexual punning is suggested as well in the next few lines of the aria. According to early treatises on the art and therapeutic value of sex, the "Yellow River" was a technical term for the flow of energy supposed to exist along the spine when semen is diverted during intercourse. The images of the recumbent dragon, the flying bolt, and of the Yellow River breaking through its restraining dikes are all fit symbols for male lust and for the rampant sexuality that will dominate the action of the play:

> Bamboo hawsers cable together the floating bridge,
> On the water a steel-blue dragon reclines.
> East and west it breeches into the Nine Regions,
> North and south it threads together a hundred streams.
> A homing vessel: Is it fast or not? How does one see it?
> Like a crossbow bolt's sudden leaving of the string.[17]

But it is the next song in the suite that establishes the mirror worlds of the play:

> [*Tianxia le*] (Student sings:)
> Just as if the Silver River dropped through the Nine Heavens:
> From its deep fount beyond the clouds suspended,
> To its entering into the Eastern Sea — it cannot but pass here.
> It irrigates the thousand kinds of flowers of Luoyang,
> Enriches the myriad-acre fields of Liangyuan,
> And once it floated a raft to the edge of sun and moon.[18]

The first line of this aria (adapted from a famous poem by the Tang poet, Li Bai 李白, 701–762)[19] equates the Yellow River with its astral counterpart, the Milky Way. The next two lines refer to the famous gardens of Luoyang 洛陽 and Liangyuan 梁園, the former renowned for its many flowers, especially peonies,[20] and the latter, a pleasure garden constructed by an ancient prince near modern Kaifeng, also denotes locations of pleasure. As we shall see below, the peonies for which Luoyang was justly famous have a particular significance within the play.

It is the final line, however, that serves to strengthen the associations drawn between the Milky Way and the Yellow River, and which ultimately sets the action of the play within two separate realms. It is an allusion to the story first found in the *Bowu zhi* 博物志 (Record of Wide Learning), in which a man who dwelt by the sea saw a raft float by every year in the eighth month. He prepared clothing and supplies, and boarded it one year. After a long period of travel, he finally arrived at a city with walls and residences, wherein he saw a woman who was weaving at a loom and met a man who was leading an oxen to drink in the river. When he asked where he was, he was told to wait until he reached Shu (the area of modern Sichuan) on his return voyage and there to question a certain Yan Zhong-ping 顏忠平 , who turned out to be a famous astrologer. The man did as he was instructed and was then told that "on a certain day of a certain month, a transient star had encroached upon the Islet of the Ox", which is the name of a constellation in the Milky Way. It was then that he knew he had actually floated beyond the confluence of the Yellow River and the Milky Way and out onto the Milky Way itself. There, he had encountered the Herd Boy and the Weaving Girl (Chinese names for constellations that are roughly in the area of the stars Altair and Vega), two lovers who are separated by the Milky Way. These celestial lovers were allowed to meet only once a year, on the seventh day of the seventh month, when magpies flew up from earth to form a bridge for them to cross. In later times and in the popular mind, the traveller on the raft became associated with Zhang Qian 張騫 , a famous explorer of the Han period who travelled extensively in Central Asia. Sharing the same surname as our young student, this explorer of wild and uncharted waters is an apt allusion to suggest the young Student Zhang and the adventure upon which he is about to embark.[21]

More importantly, however, the allusion clearly lends a mythic dimension to our love story as it establishes a strong link between the two domains of heaven and earth and between pairs of lovers: Student Zhang and Oriole and the Herdboy and Weaving Maiden. This brings the earlier puns on Qin and Jin and on "cut off secret meetings" more clearly into focus, and suggests that the Yellow River serves as a paradoxical image of foreshadowing — it will transport the student to his loved one, but also, like the Milky Way, it signals separation and obstruction to the young lovers.

Oriole

The characterization of Oriole also unfolds along these two separate planes, and she is described in celestial terms as an ethereal goddess of the

moon and in mundane terms as a stunning physical beauty. The double
nature of her beauty is bespoken in the scene where Student Zhang first
sees her as he makes the rounds of the Monastery of Universal Salvation.
His narration of locations within the temple, in which each place is
described in a single line or less of a song, creates a steady cadence that
builds to a crescendo with his counting of the arhats and his obeisances to
the Bodhisattvas. At the climax of this religious visitation he suddenly
encounters Oriole, who appears twirling a sprig of red flowers, a daunting
image of sexual congress and a brilliant spot of colour in an otherwise
colourless world:

> I've strolled through the grotto cells,
> Climbed the Holy pagoda,
> And wound my way along twisting corridors.
> I've finished counting the arhats,
> Paid my respects to the Bodhisattvas,
> Made my obeisances to the Holy One…
>
> (Female lead enters leading Crimson and twirling a flowering sprig. She
> speaks:)
> Crimson, let's go and play around in the Buddha hall.
> (The male lead acts out seeing her:) Wow …!
>
> [*Cunli Jiegao*] (Student sings:)
> …
> And now I run smack into my alluring karmic sentence from five centuries
> ago![22]

His first description of Oriole is a rather flip comparison of her with the
dangerous loves of Tushita Palace, home of lovely sylphs, but this other-
worldly quality is soon overshadowed by the power of her physical
presence:

> [*Yuanhe ling*] (Student sings:)
> Stunning knockouts — I've seen a million,
> But a lovely face like this is rarely seen!
> It dazzles a man's eyes, stuns him speechless,
> And makes his soul fly away into the heavens.
> She there, without a thought of teasing, fragrant shoulders bare,
> Simply twirls the flower, smiling.
>
> [*Shangma jiao*] (Student sings:)
> This is "Tushita Palace",[23]
> Don't guess it to be the "Heaven of Separation's Regret".[24]

Ahhh...who would have ever thought that I would meet a divine sylph,
I see her spring-breeze face, fit for anger, fit for joy,
Just suited to those kingfisher-feather-pasted flowered pins.

[*Sheng hulu*] (Student sings:)
See her palace-style eyebrows, curved like a crescent moon,
Invading the borders of her clouds of locks.

(Female lead speaks:) Crimson, look ...

Lonely, lonely monk's chambers where no one goes,
Covering the steps, padded by moss, the red of fallen flowers.

(Student speaks:) I'm dying ...

(Student sings:)
Bashful in front of others before she even speaks,
Cherry fruits split apart their redness,
Jade grains reveal their whiteness,
Time passes before she speaks.

But these strong sensual images dissolve once again into a description of
her ethereal beauty and Zhang returns again to the metaphor of celestial
beings:

[*Houting hua*] (Student sings:)
...
Slowly, she meanders,
Until she reaches the doorway,
And then a final step takes her far away.
She had just shown her face for a moment,
But has driven to madness this Laureate Zhang.
Like a divine sylph returning to her grotto heaven,
Emptily she leaves behind the mists of willows,
Where all that can be heard is the chattering of sparrows.[25]

The earlier concreteness of his physical descriptions gives way here to the
haziness of newly greening willow branches and the singing of birds —
the vestigial resonances of her lithe body and trilling voice. Having seen
but a glimpse — he has, in fact, only quick and ever-shifting sight of her
until the scene with the mass in the last act of the first play — he now
remembers her only as an apparition of a heavenly sylph returned to her
grotto. She has disappeared and left behind in the mortal world only the
redolent fragrance and faint tinkling of her presence:

[*Jisheng cao*] (Student sings:)
The scent of orchid musk lingers still,
The sound of hanging pendants moves slowly away.
The eastern wind sways, then drags up, strands of weeping willows,
Floating threads catch and stir up petals of peach blossom,
The pearly curtains now hide, now show, her hibiscus face.
You say she is the family of his Excellency, Executive of Hezhong Province,
I say she is the apparition of Guanyin, contemplating moonlight in water.[26]

The shimmering vision of the white-robed Oriole reminds him of the
Bodhisattva Guanyin 觀音 who is known as the compassionate saviour of
humanity and who is often associated with moon imagery. This trope of
the celestial beauty and her mortal lover is played out throughout the first
three plays of the drama. For instance, in the third act of play I, Zhang
steals into the flower garden to try and catch his first real glimpse of
Oriole. In this passage he shows every sign of the mortal suitor waiting in
expectancy for the manifestation of a heavenly lover:

[(*Yue modus*:) *Dou anchun*] (Student sings:)
The jade vault is without dust,
The Silver River drips light,
Moon's colour straddles the void,
Flowers' shade fills the courtyard.
My silken sleeves grow cold,
My fragrant heart is on alert.
I cock my ear to listen,
Walk with quiet step,
Silent so silent,
In darkness so dark,
Hiding, hiding,
I wait and wait and wait.[27]

When she finally appears in the garden, he again compares her to divine
beauties, this time to the goddesses of the Xiang River and to Chang E, the
goddess of the moon.

(Student chants:)
It must be that this springtime beauty is fed up with confinement,
And has flown freely out of her Palace of Spreading Frigidity.

Her whole face still covered with powder, one shoulder of her body bare, she
lets her fragrant sleeves fall without word, and trails her river-goddess skirts
without talking — she's just like the Consorts of the Xiang Tomb, leaning

against the red doors of Shun's Temple, or like Chang E in the Moon Hall, barely visible in the Golden Hall of the Ecliptic Toad. What a fine girl!

[*Tiaxiao ling*] (Student sings:)
I've just seen her lithe gracefulness,
And compare her to Chang E in the Moon Hall, who is not so fine a piece.
Now blocked from view, now hidden, she threads the fragrant path,
I can imagine how hard for her to walk on such tiny feet.
A hundred seductions spring from the face of this delightful lass,
Oh, it steals a man's soul away![28]

By the late mediaeval period, original myths of goddesses and divine beauties had become intermingled and in most cases, as clearly shown here, were hopelessly conflated. For instance, the consorts of the Xiang Tomb were, in their original form, the goddesses of the Xiang River, Xiangjun 湘君 (Mistress of the Xiang) and Xiangfei 湘妃 (Lady of the Xiang). They were also known by the style names Ehuang 娥皇 and Nüying 女英 (Fairy Radiance and Maiden Bloom)[29] and were assimilated into the legend of the Great Sage King Yao 堯 as filial daughters who were given in marriage to his successor and the next Sage King, Shun 舜 , as consorts. According to legend, Shun died on a southern journey and his two consorts could not reach him before his demise, and so wept at his tomb. Their tears fell upon and spotted the bamboos along the Xiang River. The anecdote is at once a legend of tragic love and a tale on the origin of the spotted bamboos of the Hunan area. It was believed as part of late medieval lore that Ehuang was also another name for Chang E, fairy goddess of the moon.[30] As Edward. H. Schafer has pointed out, this is not unusual, given the normal associations between water, the moon, and women.[31] Chang E was renowned for her fairness of skin and it was believed that she lived in the moon accompanied only by a hare that ceaselessly pounded out the elixir of immortality beside a cassia tree.[32]

The myth of this nocturnal goddess was also conflated in popular imagination with a story of the famous Tang emperor, Xuan Zong 玄宗 (r.712–756), who once roamed in a celestial journey to the very wheel of ice itself:

Minghuang of the Tang roamed in the palaces of the moon where he saw a heavenly precinct, the lintel tablet of which read, "Precincts of Spreading Frigidity and Clear Nothingness". There were more than ten untouched beauties, dressed in snowy clothes and riding white simurghs that danced beneath the cassia walls.[33]

One can clearly see emerging in these passages an interwoven net of references that traces a delicate tapestry of white light in the night and dark grottoes of mysterious beauty. The constant references to these other-worldly women keep the actual image of Oriole as insubstantial as a mirage, the shimmering beauty of which is caught in the next song:

> [*Xiaotao hong*] (Student sings:)
> In night's depth, mists of incense disperse through the empty courtyard,
> The curtains of the door are stilled in the eastern breeze.
> Her bows finished, she leans on the curving balustrade,
> And sighs deeply three or four times.
> The perfectly round moon like a mirror suspended:
> This is neither the slightest cloud nor thinnest haze,
> But is all smoke of incense and human breath,
> Wafting inseparably upward together.[34]

But, of course, Chang E is more than just beauty, as the name of her abode suggests. Engraved on the educated reader's or onlooker's mind would of course be the poem of the Tang poet Li Shangyin 李商隱 (812–858) about Chang E that stresses, among other things, her isolation and loneliness:

> Cloud-mother[35] screens the wind, lamp's shadows deepen,
> The Long River gradually falls, dawn's stars sink;
> Chang E should now regret having stolen the magic herb,
> In an azure sea of blue sky, in her heart, night after night...[36]

In this poem we see another phase of the myth. In one tradition, Chang E had been thought to be the wife of the archer Hou Yi 后羿. She stole from him an elixir of immortality that had been a gift of the Queen Mother of the West and fled to the moon. While her original intent had been to attain immortality, what it cost her was an eternity of loneliness, locked away in the her cold palaces, deprived of love and companionship. This is clearly the image of Chang E with which Oriole compares herself after the old lady has gone back on her word to marry Student Zhang to Oriole:

> ([Female lead] speaks:) What good does it do to burn incense, now that the affair has fallen apart. Oh, moon, how can I bear your fullness?

> [(*Yue* modus:) *Dou anchun*] (Female lead sings:)
> Clouds gather away in the clearing void,
> The icy wheel suddenly wells up,
> The breeze sweeps away tattered red,
> Scattered into piles on the fragrant steps.

A thousand kinds of parting sorrows,
A myriad sorts of idle grief.

(Crimson speaks:) Sister, look at the bright moon. A full moon means there
will be wind as well.

(Female lead speaks:)
Breeze and moonlight are there at heaven's edge,
But in this world of men there is nothing good.

[*Xiaotao hong*] (Female lead sings:)
Look in the human world:
A jade countenance is locked away within embroidered bed hangings,
Out of fear that someone might sport with it.
Think of Chang E:
Sinking in the west and rising in the east, who keeps her company?
How she resents her heavenly palace —
No Pei Hang has yet to make his dream of cavorting with immortals.
These clouds are like the layers of my silken bed hangings that,
For fear Chang E might be aroused,
Now close off the Palace of Spreading Frigidity.[37]

This song is an elaborate conceit that conflates the myth of Chang E with
an account found in a Tang Dynasty classical short story about a failed
scholar named Pei Hang 裴航 . After failing in the examinations and roaming about, Pei visited his old friend Chancellor Cui (the same name
as Oriole's father) and borrowed the money to return to the capital.
He encountered a beautiful woman on the boat to whom he sent a poem
via her maid-servant. She did not respond to his advances, but, when
he was invited to visit her chambers, which were bright and luminous,
she there explained to him that she was married. He treated her with
utmost respect for the rest of the journey, and upon leaving she gave him a
poem:

Once you drink the chalcedony liquor, a hundred feelings are born,
When the Dark Frost is pounded to the end, then you will see Cloud's
    Blossom;
Indigo Bridge is indeed the cave of spiritual transcendents,
Why must you spur off, up to the Jade Capital?

Later, at the Hostel at Indigo Bridge, Pei asked for a drink from an old
crone. She sent out a girl named Yunying 雲英 (Cloud's Blossom) to give
it to him. He was so struck by the girl's beauty that he could not proceed on
his journey. When he asked to marry her, the old crone explained that she

must first have a block of "magic cinnabar" ground to powder in a mortar and pestle made of jade. Pei sold all of his goods, his horse, and his servants in order to purchase such a pestle and mortar. He ground by day and slept by night, peeking once after dark to see a hare busy at the pestle. The old woman collected the powder daily, and after a hundred days, she had enough to take. She then ascended to heaven, asking Pei to wait at the hostel. From there he was also transported into the fairy precincts where he met again the beautiful woman he had first met on the boat and who turned out to be the elder sister of Cloud's Blossom. He was then also transformed into an immortal and lived forever.[38] The connection between the two stories is obviously the hare and the elixir of immortality that she pounds out on the moon. Chang E (Oriole), alone in her cold palace, hopes that her own Pei Hang (Student Zhang) will rescue her, trapped as she is by the obligations to her mother.

All of these allusions are inter-referential, spinning about the central mythic node of Chang E, who is also known by her other epithet as "the jade lady". The student's description of Oriole as one of the several lunar women, and the young girl's adoption of the moon fairy as a conscious persona point to an almost absolute identification of the moon and Oriole. This identification was clearly an accepted tradition by the Ming, as a set of songs, written to describe the vacillating thoughts of Oriole, show by their title, the *Guiyuan changong* 桂苑蟾宮 (Boudoir Laments in the Toad Palace).[39] Only when we realize that, in many cases, the moon *is* Oriole can we understand its daily cycle of rising and setting as an analogue to both her appearance within the play and to the progress of their love. Virtually every appearance by Oriole in the play is in the luminosity of the moon. Even in the scene of the mass for her late father, the moon appears at the beginning of the act just as she does:

> [(*Shuang* modus:) *Xinshui ling*] (Student sings:)
> The wheel of the moon is high above the Hall of the Brahma King,
> Auspicious mists encage the azure tiles,
> The incense smoke forms a canopy of clouds,
> The chanted incantations swell into ocean billows,
> The shadows of the pennants toss and flutter,
> And all of the temple patrons are here.[40]

And disappears again when she leaves at the end of the act:

> [*Yuanyang sha*] (Student sings:)
> Better not to have a heart than to have one,

> "Those full of feeling are vexed by those without";
> I've been bustling around all night,
> The moon sinks, the bells sound out, the cock cries:
> True it is, "The Jade Lady has returned too hastily",
> This good affair is concluded too soon.
> The ceremony finished, everyone disperses,
> All return to their homes in the dark —
> All befuddled, they've raised hell until dawn.[41]

Nowhere does the moon figure more importantly as a symbol of their love than in the famous scene where Student Zhang misinterprets a poem sent to him by Oriole. By the time that this verse reaches him, he has already exchanged other poems, including the one that follows here, with the young girl in which it is clear that the moon had become a code for sexual congress:

> A night bathed in moonlight,
> A spring desolated by flowers' shadows
> Why, under the hoary sycle,
> Do I not see the lady in the moon?[42]

He could hardly have misinterpreted Oriole's response to this poem, with its double entendre in the first line and the indirect allusion in the last to Chang E's lonely sighing in the moon:

> Long has my orchid chamber been lonely,
> No way to pass the fragrant spring;
> I reckon that he who walks and chants,
> Will take pity on the one who heaves a sigh.[43]

At this point, of course, there have been no prohibitions to their meeting, except those normally in place for young people of opposite gender, and Oriole is clearly interested in the student. But after the old lady goes back on her promise to have them married and destroys the possibility of a relationship legitimized by society, Student Zhang continues his pursuit while the girl becomes involved in a web of lies and self-deception. The image of the moon takes on here yet another layer of meaning, symbolizing the waxing and waning of Oriole's response to his overtures.

Sick and despairing over yet another refusal, Zhang sends Oriole a final poem, hoping that it will arouse her interest. The verse follows on his attempt to seduce her with his zither playing, which despite its eventual success does not produce immediate results:

> The vexations of love's longing grow stronger,
> In vain I played the jasper zither;
> From happy affair to encountering spring,
> Your fragrant heart must also have been moved.
> Such passion cannot be denied,
> What need to cling to empty reputation?
> Do not betray the brightness of the moon,
> But covet the heaviness of flower's shadows.[44]

Despite Crimson's warnings that the love has ended ("The moon has darkened over the Western Wing"), Zhang holds out hope and appears to be rewarded with a titillating poem from Oriole:

> Wait for the moon beneath the Western Wing,
> Welcoming the breeze, the door is half opened;
> When separated by the wall, flowers shadows move,
> I guess it is the Jade One coming.[45]

Neither Zhang nor the reader at this point have any clue to the real meaning of the piece. His interpretation that the poem calls for a rendezvous is not only plausible but, considering the freight that the image of the moon has carried to this point, the only likely reading:

> (Male lead speaks:) "Wait for the moon beneath the Western Wing": that's ordering me to come when the moon has come up. "Welcoming the breeze, the door is half opened": that means she will open the door and wait for me. "When separated by the wall, flower shadows move, I guess it is the Jade One coming": that means she wants me to jump across the wall.[46]

But when he actually carries out these actions, he is berated by Oriole and Crimson for his presumption and even accused of forcible entry for the purpose of rape. While on one level the poem Oriole sends surely expresses her real desires, she makes ironic use of the moon, an image that to this point has been identified as a romantic and sexual code. When Zhang Gong actually goes to the garden, he is severely upbraided and even threatened with exposure to the old lady. Thus, the poem has frustrated both the student and the reader, who have mistakenly placed their faith in the constancy of the moon, forgetting that, like love and petulance, it rises and sets, waxes and wanes.

Another aspect of Oriole's characterization is adapted from the topoi of the *caizi-jiaren* 才子佳人 stories, most specifically that of Sima Xiangru 司馬相如 (179–118 B.C.) and Zhuo Wenjun 卓文君,[47] a structuring element of the play that provided the model for the love of Student Zhang and Oriole, and set once and for all the parametres of the treatment of that story in later vernacular fiction.[48] The constituents of the story as found in early sources may be summarized as follows. Sima Xiangru, the son of a rich family of Chengdu, despite his literary talents, fails in his first attempt to make a career at court. He returns home to find his family estate in ruins and has to rely on the good graces of a friend, the magistrate of Linqiong 臨邛, who finds a place for him to live in a public hostel, but nevertheless treats him with utmost respect and courtesy. A certain Zhuo Wangsun 卓王孫 is impressed with Sima and invites him to party at his house. There the poet plays a zither for entertainment and Zhuo's recently-widowed daughter, Wenjun, espies the talented young man and falls in love with him. Sima Xiangru bribes a servant to send her a love note and they elope that night. Her father is, of course, extremely angry and completely cuts her off financially. They go back to the town of Linqiong, and there open a wine shop. Their predicament naturally causes embarrassment for her father, who provides for the couple. Later, Sima Xiangru's fame as a writer spreads to court and the emperor employs him as an envoy to the South-western barbarians. When he is accorded the highest honours by the officials in Shu (modern Sichuan), Zhuo Wangsun gives Zhuo Wenjun her full dowry inheritance. Sima returns to the capital where he is appointed keeper of the funerary park of emperor Wen and retires to Mouling.[49]

From the anecdotes about Sima Xiangru in the miscellany from the later Han, *Xijing zaji* 西京雜記, one account is added concerning a dalliance between Sima Xiangru and the concubine of another man in Mouling. When Zhuo Wenjun heard about it, she purportedly wrote a rather famous poem entitled the *Baitou yin* 白頭吟 (Lament of the White Hairs), in which she lamented her rejection because she had grown older, and in which she longed for a true and lasting relationship. The important point of this spurious addition to the story (both of the transmitted texts of the *Baitou yin* are written in a poetic form that was not extant at the time of her life) is that it changes the direction of the story from its original focus. It henceforth provided a model literary structure for tales about women of good family who had been courted and seduced by a talented young scholar and who then had to suffer the fear or actual ignominy of him selecting another young bride when away at a capital post.[50]

The adaptation of this model of the *caizi-jiaren* for the *Xixiang ji* has allowed the playwright to retain Dong Jieyuan's version of the story in which Oriole, who had originally played the zither in the "Tale of Oriole", is replaced by Student Zhang, who plays it to win her heart. This allows, of course, for the use of the famous scene of this stringed seduction, but through the association with the tradition of the *Baitou yin*, the story also allows the playwright to exploit the dramatic potential of Oriole's rejection which concludes the Tang Dynasty tale. These stories of scholars and beauties have two distinct possibilities as endings: either a happy reunion where lovers are united forever or a dissolution of the romance and rejection of the woman as the man moves on into the public world of Confucian society. In such a way, the story of Sima Xiangru and Zhuo Wenjun provides a background dramatic tension as the final acts unfold. After Oriole has given herself to the student and thereby risked ruining her family and social standing, she tells him in the hopes that he will not reject her:

> In a single second I have thrown away my body, precious as a thousand gold. My body and my life I entrust to you forever. May you never "disdain me in the future and made me lament my white hairs".[51]

The opposition of Oriole is the student, and casting him in the role created for Sima Xiangru allows for a complete expression of his sensitive soul. For it is really his cultural accomplishments that win Oriole over — his poetry chanted over the wall, his zither playing, the poetic *billet-doux* that he sends her in his passionate love-longing. Preconditioned by her awareness of the passing of spring and of her own youth, this paradigm of the perfect scholar triggers within her a passion keening in the green of spring. One of the marvellous features of the play is that this model is not just a literary dramatic structure, but is also the consciously-adopted persona of both Oriole and Student Zhang. For instance, after being aroused by her physical beauty, Zhang Gong's next impression is of her poetic talent:

> [*Tuse er*] (Student sings:)
> Already struck by a vexing loveliness heaped up by her face,
> I'm now perplexed by the quick intelligence stored away in her heart;
> She matched, oh, so well, the metre of my new poem,
> Each word, one by one, tells true feelings — what a pleasure to hear.
>
> [*Shengyao wang*] (Student sings:)
> The lyrics are fresh,
> The prosody flows easily,
> No accident that she has been given Oriole as a name.
> If she were to fix her eyes on me,
> Then we would banter verses across the wall until dawn.

Just now I believe the saying, "Since ancient days the bright love the bright."[52]

Later on, when he receives her letter in the post house, he also vaunts her literary talents and skills.[53] This appreciation of talent is matched perfectly by Oriole's appreciation of his skill:

[*Nuojia ling*] (Female lead sings:)
Normally, whenever I saw a stranger,
I would immediately scowl;
Whenever I saw a traveller,
I would instantly retreat;
But since seeing that man,
I precipitously wanted to get close.
Thinking about his poem of last night —
Using his earlier rhymes,
I responded with freshness and originality.

[*Quetazhi*] (Female lead sings:)
He chanted the lines so evenly,
Recited the words so true;
His new poem that sang of the moon,
Far surpassed the palindrome woven into brocade.
But who is willing to take the needle and draw the thread,
And transmit the utter devotion of this eastern neighbour?[54]

There is such a conscious adoption of the stereotyped roles of the "talented scholar" and "beautiful girl" by the characters, that no less an authority than Crimson accuses them of being *poseurs* who adopt these roles as much out of perversity as out of passion. There are three separate points in the play where Crimson castigates them for acting out their roles so well and or failing to break out of that role to act out real human feelings:

[*Chao tianzi*] (Crimson sings:)
It's not just this student alone,
But all young man of few years,
Who've just learned to suffer love sickness —
[And young girls] of intelligent nature by virtue of birth,
Dressed up in immaculate white,
Night after night they have to be all alone —
Our poet passionate,
Our beauty fickle.
Oh, aren't peoples' fates thwarted?[55]

And:

[*Jianger shui*] (Crimson sings:)
Beauties have always been unlucky,
Budding scholars are always weaklings.
One, a headless goose killed by gloom,
One, an article sold at loss, still rejected.[56]

And:

[*You hulu*] (Crimson sings:)
So haggard is our young master Pan that his temples are streaked,
Our Du Weiniang is no more her former self:
She — her belt has loosened, shrunk to nothing is her emaciated waist,
He — he sleeps in a stupor, with no desire to look at canons or histories;
She — she is unsettled, too listless to pick up her needlework,
He — he played out on silk and paulownia a score of separation's grief.
She — on flowered stationary she erases away a poem of broken hearts,
She — from her brush are written out her hidden feelings,
He — from his strings are transmitted heart's affairs.
Both — both suffer alike from love's longing.

[*Tianxia le*] (Crimson sings:)
Now I believe that "poets and beauties really exist",
But in Crimson's eyes, they are a bit perverse —
It seems to me that passionate people who do not get their heart's desire are
    like this:
What I see is that they suffer so much they become bewitched,
And what I find is that they never give a second thought,
But immediately bury their heads to prepare for a wasting death.[57]

Crimson's position in the play, among other things, is to speak for common sense and for human feeling stripped of all pretence or obscured by questions of social position. She is constantly critical of this kind of role-playing by the student and the young girl and in the end she counsels the student to forget Oriole and get underway with his studies. In a curiously ironic way she, who of all the females has been the most manipulative and critical of his feelings, is the one to urge him to leave.

Her criticism of their role-playing finds a parallel much later in the *Honglou meng*, where Grandmother Jia gives a long lecture on the falseness of this stereotyped convention of the talented beauty and young scholar:

"These stories are all the same," said Grandmother Jia, "so tedious!" Always the same ideally beautiful and accomplished young ladies — at least they are supposed to be ideal, but there's certainly nothing ideal about their behaviour — in fact there's nothing very ladylike about them at all. Invariably we are told how well-born they are. Their father has been a Prime Minister, or a First Secretary at the very least. They are always their father's only child and the apple of his eye. They are always amazingly well-educated, a model of decorum, a regular paragon of virtues — that is, until the first presentable young man comes along. As soon as he appears on the scene — it doesn't matter who or what he is — all their book-learning and the duty they owe their parents fly out the window and the next moment they are "making their plans for the future" and generally carrying on in a way that would bring blushes to the cheeks of a cat-burglar — certainly not in the least like respectable, educated young ladies. You would hardly call a young woman who conducted herself like that a "paragon", however many books she might have read — any more than you would acquit a young fellow charged with highway robbery on the grounds that he was good scholar. The people who make up these stories give themselves the lie every time they open their mouths.[58]

Although the prototypes of the scholar-beauty stories go back to the Tang Dynasty classical tale, it was the *Xixiang ji* which provided the model of that convention for vernacular literature. In the drama, however, this matched pair of young lovers is also buried within another set of relationships that are much more explicit about sex and love. That is the double-triangle relationship between a sing-song girl, maid, and poor student on one axis and between the sing-song girl, madam, and poor student on the other. Many years ago the eminent Sinologist Chen Yinke 陳寅恪 suggested that Oriole indeed might not have been the daughter of a good family, but rather a prostitute.[59] He was indeed on the right track, but as a historian his empirical proofs fell short of solving the problem. What I think he saw, but did not recognize, was that the relationship between Oriole, Madam Cui, and Crimson has clear parallels with the triangle of the old lady, the sing-song girl, and the young hand-maiden, a trio who populate Tang literary tales and later plays about courtesans in the Yuan and Ming period.[60] While the comparison is never explicitly drawn it certainly provides a hidden, but significant structure of action. In these courtesan plays, the old lady is usually insistent that the sing-song girl marry the man of the old lady's choice — usually an ugly merchant. The sing-song girl, on the other hand, has fallen in love with the poor scholar; the maid acts as a go-between for the scholar and the courtesan. We have very close parallels in this play. Madam Cui is insistent that Oriole marry the repugnant Zheng Heng 鄭衡 ; this is clearly based on the model of the madam and the merchant. Student Zhang is the poor and unknown scholar that Oriole refuses to repudiate; Crimson acts as the liaison between the two in the face of the madam's wrath.

That this structure, though unstated, is implicit in the text is substantiated by an early and stray comment by Zhu Youdun in one of his many *zaju*, that the role of Oriole was played by a *huadan* 花旦 or "painted female lead", a role type that usually did courtesans and comparable risqué characters.[61] The name itself stems from the common use of the term "flower" or "blossom" to designate women of pleasure. In the context of the play, however, flowers are most often associated with sex. Oriole's first appearance in the play holding a sprig of flowers unleashes a torrent of floral imagery. At crucial points in the play, the image of red flowers floods the scene — jumbles of red petals are left behind on the paths as she leaves, red blossoms are felled by the eastern wind; they become the indelible print of the girl herself. The association between flowers and prostitutes is subtly reinforced by Crimson, who in her counsels to Zhang, reminds him several times that Oriole is no "roadside willow" or "tattered blossom". Zhang himself is referred to as the *Tanhua lang* 探花郎 , "the flower-plucking gentleman", a term used to designate the third-place candidate in the examinations. While the play clearly states he is the first-place finisher (*zhuangyuan* 狀元), he is commonly called *tanhua lang*, to keep the metaphor of sexual conquest an active part of the play. He is chided by Crimson for being a "flower-filcher" and a "plucker of blossom". He, in turn, calls Oriole a "flower that speaks" and several times Crimson refers to Oriole's acquiescence to Zhang's desires by describing her "as a flowering with stem bent low", ready to "receive the Eastern Wind". From the very opening description of the Yellow River "irrigating the peony gardens of Luoyang", floral imagery leads us to the inevitable seduction scene. "Flower's shadow" and "flower's shade" both refer in traditional sexual lore to the female genitalia, "flower's heart" is the common term for the clitoris, and the red peony, especially, has come to symbolize the vagina in full flush of engorgement. All of these terms are used frequently in the play and figure in the various contexts of the surface narrative, where they describe the physical reality of spring's last blossoms falling before the warming winds from the east. But they also foreshadow the seduction scene itself: ·

[*Sheng hulu*] (Student sings:)
Here to my breast I press her pliant jade and warm perfume,

Ai,
Ruan Zhao has reached Mt. Tiantai.
Spring has come to the world of men, flowers sport their colours!
Gently, she adjusts her willowy waist,
Lightly splits the flower's heart:
Dew drips as the peony opens.[62]

But, I suspect, the triangle goes deeper, and is in fact congruent with another that is based on traditional Chinese lore about the theory and practice of sex and is the one that powers the sexual allegory within the play. According to these beliefs, a man is endowed with a limited amount of qi 氣, or "vital energy", the physical manifestation of which is semen (jing 精). The unmonitored squandering of vital essence detracted from one's physical well-being and hindered the quest for long, and according to some beliefs, even immortal life. Traditional sex practices, then, revolved around the need to restrict the emission of semen during intercourse. Actual ejaculation was limited only to those occasions when a man copulated with his principal wife and then solely for the purpose of producing male offspring. By practising *coitus reservatus*, either by withholding ejaculation or by diverting semen into the urethra, a man could nurture his vital energy and send it along the marrow of his spine — called the Yellow River — where it flowed upward to re-energize his brain. He could even reinforce his own vital energy by absorbing the vaginal fluids of the female, and great abundance was to be had if the man could harness his own *yang* power and simultaneously imbibe the *yin* energy produced by a woman at orgasm. If we read sexual manuals from the Han to the present, we can see a recurrent theme of initiation of an emperor (usually the Yellow Emperor) into the glories of sex by two, sometimes three women. These females, who are divine creatures, are usually known as Sunü 素女, the White Girl and Cainü 彩女, the Rainbow Girl. In the form of a physical catechism, they instruct the emperor in the ways and wiles of sex, initiating him into the physical pleasure while conveying to him the secrets of nurturing his *yang* power. This triad, I believe, lies at the very heart of understanding the archetypical structure and meaning of sex in the play. Oriole, for instance, dressed solely in white throughout the play, reflects the original Sunü; Crimson, literary named "The Red Maiden" suggests the counterpart, Rainbow Girl. This is also borne out by the fact that Crimson, whose main function in the play is something like a detective — revealing the hypocrisy of the old lady and exposing the two lovers as *poseurs* consciously adopting the *caizi-jiaren* model to interact with each other —

also has a secondary role as Student Zhang's instructress in love and sexual informant. When she first thinks that Zhang and Oriole will be married, she gives him some advice on lovemaking:

> (Crimson speaks:) I'll give you some good advice…
> [*Sibian jing*] (Crimson sings:)
> In your happy union tonight,
> Could our delicate Oriole
> Have had any experience?
> You must be tender and gentle,
> When you twine your mandarin duck necks below the lamp.
> After you've looked carefully at "your wretch",
> You'll so die of happiness that it won't come out clean![63]

She repeats this advice later on what she believes to be the night of consummation:

> [*Tianshui ling*] (Crimson explains the female lead to the student, singing:)
> This fine night will go on and on,
> The quiet courtyard is deserted and still,
> Flower stems bend low and rustle.
> She's a young girl,
> You should pamper her temper,
> Massage her with words.
> Blend with her moods:
> Dont's guess her to be a broken willow or tattered blossom!
>
> [*Zhegui ling*]
> She's an oh, so loveable, beautiful jade without flaw:
> Her powdered face engenders spring,
> Her cloudy locks are like piled-up raven feathers.
> She's oh, so timid, oh, so fearful.
> And she does not scheme for any free wine or idler's tea.[64]
> But once between the sheets you should give it your all,
> And when your fingertips report back from duty all worn out,
> Then you can stack away your moans and sighs,
> And when you have done with your concerns and anxieties,
> When you have cleared away frustrations and sorrows,
> Then be prepared to be happily stuffed.[65]

Crimson, saucy, impudent, and even bawdy at times becomes his accomplice in seduction and a voyeur of their lovemaking. As a maid-servant, of course, she has her own self-interest at stake. A happy marriage

between such a finely matched couple means for her release from inden-
tured status and acceptance as a concubine in the household — she will
become the third in a sexual partnership that fulfills the archetypical trio of
celestial lovers.

The *menage* of the sexual manuals is also suggested by Student Zhang
descriptions of Oriole as a divine being. The most consistently used comparison is to Chang E, goddess of the moon, but he describes her at times
as Guanyin, as a Taoist immortal, and as a heavenly sylph descended from
heaven for a tryst with a mere mortal. In all of these circumstances, the
descriptive lines are at the margins of her appearance — the deep and
silent mystery of her approach, heralded by soft breezes and the delicate
fragrance of flowers or the lingering tastes and smells left on her departure
— there, but as delicate and arabesque as newly greening willows or the
fading coos of love birds. The numinous quality of such descriptions are
meant to signal the rarefied contact between celestial goddesses and mortal
men, but they are significantly interwoven with descriptions of her face
and her body. Such a set of inter-related references firmly ground Oriole's
existence both in the other-world and in actual physical presence. Such a
careful interweaving of images is probably meant to illustrate how sexual
and divine knowledge are affiliated and to stress that comprehensive
knowledge and salvation are not constituted in "escape from the flesh" but
in an actualization of body and mind together in a single act.[66] That is why,
at the moment of climax quoted above, Student Zhang expresses his feelings both as physical gratification and as transcendent enlightenment
(Ruan Zhao has reached Mt. Tiantai).

The down side — at least to the modern reader — of this theory is the
fear and repression of female sexuality. The original myth of sexual in-
doctrination in which women are instructresses is closely related to the
conception of women as temptresses or succubi.[67] The basic premise of
the myth is that a man has a finite amount of *yang* energy that must be at
least retained, and at best vivified and replenished through a regimen of
sexual exercises in which the male is taught to retain control of ejaculation
while inciting a woman to orgasm. The unspoken corollary to this premise
is that intercourse is fraught with danger if a man allows himself to be
exploited or weakened by sex. The same women who were such excellent
teachers were also considered to be insatiable and unless a man remained
in complete control, he stood a chance of debilitating himself through
congress with a woman who sought to reinforce her own vital powers
through inciting a man to ejaculation. Small wonder, then, that in

vernacular literature a woman is often likened to a killing blade and was said to "carry a sword between her thighs!" One frequently quoted line in drama is "The gate that gave us birth is the door of our death." The Chinese imagination never tired of creating vixen or female ghosts who assumed human form so that they might rob the vital powers from men who were foolish enough to seduce them.

Likewise, in the play, the beauty of Oriole is extremely devastating, upsetting the neutered and orderly world of the monastery, diverting Student Zhang from the pursuit of his rightful ambitions, and even calling down the siege of the monastery. In this fear of her beauty one certainly finds an echo of the judgement of Student Zhang in the *chuanqi* 傳奇 upon which it was based. In that earlier story, Zhang rejected Oriole out right, describing her to his friends as a *youwu* 尤物, a succubus whose sexual allure would lead him into danger. This deep-seated fear of women and of female sexuality goes far back into history, and in those pages there are a plethora of attractive women who have led their kingdoms to a downfall.[68] Oriole is, in fact, compared with several of these women in the play: with Xi Shi 西施,[69] who led the kingdom of Wu to its downfall, to the sister of Li Yannian 李延年,[70] and to Yang Guifei 楊貴妃 (719–756), the notorious consort of Emperor Xuan Zong 玄宗 of the Tang. In each of these cases, Oriole is first compared to one of these women and then called a *qingguo se* 傾國色, a "state-toppling beauty". For instance, when the Flying Tiger General surrounds the monastery, he vaunts Oriole's beauty in these terms:

(Clown, costumed as Flying Tiger Sun enters and opens:) I am surnamed Sun, named Biao, and called the Flying Tiger. At this moment Emperor De Zong has ascended the throne and all under heaven is in turmoil. Because the Commander-in-chief, Ding Wenya has lost control, I, Biao, guard the River bridge and lead some five thousand men and horse to plunder the good citizens of their valuables and goods. Recently I learned that Oriole, the daughter of the former Chancellor Cui Jue, who has the "looks to topple cities and states", and a face of Xi Shi or Precious Consort Yang, is now staying at the Monastery of Universal Salvation. I've thought it over, and it seems that right now is just the time to exercise military might. When the Commander-in-chief is not acting right, why should I alone be incorruptible? My troops listen to my order — the men will all wear gags, the horses will all have bits. We will march this very night to Hezhong Prefecture. If I can snatch Oriole for my wife, then all my life's desires are fulfilled.[71]

In the case of Yang Guifei, there are numerous other subtle allusions and comparisons between the Tang Dynasty vamp and Oriole. Yang Guifei

was the young consort of the elderly Emperor Xuan Zong of the Tang
Dynasty. He first fell in love with her when he saw her plump, alabaster
body emerge from the hot springs at Huaqing Palace 華清宮. Since she
was married to one of his sons, in order for her to become his concubine,
she first had to become a nun. As in the case of Oriole and Student Zhang,
there are over-tones of incest in his infatuation. Consort Yang had been
Xuan Zong's daughter-in-law, and in the play the old lady very cleverly
established a brother-sister bond between our young lovers. There are
other points in the text where Student Zhang makes much more subtle
allusion to the similarities between Oriole and Yang Guifei, for instance,
when he calls her "a flower that can speak", which refers in turn to a
famous anecdote about the aging emperor Xuan Zong's infatuation with
Precious Consort Yang.[72] These are the comparisons that Oriole also sees
when she finally becomes aware that her beauty has power to devastate the
normal course of events, and that it has provoked the assault upon the
monastery:

> [*Reprise*]
> Those louts have heard a rumour on the wind,
> Saying, "The kohl of her eyebrows frowns darkly,
> And her lotus face engenders spring,
> Just like a city-and-state-toppling Precious Consort Yang."
> Won't I send these three-hundred monks to their deaths?
> Half a myriad mutinous troops,
> In half a second will cut them down like grass and root them out.
> For neither state nor dynasty have these louts, trust or loyalty,
> And they plunder the citizens at will.
> Even this building constructed like a heavenly palace they will burn to the
>   ground.[73]

Oriole is also called a "state-toppling beauty" by the Student and by
Facong 法聰, the monk. No matter what the roles of these male players —
bandit, student, or monk — they can "all assign the devastating power of
her charm to her; by enlisting the conventional cliché of overt and rampant
sexuality — the state-toppling beauty — none of them have to accept any
responsibility for their own desire".[74] In the play, to be sure, the devastating power of her beauty also has a didactic function. Since Oriole has been
left to wander freely around the monastery — despite the warnings of her
mother — she and the reader are made suddenly aware that beauty beyond
its logical confines is dangerous to the normal course of events and, as the

siege of the monastery shows, calls down a curiously symmetrical punishment for her overt sexual attraction in the form of violence or even rape.

But Oriole is more, of course, than this simple bundle of conventional roles and residual myths. In the play she is a bundle of contradictory feelings. She senses in the very opening scene of the play that her youth is passing, she falls madly in love with the young scholar, she is headstrong with her mother, and yet is also extraordinarily passive and filial at times. Her sincere devotion to her father is clear in the text and the suppression (or attempted suppression) of her feelings of love for the student seem to stem from a true desire to abide by her mother's wishes.

Her feelings for her mother are furthermore complicated by something akin to a lack of self-esteem. One has only to note her conception of her mother's opinion of her as "worthless goods" to be sold at "two for the price of one", to sense that Oriole's duty to her mother operates not only in the realm of love and compassion, but also within the abused relationships of authority and filial response. The tension developed between the filial devotion of the proper child and the demands and needs of sexual and emotional fulfilment exploit this boundary between human feeling and duty to the fullest. Except for moments as those mentioned above, in which she realize the effect of her beauty, her sexuality seems to be, indeed, a mystery to her; She is almost unconscious of it. Its charms are apparent to everyone else, and in fact, is described solely and exclusively by other characters in the play. But to her, awakening sexuality remains a mysterious part of contradictory and poorly defined, much less understood, feelings.

Her inability to sort out these feelings leads to charges of insincerity by the student and of lying by her maid-servant. Yet, if one were to accept a cynical point of view, she is the only person who stands to suffer loss in this love relationship. The student is a free agent, alone and directed toward a career; he can, if he chooses, be exploitative, seduce her and then either leave her behind as one more stop along the road to the capital, or abandon her for a better match later. Dramatic conventions based on the *caizi-jiaren* stories (in which the male may either return to marry the woman or else abandon her), the constant allusion in the play to dangerous and wanton women, and the use of the "flowery female lead", all suggest such a rejection as a possibility until the very end of the play. Her own fear that she expresses so clearly after the seduction scene echoes the feelings of Zhuo Wenjun, author of the *Baitou yin*, when she thought that Sima

Xiangru had abandoned her. Here it might be said that her acknow-
ledgement of that similarity represents her awareness that they are acting
out the roles prescribed for them by the *caizi-jiaren* model, but it also
signals a real change in her personality. While heretofore she was, in her
indecision, master of the student and was the one in control of the situation, once her bargaining chip of chastity is played, she is completely at his
mercy. It is anxiety, indeed, that stamps her feelings after the affair is
discovered and Zhang goes off to the capital for the examinations — as if
she waits in expectation for the rest of that well-known story of use and
rejection to unfold and for him to turn heartlessly against her. This certainly also foreshadows Zheng Heng's return to claim her and her willingness
to believe that the student had, indeed, taken another wife.

In general, what seems like an ambivalence toward the student that
he reads as heartlessness is indeed the unresolved desire of a girl struggling
to make a choice between love and responsibility. There are three clear
points in the drama when she is ready to give herself to him. The first is
when she sees him and hears his first poem chanted over the wall. The
opening scene of the next act, just before the monastery is surrounded, is
given over to her expressions of love. The possibility that she might have a
relationship with him is then endangered by the siege, for the repulse of
which she is ready to give up either her body or her life. The second, and
most significant opportunity, is when the old lady promises her to Student
Zhang if he can lift the siege. She is plainly excited about this possibility,
but that is also ruined by the duplicity of her mother, who reneges on her
promise. Finally, she is seduced by his poetry and by his zither, but at the
crucial point where she might give herself to him, she overhears him
accuse her of lying.

Her relationship with her mother makes these decision even more
difficult. There appears to be little mutual trust between the two. It is
apparent that Crimson's main job, from the old lady's point of view, is to
follow Oriole around and make sure that she stays out of trouble. Oriole's
behaviour had already occasioned one strong rebuke from her mother, but
in Oriole's eyes (as she blurts out in a moment of exasperation), she is
simply a piece of goods to be traded for status and family ties. Her bitter
reaction to her mother's duplicity in regard to the marriage promise to
Zhang is followed in the play by an intriguing aria in which it is not the
situation itself that comes under scrutiny, but rather what she sees as a
pathological and untrustworthy side of her mother — that she is a liar:

[*Qiaopaier*]
The old lady is a slippery bolt that can't be pinned down,
A wordless riddle that can't be solved.
In hidden corners she deceives people with honeyed words,
But when she summons them she makes them miserable.[75]

[*Litingyan dai xiezhi sha*]
My mother has felled him from the sky with honeyed words,
And has cheated me badly with false pretences.[76]

She decries the fact that her mother's deceit is "as big as heaven". Earlier, when she learns that her mother is going to simply put on a small banquet to honour Zhang, she laments to her maid that her mother has no real concern for her:

[*Jiao zhengse*] (Female Lead sings:)
She's afraid that I'm just goods to be sold at a loss,
But, when it's two for the price of one, then the deal is on.[77]

And, then again, after she's discovered that the old lady has gone back on her word, she again ponders that "he's just a headless goose, killed by gloom / and I'm just an article to be sold at a loss, and even then rejected!"[78] Without that basic level of trust between mother and child, what is substituted is a hierarchical relationship that not only abuses its authority and power, but invalidates the trust that should be developed therein by the exercise of humanity and compassion. Small wonder that Oriole feels that she is simply a commodity that can be offered for sale, withdrawn, and re-offered to someone of higher station in order to bolster family status.

While the transactional nature of the relationship between mother and daughter is certainly related to the structural element of the courtesan-madam-student triangle, the casting of Oriole as a *huadan* also allows the conflict between innocence and erosive beauty to be perfectly caught. Casting a young woman, just emerging from the torpor of adolescent longing, with the trappings of a courtesan, the play manages to capture that contradictory period of life when allure and sexuality, normally only openly displayed by easy women, can be presented as a mysterious and innocent longing of a young woman who has yet seen the need to hide this powerful force from public view. Except for moments as those mentioned above, Oriole seems unaware of the effect of her beauty and her own sexuality seems to be a mystery to her, something of which she is completely unconscious and which are simply part of contradictory or otherwise poorly understood emotions that are complicated by a lack of sense of self-worth. This is an intensely human situation, but it is one not just created from what we might like to call psychological realism. It is rather wrought from deep-seated cultural myths about the power and danger of feminine sexuality, about lonely moon-goddesses and celestial lovers, about lovers who are perfectly-matched cultural models, but in the end also created from the conventions of the stage itself — the "flowery female lead".

Notes

1. Portions of this paper are drawn from Stephen H. West and Wilt L. Idema, *The Moon and the Zither: Wang Shifu's Story of the Western Wing* (Berkeley: University of California Press, 1991).

2. The Hongzhi edition is available in a photographic facsimile reproduction: *Xinkan qimiao quanxiang zhushi Xixiang ji* 新刊奇妙全相注釋西廂記 (Shanghai: Shangwu yinshuguan, 1955). The Hongzhi edition of the *Xixiang ji* also constitutes, in a much reduced size, the first two volumes of the *Guben xiqu congkan* 古本戲曲叢刊, *chuji* 初集 of 1954. Both reproductions have been repeatedly reprinted. Also see Jiang Xingyu 蔣星煜, "Hongzhi ben *Xixiang ji* de tili ji 'Yueke' wenti" 弘治本西廂記的體例及岳刻問題, in his *Ming kanben Xixiang ji yanjiu* 明刊本西廂記研究 (Beijing: Zhongguo xiju chubanshe, 1982), pp. 26–37. The publisher's advertisement describing the compilation and cutting of both the text and the woodblock illustrations is found on p. 161b.

3. This *Huitu xinjiaozhu guben Xixiang ji* 繪圖新校註古本西廂記 was photo-mechanically reproduced in facsimile in 1927 in Beijing by Fujian shushe and Donglaige shudian.

4. The chantefable is well represented in modern philological literature and in translation. See *Dong Jieyuan Xixiang ji* 董解元西廂記, collated and annotated by Ling Jingyan 凌景埏 (Beijing: Renmin wenxue chubanshe, 1962). Another annotated edition has been produced by Zhu Pingchu 朱平楚 as *Xixiang ji zhugongdiao zhushi* 西廂記諸宮調註釋 (Lanzhou: Gansu renmin chubanshe, 1982). Dong's work was translated into English by Li-li Ch'en as *Master Tung's Western Chamber Romance (Tung Hsi-hsiang chu-kung-tiao), A Chinese Chantefable* (Cambridge: Cambridge University Press, 1976), and into Dutch by W. L. Idema as Mijnheer Dong, *Het verhaal van de westerkamers in alle toonaarden* (Amsterdam: Meulenhoff, 1984).

5. Ling Mengchu's edition of Wang Shifu's *Xixiang ji* was reprinted by Liu Shiheng 劉世珩 in his *Nuanhongshi huike Xixiang ji* 暖紅室彙刻西廂記 .

6. John Ching-yu Wang, *Chin Sheng-t'an* (New York: Twayne Publishers, 1972) provides a succinct but lucid survey of Jin's life and criticism.

7. Ibid., pp. 82–104.

8. At least three very recent modern typeset editions of Jin Shengtan's version of the play are available: *Guanhuatang diliu caizishu Xixiang ji* 觀華堂第六才子書西廂記 , collated by Fu Xiaohang 傅曉航 (Lanzhou: Gansu renmin chubanshe, 1985); *Guanhuatang diliu caizishu Xixiang ji*, collated by Cao Fangren 曹方人 (Nanjing: Jiangsu guji chubanshe, 1986); and *Jin Shengtan piben Xixiang ji* 金聖嘆批本西廂記, collated by Zhang Guoguang 張國光 (Shanghai: Shanghai guji chubanshe, 1986). This portion of the paper is summarized from Stephen H. West and Wilt L. Idema, *The Moon and the Zither*.

9. Wang Shifu's *Xixiang ji* has often been translated into Western and Eastern languages. (See Wang Lina 王麗娜, "*Xixiang ji* de waiwen yiben he Man Meng wen yiben" 西廂記的外文譯本和滿蒙文譯本 , in *Wenxue yichan* 文學遺產, No. 3, 1981, pp. 148–154; Jiang Xingyu, "*Xixiang ji* de Riwen yiben 西廂記的日文譯本", in *Wenxue yichan*, No. 3, 1982, p. 32.) The earliest translation into a European language dates to the French version of the eminent sinologue Stanislas Julien, which first appeared in 1872 in the pages of a periodical and was reissued in book form in 1880 as *Si-siang-ki ou l'Histoire du pavillon d'occident, Comédie en seize actes* (Geneve: H. Georg, Th. Mueller). From the very start of his career, Julien had been a student and translator of Yuan drama. He attempted to redress the eighteenth century prejudices against Chinese drama that stemmed from Prémare's early rendition of Ji Junxiang's 紀君祥 *Zhaoshi guer* 趙氏孤兒 (Orphan of Zhao) with a new translation in 1839 and his translation of Li Xingdao's 李行道 *Huilan ji* 灰蘭記 (The Chalk Circle) indirectly influenced Bertold Brecht in his conception of *Der kaukasische Kreidekreis*. The translation of the *Xixiang ji* was the crowning achievement of his lifelong involvement with Chinese vernacular literature. As in the case of all other Western translators so far, Julien based himself on the Jin Shengtan edition of the text and accordingly only translated the four "authentic" plays of the cycle. His translation was primarily intended as a crib for students and was accompanied by extensive notes and even the Chinese text of the arias.

The next Western language translation to appear was the German rendition of all five plays by Vincenz Hundhausen in 1926, which was entitled *Das Westzimmer, Ein chinesisches Singspiel aus dem dreizehnten Jahrhundert* (Eisenach: Erich Roth Verlag). This is a very free adaptation in the German tradition of *Nachdichtung* or "re-creation" which allows the translator a very wide leeway in superimposing his own thoughts and fancies on the text of his choice. Nevertheless, his work created quite a scandal upon its appearance because Hundhausen was accused by one of his reviewers of having plagiarized Julien's translation. Hundhausen sued the reviewer for libel and many members of the German sinological community one way or another became involved in the imbroglio. (See the review of Hundhausen's translation by E. Haenisch in *Asia Major*, 8 (1932), pp. 278–282.) Hundhausen went on to produce a *Nachdichtung* of Tang Xianzu's 湯顯祖 (1550–1617) famous sentimental melodrama *Mudan ting* 牡丹亭 (The Peony Pavilion) in 1933.

In the mid-thirties two English language versions of the *Xixiang ji* appeared almost simultaneously. In 1936, Stanford University Press published Henry H. Hart's *The West Chamber, A Medieval Drama*. Hart again limited himself to a translation of the first four plays and even omitted the final act of the fourth play as "it is an anticlimax and adds nothing to the interest of the play" [sic!] (*The West Chamber, A Medieval Drama*, p. x). In his preface, Hart chided Hundhausen for casting his rendition of the arias into rhymed couplets and called it "an effort which more often than not distorts the sense of the original" (Ibid., p. ix). Accordingly, Hart presented the arias in his translation as free verse. Ironically, Hart's version has been "poeticized" by Henry W. Wells, who in 1972 published an adaptation of Hart's translation in which all prose-passages had been recast into blank verse and all arias had been rhymed! (See "*The West Chamber (Hsi-hsiang chi)*, Attributed to Wang Shih-fu, Rendered into English Verse by Henry W. Wells", in *Four Classical Asian Plays in Modern Translation,* compiled and edited by Vera Rushforth Irwin, Baltimore: Penguin Books, 1972, pp. 95–230.)

The publication of Hart's rendition was preceded by one year by the publication of another, soon-to-become-standard, English language version by S.I. Hsiung as *The Romance of the Western Chamber (Hsi-hsiang chi)* (London: Methuen and Co., 1935) in which Hsiung translated all five plays. This edition was reissued as late as 1968 by Columbia University Press with a new introduction by C. T. Hsia, who regretted that the translator based himself on the Jin Shengtan edition instead of one of the earlier Ming editions. Still, Hsia credited him with having done "a conscientious job of reproducing in English the paraphraseable meaning of his adopted text". (See C. T. Hsia, "A Critical Introduction", in *The Romance of the Western Chamber*, p. xxxi.) In his critical introduction, Hsia made it abundantly clear that in his opinion the translator had failed to do justice to the stylistic variety of the original. However, we should not forget that, whatever the modern view of scholarly translation may be, these earlier translations for their times and for the sources available to them constituted quite creditable, even excellent achievements.

10. Cao Xueqin 曹雪芹, *The Story of the Stone*, Vol. 1, translated by David Hawkes (Harmondsworth: Penguin Books, 1973), p. 464. For the Chinese text, see, for example, *Honglou meng bashihui jiaoben* 紅樓夢八十回校本,

collated by Yu Pingbo 俞平伯 with the assistance of Wang Xishi 王熙時 (Beijing: Renmin wenxue chubanshe, 1958), Vol. 1, p. 234.

11. Cao Xueqin, *The Story of the Stone*, Vol. 2, translated by David Hawkes (Hammondsworth: Penguin Books, 1977), p. 333. For the Chinese text, see, for example, *Honglou meng bashihui jiaoben*, Vol. 2, pp. 448–449. *The Lute Player* refers to Gao Ming's 高明 (d. 1359) famous southern play *Pipa ji* 琵琶記, which was translated into English by Jean Mulligan as *The Lute: Kao Ming's P'i-pa chi* (New York: Columbia University Press, 1980). *A Hundred Yuan Plays* is an alternative designation of the *Yuanqu xuan*, an anthology of one hundred *zaju* plays from the Yuan and early Ming Dynasties, compiled by Zang Mouxun (1550–1620) and published in 1615/1616. This anthology, which does not include Wang Shifu's *Xixiang ji*, quickly established itself as the most authoritative collection of *zaju*.

12. Ibid., p. 515. For the Chinese text, see, for example, Cao Xueqin, *Honglou meng bashihui jiaoben*, Vol. 2, p. 550. *The Soul's Return* refers to *Mudan ting huanhun ji* 牡丹亭還魂記 by Tang Xianzu. This play was translated into English by Cyril Birch as *The Peony Pavilion (Mudan ting)* (Bloomington: Indiana University Press, 1980).

13. The modern scholar Jiang Xingyu has devoted a number of articles to a discussion of various aspects of the complex relations between the *Xixiang ji* and the *Honglou meng*, "Guanyu Baoyu, Daiyu suo du de shiliuchuben *Xixiang ji*"關於寶玉、黛玉所讀的十六出本西廂記, in his *Ming kanben Xixiang ji yanjiu* , pp. 210–214; "*Xixiang ji* de 'Zhuangtai kuijian' yu *Honglou meng* di ershisan hui"西廂記的"妝台窺見"與紅樓夢第二十三回 Ibid., pp. 293–296; "Cao Xueqin yong xiaoshuo xingshi xie de *Xixiang ji* pipingshi"曹雪芹用小說形式寫的西廂記批評史, in his *Zhongguo xiqushi tanwei*中國戲曲史探微(Jinan: Qi Lu shushe, 1985). The vehement denunciations of our play as reading matter should perhaps be related to the traditional reading practice: students were trained to read a text repeatedly and intently until they knew its words by heart and had internalized its values. Information to this point has been adapted from Stephen H. West and Wilt L. Idema, *The Moon and the Zither*.

14. *Huitu xinjiaozhu guben Xixiang ji*, 1.7a. In his annotations, Wang Jide also cites Xu Wei's comment that, in fact, the long geographical description that follows echoes Student Zhang's trip up the Yellow River.

15. I.1.34a. *You hulu*. The location within the plays will be noted as follows: (I.1.34a. *You hulu*):

    I: Play one (of one to five).

    1: Act one (of one to five).

    34a: Page number in the Hongzhi edition.

    You hulu: Appropriate Tune title.

16. II.1.61b. *Qing geer*.

17. I.1.34a. *You hulu.*
18. I.1.34a.
19. The poem is one of a series of two on the famed Mt. Lu:
   The sun burns Incense Censer, producing violet smoke,
   Far off, looking at the waterfall suspending what was stream before;
   Flying currents plummet straight down three thousand feet,
   Could it be the Silver River falling through the Nine Heavens?
   (Incense Censer was a name of one of the peaks)
20. The peony is known, in fact, as the "flower of Luoyang" (*Luoyanghua* 洛陽花); Ouyang Xiu 歐陽修 (1007–1072), the famous Song statesman and scholar, wrote a long treatise on the peonies of Luoyang, identifying hundreds of varieties, called *Luoyang mudan ji* 洛陽牡丹集, see *Ouyang Wenzhonggong quanji* 歐陽文忠公全集(*Sibu beiyao* ed.) 72. 1a–7a.
21. The *Bowu zhi* is a collection of anecdotes traditionally attributed to Zhang Hua 張華 (232–300), but shown to be a compilation of diverse stories by a later editor or editors. The story of the raft is found in (*Sibu beiyao* ed.) 3.3a; there are also references to Zhang Qian on 1.1b. By the late Six Dynasties, these myths were conflated as indicated by the amalgamated story's appearance in the late seventh century *Jing Chu suishi ji* 荆楚歲時記(A Record of the Annual and Seasonal Customs of the Areas of Jing and Chu).
22. I.1.35b-36a. *Jiegao.*
23. In popular lore a palace where one meets "divine sylphs".
24. In popular lore there were thirty-three heavens, and that of "Separation's Regret" was the highest and was the home of thwarted lovers who had to endure eternal separation. One finds in Yuan drama the common saying:
   "Thirty-three heavens: Separation's Regret is the highest.
   Four hundred and four ailments: the illness of love's longing is most bitter."
25. I.1.37b.
26. I.1.38a.
27. I.3.49b. *Dou anchun.*
28. I.3.49b.
29. The translations for these names are taken from Edward Schafer, *The Divine Woman: Dragon Ladies and Rain Maidens* (Berkeley: University of California Press, 1973), see especially pp. 48–53.
30. Ibid.
31. Ibid.
32. In some traditions, Chang E is actually transformed into the hare.
33. This story originated in the *Longcheng lu* 龍城錄, which has been attributed (incorrectly) to Liu Zongyuan 柳宗元. For a complete account of the affair see, instead, the Song work, Wang Zhuo 王灼, *Biji manzhi* 碧雞漫志(An Occasional Record of the Azure Fowl Ward), Vol. 3, pp. 124–128.
34. I.3.51a.

35. i.e., the mica used for panels in the folding screen.

36. See Li Shangyin, *Li Shangyin xuanji* 李商隱選集, annotated by Zhou Zhenfu 周振甫 (Shanghai: Guji chubanshe, 1985), pp. 299–300; see also James J. Y. Liu, *The Poems of Li Shangyin* (Chicago: Chicago University Press, 1969), p. 99.

37. I.5.83a–83b.

38. "Pei Hang", in *Taiping guangji* 太平廣記 (Beijing: Zhonghua shuju, 1958), Vol. II, 50, pp. 312–315.

39. See Book I, 2a–3b.

40. I.4.53b.

41. I.4.56a.

42. I.3.51a.

43. I.3.5lb.

44. III.1.54a.

45. III.2.100a.

46. III.2.100b.

47. See the biography of Sima Xiangru in Sima Qian, *Shiji* (Beijing: Zhonghua shuju, 1959), V. *liejuan* 117, pp. 2999–3074, translated by Burton Watson, *Records of the Grand Historian of China* (New York: Columbia University Press, 1961), Vol. II, pp. 297–342, translated by Yves Hervouet, *Le chapitre 117 du Cheki* (Paris: Presses universitaires de France, 1972). Hervouet had earlier published an extensive study of the poet's life and work in *Un Poète de cour sous les Han: Sseu-ma Siang-jou* (Paris: Presses universitaires de France, 1964). See also W. L. Idema, "The Story of Ssu-ma Hsiang-ju and Cho Wen-Chün in Vernacular Literature of the Yüan and Early Ming Dynasties", *T'oung Pao*, 70 (1984): pp. 60–169.

48. Ibid. and W. L. Idema, "Satire in All Keys and Modes", especially the section entitled "Social Satire and Sexual Allegory in the *Hsi-hsiang-chi chu-kung-tiaon*", in Stephen H. West and Hoyt Tillman, *Thought and Culture in North China, 1115–1234*, forthcoming.

49. Idema, op. cit., p. 64.

50. Wang Jisi 王季思, "Cong *Fengqiuhuang* dao *Xixiang ji*" 從鳳求凰到西廂記, in *Yulunxuan qulun xinbian* 玉輪軒曲論新編 (Beijing: Zhongguo xiju chubanshe, 1983), pp. 17–24.

51. IV.1.117a.

52. I.3.51b.

53. V.2.142a–142b. *Shang xiaolou*.

54. II.1.59a–59b.

55. II.2.72b.

56. II.3.79a.

57. III.1.92a.

58. Cao Xueqin, *The Story of the Stone*, Vol. 3, p. 30; for the Chinese text, see

Honglou meng bashihui jiaoben, Vol. 2, p. 679.

59. Chen Yinke, "Du Yingying zhuan" 讀鶯鶯傳 (reprinted in 1964) *Chen Yinke xiansheng lunji* 陳寅恪先生論集 (Zhongyang yanjiuyuan lishi yuyan yanjiusuo), Special Issue 3, Taipei: Zhongyang yanjiuyuan, 1970, pp. 394–400.

60. See Zheng Zhenduo 鄭振鐸, "Lun Yuanren suoxie shangren, shizi, jinü jian de sanjiao lian'ai ju" 論元人所寫商人、士子、妓女間的三角戀愛劇, *Zhongguo wenxue yanjiu* 中國文學研究 (Beijing: Zuojia chubanshe, 1957).

61. This fact is mentioned in Zhu Youdun's *zaju* entitled *Xiangnang yuan* 香囊怨. See his *Xinbian Liu Panchun shouzhi Xiangnang yuan* 新編劉盼春守志香囊怨 (fifteenth century woodblock edition), p. 5a; *Xiangnang yuan* (in *Shemotashi qucong erji*, compiled by Wu Mei), p. 3a; and Wilt L. Idema and Stephen H. West, *Chinese Theatre 1100–1450, A Source Book*, p. 394. This categorization of our heroine may also lie behind her characterization in Li Kaixian's 李開先 (1502–1568) *Yuanlin wumeng* 園林午夢 (Noontime Dream in a Garden Grove), a little skit that pitches Oriole in a shouting match against a courtesan, Li Wa 李娃, famous for her destruction and rehabilitation of the student Zheng Yuanhe 鄭元和. For a discussion and translation of this skit, see W. L. Idema, "*Yuan-pen* as a Minor Form of Dramatic Literature in the Fifteenth and Sixteenth Centuries", in *Chinese Literature, Essays, Articles, and Reviews 6* (1984), pp. 53–75, and see also the revised translation in West and Idema, *The Moon and the Zither*, Appendix II.

62. IV.I. 117a.

63. II.III.72b–73a.

64. She's not a woman who is paid to accompany men.

65. III.III.105a.

66. Patricia Sieber, "Centre, Gaps, and Margin: Sexuality in the *Xixiang ji*", unpublished paper, 1988, p. 7.

67. In the original short story on which this play is based, Zhang Sheng rejects Oriole because she is a *youwu*, a succubus who poses danger to him.

68. For example, in the *Shijing* 詩經 (Book of Songs), the ode "Zhengyue" 小雅 · 正月 recounts the story of the woman Baosi 褒姒, for whom the last king of Western Zhou was besotted with love (Mao ode 192) and also spells out the dangers of "wise women" who can topple cities with their tongues as well as their beauty; see also the song entitled "Zhanang" 大雅 · 瞻卬 (Mao ode 264). James Legge, *The She King* (Hong Kong: The Chinese University Press, 1960, reprint of 1895 edition), pp. 319, 661, respectively.

69. Xishi was a beauty of the sixth century B.C. who was enlisted by a minister of the state of Yue 越, Fan Li 范蠡, to subvert the state of Wu 吳 by distracting the King, Fu Cha 夫差, with her good looks and many charms. There are two legends of her fate after the fall of Wu. Even though one account says that she went away with Fan Li, another relates that the people of Yue, fearful of the effects of her beauty on their own monarch, drowned her in the Yangtze;

whatever the case, she becomes in literature the archetype of the destructive woman.

70. He calls her a beauty that can set empires awash, a reference to the performer and sister of Li Yannian, who was so lovely that she was introduced to the Martial Emperor of the Han (Han Wudi 漢武帝) with the following poem:

> In the north is a beautiful woman,
> Without compeer, she stands alone.
> A single glance topples a city,
> A second glance topples a state.
> Of course, one knows she can topple a city, topple a state,
> But such a beauty is not to be found again.

From the biography of the woman Li, consort to the emperor. It should also be noted that both she and her brother were performers. See Ban Gu 班固 , *Hanshu* 漢書 (Beijing: Zhonghua shuju, 1962), Vol. 8, Juan 67 "waiqi zhuan" 外戚傳, p. 3951. The words of Li Yannian's poem echo Mao ode 264. See previous note.

71. II.I.57a.

72. The anecdote refers to a feast that Xuan Zong and his court ladies held to view some blooming white lotuses. Everyone present sighed in admiration over their beauty when Xuan Zong pointed out Yang Guifei to those around him and said, "But can they compare with my flower that speaks?" See Wang Renyu 王仁裕 , *Kaiyuan Tianbao yishi* 開元天寶遺事 in *Kaiyuan Tianbao yishi shizhong* 開元天寶遺事十種 , edited and collected by Ding Ruming 丁如明(Shanghai: Shanghai guji chubanshe, 1985), p. 96.

73. II.1.59b–60a.

74. Sieber, op. cit., p. 8.

75. II.3.79a.

76. II.3.79a–79b.

77. II.3.76b.

78. II.3.79a.

3

The Tale of Liu Yi and Its Analogues

Glen Dudbridge

One day in the twelfth century a Jinling 金陵 woman selling fried food in the market heard the words of a beggar's song (*Lianhua lao* 蓮華樂):

> If Liu Yi had not delivered that letter,
> How could he have reached the mountain in Dongting?

The woman experienced full enlightenment, threw aside the tray of food and became a recognized transmitter of teachings in the line of the Chan Master Yongqi of Langye 瑯琊永起禪師.[1] For literary historians this episode holds both interest and irony. It offers the clearest evidence I know that the famous literary story of Liu Yi 柳毅 and the dragons of Lake Dongting 洞庭湖 passed early into the humblest levels of popular currency. Yet the beggars of the Song market-place distilled from that complex and sophisticated creation a single prominent feature — the delivery of a letter — which had in fact come down from traditions centuries older than the tale of Liu Yi itself. There lies the irony. But the song and its surrounding anecdote do bear a richer significance: they show the act of communication by a mediator (Liu Yi for the dragons, the food seller for the *Chan* initiates) giving access to a transcendent destination. There lies the interest — and also, in brief, the point of the present paper: we can watch simple materials worked into a subtle and elaborate creative scheme.

For all its literary fame, popular currency and mythical resonance in the Chinese world, we remain quite ignorant of the story's provenance. We know the author's name — Li Chaowei 李朝威 — but nothing else about him. We can use the internal time-scheme to construct, but only roughly, an early limit for composition: the main action spans the period from Yifeng 儀鳳 (676–678) to the end of Kaiyuan 開元 (741); it then requires the passage of up to fifty more years, and so implies a date no earlier than, say, 790. Eventually a text of this story appeared in the ninth-century anthology *Yiwen ji* 異聞集 , a lost book which seems to date from after 840.[2] And later in the same century other texts began to refer to it. A story in the collection *Chuan qi* 傳奇 by Pei Xing 裴鉶 had a man ask the question: "Recently in human society someone has reported the matter of Liu Yi's divine marriage: Did that really happen?"[3] And a character in the anonymous *Lingying zhuan* 靈應傳 spoke of a "historical account" (史傳) recording the family feud in the dragon world which Liu Yi brought to a climax.[4] But to conclude from all this that the tale of Liu Yi as we know it first appeared between the late eighth and the mid-ninth centuries scarcely stirs the blood — we have simply identified yet again, but in loose terms, the liveliest and most creative period of Chinese literary fiction.

The tale of Liu Yi has attracted some attention from modern scholarship. There are studies of its echoes from Indian tradition,[5] of parallel motifs in Chinese literary sources,[6] of archetypal images deployed in the story.[7] This paper will not attempt to duplicate or repeat the conclusions of that earlier work. But it will aim to examine and add to certain sources brought out in it and to form an integrated view. The argument will grow from one central position: that the tale of Liu Yi owes its characteristic tensions, conflicts and complexity to a vertical structure. It superimposes distinct and recognizable layers of story material upon one another; it also articulates the social and ethical values generated or implied in each of them. *Liu Yi* thus becomes an arena for ethical confrontation, challenge and ultimately reconciliation. And through the whole structure runs a shifting and subtle ambiguity of status: man faces dragon, and they struggle with the conflicting hierarchies of ethics, power and mortality.

We shall conduct this anatomy by relating the tale *Liu Yi* to three analogues from Tang literature. The term is chosen with care. By calling them analogues I expressly draw back from any presumption of source-relationship or direct influence. Enough to say that these short pieces certainly date from a period before the composition of Li Chaowei's tale of Liu Yi; and in their several ways they certainly belonged to a literary culture which Li Chaowei perhaps knew well, but which we know only imperfectly. In circumstances like this notions of derivation and influence will always hover temptingly near, but they will not be necessary to the formal work of this analysis. The analogues are mere specimens. They prove that stories of a given shape or character did have a place in the mid-Tang literary record; but we shall not treat them as Li Chaowei's raw material.

A story as familiar as *Liu Yi* needs no new translation, summary or introduction here. But comparison with its analogues will be easier if the course of the story can be expressed in terms of discrete narrative units. The story elements in the list that follows below have no theoretical status: they define themselves simply as the needs of comparison require.

L1 Liu Yi fails the metropolitan examination and leaves the capital on his journey home.

L2 A bird startles his horse, which bolts and takes him to an unknown place.

L3 He meets a dragon maiden there.

L4 She is expecting him.

L5 She is woebegone, because neglected and ill-treated by her husband.

L6 She asks him to carry a letter to her dragon father in Lake Dongting and gives him directions for access to the underwater realm, including knocking on a tree. Liu Yi agrees.

L7 They exchange flirtatious remarks.

L8 Liu Yi delivers the letter as directed, gaining access to the lake through a gate by the tree. He is escorted into the dragon king's palace and presence, delivers the letter. It causes dismay and grief in the palace.

L9 The king's brother, a violent and impulsive character, breaks out of confinement, intent on rescuing and avenging his niece.

L10 Liu Yi is terrified by the dragon's appearance and wants to leave. The dragon king persuades him to stay.

L11 The avenging uncle returns after wreaking extensive damage and devouring the husband.

L12 The dragon maiden returns, looking radiant.

L13 Liu Yi is feasted by the grateful dragons.

L14 The dragon king's brother proposes that Liu Yi marry his niece.

L15 Liu Yi refuses on ethical grounds to marry a widow when he shares responsibility for her husband's death.

L16 The brother backs away apologetically.

L17 Liu Yi is rewarded with fabulous riches as he leaves. He moves to Jinling, a wealthy and socially prominent man.

L18 He marries twice, both wives die. His third wife, a widow, looks like the dragon maiden but evades questioning on the point.

L19 She declares her true identity only when she and her baby son establish themselves in society at the "one month old" party. In conversation with Liu Yi she recalls the progress of their relationship.

L20 Her motive in seeking to marry him was to discharge a debt of gratitude.

L21 Although Liu Yi's original casual flirtation (L7) was neutralized by the events of **L14–L15**, he now loves her more seriously.

L22 She leads him back to the lake palace with a promise of immortality. They live opulently for decades in Nanhai 南海 and retire finally to the Lake.

L23   Liu Yi's cousin meets him at a mountain risen from the Lake, receives some life-extending pills from him.

L24   The author concludes with approving remarks about the dragons' moral characteristics.

The Imperial Guardsman

The short tale that serves as our first analogue survives in the *Taiping guangji* 太平廣記, whose editors took it from a collection, now lost, called *Guang yi ji* 廣異記.[8] This seems to have been assembled during a period ending around 780 by Dai Fu 戴孚, a career official whose experience in the provincial service offered him a rich supply of anecdotes reflecting local cults, traditions and religious practices.[9] "The Imperial Guardsman" 三衛 belongs to a group of stories about the god of Mt. Hua 華嶽 and his temple cult in southern Shaanxi, a subject on which I am preparing a more detailed study.[10]

> At the beginning of the Kaiyuan period a certain imperial guardsman was returning from the capital to Qingzhou. Arriving in front of the Mt. Hua Temple he saw a servant-maid, clad in old and shabby clothes, who came up to speak to him.
>
> "My mistress wishes to meet you," she said, and led him forward to meet a woman of sixteen or seventeen years, looking woebegone and distressed.
>
> She said: "I am no human: I'm the third bride of Mt. Hua. But my husband is very cruel. My own family is in the Northern Ocean: for three years no letter has passed between us, and on this score I have suffered even worse treatment from the prince of the Mount. Now that I hear you are bound on the long journey home, sir, I should like to place a letter in your kind charge. If you can deliver it for me, my father will richly reward you."
>
> Upon which she handed him the letter. The man was a gentleman of his word, and asked her where in the Northern Ocean it was to be taken.
>
> The woman replied: "Simply knock at the second tree upon the coast,[11] and there will be someone to answer." With these words she took her leave and departed.
>
> When he came to the Northern Ocean he set about delivering the letter as directed. After knocking on the tree he suddenly saw a red gate beneath it, with someone coming out to attend to his business. He handed over the letter. The man withdrew for a while, then reappeared to say: "The Great King invites his guest to enter!"

He followed behind the man for a hundred paces or more. They went through another[12] gate. And there was a man in crimson robes, more than ten feet tall, with many thousands of maidens in attendance. They duly took their seats.

The man then declared: "I have not had a letter from my daughter for three years!" But when he had read the letter he cried out in a fury — "How dare that slave do this!" — and gave orders to summon his palace surveillance officers of left and right.

Before long these appeared — both more than ten feet tall, most evil-looking, with huge heads and great snouts. He commanded them to mobilize 50,000 troops and march west on the fifteenth of the month to attack Mt. Hua, making quite sure they won a victory. The two men received their orders and marched out.

Then, addressing the imperial guardsman — "I have nothing special to offer you in token of gratitude." — he ordered his attendants to pick out two rolls of silk and present them to this messenger.

The guardsman was displeased and grumbled to himself that two rolls were not enough. But as he prepared to leave[13] the man in the crimson robes said: "Sell these two rolls of silk only when you can get 20,000 strings of cash for them! Be sure not to part with them too cheaply!"

On returning to the outside world the guardsman wanted to see for himself what would happen, so he went back to Huayin. On the fifteenth of the month, when evening fell, he saw far off in the east a cloud of black vapour like a canopy moving gradually toward the west. Thunder rolled and lightning played — the noise could be heard a hundred *li* away. And in a moment a great wind on Mt. Hua, strong enough to bend trees, blew up a cloud from the westward. The cloud built up more and more powerfully and came right up to Mt. Hua. Thunderbolts pressed clamorously about it, and the entire mountain looked parched and red. Not for a long time did this come to an end, and when it grew light the mountain had a black and scorched appearance.

The guardsman now went into the capital to sell his silk. When buyers heard he was asking 20,000 they all laughed in amazement and took him for a madman. Then, some days later, a man on a white horse came to buy the silk and paid the price of 20,000 without further hesitation. The cash sum was already on deposit in the West Market.[14] The guardsman now asked for what purpose he was buying the silk, and the man said: "The god of the River Wei is arranging his daughter's marriage: he will use this as a gift. No silk in the world is as fine as that from the Northern Ocean, and he was just about to send for some to be bought when he heard that you were selling Northern Ocean silk. That is why I have come."

The guardsman took possession of the cash, spent some months in trading, and then set off eastwards back to Qingzhou. He had come as far as Huayin when he once again saw the same servant-girl as before.

She said: "My mistress has come specially to give thanks for your kindness." And he saw an ox-drawn carriage with dark blue[15] canopy coming down the mountain, flanked by a dozen attendants. It came up to him, and there alighted the very young lady he had met before. Clothes and countenance now bright and shining, gaze alert and clear — she was almost unrecognizable.

Seeing the guardsman she bowed to him and said: "You showed me great kindness in taking that message far away to my parents. Since the battle was fought,[16] my husband's affection has grown much warmer. The one thing that troubles me is that I have no way to repay you. But the Third Son[17] has turned his wrath against you for delivering my letter and is now waiting for you at the Tongguan pass with five hundred troops. You will certainly come to harm if you go there, so for now you should go back to the capital. Before long the imperial suite will make a progress to the east: spirits and demons have a terror of the drum,[18] so if you sit in the drum carriage, you will have nothing to worry about." And with these words she disappeared.

The imperial guardsman was really frightened and at once went back to the capital. A few weeks later it happened that Xuan Zong was to make a progress to Luoyang. The guardsman gave the drummer some cash and came out through the pass in the drum carriage. Thanks to this he was free of worry.

Three categories of guards (三衛) — "Bodyguard" (親衛), "Distinguished" (勳衛) and "Standby" (翊衛) — all of them ranking officials, staffed various guards corps in the imperial palace. Their tours of duty were defined by the distance of their homes from the capital: eight tours of one month were required of those living between 1,000 and 2,000 *li* 里 away.[19] The hero of this story is no doubt returning from one of these short spells of duty in the capital. To follow his adventures we must grasp the 600-mile line of communication along which he travels east and west, back and forth, throughout the story. The capital Chang'an 長安 marks its western extreme, the coastal prefecture Qingzhou 青州 , on the present gulf of Bohai 渤海 , the eastern. Between them in Tang times ran a major government post road, and its landmarks are the scenes of this story's events: Mt. Hua, towering south of the road some seventy miles east of the capital; its presiding god's temple outside the nearby county town of Huayin, fronting on the north side of the road; the strategically narrow neck of the Tongguan 潼關 pass, where the Yellow River rounds the south-west angle of modern Shanxi;[20] the Eastern Capital Luoyang, from which the Tang post road curved north-east towards the prefectures of the Shandong peninsula.

Against this solid background the guardsman enjoys a privileged glimpse into the spirit world that enriches our own knowledge of ethnography and mythology for the period. The family quarrel among landed aristocracy of the other world shows him, and us, one more view of Mt. Hua's turbulent domestic affairs. The guardsman also learns details of laws and procedure in the other world — a battle takes place, like the major lunar festivals, on the fifteenth of the month, the day of the full moon; Tongguan, where Third Son attempts his ambush, presents a barrier through which spirits cannot easily pass;[21] ghosts and spirits fear the drum — hence the crucial importance of the drum carriage in Chinese ritual processions, including (we now learn) those of the Tang emperors as they moved across the land; the bride of Mt. Hua travels in a blue-canopied carriage (青蓋犢車), like Chinese imperial princes from Han times on.[22]

Uchida Michio was the first to point out this story's obvious similarity to *Liu Yi*.[23] His analysis covers the parallel opening sections (**L3–L6, L8**), showing how ancient and rich was the literary tradition of mortals gaining directed access to the other world by knocking on a tree and spanning a gap of communication between the gods.[24] He notes the parallels in climax and resolution, in which violence wreaks due justice and secular wealth rewards good service (**L9, L17**). He cites some detailed points of narrative similarity to match the broadly similar construction. But beyond this Uchida observes merely that the tale of Liu Yi proceeds to further episodes which explore human relationships more fully than the simple "Imperial Guardsman".[25]

Our analysis begins at this point. From traditional materials like the mortal-borne message, the knocked tree and the mean-looking gift that comes to be worth a fortune, "The Imperial Guardsman" sets up a balanced, organic action. To be precise, it resolves three distinct social transactions: (1) grounds for conflict exist among the gods — actual conflict discharges them; (2) by delivering a letter the man puts the family of gods in his debt — they discharge the debt with their gift of silk; (3) by relieving the bride's suffering the man makes her personally obliged to him — she repays him by neutralizing the threat of a further, unrealized transaction (Third Son's planned revenge on the guardsman). Each transaction implies an ethical scheme. The first grows from the principle that marriage is a negotiated union between families, and thus that marriage abused may turn amicable union into enmity between families; it follows that the natal family of a wronged wife feels entitled, even obliged, to claim satisfaction for her wrongs. The second and third affirm a principle of reciprocity in all social dealings — a favour granted requires a matching return. These ethical values were deeply established in Chinese traditional life, may even be said in some part to define it. So axiomatic are they that the story needs no ethical argument to acknowledge or justify them. The god of the Northern Ocean simply speaks of his "token of gratitude", his married daughter comes to "give thanks" for kindness and "repay" the service. Only the guardsman himself, at the moment when he accepts the mission to deliver her letter, attracts the description "a gentleman of his word" (信士) — significantly, because his act now takes on a positive moral quality and calls for a fitting return. So, with care and with symmetry, the story defines and balances out its social transactions.

The tale of Liu Yi puts similar narrative material and similar social transactions to work. Li Chaowei characteristically gives them a sharper ethnographic focus. The tree at which his human messenger must knock (**L6**) is now an "orange-tree soil-god" 橘社 :[26] the tree genuinely belongs to the southern soil and serves its local community as a god in a way which we recognize from polemical religious literature of the period.[27] The work of revenge against the callous husband is done, not by army officers and their troops, but by the wronged wife's paternal uncle, making it expressly an act of family responsibility discharged. We shall return to this relation again below.

These adjustments may seem like matters of detail or style. But a comparison of the *transactions* in the two stories raises new and interesting questions. Conflict between the gods grows out of exactly the same social situation as before (**L5**), but retaliation now rises to a different level of severity: the husband pays with his life and gets eaten by his punisher (**L11**). Where "The Imperial Guardsman" offers discipline, restoring the old marriage contract to health, *Liu Yi* brings destruction, returning the widowed daughter to her family (**L12**). The orderly, balanced shape of the simpler story has collapsed. Movements of reciprocity between man and gods also seem to run out of control: Liu Yi's reward of prodigious wealth is straightforwardly traditional (**L17**), but the transaction suffers discord and disturbance when the gods vainly propose to unite Liu Yi himself with the widowed dragon daughter (**L14–L16**). Intimately involved with this is the dragon woman's own debt of gratitude. To discharge it she achieves the union with him, even against his expressed wish, by guile, and she protects it by concealment (**L18–L19**). The parity of act and response no longer seems so clear when the delivery of a letter leads a man, despite his protests, unknowingly into the ultimate commitment of immortal marriage (**L20–L22**). Liu Yi first sets out on his adventure in a simple spirit of chivalry (義), but it leads him into consequences which seem to reflect another order of values. With these complexities the first analogue gives us no help at all.

The Nāgas of Udyāna

A second analogue, pointed out more than fifty years ago,[28] has lain neglected ever since. I find this surprising and regrettable, for it offers more useful insights into the tale of Liu Yi than any other. In essence it is not a Chinese story, but originates from the mountainous area in the north of modern Pakistan through which flows the river Swāt. It came to the Chinese early in the seventh century, when Xuanzang's 玄奘 (602–664) great description of the Western Regions, *Da Tang xiyu ji* 大唐西域記 , included it in an account of the Mahāyāna Buddhist kingdom of Udyāna.[29] A translation of this material by Samuel Beal has been available and widely used for more than a hundred years,[30] but I give a new version here, because Beal misinterpreted several key phrases in the text of the story.

> Some 140 or 150 *li* north-west of the image of Bodhisattva Guanzizai we come to Mt. Lanbolu. By the mountain ridge there is a Nāga Lake more than thirty *li* round, with limpid waves spreading broad and far and pure waters showing crystal clear.[31]
>
> Long ago, when King Viruûdhaka marched against the Śākyas, four of them who resisted his armies were cast out by their kinsmen, and each took flight for himself. One of these Śākyas, having escaped from his country's capital, was exhausted from hard travelling and came to a halt halfway along the road. At that point a wild goose flew down in front of him. Finding it tame and friendly he got astride, and the goose took wing and soared aloft. It landed by the side of this lake. Travelling through the air the Śākya clansman had come a great distance to a strange land: he was lost and ignorant of the way, and took a short sleep in the shade of a tree.
>
> The young daughter of the Nāga of the lake was promenading by the water's edge when she suddenly caught sight of the Śākya. She changed into human form, for otherwise she feared it would be unsuitable, and then stroked and patted him. The Śākya awoke with a start, and made some demur: "Why do you show a worn-out traveller like me such tender care?" But then he

made passionate advances to her and would have forced her to sleep with him.

She said: "I dutifully obey my parents' instructions. Even though you favour me with your kind attention, we do not have their consent yet!"

The Śākya asked: "Where among these gloomy mountains and gorges is your home?"

She replied: "I am a Nāga maiden from this lake. I learned with respect that your sacred clan are wandering abroad as refugees and by good fortune, as I took my promenade, made bold to comfort you in your weariness. You now want me to join you in the privacy of the bedroom, but we have not yet received permission. What is more, through accumulated misfortunes I have received this Nāga body. Man and beast walk different paths — it would be something unheard of!"

The Śākya said: "One word of consent from you and your long-cherished wish may be had!"[32]

The Nāga girl said: "I will humbly obey you in whatever you require."

The Śākya now made a vow: "May all the blessed power of my good deeds cause this Nāga woman to take on a fully human form!" Upon which, in response to that blessed power, the Nāga was transformed and, finding herself now with a human body, greatly delighted.

She thanked the Śākya in these words: "I built up for myself an accursed fortune and migrated through evil forms of birth. Happily now, favoured by your kind offices and through dint of your blessed power, that vile body which I bore through long kalpas has been transformed in a moment. Even the gift of my life would not be thanks enough to repay your goodness. My heart longs to join you in your wanderings, but we are held back by what the world would say. I want to speak to my parents before we solemnize the marriage."

She returned to the lake and addressed her parents: "Today on my promenade I came upon a Śākya clansman, who by the working of his blessed power has transformed me into a human. We are in love, and I make bold to lay the truth before you."

The Nāga King was delighted with her human incarnation and impressed by such noble stock. He granted his daughter's request and came out from the lake to express his thanks to the Śākya: "You have not scorned a kind not your own, but have lowered your honoured station to join a baser one. If you would consent to visit my home, I will humbly wait on you there!"

The Śākya accepted the Nāga King's invitation and moved on at once to his dwelling. Upon which, in the Nāga palace, they performed in full the ceremony of "Meeting the bride in person"[33] and celebrated the nuptial feast,[34] revelling and making merry to their hearts' content.

The Śākya clansman felt both dread and disgust as he viewed the Nāgas' physical shape, and wanted to take his leave and go. But the Nāga King stopped him: "I hope that you will not distance yourself from us, but make your dwelling nearby. I will make you master of the land, holder of the royal title, commander of both courtiers and commoners: your blessings shall last for ages long!"

The Śakya expressed his thanks: "I never expected to hear words like these!"

The Nāga King placed a jewelled sword into a case, which he covered over with the finest white cotton cloth. He said to the Śakya: "I should like you to take this cotton as a presentation to the king of the land. When a traveller from far away brings tribute the king will certainly receive it in person, and that is the moment for you to take his life. Then you seize his kingdom! A good plan, surely?"

Accepting these instructions from the Nāga King, the Śakya went to make his presentation. As the King of Udyāna personally picked up the cotton, the Śakya gripped his sleeve and ran him through. And while the courtiers and guards broke into hubbub and disorder about the dais, the Śakya brandished his sword to announce: "This sword that I wield was conferred on me by a divine Nāga to kill recalcitrants and put rebels to death!"

All feared this divine warrior: they exalted him to the highest place. Upon which he brought good rule where before there had been corruption, he celebrated merit and pitied misfortune. Then, mustering a huge following and preparing an imperial coach, he proceeded to the Nāga palace to report on his mission. And he escorted the Nāga woman back to his royal seat.

But the Nāga woman's predestined lot was not yet discharged, and some retribution still remained to pay. Whenever she retired to the privacy of the bedroom a ninefold Nāga hood would grow out of her head.[35] The Śakya felt fear and disgust, but could think of no better plan to deal with it than to wait for her to fall asleep and cut the hood away with a sharp blade.

The Nāga woman awoke with a start and said: "This will not be a good thing for future generations. Not only will my life receive some ill consequences, but your descendants will suffer from headaches!"

That is why the royal family of the land regularly suffer from this complaint, not continuously, but in sporadic outbreaks.

When the Śakya clansman died his heir succeeded to the throne. This was King Uttarasēna (in Chinese: "Superior Army").

This story belonged to two cultures. In the context of northwestern India it plainly served the ancient kingdom of Udyāna as a dynastic myth, validating the title of its ruling house with a certificate of descent from the royal Śakya 釋 clan (in common with the Śakyamuni Buddha) and the divine Nāgas (龍), serpent gods whose power overshadowed the region. The use of a Nāga-given sword to slay an earlier ruler affirms the same

claim to divine legitimacy. And even the genetically inherited family af-
fliction of headaches is made to serve a legitimating purpose by finding its
matching episode in the myth. As reported in Chinese by Xuanzang all this
had the status of an ethnographic document: it stood in what amounted to
an imperial survey of the lands in the Far West. But that famous book,
current in manuscript versions and printed in the early Buddhist canons,[36]
was itself a Chinese cultural asset, and the stories to be read there, couched
formally in well-crafted parallel prose, were poised to enter directly into
Chinese experience.

Among the many subtle cultural adjustments that Xuanzang's language brought to these alien documents, one is crucial to our present study.
After the ancient wont of Chinese Buddhist translators he rendered the
Indian term Nāga with Chinese *long* 龍 . The most familiar classic locus of
this rendering lay certainly in the *Lotus Sūtra* (chapter 12) with its story of
the daughter of the Nāga-king Sāgara: in a single act of spontaneous
change she transcended the limitations of a woman's body to become a
male and to gain perfect enlightenment.[37] But the *Lotus Sūtra* also displays
for us the scale of beings, human and divine, who attend devoutly upon the
Buddha's preaching. Stated in a fixed order, this ranking seems to express
a hierarchy of closeness to the condition of enlightenment: after the senior
disciples, the monks and nuns, the male and female lay devotees, come
Devas (天), Nāgas, Yaksas (夜叉), then Gandharvas, Asuras, Garudas,
Kinnaras, and Mahoragas.[38] So Nāgas, in the light of Buddhist truth, lie
below the condition of men and women. No wonder the Nāga maiden in
our analogue deplores the cursed migrations that led her into such a shape,
and no wonder she craves the gift of merit which can release her from it.
The physical presence of Nāgas inspires disgust and fear in the Śākya
youth, and their king readily admits their low estate as he grovels before
his daughter's human benefactor.

Yet the story does not flinch from its central paradox. Nāgas are gods,
worshipped by men. They belong to India's most ancient company of
deities, associated with trees, pools, wells and waterways, whose cults
come down from times before its Aryan civilization began and survive into
the present.[39] They have power to protect or to harm,[40] and men are wise to
fear and serve them. No sooner is the Śākya youth withdrawing in dread
from the Nāgas' presence than their king is offering him the means to royal
power and blessings in perpetuity — an offer which the Śākya accepts
without demur. And his marriage bonds the Nāgas to his line for ever.

Here is a mirror image of Liu Yi's world. He too confronts divine beings who have ruled rivers and lakes since the beginning of mythological time. The Lord of Dongting identifies his violent brother as the dangerous tidal River Qiantang 錢塘 , capable of vast flood damage, kept under precarious restraint, daily waited upon by the local population; and he makes a comically overstated reference to the mythical struggles of Yu the Great to master the primeval floods caused by this same brother.[41] Liu Yi like the Śākya finds the dragon's physical form terrifying and tries to leave its presence at once (**L10**). But, echoing his culture's ancient wisdom, he insists on the superiority of the human race,[42] and fearlessly defines it in terms of Confucian moral values:

> Truly, I never knew that the Lord of Qiantang was as wretched as this! ... If I had met you among mighty waves or amid gloomy mountains, flourishing whiskers and scales and robed in clouds and rain as you pressed me to the point of death, then I would have regarded you as a mere beast and would have no grounds for complaint! But now you are clothed in cap and gown, you sit talking of ritual decorum and moral right, you have a commitment to the Five Relationships, a command of the nuances of conduct that would surpass some of the best in the world of men, let alone the deities of the rivers! Yet, with hulking body and violent temper, fortified by strong drink, you want to put pressure on another man. Is that anything like honest behaviour?[43]

The onslaught has its effect (**L16**): Liu Yi succeeds in dictating the values to which the dragons ought to aspire, and they abjectly submit to his judgment. Yet at once the story twists them round with paradox. Not only do the dragons make Liu Yi rich (**L17**), but through marriage with their daughter they give him access to a world where he enjoys the endless pleasures of a Taoist paradise (**L22–L23**). And the story ends by discarding the values of secular Chinese society to endorse those of divine immortality:

> When the Kaiyuan period came the emperor fixed his mind on matters of transcendence and immortality and diligently sought out Taoist techniques. [Liu] Yi had no peace, and so retired in company [with his wife] to Dongting.[44]

In the event the divine dragons serve Liu Yi, as the Nāgas serve the Śākya, with all that is great and desirable in his lot. The two stories share a common thrust: each shows a rejected hero (the Śākya driven out by his kinsmen, Liu Yi failed in the examination) brought by divine intervention (the friendly goose, the horse startled by a bird) towards a liaison with the spirits of the waters, who through marriage help him to a triumphant and transcendent destiny. In each case the shifting notions of hierarchy, the simultaneous looking up and looking down, form an essential context for the mutual favours and bargains which make that resolution possible. Yet once again, when we begin to examine the pattern of those transactions, the tale of Liu Yi breaks up into complexity.

The "Nāga" analogue, like "The Imperial Guardsman", presents a methodically balanced action. Its transactions begin with the chance meeting between Nāga maiden and Śākya youth that leads him to desire her sexually.[45] They are then ready for the personal bargain in which, by liberating her into human form, he grants a favour for which "even the gift of my life would not be thanks enough", and for which marriage is an accepted personal return. The broader political transaction between Nāga king and human prince rewards the same act with dynastic power. The marriage serves as key to the whole structure: desired by the prince, it becomes possible when he neutralizes the problem of alien breeds ("man and beast walk different paths"); reciprocally granted by the Nāgas, it leads on to his dynastic success.

For Liu Yi too his dragon marriage becomes ultimately his strongest, most desirable asset. By any reckoning it counts as essential to the story. Here too the dragon woman expresses her commitment in terms of a debt of gratitude ("favoured by your kindness, I vowed in my heart to seek to repay you"衙君之思，誓心求報).[46] But Liu Yi never seeks marriage as a return for his service, and indeed magnificently refuses the direct offer (**L14–L15**). A tension has entered the story to destroy its orderly discharge of bargains and to threaten its due resolution. Our use of the first two analogues now puts us in a position to explain that tension: it follows inevitably from the simultaneous use of the two distinct story moulds that they represent. To the extent that *Liu Yi* follows the first mould it portrays a man external to the affairs of the other world, involved as a mere messenger and rewarded as such; his act should serve to heal and restore an established marriage between gods. But *Liu Yi* is equally committed to the second mould, in which a service to the dragons wins the desirable hand of their unmarried daughter and all the benefits that flow from it. The two cannot be reconciled without damage and conflict.

The most obvious problem is the woman's availability. Liu Yi begins by helping a married dragon-woman, he ends by marrying her himself. That first consequence of mixing the two moulds demands a radical plot adjustment. The murderous revenge of Lord Qiantang (**L11**) becomes a structural necessity to the story. Its result is to create a widow available for remarriage — and of course the widowed status is not forgotten when Liu Yi eventually marries for the third time and accepts a widow, only later learning who she really is (**L18–19**). The creation of this available widow can be seen as following necessarily from the mixed structure of the new story.

By observing that mixed structure we can also explain the "distorted balance between act and response" which stood out as a problem under the first analogue. Liu Yi's initial service belongs to one mould, his ultimate reward to the other — they were never designed to fit together. The story pleasantly disguises them with the light flirtation that adorns Liu Yi's first meeting with the girl (**L7**) and the deeper affection that draws him to her later (**L21**). As elements of the plot these are really cosmetic additions. But can we say the same of that other problem at the centre of the story — Liu Yi's refusal of marriage — which breaks the pattern of both moulds? For this we shall need a third analogue.

A Man of Ruyin

The original source, once again, is *Guang yi ji*.[47]

> There was a man of Ruyin called Xu, orphaned since childhood. He was fair-skinned and handsome, loved smart clothes and fine horses, and roamed wild and free. Often he would lead out yellow hunting-hounds to chase game through wilderness and mountain streams.
>
> He [once] rested beneath a great tree more than 100 feet tall and several dozen spans in girth. High branches stretched out to either side, casting shade over several *mu*. He glanced up into the branches, and hanging there was a purse made of many-coloured silks. Thinking someone had left it by mistake he retrieved it and took it home. But the knot could not be undone. He prized the purse highly and put it in his personal case.
>
> As evening approached it changed into a girl, who came straight up to him with a name-card in her hand and said: "The King's daughter has instructed me to pay you her respects." Thus announcing her name, she departed.
>
> Shortly afterwards a strange fragrance filled the room and the sound of horses and carriages gradually became audible. Xu went outside and saw in the distance a line of torches. In front there was a youth on a white horse attended by a dozen riders, who came straight up to Xu and said: "My younger sister, though of mean family, humbly admires your fine character and wishes to join herself in marriage to a true gentleman. What do you think?"
>
> Xu dared not refuse too hard, for these people were gods. So the youth

commanded his attendants to sweep and clean out a separate chamber. And before long the girl's carriage arrived. The road was filled with fragrance and light.

There were dozens of maidservants mounted on horseback, all of them beautiful, who held up windbreaks as they clustered around the alighting maiden and invited her into the separate chamber.

Drapery and mattresses were there in complete supply, to the amazement of Xu's family, all of whom could see it for themselves when they went to look. The youth urged Xu to bathe and presented him with new clothes. Then the maids ushered him into the girl's chamber. She was sixteen or seventeen, peerlessly lovely, dressed in a long wedding gown of dark blue, and wearing pearls and jades in profusion. Down from the dais she came to respond to his bow, and together they went up to the top of the hall. The youth now left them, while in their chamber were set up mica screens and blue-green lotus-patterned curtains, with partitions of hanging brocade marked with lucky deer symbols[48] to face all four walls. There was a lavish spread of fine meats and many kinds of exotic fruit, sweet and fragrant such as we never find in this world. The vessels were seven-nut goblets, nine-branched dishes, whelk-shaped cups and lotus-leaf bowls — all these patterned with faint lines of gold and studded with fine blue-green stones. There was a jade urn containing Central Asian grape wine with a really strong bouquet. Over their seats were placed wax candles with a common wick[49] in a stand made of purple jade. The illumination was as bright as day.

Xu, always a frivolous, thoughtless type and now dazzled by all these fine wares, was highly pleased. They took their seats, and Xu asked: "A mean and humble man like me in a low and cramped hovel like this never expected to receive such generous attention. I feel joy and gladness mixed together, and really don't know what to do!"

She replied: "My father is General of the Southern Command at the Central Peak.[50] If, sir, you do not [object to][51] my obscure and lowly origins, I want to have myself given to you in marriage and to offer you my most diligent service. Truly I am deeply happy at my good fortune in enjoying this fine occasion!"

Xu then asked: "What would the General of the Southern Command's position be in our modern establishment?"

She said: "It is a divisional appointment under the Lord of Mt. Song, like the Generals of the Four Commands in times of old."

When they had drunk deep she sighed and recited the lines:

"What a night it is tonight, that I should meet this fine man!"[52]

The verses were more sweet and clear than he had ever heard before. Then taking up a zither she played "The flying goose takes leave of the crane"[53] and sang it, with head inclined, to entertain Xu as he drank. The pure notes were plangent and mournful, the singer's attitude so transported that she scarcely seemed in control of herself. Xu could master his feelings no longer. He went up and embraced her. She smiled with a little sidelong glance at him and said: "You have done what the poet mocks — 'touched my hand-kerchief'; you've committed the offence in that joke about the courtier and his tassel:[54] so now what should we do?"

She turned and ordered the feast cleared away. They removed the candles and went to bed, where they freely enjoyed the intimacy of love. She was full-fleshed and tender boned, soft and smooth as syrup.

The next day they invited in all his kin, and she carried out in full the married woman's ritual duties, bestowing generous gifts upon them. When the third day came the young man he saw before reappeared and said: "My father feels deeply in your debt and would like to meet you. He has sent me to make you welcome." So Xu went with him.

They came to the spot where he had been hunting, but the great tree was no longer there. He saw only vermilion gates and white walls, like those in a grand official residence of our own times. Formed up on either side were armed guards, all bowing in welcome. The youth led him inside to meet the Commander. He was crowned with the flat-topped turban, robed in the crimson muslin, and sat enthroned in a lofty hall, with halberds and pennons arrayed in the courtyard.

Xu bowed as he came before him. The Commander responded by standing up and gave him precedence as they mounted the steps. He addressed Xu with polite, concerned enquiries, and went on: "My young daughter lost her mother in childhood, but she was fortunate enough to become wife to a man as brilliant as you, which gives great cause for rejoicing. Indeed, this must have been decreed in the world of the shades. It could never have come about unless you two had been bound in a close spiritual affinity!"

Xu thanked him. And now they went together into the private suite. The gates and buildings were impressive and deeply set back, with a connecting network of winding passageways and raised walkways. In the centre of the main hall a grand reception took place, and when the feasting and revels were at their height a performance of music was commanded. Pipes and strings blended intricately together, their tunes novel and fresh, while the several dozen singing-girls were all ravishing beauties.

At the end of all this Xu was given rich gifts of gold and silk and furnished with servants and horses. In consequence his family was well provided for and he built a residence for them in their village, in all points luxurious and splendid.

The young lady was well versed in "nourishing life" by means of sexual techniques,[55] and Xu came to enjoy an excellent physical condition — twice as fit as normal. By this he knew that she was indeed a divine being. In due course he went back again, each time in company with the young lady. The Commander would always shower him with gifts. Over several decades she bore five sons, without suffering any loss in good looks. Later Xu died, and she departed, taking her sons with her. We know nothing of their whereabouts.

Ruyin 汝陰 county (Fuyang 阜陽 on modern maps) was prefectural seat of Yingzhou 穎州 in the Tang province of Henan. It lay in the well watered area through which streams born in the Mt. Song massif find their way to the River Huai. But Mt. Song itself lies more than 300 km to the north-west, and to reach this far the Central Peak's ritual authority must cover a large tract of land. The bride identifies her father with care. His "divisional appointment under the Lord of Mt. Song (嵩君), like the Generals of the Four Commands (四鎮將軍) in times of old" has a con-scious historical reference. Generals of the Four Commands (north, south, east, west) served in the military establishments of the Northern and Southern Dynasties (420–589).[56] (Ruyin lay in the territory of each in succession.) And the Commander, when young Xu 許 meets him, wears the ceremonial headgear of military officers since the Southern Qi.[57] It is as though, in the eyes of the eighth century, the Lord of Mt. Song has the characteristics of a ruler of one of the old southern dynasties. The splen-dours of the Commander's headquarters match what we see pictured on the walls of eighth-century royal tombs: gate fortifications (woodwork in red, walls in white), armed guards in formation, ceremonial halberds ranged in wall-racks, pennoned banners borne by guards of honour — all these con-firm the author's comparison with "a grand official residence of our own times".[58]

   With echoes of secular pomp, fertile union with a goddess, nourishing of physical condition, paradisiacal fulfilments, it is not difficult to see a loose parallel with the tale of Liu Yi. But no more than that: we could never claim to find here a close analogue of the kind which demands attention as the others do. And needless to say, no previous critic has tried to involve it in the discussion. I use it here for a special reason which has to do with the story's opening sequence, leading to the gods' proposal of marriage. Their contrived introduction of a hopeful bride is no other-worldly fantasy, but reflects the actual practice of families in certain parts of China seeking a "ghost marriage" alliance for their dead daughter with a living man. The anthropologist Arthur P. Wolf reports from a village in modern Taiwan:

Elderly people in San-hsia say that in "the old days" a girl's parents could rid themselves of the responsibility for her soul by trapping a husband for her. The girl's name and horoscope were written on a piece of red paper, which was concealed in a purse or some other attractive bait and placed beside the road. The girl's brothers then hid nearby and waited until some unsuspecting passer-by discovered the purse. The fact that he picked up the girl's horoscope was taken as evidence that he was fated to marry her, and so he usually did, in return for a small amount of money offered as a dowry.[59]

Here, point for point, is what we find also in the "Ruyin" story: "name card" in attractive purse, casual discovery, brother in wait nearby, dowry, inference of predestined union. In real society, as Wolf's later analysis makes clear, the ghost marriage brings relief to a dead girl's family. Unmarried at death, she may harm her family with real or threatened malignancy; ceremonially married to a living man, she will become entitled to service from his living children, and the threat is neutralized. For this reason ghost marriage plays an integral, if marginal, role in traditional society,[60] and we can trace the practice within the sphere of strictly human relations elsewhere in the pages of the eighth-century *Guang yi ji*.[61] The "man of Ruyin" story implies a parallel between ghost marriage and divine marriage, and this deserves exploring for possible insights.

Each marriage contract in these stories has two main parties — the bride's family and the groom (whose own family makes no significant appearance in any). Initiative lies with the bride's family, whose spokesman is a junior male (her own brother, her father's younger brother). They identify the husband they want and through their spokesman approach him. Their strategy aims to set up either an obligation or a disposition in him to accept. So the trick with the purse in "A man of Ruyin", and in the village traditions of modern Sanxia, is understood to express a predestined affinity: the groom must feel that circumstances are pressing him to accept, and gifts from the family help make up his mind. There is an implication that, left to himself, the man might well refuse. Marriage with spirits seems not to be desirable in itself, if only because sexual union with a spirit can dangerously deplete the vital essence.[62] Revealingly, the man of Ruyin "dared not refuse too hard, for these people were gods"; and to their power he responds with awe and obedience. Later, of course, he has no cause for regret: sexual union with the truly divine is a physical tonic — "by this he knew that she was indeed a divine being".

Feasting drunkenly with the dragons in their lake palace, Liu Yi finds himself facing the same situation. Now that the dragon-woman is widowed and unattached her family respond as a mortal family would. Circumstances have picked out the likely husband, and the moment has come for the family spokesman to pressure him. The "junior male relative" here is the same agnatic uncle who avenged her earlier wrongs on the first husband.[63] His chosen form of pressure is to create an appeal to moral obligation:

> "We hope to entrust her to a man of lofty principle, to be kin of ours for generations to come, so that she who received your kindness will know the man she is joining, and we who hold her dear will know the man we are giving her to. That surely is the way for a true gentleman to see through his work to the end!"[64]

Liu Yi knows well that other kinds of pressure might threaten — he has after all seen what bestial violence that same uncle can inflict. In such a situation, the third analogue suggests, natural inclination might urge him to refuse, but common prudence might lead him to agree. In fact, as we know, he famously resists the offer and later defends his stand on moral grounds:

> "When Qiantang put pressure on me there was something in the principle of the thing that could not be put straight — that alone provoked me to anger. You see, my first intention had been to act with chivalry — so how could I possibly get a husband put to death and then accept his wife in marriage? That was one thing wrong with it. And I have always given highest priority[65] to maintaining my integrity. How could I compromise myself to surrender to my heart's affections? That was the second thing wrong with it."[66]

With this gesture and this argument Liu Yi steps out beyond the bounds of traditional analogues. But they will of course close in on him again, to require a fulfilled divine marriage at the end. And the third analogue even invites us to ask whether the rapid deaths of his two mortal wives (**L18**) might not reflect the menacing power of a spirit-woman denied the marriage she desires. At first sight all this work of analogy has a destructive effect. It finds out broken continuity and distorted balance in the tale of Liu Yi. The story's play of human relationships and ethical conflict easily seems, in this light, a superficial overlay upon its patched-together plot. But taking a closer look, we can turn the whole system round and find in it more positive insights. The very points in the story that betray signs of breaking traditional moulds correspond to its liveliest scenes of ethical challenge and debate. Lord Qiantang devours his niece's first husband (**L11**): we lose sight of the first analogue and become aware of the gulf that separates dragon from man. Yet at once Qiantang is proposing her marriage to Liu Yi and using human ethical values to sanction and support the idea. The three analogues are now seriously at odds — the first quite discarded, the second finding its motivation confused, the third intruding on the expectations of the other two. Yet the forceful response by Liu Yi, in which he defies the dragons' appeal by affirming a still higher order of moral values, gathers the confused ends of the plot into a single, absorbing problem. All the reader's cultural preparation leads him to share with the dragons their hope that Liu Yi will end by marrying their widowed daughter. Liu Yi's private affections long for the same end too, as he later confesses. The plot must eventually, we know, find its way to that resolution. Yet Liu Yi's conscience stands firmly in the way.

The problem in fact restates in terms of Confucian ethics what once divided the Śākya youth from his Nāga lover — "man and beast walk different paths". Liu Yi can achieve this marriage only by losing the moral integrity for which he claims superiority over the dragons. Even they look up to his "lofty principle" as the Nāgas looked up to the condition of human incarnation. Neither side, it seems, would want marriage at the price of moral betrayal. But alas, the miraculous powers of transferred Buddhist merit are not available or relevant here to set the problem easily aside. The situation is deadlocked. So to find its solution the story moves beyond the simple mechanisms of the analogues to a new level of sophistication. Direct answers give way to indirect. The dragons respect Liu Yi's precious, inviolable conscience by outflanking it: he marries their widow in safe ignorance of the truth. And secured by fertility, the marriage stands firm. That too is a miracle, but a suitably urbane one. It comes with an attractive sense of paradox: these dragons have solved their problem not with the arbitrary directness of divine beings, but with all the devious manipulation of compromise that belongs to true human society. Throughout the literature we like to call Tang fiction there runs a lasting interest in relations between alien forms of being.[67] In *Liu Yi* that interest finds perhaps its wittiest and most dynamic statement. Author and reader know well the traditional models from which the story grows. Together they follow the twists and turns by which traditional expectations are set aside, postponed, or deviously fulfilled. But more particularly they savour the ironies and ambiguities of Liu Yi's changing relations with the dragons. Even after the transcendent splendours of the closing scene the author speaks up yet again on that insistent theme:

Here[68] we can see how, among creatures of the five breeds, pre-eminence always comes from spiritual power.[69] Man is the naked breed, but he can communicate his good faith to the scaly breed. Dongting's forbearance and uprightness, Qiantang's impetuosity and frank openness — these should be handed down....[70]

Li Chaowei's own voice confirms what our study of analogues has clearly shown: the story's crux lies in that eloquent centre-piece played out in the depths of the lake. Alien breeds confront and engage, ethical values clash and lock; traditional tales pile up in layers, a paradoxical synthesis takes charge.

Notes

1. Zhengshou 正受 (1146–1208), *Jiatai pu deng lu* 嘉泰普燈錄, reprinted in *Dai Nihon zoku zōkyō* 大日本續藏經 1, 2B, 10, 1, 11.95b; also Puji 普濟 (1179–1253), *Wu deng hui yuan* 五燈會元, edited by Su Yuanlei 蘇淵雷 (Beijing: Zhonghua shuju, 1984), 19.1271–1272, and *Xu chuan deng lu* 續傳燈錄, *Taishō shinshū daizōkyō* 大正新脩大藏經, edited by Takakusu Junjirō 南楠順次郎 and Watanabe Kaigyoku 渡辺海旭(Tokyo:1924–1929), Vol. 51, no. 2077, 3.627b. The position of these persons in the Chan patriarchal succession is shown diagrammatically in *Zengaku daijiten* 禪學大辭典, Suppl. Vol. (Tokyo: Daishūkan Shoten, 1978), pp. 2 and 13. The significance of this anecdote for the history of the *Lianhua le* performance is discussed by Zhou Yibai 周貽白 in *Zhongguo xiqu fazhan shi gangyao* 中國戲曲發展史綱要 (Shanghai: Shanghai guji chubanshe, 1979), pp. 515 ff.

2. In many respects the story's textual history parallels that of *Li Wa zhuan* 李娃傳, which I have discussed in *The Tale of Li Wa: Study and Critical Edition of a Chinese Story from the Ninth Century* (London: Ithaca Press, 1983), pp. 1–14, with p. 1 on *Yi wen ji*. The corresponding references in other sources discussed there are: *Taiping guangji*, compiled by Li Fang 李昉 et al; reprinted by Beijing: Renmin wenxue chubanshe, 1959; revised edition, Beijing: Zhonghua shuju, 1961, 419.3410–3417; *Lei shuo* 類說, compiled by Zeng Zao 曾慥, ca 1136; reprint of 1626 edition (Beijing: Wenxue guji kanxingshe, 1955), 28.10a–12b; Luo Ye 羅燁, *Zui weng tan lu* 醉翁談錄 (Shanghai: Gudian wenxue chubanshe, 1957), xin ji, 1.83–87; *Lü chuang xin hua* 綠窗新話, edited by Zhou Yi 周夷 (Shanghai: Gudian wenxue chubanshe, 1957), A.40; *Yu Chu zhi* 虞初志, Anon. (late-Ming edition in National Central Library, Taipei), 2.7a–18b.

3. *Taiping guangji*, 311.2460. The crediting of this item to *Chuan qi* rests on a variant in the Ming MS., but is supported by *Lei shuo*, 32.1ab, by *Gan zhu ji* 紺珠集, reprinted as *Yingyin Ming kan han chuanben Gan zhu ji* 影印明刊罕傳本紺珠集 (Taipei: Taiwan shangwu yinshuguan, 1970), 11.8a,

and by Yao Kuan 姚寬 (1105–1162) in *Xi qi cong yu* 西溪叢語 , *Jindai mi shu* 津逮秘書 edition, A.8a. See *Pei Xing chuan qi* 裴鉶傳奇 , edited by Zhou Lengqie 周楞枷 (Shanghai: Shanghai guji chubanshe, 1980), p. 84. The known events of Pei Xing's life date from the 860s and 870s: see Wang Meng'ou 王夢鷗 , *Tang ren xiaoshuo yanjiu* 唐人小說研究 (Banqiao: Yiwen yinshuguan, 1971), Vol. 1, p. 78. Uchida Michio 内田道夫 unfortunately used the ascription to "Zhuan ji" 傳記 given in printed versions of *Taiping guangji*, and was left with problems of dating he could not resolve. See his 1955 article, "*Ryū Ki den* ni tsuite — suishin setsuwa no kenkai o chūshin ni" 柳毅伝について——水神説話の展開を中心に , reprinted as chapter 6, "Tōno ikō sakuhin (1)" 唐の中期以降の作品 (一), *Chūgoku shōsetsu kenkyū* 中国小説研究 (Tokyo: Hyōronsha, 1977), pp. 106 and 111, n.4.

4. *Taiping guangji* 492.4040. On the late ninth-century dating of this piece see Wang Pijiang 汪辟疆 , *Tangren xiaoshuo* 唐人小説 , revised edition (Shanghai: Gudian wenxue chubanshe, 1955; Hong Kong: Zhonghua shuju, 1958), pp. 75–76.

5. See Huo Shixiu 霍世休 , "Tang dai chuanqi wen yu Yindu gushi" 唐代傳奇文與印度故事, *Wenxue* 文學 2.6, 1934, pp. 1051–1066; with pp. 1061–1063 on Liu Yi.

6. Uchida Michio, *Chūgoku shōsetsu kenkyū*, chapter 6; Qian Zhongshu 錢鍾書 , *Guan zhui bian* 管錐篇 , 4 vols. (Beijing: Zhonghua shuju, 1979), pp. 805–806. See also Wang Pijiang, *Tang ren xiaoshuo*, p. 69.

7. Curtis P. Adkins, "The hero in T'ang *ch'uan-ch'i* tales", *Critical Essays on Chinese Fiction*, edited by Winston L.Y. Yang and Curtis P. Adkins (Hong Kong: The Chinese University Press, 1980), pp. 17–46.

8. *Taiping guangji* 300.2383–2384.

9. I have documented the textual history elsewhere: Du Deqiao 杜德橋 , "*Guang yi ji* chu tan" 廣異記初探 , *Xinya xuebao* 新亞學報 15, 1986, pp. 395–414. See also Uchiyama Chinari 山内知也 , "Chū Tō shoki no shōsetsu — *Kōiki* o chūshin to shite" 中唐の初期の小説——広異記を中心として, in *Kaga hakushi taikan kinen Chūgoku bunshi tetsugaku ronshū* 加賀博士退官記念中国文史哲学論集 (Tokyo: Kōdansha, 1979), pp. 527–541. Uchiyama's figures for internal dating are slightly different from my own. His reconstruction of Dai Fu's career, assuming first appointment in or after 787, is not based on hard evidence: see his pp. 531–532.

10. Some summary remarks appear in my paper "Tang Tales and Tang Cults: Some Cases from the Eighth Century", *Proceedings of the Second International Conference on Sinology*, Section on Literature (Nankang: Academia Sinica, 1990), pp. 335–352, in particular pp. 337–343.

11. "coast": For 海池 read 海地 , accepting the variant given by Sun Qian 孫潛 in his seventeenth-century collation of an early MS.: reported in Yan Yiping 嚴一萍 , *Taiping guangji jiaokan ji* 太平廣記校勘記, vol. appended to reprint

of *Tan Kai's* 談愷 1567 edition of *Taiping quangji* (Banqiao: Yiwen yin-shuguan, 1970), p. 112b.

12. "another": For 後 read 復 , with Sun Qian.

13. "prepared to leave": For 持別 read 將別 , with Sun Qian.

14. The sale transaction is interesting on two counts: as an example of the tale-type in which a stranger, often a foreign merchant, buys a rare treasure for a high price — see Ishida Mikinosuke's 石田幹之助 classic studies on the subject reprinted in his *Zōtei Chōan no haru* 增訂長安の春 (revised edition, Tokyo: Heibonsha, 1967), pp. 210–281; and as one of the earliest references to safe-deposit banking in China — cf. *TPGJ* 243.1877, *Lei shuo* 7.19a, *Tang da zhao ling ji* 唐大詔令集 , compiled by Song Minqiu 宋敏秋 (1019–1079) (Beijing: Shangwu yinshuguan, 1959), 72.404; also Tao Xisheng 陶希聖 and Ju Qingyuan 鞠清遠 , *Tang dai jingji shi* 唐代經濟史 (Shanghai: Shangwu yinshuguan, 1936), pp. 107–113; Kato Shigeshi 加藤繁 , "Kihō kō" 櫃坊考 , *Shina keizai shi kōshō* 支那經済史考證 (Tokyo: Tōyō bunko, 1952), Vol. 1, pp. 489–492; and Lien-sheng Yang, *Money and Credit in China* (Cambridge, Mass.: Harvard University Press, 1952), p. 79.

15. "dark blue": For 香 read 青 , with Sun Qian.

16. "fought": For 鬧 read 鬪 , with Sun Qian.

17. The god of Mt. Hua bore the familiar name Third Son through most of the Tang period. Positive identification comes quite late, probably in the tenth century, at Dunhuang. Wei Zhuang's 韋莊 (836–910) famous but long lost poem "Qin fu yin" 秦婦吟 , finally recovered in manuscript from the Dun-huang cave library, contains a passage on this god. In one MS. (P 2700) his title Metal Heaven God 金天神 is glossed "Third Son, Mt. Hua" 華嶽三郎. See Lionel Giles, "The Lament of the Lady of Ch'in", *T'oung Pao* 24, 1926, p. 333.

18. "the drum": Omit 車 , with Sun Qian.

19. *Da Tang liu dian* 大唐六典 , edition of Konoe Iehiro, 1724, reprinted Taipei 1962, 5.13b–14b; Robert des Rotours, *Traité des fonctionnaires et traité de l'armée*, revised edition (San Francisco: Chinese Materials Center, 1974), p. 105, n. 2 and p. 503, n. 3.

20. See the detailed comment in *Yuanhe jun xian tu zhi* 元和郡縣圖志 , compiled by Li Jifu 李吉甫 (758–814) (Beijing: Zhonghua shuju, 1983), 2.35–36.

21. Compare another story from *Guang yi ji* in *TPGJ* 333.2647: "When they reached Tongguan they were stopped by the other-world frontier officers and could not get through for several days."

22. "Yu fu zhi" 輿服志 , *Xu Han shu* 續漢書 (ap. *Hou Hanshu* 後漢書 , 29.3647).

23. Uchida, pp. 106–111.

24. Uchida, p. 104; and, more copiously, Qian Zhongshu, pp. 805–806.

25. Uchida, pp. 109–110.

26. The textual reading *she ju* 社橘 in *TPGJ* 419.3410 is certainly a misprint: it is

corrected later in the same text (419.3411), and the corresponding phrase in other early texts correctly reads *ju she*: see *Lei shuo* 28.10b; *Zui weng tan lu, xin ji*, 1.83 and 84; *Lü chuang xin hua* A.40; *San dong qun xian lu* 三洞羣仙錄 compiled by Chen Baoguang 陳葆光 , preface 1154 (*Dao zang* 道藏 , Harvard-Yenching no. 1238), 12.15b, which adds a further remark — "the country districts sacrifice to it".

27. The archaic Altar of the Soil (*she* 社) consisted of an earthen tump, a tree growing upon it, and a "tablet" (*zhu* 主) in the form of a wooden post or stone marker. The territorial god worshipped there was associated with the earth and with the *yin* force in nature, and received prayers for rain in times of drought. All this is documented in Chavannes' classic study "Le dieu du sol dans la Chine antique", in *Le T'ai chan: essai de monographie d'un culte chinois* (Paris: Leroux, 1910), pp. 437–525. By the fifth and sixth centuries A.D. the trees on state altars had become obsolete enough to stimulate Liu Fang 劉芳 to write a learned memorial urging restoration: *Wei shu* 魏書 (Beijing: Zhonghua shuju, 1974), 55.1225–1226; Chavannes, p. 466, with note 2. On the other hand, an "anti-Taoist Buddhist pamphlet of the sixth or seventh centuries (*Kuang hing-ming* [read *hung-ming*] *chi* 12, *Pien-huo p'ien* 辯惑篇 , *T* LII, 2103, p. 171a) ridicules Taoists who 'mark trees in order to make them into soil gods'. The purpose of all this is to beg for help in case of danger, or to pray for rain." See Rolf A. Stein, "Religious Taoism and Popular Religion from the Second to Seventh Centuries", in *Facets of Taoism*, edited by Holmes Welch and Anna K. Seidel (New Haven and London: Yale University Press, 1979), p. 72, n. 67. The link between orange-tree, soil god, prayers for rain and the dragons who control rainfall is clear. On the orange (perhaps more precisely tangerine) in southern China, see Joseph Needham, *Science and Civilisation in China*, Vol. 6, Part 1 (Cambridge: Cambridge University Press, 1986), pp. 104 ff.

28. Huo Shixiu, pp. 1061–1062. The link is noted again, but not further studied, by Ji Xianlin 季羨林 (in "Yindu gushi zai Zhongguo" 印度故事在中國 , *Wenxue yichan* 文學遺產 1980.1, p. 148) and by Liu Shouhua 劉守華 (in "*Da Tang xiyu ji* de minjian wenxue jiazhi" 大唐西域記的民間文學價值 , *Minjian wenxue jikan* 民間文學季刊 1982.2, p. 175).

29. Xuanzang 玄奘 , *Da Tang xiyu ji* 大唐西域記 , edited by Zhang Xun 張巽 (Shanghai: Shanghai renmin chubanshe, 1977), 3.63–64.

30. Samuel Beal, *Si-yu-ki: Buddhist Records of the Western World*, 2 vols. (London: Kegan Paul, Trench, Trübner, 1884) with pp. 128–132 on the Nāga Lake.

31. A close examination of this topographical reference was made by a British officer, Major H. A. Deane, in "Note on Udyāna and Gandhāra", *Journal of the Royal Asiatic Society*, 1896, p. 661: "This measurement brings us exactly to the head of the Aushiri valley, which drains into the Panjkora near Darora.

How the Pilgrim got his distance over several valleys and intervening high spurs, it is difficult to conjecture. But on the hill to which it brings us there is found a large lake, more than a mile in length. It is apparently fed by snow."

32. Beal's wrestling with the term *su xin* 宿心 (p. 129, n. 32) seems to miss the point. The Śākya youth is offering a bargain in which the Nāga girl's consent to marriage will earn his consent to perform the transformation of her body that she strongly desires. The bargain is then fulfilled in word and deed.

33. "Meeting the bride in person" 親迎 : The final item in the ancient Six Rites of marriage, in which the groom went to the bride's home for their joint ritual salutations. See "Shi hun li" 士昏禮 in *Yili* 儀禮, Song edition reprinted by Ruan Yuan 阮元 in *Chong kan Song ben shisan jing zhu shu* 重刊宋本十三經注疏 (Changsha: 1815–1816), 4.1a–5.4b.

34. "nuptial" 燕爾 : A phrase implying marriage celebrations since the line 宴爾新昏, "You feast your marriage-kin", in *Shi jing* 35, "Gu feng" 谷風. Beal (p. 131) overlooked these nuptial references and so left the story without a marriage ceremony.

35. Thus reflecting the common iconic form of Nāga images in Indian society — "the human form universally characterized by means of the polycephalous serpent-hood... In art the number of heads varies, but is always uneven; it may be three, five, or seven": J. P. Vogel, *Indian Serpent-lore or the Nāgas in Hindu Legend and Art* (London: Probstain, 1926), pp. 37–38.

36. Three MS. fragments are extant from Dunhuang: S 2659, 0958, and P 3814. On these and the Buddhist canonical editions, see *Da Tang xiyu ji*, editorial note, pp. 1–2, and *Da Tang xiyu ji guben san zhong* 大唐西域記古本三種, edited by Xiang Da 向達 (Beijing: Zhonghua shuju, 1981) preface, pp. 1–15.

37. Compare H. Kern, *The Saddharma-pundarika, or The Lotus of the True Law* (Oxford: Clarendon Press, 1909), Chapter 11, pp. 250–254, and Kumārajīva's version, *Miao fa lian hua jing* 妙法蓮花經, in *Taishō shinshū daizōkyō*, Vol. 9, no. 262, 12.35bc.

38. Kern, ch.1, p. 7; Kumārajīva, 1.2b.

39. A progress surveyed by Diana L. Eck, *Banāras, City of Light* (London: Routledge & Kegan Paul, 1983), pp. 51–54. On pp. 264–265 she describes and illustrates the seasonal propitiation of Nāga deities with offerings.

40. A power well illustrated by Xuanzang's other Nāga myth from Udyāna, concerning the spring of Nāga Apalāla: *Da Tang xiyu ji* 3.60; Beal, pp. 121–123.

41. *TPGJ* 419.3412. Myths of Yu the Great in conflict with dragons are reflected in Warring States and Han literature. See *Huainan zi* 淮南子, *Si bu cong kan* edition, 7.7ab ("Jing shen" 精神); Wang Chong 王充, *Lun heng* 論衡 in *Lunheng ji jie* 論衡集解, edited by Liu Pansui 劉盼遂 (Beijing: Guji chuban-she, 1957), 5.103, 6.130; *Lüshi chunqiu* 呂氏春秋 in *Lüshi chunqiu jiaoshi*

呂氏春秋校釋 4 vols., edited by Chen Qiyou 陳奇猷 (Shanghai: Xuelin chubanshe, 1984), 20.1346.

42. "Among the creatures produced by Heaven and Earth man being the noblest, the dragon must be inferior": see Wang Chong's *Lun heng* 6.131, *Lun-hêng, Part I: Philosophical Essays of Wang Ch'ung*, translated by Alfred Forke (Shanghai: Kelly & Walsh, etc., 1907), p. 352.

43. *TPGJ* 419.3414.

44. *TPGJ* 419.3416.

45. The seductive charm of Nāga maidens is widely met in Indian legend, and descent from marriages with them was claimed for other royal houses of ancient India: J. P. Vogel, pp. 33 ff.

46. *TPGJ* 419.3415.

47. *TPGJ* 301.2387–2388.

48. "lucky deer symbol" 鹿瑞 : The symbolism is based on a pun — *lu* 鹿 (deer) and *lu* 祿 (blessing, prosperity).

49. **"common wick": To symbolize linked hearts.**

50. "Peak": For 樂 read 嶽 , conjecture.

51. "object to": Supplied by conjecture.

52. A line from *Shi jing* 118, "Chou mou" 綢繆 . This piece was anciently interpreted as a marriage song.

53. An echo of the Tang zither repertoire. A tune called "Parting Crane" 別鶴操 appeared as one of the four main zither pieces in the *Qin pu* 琴譜 used by Guo Maoqian 郭茂倩 in his *Yuefu shi ji* 樂府詩集 (Beijing: Zhonghua shuju, 1979), 58.844–847, where its mournful theme of stern separation imposed on a devoted wedded couple resounds through poetry from the fifth to the ninth centuries.

54. The words "touched my handkerchief" come from *Shi jing* 23, "Ye you si jun" 野有死麕 , traditionally read as a song of courtship in which the disturbed handkerchief is worn at the girl's girdle. For the "joke about the courtier and his tassel", see *Han shi wai zhuan* 韓詩外傳 in *Han shi wai zhuan ji shi* 韓詩外傳集釋 , edited by Xu Weiju 許維遹 (Beijing: Zhonghua shuju, 1980), 7.256–257: in the anecdote a consort of King Zhuang of Chu removes the tassel from the hat of a courtier who has pulled at her clothes in the dark.

55. Literally, "the techniques ... of Xuan and Su", celestial women whose teachings on sexual therapeutics formed the content of two ancient manuals — *Xuan nü jing* 玄女經 and *Su nü jing* 素女經 — circulating in Tang China: see reprint of *Su nü jing* by Ye Dehui 葉德輝 in *Shuang mei jing an congshu* 雙梅景闇叢書 ,with his editorial preface.

56. *Song shu* 宋書 (Beijing: Zhonghua shuju, 1974), 39.1225; *Nan Qi shu* 南齊書 (Beijing: Zhonghua shuju, 1972), 16.313. In the Sui the group expands to eight: *Sui shu* 隋書 (Beijing: Zhonghua shuju, 1973), 26.736.

57. *Nan Qi shu* 17.342. I take *ping tian ze* 平天幘 to mean the same as *ping ze*

guan 平幘冠 ; cf. Wang Pu 王溥 , *Tang hui yao* 唐會要 , *Guoxue jiben congshu* edition (Shanghai: Shangwu yinshuguan, 1935), 31.577–578(*ping jin ze* 平巾幘). For the Commander's crimson muslin gown, see *Nan Qi shu* 17.341.

58. Compare *Tang Li Chongrun mu bihua* 唐李重潤墓壁畫 (Beijing: Wenwu chubanshe, 1974), plates 1–16.

59. From "Gods, Ghosts and Ancestors", *Religion and Ritual in Chinese Society*, edited by Arthur P. Wolf (Stanford: Stanford University Press, 1974), p. 150.

60. For similar reports, also based on Taiwan fieldwork, see Li Yih-yuan, "Ghost marriage, shamanism and kinship behavior in rural Taiwan", in *Folk Religion and the Worldview in the Southwestern Pacific*, edited by N. Matsumoto and T. Mabuchi (Tokyo: Keio Institute of Cultural and Linguistic Studies, 1968), pp. 97–99; and David K. Jordan, *Gods, Ghosts, and Ancestors: The Folk Religion of a Taiwanese Village* (Berkeley: University of California Press, 1972), pp. 140–155.

61. *TPGJ* 333.2647–2648; 334.2650–2651; 380.3023. In these three cases the ghost wedding is performed when both parties are dead.

62. Wolf, "Gods, Ghosts, and Ancestors", p. 151. Compare the man interviewed by Jordan (p. 143): "Of course no one wants to marry a spirit! You only marry a spirit when there is nothing else you can do."

63. Brief but subtle discussions of the role of the bride's agnates in her wedding rites and married life are given by Maurice Freedman in papers reprinted in *The Study of Chinese Society*, edited by G. William Skinner (Stanford: Stanford University Press, 1979): see pp. 269–271 and 294–295.

64. *TPGJ* 419.3414.

65. "highest priority": For 志尚 read 之尚 , by parallelism with previous sentence.

66. *TPGJ* 419.3416.

67. I have explored this idea in *The Tale of Li Wa*, pp. 61–78.

68. For 別 I read 則 : an emendation which is conjectural here, but widely attested elsewhere in *TPGJ*.

69. "five breeds" 五蟲 : Five classes of living creature, distinguished as feathered, hairy, shelled, scaly and naked — the human race belonging to the last. The underlying idea of pre-eminence (長) within these individual classes appeared already in the *Lun heng* chapter on dragons (6.131): "Man ranks first among the naked creatures, as the dragon is the foremost of the scaly animals. Both take the first place among their kindred." See Forke, *Lun-hêng*, p. 353.

70. *TPGJ* 419.3417.

4

Subculturalness as Moral Paradox: A Study of the Texts of the White Rabbit Play

Henry Y. H. Zhao

Defining the Field

The aim of this article is to examine the particular fashion in which subcultural texts of Chinese popular literature perform their moral function within the framework of Chinese culture. This being too ambitious an aim for a short article, it is particularly unwise to be involved in the argument on the definition of such concepts as "popular literature", and "subculture", both of which are notoriously elusive. Neverthless, before starting my discussion, I have to draw the boundaries so that my article will not look like a wild goose chase. Though the definitions I shall suggest below have no claim to universality, it is hoped that they will at least serve the needs here.

Popular literature, in this article, is viewed as a generic category historically definable by critical consensus, often retrospectively. Some genres of a historical period are considered popular by literary critics at a certain time, but no longer so at other times. The *sanqu* 散曲 of Yuan, for instance, nowadays no longer considered a popular genre, was for a time held as one. Zheng Zhenduo 鄭振鐸 discussed *sanqu* in his *Zhongguo su wenxue shi* 中國俗文學史 (A History of Chinese Popular Literature) despite the fact that many *sanqu* works were composed by literati authors like Yuan Haowen 元好問 (1190–1257), Ma Zhiyuan 馬致遠 (1250?–1324?) and others. "Popular literature" is therefore a generic category that covers all the works of the genres in question, irrespective of the characteristics of specific works. Chinese vernacular fiction of the thirteenth to nineteeth centuries is still considered a popular genre even though many of the works are generally regarded as classics. In the light of this understanding, one is entitled to argue that the sixteenth century versions of some vernacular "fictional masterpieces" could be studied as "literati novels", as Andrew Plaks did.[1] Within one popular genre there may exist texts of widely different cultural status.

"Subcultural text", on the contrary, is a functional concept that is decided by the performance of the text itself in the culture. Culture, in this article, is viewed as composed of all discourses and all activities — "texts" in the broadest meaning of the term — that impart meanings relevant to social life. Thus, a culture is the conglomeration of all meaning production and transmission in a society. But the texts in a culture "are differently ranked, and stand in opposition to one another, in relation of domination and subordination, along the scale of 'cultural power' ".[2] This is especially so with traditional Chinese culture which demonstrates a distinct "paradigmatic structure" where the various texts rank in a strict hierarchy with top genres possessing absolute meaning-power.[3] Subcultural texts are those situated on the lowest rungs of the hierarchy. Since they are subordinated to the higher texts in their mode of signification, production and expected interpretation, they do not secrete the value legitimacy carried by the latter.

A certain text is considered subcultural on account of the particular mode of its performance of cultural functions. Though the performance by a specific text is difficult to examine retrospectively since the various socio-cultural data we can gather often provide us with only a vague picture, the intrinsic characteristics such as stylistic features, plot typology, composition of the motif-sequence, etc., can still provide more or less reliable evidence for determining its cultural status.

This article will focus on the difference between the subcultural texts and the culturally higher texts in their performance of socio-cultural, especially moral, functions. The ideal texts for such an examination would be texts of the same popular genre, or preferably, different versions telling the same story based on different cultural levels.

Fortunately, such examples are not difficult to find as constant recension was, for many centuries, the very mode of existence of Chinese popular literature. Most works of popular literary genres, whether fiction, drama or ballad, were constantly rehashed. Printing, having become the major channel for literature, might be expected to deprive the texts of the non-repeatability they enjoy in oral presentations, as books are both re-readable and re-printable. But for the texts of Chinese popular literature, each printing was almost unexceptionally a recension (which is very different from the texts of privileged genres like poetry, where textual alterations by editors are never tolerated unless his textual criticism can prove them more authentic). So the printed texts of popular literature only enjoyed a semi-unrepeatability, as they are re-readable but not re-printable.

In constant rehashing, the authorship of the text was then reduced to a social average, and, as a result, situational context took the place of intentional context as the more important factor in controlling the interpretation.[4] The audience intentionality then substitutes the authorial intentionality, more securely anchoring those texts at subculturalness.

It seems that this sequence of rewritings should eventually be brought to an end by an author who is able to provide a satisfactory and somewhat literati shape to the text, as indeed happened to many of the best known early Chinese vernacular novels. Yet this often does not disallow the rehashing to continue in other popular genres or subgenres. Guan Hanqing's 關漢卿 (1230?–1300?) *zaju* 雜劇 version of *Baiyue ting* 拜月亭 did not prevent it from being rewritten into *nanxi* 南戲, nor did Feng Menglong's 馮夢龍 (1574–1646) *ni huaben* 擬話本 fiction version of the same story prevent its being rewritten into a *tanci* 彈詞 ballad.

But even within one genre, the most "refined" version was not always able to halt the virtually unstoppable reprinting/recension. In fact, some stories are so essentially bound to their subculturalness that they do not reward the refining efforts. Though hardly successful, those refining efforts pulled texts above the subcultural levels, which is exactly what is needed for comparative study.[5]

The White Rabbit Play[6]

The texts of the White Rabbit are not the only ones in Chinese popular literature that could meet the need of the present article. However, for more than one thousand years, the story has enjoyed a large number of recensions in different popular genres, and some of its texts are among the earliest extant texts of those genres. Though always a story favoured only by the vulgar, there was some literati effort to refine it. For these reasons it is a suitable case for my study.

According to the scanty documentation about oral literature of the Northern Song, the story of Liu Zhiyuan 劉智遠, the first emperor of the short-lived Later Han Dynasty (947–950), and his long neglected wife Li Sanniang 李三娘 seems to have been a favourite topic in oral story-telling as early as the eleventh century, when the time of the hero and heroine was still the recent past.[7] The historical figure of Li Sanniang must have been of special interest to the audience as she was originally a farmer's daughter. According to official history she was "spirited away by Liu who sneaked into the house at midnight" when Liu was a stable-boy. She became a very important political figure as the Empress and then the Empress Dowager in the later turbulent years, and her brothers all assumed important government positions.

The earliest extant text of the Liu-Li story appear in *Xinbian Wudai shi pinghua* 新編五代史平話 (The Newly Compiled History of the Five Dynasties) believed by some critics to be the only genuine Song text (i.e., before the middle of the thirteenth century) among the three earliest texts of *pinghua* 平話 fiction.[8] The basic plot of the Liu-Li story that was later elaborated in the White Rabbit play can already be found in the chapter dealing with Liu's founding of the new dynasty.[9]

At the same time as it was being performed in *pinghua* story-telling, the Liu-Li story was also finding its way into other popular genres. One of the only three extant texts of *zhu gong diao* 諸宮調 is devoted to the Liu-Li story. Out of the twelve chapters, only five have been found. But we can see that the plot of the ballad appears much more enriched than that about the Liu-Li marriage in *Xinbian Wudai shi pinghua*. What was only an episode of Liu's imperial career in the *pinghua* was now developed into an independent story — the rise to fortune of Liu Zhiyuan and the reward received by Li Sanniang for her virtues. Liu Zhiyuan's military success and his subsequent ascension to the throne seems to have developed into another lineage of texts, among them the *Can Tang Wudai shi yanyi* 殘唐五代史演義 purporting to be written by Luo Guanzhong 羅貫中 (1330?–1400?)[10] and the play *Wu long zuo* 五龍祚.[11]

The earliest dramatic versions of the Liu-Li story seems to be a *zaju* play of the Yuan Dynasty (thirteenth to fourteenth centuries). In *Lu gui bu* 錄鬼簿 there is an entry *Li sanniang madi peng yin* 李三娘麻地捧印(Li Sanniang Holds the Seal in the Hemp Field) by Liu Tangqing 劉唐卿. The play is, unfortunately, lost.[12] Judging from the title, the vicissitude of Li Sanniang's life was given greater prominence in the Yuan drama version than in the *zhu gong diao* ballad.

In the scarce documents about the early Southern opera of the Yuan Dynasty, the play of the Liu-Li marriage is repeatedly mentioned,[13] and it is known to be among the "Greatest Four" (四大傳奇).[14] Since the early twentieth century, when Chinese popular literature became a serious scholarly concern, no text of an early *nanxi* version of the White Rabbit has been available except for some of the arias preserved in *Jiugong zhengshi* 九宮正始. Among the *nanxi* versions I shall discuss, the earliest is the text unearthed in a mid-Ming grave near Shanghai in 1967, *Xinbian Liu Zhiyuan huanxiang baitu ji* 新編劉智遠還鄉白兔記, which is the earliest extant printed text of *nanxi*.[15] In the prologue it is stated that the play is printed in the Chenghua period (1465–1487) by Yongshun Tang in Beijing and written by the "talents of Yongjia Writing Club" (永嘉書會 才人). I venture to suggest that this claim of authorship or editorship is doubtful since the stunning amount of unorthographic and miswritten characters[16] in the text indicates that the script must have been recorded by a barely literate actor who learned the play orally.[17] Anyone with basic schooling should have produced a better script.[18] Though its language is so crude, both the date (mid-fifteenth century) and the similarity of many of its arias to those of the earlier versions preserved in *Jiugong zhengshi* (with tunes different) show that it is truly a "New Compilation", that is, a recension.[19] We can deduce that this print, of such miserable quality, did not have any other ambition than circulation among semi-literate readers, presumably habitual theatre-goers, who could recall the performance in their minds with the help of a crude version like this. Since no one would deliberately condone orthographic errors, the editorial hastiness possibly indicates that the print was in high demand.[20]

The plot of this version had already settled into the form that remained basically unaltered in the later drama versions: Liu Zhiyuan is now said to be a native of Xuzhou 徐州 , the birth place of the great emperor Han Gaozu 漢高祖 (r. 206–195 B.C.). A step-child, he loses all his money at gambling, and tries to steal the sacrificial chicken in a temple. He is caught but saved by Squire Li, a well-to-do farmer who hires him as stable-boy and later marries his daughter Sanniang to him as he believes Liu to be a man of destiny. Sanniang's brother and sister-in-law hate Liu and, after the death of Squire Li and his wife, play all kinds of dirty tricks to force Liu to leave the household. Liu leaves to join the army and, after marrying the general's daughter, rises up the army ranks. Meanwhile Sanniang's brother and sister-in-law try to force her into remarriage. She refuses, and is therefore punished with hard labour. She gives birth to a son by the millstone without any help and has to cut his cord with her teeth (hence the son's pet name Bittencord).[21] To save the child, an old neighbour Dou carries him to where Liu is stationed. Sixteen years later, his son, out on a hunt one day, is led by a white rabbit to a woman weeping at the well, who tells him about her life. Bittencord questions his father on the matter, and

Liu Zhiyuan decides to fetch his former wife. Disguised as a poor farm hand he comes back to Sanniang and hands her his official gold seal. At the happy family reunion, the evil persons are duly punished.

The second extant opera version is *Xinke chuxiang zengzhu zengbu Liu Zhiyuan baitu ji* printed by the Nanjing publisher Fuchun Tang in the Wanli period 萬曆 (1573–1619). The reviser Xie Tianyou 謝天祐 was a professional playwright, of whose plays only three are known today by title. He seems to have worked for Fuchun Tang for some time, as another play printed by the same publisher also bears his name as the reviser. Though we are not sure on which original this recension was based, this version of the White Rabbit play is a complete rewriting; the dialogue and arias are almost completely different from those of the Chenghua or the earlier Yuan versions,[22] though the basic story remains. The language of the text, in particular of the arias, is much more refined. Nevertheless, the recension contains a large number of simplified characters (but no miswritten ones like those abundant in the Chenghua version) not normally tolerated in the texts of higher genres.

The third extant drama version of the White Rabbit is *Baitu ji* 白兔記 in the early-seventeenth century collection *Liushi zhong qu* (Sixty Plays) compiled by Mao Jin 毛晉 (1599–1659) and printed by his own publishing house Jigu Ge. Since the collection was widely circulated, this version has been the best known among all texts of the White Rabbit play. Mao Jin was among the group of late Ming intellectuals in the Suzhou area who made a great contribution to the development of Chinese popular literature by carefully collecting and editing popular fiction, opera and folk songs. Like Feng Menglong, the most outstanding member of this group, Mao Jin showed remarkable appreciation for the "vulgar" elements in the popular texts, and, while making the text more readable, tried his best not to dilute the popular flavour. Ling Mengchu 凌濛初 (1580–1644), another great enthusiast of popular literature in the late Ming, once commented on the editing of the White Rabbit play:

> The White Rabbit and The Killing of the Dog are two of the "Greatest Four", but the texts we have now are simply unreadable. It is true that the original texts are crude and difficult to read. But some complacent people took such liberty to make such drastic alterations to the supposedly ungrammatical sentences or colloquialisms that the true form of these plays is now completely lost to us.[23]

This seems to be a criticism of the Fuchun Tang version or its like, and also to be Mao Jin's guiding principle when compiling *Liushi zhong qu*. It is due to his remarkable editing skills that, though the text remains highly colloquial, there is virtually no unorthographed character (either simplified or miswritten) in this elegantly printed edition.[24]

Apart from these three versions, there is no other complete extant text of the play printed before the twentieth century, though beginning from the late sixteenth century there has appeared a large number of "selected acts" versions of the White Rabbit, which we shall discuss later.[25]

The three opera versions of the White Rabbit belong respectively to three centuries: the Chenghua version the 1470s, the Fuchun Tang version c. the 1590s, and the *Liushi zhong qu* version c. the 1630s. It is of course hardly justifiable to compare them in a purely synchronic fashion without considering the diachronic context. In fact the production of the three versions — one recorded with hardly any editorship, the second rewritten with almost excessive refinement, and the third tidied up with moderate alteration — could be seen as an important indication of the Chinese literati's changing attitudes toward popular literature.

A Comparison of the Three White Rabbit Opera Versions

A comparison of any group of parallel passages in the three plays would bring out the differences immediately. Li Sanniang's self-introduction song when she walks onto the stage in the Chenghua version runs like this:

> [*Zuo huanglong*]
> I, Sanniang, am a pretty girl.
> My Parents are old.
> I grew up in the village
> Diligent in weaving, good at sewing.

Most of the arias in the Chenghua version, like this one, are as plain as daily speech, with hardly any poetic diction, except for arias which seem to have been taken over from the earlier, and more refined versions preserved in *Jiugong zhengshi*. The self-introduction song in the *Liushi zhong qu* version depicts a stereotypical scene of the countryside:

> [*Wei fan xu*]
> Entertaining ourselves at the family dinner
> Glad that we support ourselves as farmers

With these hundred *mu* of fertile land.
Dozens of households hearing each other's cocks crowing and dogs barking.
In the distance fishermen are singing at dusk
And we see boys dosing off on the back of the calves.

But in the Fuchun Tang version of this self-introduction song, the country girl is gentrified beyond recognition:

[*Bao ding'r*]
Alarmed at fallen flowers, pitying the tender green
I stop sewing beside the window, speechless.
Swallows and thrushes are hastening spring.
But how much of it can be called back?

Apart from the style, in the Chenghua version there are a great number of set expressions (so-called *shuici* 水詞, or diluting words) ready for the characters to use at any moment. For instance, Liu Zhiyuan repeats, "All good and evil will have its retribution in the end" (善惡到頭終有報) three times; Li Sanniang's brother repeats five times the line, "The blue sky refuses to be fooled" (湛湛青天不可欺); each time at the head of an irrelevant nonsense poem. When Brother walks onto the stage for the first time, he chants:

The blue sky refuses to be fooled.
The sadness can hardly be compared to the flowing river.
On River Wu it is not impossible to find a ferryboat.
Love of one night lasts a hundred nights.

This doggerel is repeated word-for-word in the middle of the play when Brother forces Sanniang to remarry. Another doggerel beginning with the same line:

The blue sky refuses to be fooled.
Eight crabs fly southwards.
One of them can hardly fly on,
'Cause it is a male one.

The last time the same line drags out probably the silliest doggerel ever found in Chinese popular drama:

The blue sky refuses to be fooled.
The toad in the well has no fur coat.
The eighty-year-old grandma pisses standing,
Only with nothing to hold in her hand.

The clown chants this "poem" when he is threatening to beat Liu Zhiyuan. Maybe he is just looking in vain for some weapon. Maybe these lines exist for no reason other than arousing simple-minded laughter.

We may assume that these doggerels serve to stereotype the character as a clown. However, this nonsense poem can be found with exactly the same wording in other plays, for example, the *zaju San zhan Lü Bu* 三戰呂布 (Three Battles against Lü Bu),[26] in which it is sung by a heroic warrior.

All the nonsense doggerels are deleted in the *Luishi zhong qu* version, not to mention the Fuchun Tang version. Literati authors, familiar with stage conventions, used *shuici* occasionally, as we can see in many Yuan and Ming plays,[27] and the Fuchun Tang version of the White Rabbit play is no exception. But an abuse of *shuici* is seen only in the culturally lowest texts like the Chenghua version.

Besides the crudity of the language, the Chenghua version is also characterized by recapitulation of previous events. When Bittencord returns from the hunt, Liu Zhiyuan asks him, "My child, how many mountains have you climbed? What game have you shot?" And Bittencord retells in detail the events of the previous two acts. After that Liu Zhiyuan, in an effort to appease his second wife, retells all the events in the first half of the play. This kind of repetition, also seen in pre-modern Chinese vernacular fiction, is often considered by critics to be the vestiges of oral performance where the audience, constantly coming and going, have to be informed now and then of the events that had already been enacted. Such repetitions, though greatly shortened, are also found in other versions of the play. Bittencord's retelling, 280 Chinese characters long, only takes up 180 characters in the *Liushi zhong qu* version. Liu Zhiyuan's retelling of 190 characters is shortened to 126 characters in the *Liushi zhong qu* version. In the Fuchun Tang version, the first retelling is turned into arias, and the second completely omitted.

This linguistic difference clearly marks the cultural ranking of the three versions: the Chenghua version is culturally the lowest; the *Liushi zhong qu* version is one with the play's subcultural characteristics carefully preserved but made more presentable; the Fuchun Tang version is a remoulded version to cater for the taste of more learned readers — a text of a popular genre, disengaged from its original subculturalness.

However, more important to our analysis is the difference in the motivation of the play's action, since motivation provides the ethos of the play. In this respect, the three versions show an order of progressive rationalization: the more refined the version, the more care it takes to give the heroes a noble motivation on every occasion.

For example, let us see how Liu Zhiyuan sinks into stark poverty and meets the Li family: In the *Xinbian Wudai shi pinghua*, Liu is a compulsive gambler who does not repent even after he is married into the Li family, who later flees to join the army because he has lost all his wife's dowry in gambling. In the Chenghua version, this ne'er-do-well image of Liu Zhiyuan is not much improved. Appearing on stage for the first time, Liu introduces himself, "I was driven out of the house by my step-father because I squandered my fortune. Now I fool around in the gambling house everyday and sleep in the temple every night." Liu is made a little more respectable in the *Liushi zhong qu* version where he is an unlucky man who "loses nine times out of ten". In the Fuchun Tang version, Liu's gambling is arranged by the Maming God who, appearing as a character in the play, explains, "I see that Liu Zhiyuan of Shatuo village is predestined to ascend to the throne and pass it on to his son, and that the third girl of the Lis will become the first mother of the nation. But there should be some arrangement to let them meet." So he sees to it that Liu loses all his money that day and has to get himself hired by Squire Li and eventually married into the family. Our hero, then, is no longer the village rough.

On why Brother Li hates Liu Zhiyuan so much that he tries every means to drive Liu away: In the Chenghua version, the reason is simple, as Brother complains, "This guy knows nothing of farming. Every day a gang of idlers around him practise martial arts on the threshing ground. There will come a day when he beats someone to death and flees, and we shall be held responsible." This is excusable peasant narrow-mindedness. In the *Liushi zhong qu* version Brother boasts of his virtue of diligence, and complains that Liu is an idle man. But he then goes a step further and complains that Liu has come to the family dead broke, and so should be nicknamed Liu the Penniless. This is not only boorish but snobbish. In the Fuchun Tang version, however, the motivation is rendered psychologically more complex. Ugly Sister, merely an accomplice in the other two versions, is now the main culprit. She hates Sanniang because, as she confesses, "I often lapse in feminine duty. Sanniang always reported it to my parents-in-law and made me suffer humiliation. Now the parents-in-law have died, it's time for revenge." And Brother is only a henpecked husband who dares not disobey his wife. The persecution of Sanniang is then an ethical conflict between good and evil.

On the reasons for Liu Zhiyuan's marriage to the general's daughter: In the Chenghua version he says frankly, "If I had not married her, how could I have attained such a high position?" He says the same in the *Liushi zhong qu* version with more elegance, "One step and I am now in heaven. This marriage is no coincidence." However, in the Fuchun Tang version Liu Zhiyuan first establishes himself by winning merits on the battlefield, thus putting himself on an equal footing with the general's daughter. Then when the general suggests the marriage Liu refuses on the grounds that he has a wife at home (which, in the other two versions, he does not care to mention), and the general agrees to let his daughter be Liu's second wife. So Liu's image is not tainted by the marriage of convenience.

But the most important motivation problem is why Liu Zhiyuan neglects his wife for sixteen years, leaving her at the mercy of his in-laws. In the Chenghua version this is simply left unexplained. In the *Liushi zhong qu* version a flimsy pretext is provided: when leaving the village Liu vows that he will not return till three conditions are satisfied — becoming successful, winning a high official post, and taking revenge on Brother. This poor imitation of the celebrated "Three Refusals" in the *nanxi* classic *Pipa ji* 琵琶記 (The Lute Song) was perhaps added by Mao Jin himself. But the long negligence is still barely explained away. In the Fuchun Tang version Liu has been so completely occupied with the noble cause of fighting rebels and barbarians that he does not return even to his second wife, the general's daughter, for fifteen years.

To substantiate this arrangement, the Fuchun Tang version adds nine acts recounting Liu Zhiyuan's military career, just to prove how busy he has been during all those years saving the nation. In the *Liushi zhong qu* version three acts are added to cover the sixteen years, but in the Chenghua version this is a blank. Some critics, Zhou Yibai 周貽白 for instance, argues that the Fuchun Tang version is a typical *antouqu* 案頭曲 , or closet play.[28] But the frequent anthologization in the sixteenth to seventeenth centuries (perhaps because it was the first version of the White Rabbit play in Yiyang Qiang opera which became very popular in those years) should convince us that the Fuchun Tang version was actually the text for a great number of stage presentations.

The differences among these versions also lie in their treatment of legendary events. The three versions show an order of regressive legendization: the more refined the version, the less legendary it is. For instance, on why Squire Li wants to marry Sanniang to Liu Zhiyuan: In the Fuchun Tang version it is because he thinks that this is a "good match", and in order to convince his daughter, he arranges for Liu to sweep the drawing room and let Sanniang have a look at her future husband from behind the curtain. In the Chenghua version and the *Liushi zhong qu* version it is because Squire Li sees snakes running through Liu's nostrils when the latter is asleep, and in the *Liushi zhong qu* version there is even a scene on how Liu's "imperial" snoring makes people think that a storm is coming.[29]

On the cause of Squire Li's death: In the Chenghua version, the old couple are knocked down at the wedding by Liu's kowtows as it is against the hierarchy of rites for common people to be kowtowed to by an emperor. This bizarre event is half deleted in the *Liushi zhong qu* version, where the parents-in-law feel dizzy after Liu's kowtow, and they tell others that they are not in good health. This serves as a foreshadowing of their death not long after, but it is left unexplained whether or not they are killed by Liu's kowtow. In the Fuchun Tang version there is not a trace left of this killing kowtow.

The most important legendary event, the titular one, is supposed to explain how Bittencord finds his mother. Liu Zhiyuan is stationed in Binzhou 邠州 which is quite close to the historical fact, for Shanxi was Liu Zhiyuan's base, from where he launched his triumphant expedition to the capital. One day Bittencord sees a white rabbit, which, with Bittencord's arrow shot in its side, leads him to Sanniang's village thousands of miles away from Binzhou. The writer of the Chenghua version ignores this distance as if there is no miracle involved.[30] The *Liushi zhong qu* version highlights the mystery:

> Bittencord: My old soldiers, where are we now?
> Soldiers: This is Shatuo Village.
> Bittencord: How could we be so fast?
> Soldiers: We were like riding on a cloud.

Zhou Yibai thinks that this is "the author laughing at himself" as a trip on the clouds is impossible.[31] I would rather take it as a reminder of the legend, by which the play gets its title.

The rewriter of the Fuchun Tang version feels uneasy about this legendary arrangement and tries to put it straight. In Act 32 Liu delivers a long monologue in which he says that he cannot continue to cooperate with Li Cunxu as the latter usurped the throne, and he decides to lead his army away to Shi Jingtang 石敬塘, his old colleague, and also to make preparations against the Qidan 契丹 barbarians who are threatening to invade China again. On this long expedition he plans to visit his second wife Yue, whom he has not seen for fifteen years, and to try to find his first wife Li Sanniang whom he left sixteen years ago. He gives the command of the vanguard to his son who, in due course, marches to the village and finds his mother.

Then why bother about the rabbit? In fact the rabbit disappears completely from the play though it still carries the title "The White Rabbit". The only vestige of the legendary rabbit surfaces when Bittencord reports to his father and mentions briefly that a rabbit metamorphosed into an old man who led him to the woman weeping at the well.

It is not that there is no legendization in the Fuchun Tang version. On at least three occasions supernatural beings come into the play. But those legendary events themselves lack dramatic interest as they are only arranged to forward the hero's career.

The Farcical

The culturally lower versions abound in farcical scenes. These passages hardly contribute to the characterization of the heroes and are at odds with the composition of the plot. As the hero never participates in the farce, he looks, in his aloofness, awkwardly out of place amid the hilarious clowning.

The beginning scene in the Chenghua version features Liu's sworn brother Shi Hongzhao 史弘肇 and his wife treating Liu Zhiyuan to noodles. Shi's wife, in the role of a clown, cracks nonsense jokes all along, and finally adds dust to the flour to make the noodles. In the *Liushi zhong qu* version she makes noodles out of the flour for "starching foot-wrappers". When she cannot find the kneading board, she makes her husband go down on all fours so that she could make noodles on his back. This man-turned-prop slapstick seems to be a stock technique of early *nanxi*.[32]

Such acts seem to be meant to provide an opportunity for free clowning. That is why the arias and dialogues in this act of the Chenghua version are completely different from the *Liushi zhong qu* version. In the Fuchun Tang version, this irrelevant first act is omitted.

In the Chenghua version Brother forces Liu to write the divorce bill. He then makes Liu fingerprint it, while he himself makes his toe-print, and Ugly Sister volunteers to sign with her "ass-print". This scene of low comedy could bring down the house. But Liu Zhiyuan's writing the divorce bill while weeping ruins his heroic image as a man of destiny. In the *Liushi zhong qu* version this scene is less side-splitting but still uneasy for Liu Zhiyuan. In the Fuchun Tang version, Liu makes fools of Brother and Ugly Sister by dictating a false divorce bill, thus showing himself intellectually superior to the clowns.

Clowning enjoyed a great prominence in early *nanxi* plays. Judging from the few extant texts, we can see that after nearly every serious scene, there is a scene where clowns dominate. This tradition was discontinued in the main-stream *chuanqi* 傳奇 plays of Ming which came to be ever more refined. But, judging from texts like the *Liushi zhong qu* version of the White Rabbit, it persisted in subcultural plays.

Since the basic story is the same from one version to another, the localized legendary and farcial parts are what give the various versions their uniqueness. Each recension seems to contain its own particular farcical scenes, to be changed yet again at the next recension.

Any new rewriting was, in the intention of the rewriter, an improvement. The culturally lower texts, it seems, tend to retain the localized legends and farcical scenes, while the culturally higher versions would endeavour to weed out the localized parts in their effort to totalize the whole play rationally.

This rule, if true, offers some indication of the lineage of evolution of those versions. There remain a small number of localized passages in the Fuchun Tang version that the rewriter Xie Tianyou could not have invented by himself. For instance in Act 37, before Bittencord comes back from the hunt, there appears a miserable monk who sings:

> [*Qing Xuan he*]
> Poor me, I wake at midnight
> And my feet are so cold,
> Feet so cold.
> How I long to have a pretty partner.
> But I am afraid, as adulterer,
> I shall be dragged to court by the patron.

The monk is an unnecessary character appearing briefly on the stage, only to prepare for Liu's arrival at the temple where he would hear his son's report. It is possible that this was a passage in the version on which the Fuchun Tang version is based, which was, somehow, not weeded out. Since the Chenghua version does not contain this passage, we may deduce that it cannot be the basis of the Fuchun Tang version.[33] The *Liushi zhong qu* version bears striking similarity to the Chenghua version in many parts, especially in the arias. But there are also some localized parts that are quite different. For instance, in Act 9 of the *Liushi zhong qu* version the Ugly Sister eats the noodles prepared for the monks whom the Lis hire to chant sutras, and she adds her snot to the noodles to let it pass for over-stewed noodles. It is unimaginable that Mao Jin the literati-rewriter could have produced such a coarse joke, though he may have appreciated it enough to let it remain. Since the Chenghua version does not contain this or many other vulgar jokes, the basis for the *Liushi zhong qu* version must be another lost version.[34]

The localized parts in culturally lower *nanxi* texts form an evident structural dualism, which, as I shall show in the following sections, could lead to a moral dualism.

Chinese Cinderella, the Moralist

The plot of the White Rabbit play is a combination of two success stories — Liu Zhiyuan's rise from poverty to eminence, and Li Sanniang's rise to fortune through her feminine virtues. This is a typical case of the highly ethical Chinese variation of the Cinderella formula.

The basic Cinderella formula contains the following steps or "functions":

1. Although the protagonist suffers unfair treatment at the hands of evil people, blocking her way to success,
2. she displays impressive merits which
3. win her the deserved reward
4. and the evil people are punished.

Li Sanniang's story proceeds neatly along the four steps. Compared with her Western counterpart, we can see that this process of reversing fortune in Chinese drama is always ethically encoded.

Sanniang's suffering is the result of her brother and sister-in-law's pressure on her to divorce and remarry which goes against the Chinese moral codes for family life; Sanniang's merit for redemption is her sixteen years of chastity and hard labour, and most importantly, her giving birth to Liu's eldest son, whereas the Western Cinderella's merit seems mainly to be her attractive appearance; Sanniang's situation is that the man she has married is able to fight his way up, while the Western Cinderella's opportunity is having a handsome prince fall in love with her; Sanniang's reward is family reunion; the Western Cinderella's is marriage.

In late medieval Chinese opera there are hundreds of plays following the Chinese Cinderella formula.[35] If we include the "twisted" variations in which the man betrays the woman of virtue but later repents (generally after the woman's attempted suicide) and goes back to her, our list could be much longer. Thus the man who obstructs success is the same one who creates the opportunity for redemption.

To sum up the East-West difference, the Western Cinderella succeeds mainly because of her beauty, the Chinese Cinderella because of her chastity; the Western Cinderella story promotes the exertion of one's rights endowed by nature, the Chinese Cinderella story prizes the rights won by moral constancy.[36]

If the ethical logic in literary works can have both expressive and instrumental functions, then the morality in the Chinese Cinderella formula can be said to express the interest of the Chinese open-elite power system.[37] This system is more ethically based. Since ancient times, Western sages have always held that politics runs counter to man's moral self-cultivation.[38] In Confucianist ethical philosophy, since politics is the manifestation of man's self-cultivation, rising to a high position is itself the peak of moral perfection.

Now the question arises: why is this dramatic admonition on how to deal with changes in fortune so welcomed by popular audiences? After all, few villagers could dream of becoming a governor, much less an emperor. Obviously what works here is the instrumental function of morality in literature, not the expressive function.[39] The consolidation of the family is always seen in China as an antidote for disorder in society. That is why the Chinese Cinderella must always be a married woman, at least a girl already engaged, so that she can have a chance to display her faithfulness to the family and invite the whole audience to join in the celebration of the final victory of the social moral codes.

The Moral Conservatism of Popular Drama

We can see that among the two types of recensions of the White Rabbit plays, the culturally lower versions are even stricter than the culturally higher recensions in their moral adherence.

The sufferings Sanniang has to endure are more graphic in the culturally lower versions. In the *Liushi zhong qu* version, Sanniang is made to carry water with a pair of "olive-shaped" buckets with pointed bottom so that she would not be able to sit and rest on her way, and a hole is drilled in the water vat so that it would never be full. In both the Chenghua and the *Liushi zhong qu* versions, Ugly Sister comes to grab Sanniang's new-born baby and tries to drown him in a pond. Such treatment, more likely to be found in folklore, is replaced in the Fuchun Tang version by almost two whole acts of Sanniang's arias complaining about her ill fate.

Sanniang more staunchly refuses to remarry in the culturally lower versions. In the Chenghua version, Brother lies to her that he has just received a letter from Binzhou saying that Liu has been killed in battle. Sanniang says nothing beyond repeating: "One saddle to one horse, one wife to one husband, I will not marry another man all my life." So her constancy seems to be a faithfulness more to the norm than to her husband.

The culturally lower versions centre more on the ritual significance of redemption. In the Chenghua version, Liu Zhiyuan comes back to the village in disguise and meets Sanniang at the mill:

> Liu: I shall come back to you with a brocade robe and a gold head-dress to take you away with me as a noble lady.
> Sanniang: My husband, if you really want to take me away, what pledge would you give me?
> Liu: Here I give you my official seal made of forty-eight taels of gold. This is *"Li Sanniang holds the seal in the hemp field, and Liu Zhiyuan returns home in a splendid garb"*.

The last sentence Liu says is possibly the full title of the lost *zaju*, but it is not in agreement with the plot of the *nanxi* versions, as the scene is now not set in the hemp field, and Liu is at this moment dressed in the ragged clothes of a farm-hand. Still more surprising is that the pronouncement should be made not in his role of Liu Zhiyuan. He is actually stepping out of the dramatized world into the dramatizing world to make an announcement, in the capacity of the actor, to call the audience to join in the celebration. This "stepping-out" is deleted in the *Liushi zhong qu* version, but the handing over of the seal as pledge remains. But this event is actually superfluous so far as the plot is concerned, since there is no last twist before the family reunion. (In the *zhu gong diao* ballad and, probably, in the *zaju* versions, Sanniang is kidnapped by gangsters. It takes Liu a fierce battle to get her back.) In the Fuchun Tang version, the whole scene is omitted, replaced by Sanniang's long aria on her years of suffering, thus making this act more realistic but less emotionally redemptive.

And finally the punishment. In the *pinghua* fiction and the *zhu gong diao* ballad versions of the Liu-Li story, the evil in-laws are pardoned after a severe censure. This is also true of the Chenghua version. In the Fuchun Tang version, they are still pardoned, but Ugly Sister, as the main culprit, kills herself in repentance. In the *Liushi zhong qu* version, however, Ugly Sister is made to fulfil her joking vow made sixteen years ago that she would make herself into a candle should Liu become successful. When Ugly Sister is ordered by Liu to be wrapped in cloth and oil and carried away to be executed according to her word, Brother, who has just been pardoned because Sanniang wants him to carry on the family lineage, shouts: "Good burning for the bitch!" The punishment is thus made hellish to the great rejoicing of the audience. This cruel punishment, and in particular Brother's horrible cheer, could hardly have been invented by the literati editor Mao Jin.

The propensity for culturally lower texts to adhere more strictly to the moral code was already noticed by Chinese literati critics in late Yuan and early Ming. Yang Weizhen 楊維楨 , for instance, points out that the moral fervour of popular actors "could make the Confucian scholars ashamed of themselves".[40]

So we discover that for the subcultural texts, there is neither an independent interpretation system nor an independent set of values. The ideology of a society is unconditionally accepted and implemented by the lower social strata, though in appearance these values are mainly designed to regulate the behaviour of the socially privileged classes. Being culturally subordinate, the lower classes are also subordinate in ideology.

The eager adoption by subcultural texts of the dominating moral codes has been confirmed by many Western sociologists in their study of mass culture in modern times. Michael R. Booth in his study of nineteenth century English plays concludes:

> What both the reading and play-going public looked for was ... a stern morality, much positive virtue and its reward in the almost inevitable happy ending, eccentric humour, and native English jollity and spirit.[41]

Some critics hold that the moral rigidity of early Ming popular plays is ascribable to the repeated imperial decrees threatening severe punishment on immoral popular literature. Booth seems to be answering a similar challenge when he points out that "dramatists, managers, and audiences were as conservative as the Lord Chamberlain and his Examiner, whose edicts were quite in accord with the taste of the times".[42]

Modern Chinese critics have extolled popular literature as belonging to a culture independent of, and superior to, the dominating culture. For both left-wing and right-wing critics, it has been fashionable to stress the independent values of this popular culture. Zheng Zhenduo declares in unequivocal terms: "They [popular literary works] represented another society, another life, another side of China...."[43] Yet Zheng Zhenduo realizes that popular works may not necessarily live in "another world". In his discussion of Qing *tanci* ballads written by women, he says:

> Here the ethical demand is more strict as the authors demand firmer, purer chastity on the part of the women protagonists, while male protagonists are allowed several concubines without facing up to the question of morality. This kind of one-sided understanding of virtue was at that time so inveterate that even women thought it was beyond any doubt.[44]

Zheng probably did not realize that this is a direct refutation of his own statement in his preface to the book.

There were different opinions. In the early 1940s there arose a dispute among Chinese intellectuals on the "class nature" of popular literature. Hu Feng 胡風 was the representative of the minority who insisted that popular literature is "determined by, and adapted to, its feudalistic content.... Basically it tries to attract the masses with poisonous feudalistic ideas".[45] His opinion evoked intense controversy. He and those on his side were labelled "national nihilists", and were silenced.

Though their argument showed a better understanding of the conservatism of popular culture, they failed to account for the double nature of the morality of popular literature in relation to the dominating ideology. Indeed the cultural performance of popular literature defies any monolithic understanding.

The Moral Dualism in Subcultural Texts

In the two types of recensions of popular plays we have examined, the culturally higher and the subcultural, the moral message may be similar, but the fashion of imparting it is different. The rationalization we observe in culturally higher versions is, by its nature, an effort to reinforce the pervasive power of the ideological metalanguage. That is why the Fuchun Tang version spares no effort, even at the expense of rendering the play less stageable, to make Liu Zhiyuan a true national hero who deserves the reward of bringing wealth and glory to his family. Not even the smallest parts of the long play are spared this tyrannic rationalization; all that is irrelevant is weeded out. This structural integrity corresponds to a moral monism.

Such a structuring principle seems to justify the theory of organicism, which argues that literary works should be dealt with as an organic unit, and that no part of the work can be separated, or dispensed with, aesthetically or ethically. In other words, no part can be removed or altered without changing the meaning of the whole text. If this sounds rather exaggerated in describing any work, supporters of organicism may argue that the most important excellence attributable to any one part is to show that it is a necessary element of the whole.[46]

This organicist theory has not gone unchallenged. John Crowe Ransom, the modern American critic, was one of its most formidable opponents. He holds that a literary work is formed by two kinds of non-incorporated elements — the structure and the texture. According to him, structure is the logical substance or the paraphrasable core of the work, or "its ethics if it seems to have an ideology". Texture is what is not the structure in the text — the unparaphrasable, "local" substance.[47]

The dispute over organicism seems to be long over, but the two different critical approaches are still practised. And in Chinese popular drama, we observe the two different principles of text-structuring. The culturally higher texts are more likely to satisfy the critical effort to reveal an organic unity as they are structured more like integrated wholes, while the subcultural texts tend to show a distinct dualistic composition — a logical skeleton and many localized parts that are not sufficiently incorporated into the whole.

In reading the culturally higher texts, the readers are constantly reminded of its ethical logic to which every part of the text contributes. No matter whether this ethical logic is conformist or dissentient, the texts go for it in all earnestness. For instance, *Mudan ting* 牡丹亭 (The Peony Pavilion) challenges the dominating Neo-Confucianist "reason" (*tianli* 天理) ethics with "desire" (*renyu* 人慾) in such a whole-hearted way that the author claims: "Feeling and Rites do not have anything in common, and you have to sever them with a sword" (情有者理必無，理有者情必無，真是一刀兩斷語).[48] Those plays could be ethically subversive, but still morally monistic.

As a contrast, subcultural texts can hardly be morally dissentient. Since in subcultural texts the audience intentionality carries more weight than the authorial intentionality, it is very difficult to infuse dissentient ideas into the texts and ignore the reaction of the audience.

In this article we are comparing conformist, culturally higher texts and culturally lower texts that are, by definition, conformist. It is not the ethical logic that separates them but the fashion in which this ethical logic is implemented. In the latter we find the unique co-existence of the totalized and the localized. T. S. Eliot once offered a very interesting description of the structure of literary texts:

> The chief use of the "meaning" of a poem, in the ordinary sense, may be ... to satisfy one habit of the reader, to keep his mind diverted and quiet, while the poem does its work upon him: much as the imaginary burglar is always provided with a bit of nice meat for the house dog.[49]

This hungry but foolish dog is, according to Eliot, "the social censorship or the moral prejudice of the social average reader". This is reverse to the traditional concept that formal elements are an attractive decoration to make the moral logic more palatable. Thus the structural dualism becomes a moral dualism.

The ellipsis in the above quote is a note in brackets declaring that Eliot was "speaking of some kinds of poetry and not all". We are not clear what kind of texts he excludes from his theory. It seems to me that this dualism is not readily discernible in the culturally higher versions of the White Rabbit play, as in those versions there is a desperate effort to sufficiently encode all parts. Eliot's description, it seems, can be borrowed to explain the structural dualism we have observed in subcultural texts.

The Fuchun Tang version of the White Rabbit play proves that a totalizing effort does not necessarily add to the merits of the text, and a culturally higher version does not mean that it is artistically more satisfactory. Some subjects are simply not suitable for such a rational totalization, and Liu Zhiyuan's story is one of them. The stories of the heroes of the Five Dynasties are no less interesting than those of the Three Kingdoms. What complicates the matter is that three of the short-lived dynasties were established by warlords of the Shatuo, a semi-sinicized Turkish tribe (in the White Rabbit play the name Shatuo is said to be Squire Li's village). This kind of regime would not be honoured by the exclusive Confucianist historical philosophy. In history, Liu Zhiyuan rose to pre-eminence as a general under Shi Jingtang, the flagrant traitor who ceded sixteen prefectures to the Qidan "barbarians" in exchange for military help which enabled him to ascend the throne. Liu Zhiyuan, not directly responsible for this cession, filled the political vacuum by carefully avoiding conflict with the Qidan. Of course not many dynasty founders in Chinese history are of higher moral integrity than Liu Zhiyuan, but his dynasty was too short-lived to justify its sanctity. Official historians, who are often political snobs, comment, "Though fate made him rise to meet the opportunity, we do not see in him the appropriate moral integrity of an emperor."[50] I think that this was one of the main reasons why story-telling on the Five Dynasties topics gradually declined while that on the Three Kingdoms topics, equally welcomed by the populace in the Song period, evolved into a huge number of plays and the greatest historical novel in China. No matter how hard the rewriter of the Fuchun Tang version Xie Tianyou tried to rationalize the play, his effort was doomed as the subject-matter of Liu Zhiyuan, an opportunistic Turkish-Chinese emperor, is simply not suitable for ethicizing.

The notion of dual structure is more applicable to the subcultural versions of popular drama. Some critics seem to have noticed the serious localization in such texts. Piet van der Loon, for instance, notes, "une telle action ne doit pas être considerée comme une addition à l'intrigue originelle. Au contraire, l'histoire était seulement un cadre commode pour une action scénique, qui pouvait également se rerouler *de façon independante*".[51] (Italics mine.) And J. I. Crump, in his study of the White Rabbit play, concludes, "Ming drama is a form thoroughly devoted to theatrical contrivance and takes full advantage of every excuse for a dance, a skit or other types of divagation. The result is that stories often disappear in a wallow of stage business, cute tricks or divertissements (as a minor example, the playwright's fun with Liu's snores)."[52] This, I venture to say, is not true with the culturally higher *nanxi* texts which strive to eliminate the localization. He was apparently only discussing the *Liushi zhong qu* version, not the Fuchun Tang version (The Chenghua version was not yet unearthed).

But what after all are the relations between the localized and the totalized in the culturally lower texts? If they are really as irrelevant as these critics suggest, why should they co-exist in one text and be presented in one stage performance?

My suggestion is that the two are interdependent. On the one hand, the flood of localized parts threatens to drown the plot, diverting audience attention or turning the serious story frivolous. For instance, in the Chenghua version, after the parents are knocked off by Liu's kowtow, the juicy wedding song continues to be sung to celebrate the marriage, which makes the new couple seem extremely callous. After the reunion of Liu and Sanniang, Brother and Ugly Sister enter to fight Liu but end in a howling scramble on the stage, which jars with the tearful reunion scene a moment before.

Since the ethical logic of the plot is almost the same in subcultural versions as in the culturally higher versions, there appears in the former a structural-moral paradox which is actually part of the definition of the subcultural texts.

First, the paradox displays itself in the fact that the subcultural texts have to adhere more closely to the dominant ideology, for no other reason than that they have neither right nor aspiration to participate in the forming or transforming of ideology. As they are farther from the canonized texts at the top, the pressure on them to conform is accordingly higher in order for them to remain under the ideological control. This pressure in fact ensures the covering of the ideology coding over all the texts in a culture.

But this ideological covering becomes flimsier as it reaches down to the bottom of the pyramid of the cultural hierarchy in society. Though subcultural texts share the coding system, only part of these texts — the ethically logical part or the paraphrasable core — is sufficiently encoded, leaving a large amount of localized parts relatively undercoded.[53] Though the localized parts have to rely on the ethical logic to hold together in one piece and to give it a moral *reason d'être*, they are not sufficiently incorporated into the ethical logic, and on the whole they do not contribute to, but muddle or even hinder, its progress.

We can say that the ethical logic serves in the play not only as an excuse which, in Eliot's opinion, can be jettisoned as a piece of meat for the moral watch-dog. It is an essential part of the subcultural texts, and both of these — the localized and the totalized — do the real work. That is why subcultural texts may sometimes appear hypocritical when they endeavour to "camouflage" the jovial or wild passages with moral admonition. It is not actually hypocrisy but a natural manifestation of their intrinsic moral paradox, since they must have an ethical logic to hang together.[54] The doggerel cited in Section 3 of this article can be regarded as miniatures of this dualism — no matter how nonsensical the "poems" are, the leading line is likely to be a moral admonition.

The localized parts, especially the farcical ones, sometimes show a deviance from the norm. For instance, in the Chenghua version, Brother says on one occasion that he would be "first beheaded and then exiled" if he poisoned Liu, because, he says, "The rate for Tax-Paid-in-Grain is really too low in our Chenghua period." In the Chenghua and the *Liushi zhong qu* versions, when Liu has the good fortune to be picked by the General as his son-in-law because of the red-robe incident, two other soldiers come forward to ask to share the bride. After being told to shut up, one soldier in the *Liushi zhong qu* version says, "In today's world, pilferers win." In the *Liushi zhong qu* version when Old Man Dou carries Liu's son to Binzhou and finds that Liu has married again, he cracks a joke, "You are really a quicklime bag, leaving traces wherever you go" — a jovial joke which does no good at all to Liu's heroic image. Such jokes are too localized to be regarded as a political or ideological challenge. Most of the farcical scenes play on the signifier rather than on the signified, as they seem to be without definite reference. This is a major characteristic of subculture that modern sociologists find in today's urban subcultural group activities — threatening only in appearance.[55]

Sometimes this paradox seems ready to be developed into a kind of irony. The heroic image of Liu Zhiyuan in the subcultural versions is sometimes destroyed by the localized parts to such an extent that he becomes what modern critics would consider a round character: in the two subcultural versions, Liu's marriage and remarriage are both unashamedly for convenience, his long neglect of Sanniang seems to be intentional, and he is actually forced by his son to fetch his former wife. Thus his becomes a complex characterization, a combination of the images of Cai Bojie 蔡伯喈 in both the culturally lower *Zhao zhennü* 趙貞女 version and the culturally higher *Pipa ji* version — a character much more complicated than the Liu Zhiyuan in the culturally higher Fuchun Tang version where he is reduced to a flat embodiment of all virtues. But this possible complexity is the result of the interpretative deduction of today's critics. It is not something that the anonymous rewriters of these subcultural versions would ever have conceived, or something the popular audience of the time could have perceived. Structurally, it is mainly the result of sloppiness and discrepancies, and of the separation of the localized substance from the ethical logic. We would be fooling ourselves if we were to go too seriously into an "ironical" reading of these subcultural texts, even though it seems like an alluring opportunity for a critical game.

The "Selected Act" Texts of the White Rabbit Play

Starting from the seventeenth century, some other White Rabbit texts appeared, in the form of selected acts preserved in various anthologies.[56] It is not surprising that the majority of these acts contains beautiful arias, mostly derivatives of the arias in the Fuchun Tang version. The acts most often selected are *Guan hua* 觀花 (Admiring Flowers), *Sao di* 掃地

(Sweeping the Floor), *Hui qi* 會妻 (Meeting the Wife) — acts where there is little legend or clowning to interfere with the music.

What we call *zhezi xi* 折子戲 are originally selected acts from full-length plays, but later developed into texts of independently staged short pieces. There are some anthologies, beginning from the seventeenth century, that are devoted to "selected acts" plays. For instance the White Rabbit acts in *Qiu ye yue* (Autumn Night Moon) and *Zui yi qing* (Enjoyment after Drinking) are developed and expanded to such an extent that it is hard to imagine that the whole play could be stretched in like manner. The act of *Mofang xianghui* 磨房相會 (Meeting at the Mill) in *Qiu ye yue*, for instance, is several times longer than the act in any of the three complete versions, and very different from them too. It must have been a *zhezi xi* play independently staged.

In the eighteenth century, *zhezi xi* became the dominant form of stage performance of Chinese opera. In 1770 there appeared *Zhui bai qiu* 綴白裘 (The Patched White Fur Robe), the largest ever collection of *zhezi xi* plays compiled by Qian Decang 錢德蒼 which includes six acts of the White Rabbit play. In these pieces the arias remain much the same as those in the *Liushi zhong qu* version, but the clowning is expanded so much that if the play had been complete, it would have been a totally new version of the White Rabbit play.

When we have to interpret these *zhezi xi* texts, however, we find ourselves in a dilemma. We are not sure whether they should be treated as short plays or selected acts of one long play. This dilemma is actually the extension of the paradox already existing in the play — when localization is developed to a certain extent, the structure disintegrates. There seem to be some practical reasons to treat them as independent plays, since the full-length *chuanqi* play, by that time, was generally so long that only a partial stage presentation could retain the necessary dramatic tension. Nevertheless, the moral protection that could only be provided by the ethical logic of the plot in the full-length play was still needed, though the ethical logic was now kept at a convenient distance. Therefore, with *zhezi xi*, the ethical logic became a shadow that is neither totally separated from nor totally integrated into the text.

For instance, *Yuzan ji* 玉簪記 (The Jade Hairpin) is a boring exemplary play with a stereotyped plot in its *Liushi zhong qu* version of the sixteenth century. But its selected act *Qiujiang* 秋江 (The Autumn River) in *Zhui bai qiu* becomes one of the most exciting pieces of traditional Chinese opera, where the heroine Chen Miaochang 陳妙嫦, a young nun, falls in love with a young scholar who stays a few days in the monastery, and when he leaves, the nun persuades the owner of a tiny boat to carry her down the river to reach her lover. This is a bold challenge to the Chinese moral codes defining feminine virtue. Yet for those in the audience who remember the plot of the play (which most of the eighteenth century audience did), the young nun is only fulfilling her moral duty as she was engaged, unbeknown to her, to the young scholar by an arranged marriage before their birth. The enchanting and provocative short play is then morally safe under the protective umbrella of the original play.

What was preserved most in the *zhezi xi* texts of the White Rabbit play in *Zhui bai qiu* was the legendary and the farcical — the most moving scenes of Sanniang's suffering and the purely clowning scenes. They are *Yang zi* 養子 (Giving Birth), *Hui lie* 回獵 (Back from the Hunt), *Madi* 麻地 (The Hemp Field), *Xianghui* 相會 (Meeting the Wife), *Song zi* 送子 (Delivering the Child), and *Nao ji* 鬧雞 (The Fuss about the Chicken). None of the acts devoted to the heroic career of Liu Zhiyuan was chosen. The readers or audience now did not have to read or watch the strenuous ethicizing efforts in the full-length play. But the ethical logic is still indispensable as the audience was frequently reminded of it.

This is, however, not an adequate solution to the moral paradox of the subcultural texts. It is only its formal extension and interpretative deferral. In a sense, the emergence of *zhezi xi* plays marked the last phase of the development of the structure of traditional Chinese drama, as the ideology has now to work in a fragmented fashion which would eventually lead to its disintegration. The structural-moral paradox of Chinese subcultural texts now assumed a new form.

Notes

1. Andrew H. Plaks argues that these texts "exhibit many of the same pretensions to high wit and deep seriousness as those found in literati painting — pretensions that set the four works sharply apart from the popular materials out of which they are fashioned", *The Four Masterworks of the Ming Novel* (Princeton: Princeton University Press, 1987), pp. 24–25.

2. John Clarke and Tony Jefferon, *The Politics of Popular Culture: Cultures and Sub-Cultures* (Birmingham: Centre for Contemporary Culture Studies, 1973), p. 54.

3. Jurii Lotman and A. M. Pjatigorskij suggest the typological distinction be-

tween syntagmatic culture and paradigmatic culture. Their description of the two reads as follows:

> Paradigmatic cultures create a single hierarchy of texts with a constant intensification of textual semiotics such that at the summit is found a culture's Text, which has the greatest indice of value and truth. Syntagmatic cultures create a set of types of texts that comprise various aspects of reality and are thought to be equal in value. These principles are complexly interwoven in the majority of actual human cultures (*Soviet Semiotics*, edited by Daniel P. Lucid, Baltimore, 1977, pp. 130–131).

4. Modern semiotics tries to distinguish five "contexts" that may influence the interpretation of a text: the co-textual, the existential, the situational, the intentional, and the psychological. See *Encyclopedic Dictionary of Semiotics* (Berlin: Mouton de Gruyter, 1986).

5. The present paper intentionally shuns the pair of terms *histoire/recit*, which seems to be readily applicable here. Basically, the different *recits* can be regarded as presentations on the same *histoire*, with variations only on the sequence, ellipsis, focalization and other aspects of narrative mediation. But to what extent can a *recit* change the plot while still claiming to belong to the same *histoire*? To get around this critical uncertainty, I refrain from the temptation of using this seemingly neat pair of terms. Besides, I have a personal reason for the choice: ten years ago I attended a seminar offered by Professor Cyril Birch at Berkeley on reading the "White Rabbit play." Professor Birch's well-informed guidance, and the animated discussion at the seminar provided me with the stimulation to delve more deeply into the texts.

6. The texts of the White Rabbit play on which this article is based are: The Chenghua version: *Ming Chenghua shuochang cihua congkan* 明成化説唱詞話叢刊, Vol. 10, xerox reprint of *Ming Yongxun Tang keben xinbian Liu Zhiyuan baitu ji* 明永順堂刻本新編劉智遠白兔記 (Beijing: Wenwu chubanshe, 1979); The Fuchun Tang version: *Guben xiqu congkan biankan weiyuanhui yingyin Beijing tushuguan cang Ming Fuchun Tang kanben xinke chuxiang zengzhu zengbu Liu Zhiyuan baitu ji* 古本戲曲叢刊編刊委員會影印北京圖書館藏明富春堂刊本新刻出像增註增補劉智遠白兔記 (Shanghai: Shangwu yinshuguan, 1953–1954); The *Liushi zhong qu* 六十種曲 version: *Guben xiqu congkan biankan weiyuanhui yingyin Changle Zheng (Zhengduo) shi cang Ming Jigu Ge kanben baitu ji* 古本戲曲叢刊編刊委員會影印長樂鄭 (振鐸) 氏藏明汲古閣刊本白兔記 (Shanghai: Shangwu yinshuguan, 1953–1954).

7. In *Dongjing menghua lu* 東京夢華錄, it is said that in the time of the Northern Song there were renowned professional story-tellers who specialized respectively in stories of the Five Dynasties and the Three Kingdoms. The stories of the Three Kingdoms later became more popular — I shall explain why further on in this article. Liu Zhiyuan is generally considered one of the most attractive heroes in the Five Dynasties stories. See Liu Dajie 劉大杰 , *Zhongguo*

wenxue fazhan shi 中國文學發展史 (Shanghai: Gudian wenxue chubanshe, 1959), p. 363; also J. I. Crump, "Liu Chihyuan in the Chinese 'Epic' Ballad, and Drama", *Literature East and West*, Vol. xiv, 1970, p. 155.

8. Liu Dajie, for instance, holds that the extant texts of the other two early vernacular *pinghua*, *Quanxiang pinghua wuzhong* 全相平話五種 and *Da Song xuanhe yishi* 大宋宣和遺事, should be dated not earlier than the beginning of Yuan (that is, early thirteenth century). But he spares this novel. Ibid., p. 312. Not all the decreed taboo characters of the Song Dynasty are carefully avoided in the text, but that may be because it was printed by a commercial press.

9. In the late-Ming collection of short stories *Gu jin xiaoshuo* 古今小説 compiled by Feng Menglong there is a story about Shi Hongzhao 史弘肇 and Guo Wei 郭威, the two generals under Liu Zhiyuan's command. So not only Liu Zhiyuan and his wife, but other members of his military *junta* also became heroes of oral literature.

10. Zhao Jingchen 趙景琛 holds that the *pinghua* may have first been written in the Yuan period since many of the episodes were used in Yuan *zaju* plays. See his *Zhongguo xiaoshuo kaozheng* 中國小説考證 (Jinan: Qilu shushe, 1980), pp. 122–129. Obviously this *yanyi* was another product of Song story-telling on Five Dynasties topics, as the Liu–Li marriage story is not even mentioned in it. In Five Dynasties plays after Yuan, events from the *pinghua* and the *yanyi* gradually mingled.

11. See *Quhai zongmu tiyao* 曲海總目提要, Vol. 31. The play is also titled *Hou baitu* 後白兔 (The Latter White Rabbit). But this does not mean that the play in its original form took shape later than the White Rabbit play.

12. This entry is also found in *Taihe zhengyin pu* 太和正音譜 and *Yuan qu xuan mu* 元曲選目, but the title is 麻地傍印, and in another edition of *Lu gui bu* the title is 李三娘麻地傍郎. The variation of titles may indicate that there are more than one *zaju* version of the White Rabbit play, though they purport to be written by the same author.

13. For instance, Xu Wei 徐渭 mentioned the title *Liu Zhiyuan baitu ji* in his *Nanci xulu* 南詞叙錄; Zhang Mu 張牧 mentioned the title *Fengxue hongpao Liu Zhiyuan* 風雪紅袍劉智遠 in his *Lize suibi* 笠澤隨筆. In *Hui* 64 of *Jin Ping Mei cihua* 金瓶梅詞話, the title *Liu Zhiyuan hongpao ji* 劉智遠紅袍記 is also mentioned.

14. There are two different lists of the "Greatest Four": Jing–Liu–Bai–Sha 荆劉拜殺 or Cai–Jing–Liu–Sha 蔡荆劉殺. The White Rabbit (Liu) is on both.

15. There are, in fact, three *nanxi* plays preserved in the Chinese encyclopedia *Yongle dadian* 永樂大典. But the encyclopedia itself is a scribed book, and we have no evidence that the *nanxi* texts there were copied from printed editions.

16. For instance, on the page following the title page there can be found as many as twenty-five unorthographic or miswritten characters.

17. It is, of course, unfair to put the whole blame of a poor edition on the writer of

the manuscripts, but the majority of the sixteen long ballads unearthed together with this play were apparently prepared by the same carver, and they do not contain as many mistaken characters. We can only deduce that this carver was just following the manuscripts.

18. Some other extant texts of the Southern Opera also purport to be written by playwrights of other clubs. For instance *Zhangxie zhuangyuan* 張協狀元 purports to have been written by the Talents of Jiushan Shuhui of Wenzhou. We have no evidence that these claims of authorship are authentic, and the poor orthography of the Chenghua version of the White Rabbit play makes such claims even more suspicious. In fact the activities of such playwright clubs are mostly mentioned in the documents of Song, Jin and Yuan, but hardly in any of Ming.

19. Sun Chongtao 孫崇濤, after a careful comparison of the fifty-seven arias supposed to belong to the earliest *Yuan nanxi Liu Zhiyuan* 元南戲劉智遠 preserved in *Jiugong zhengshi* with the arias in the Chenghua version and those in the *Liushi zhong qu* version, concludes that the *Liushi zhong qu* version, though written two centuries later than the Chenghua version, must be based on the earlier Yuan versions. (Sun Chongtao, "Chenghua ben *Baitu ji* yu Yuan chuanqi *Liu Zhiyuan*" 成化本白兔記與元傳奇劉智遠, *Wenshi* 文史, No. 20, 1983, pp. 213–219). He points out that the arias in the Chenghua version, though quite similar to those of Yuan versions in lyrics, are set to entirely different tunes. This is a clear indication that the Chenghua version must belong to a local opera different from those Yuan versions. His argument sounds convincing.

20. This Southern opera play, with so many unorthographed characters recongnizable only to southerners, was printed by a Beijing publisher. The name of the publisher is printed on the ballads unearthed together with the play. They were obviously carved by the same person.

21. The translation of this and other names in the play are borrowed from Cyril Birch's essay "The White Rabbit Plays: The Birth at the Mill, and Other Scenes", *Chinese Literature: Essays in Honor of J. I. Crump* (forthcoming).

22. There are only several arias in the Fuchun Tang version that are somewhat similar to those of the Yuan version (as preserved in *Jiugong zhenshi*), the Chenghua version, or the *Liushi zhong qu* version.

23. Ling Mengchu, "Tanqu zazha" 譚曲雜劄, *Zhongguo gudai xiqu lilun ziliao* 中國古代戲曲理論資料(Beijing: Zhongguo xiju chubanshe, 1988), p. 186.

24. Peng Fei 彭飛 argues, "The *Liushi zhong qu* version deletes too much farcical dialogue ... and sounds too cold and cheerless though much more refined. It is not only undesirable but impossible to let actors stage this version exactly as it is." See his "Lüelun Chenghua ben *Baitu ji*" 略論成化本白兔記, *Wenxue yichan* 文學遺產, No. 3 (1983), p. 75. It seems that Peng Fei had not read the Fuchun Tang version which is far "colder" and more "refined" than the *Liushi*

zhong qu version. However, even this too "refined" *Liushi zhong qu* version was criticized by Wu Mei 吳梅 : "The language is unbearably crude. It is enough to make a person vomit." *Guqu zhutan* 顧曲麈談(Shanghai: Shangwu yinshuguan, 1944), p. 167. The two diametrically opposite comments show how the version successfully takes the middle course.

25. There are reported to be modern versions in Peking opera 京劇, Xiang opera 湘劇, Yue opera 越劇, Qin Qiang opera 秦腔, Huangmei opera 黃梅劇, and other local operas since the end of nineteenth century, but my study is limited to texts before the twentieth century.

26. Quoted in Tang Wenbiao 唐文標, *Zhongguo gudai xiju shi chugao* 中國古代 戲劇史初稿(Taipei: Linking Press, 1984), p. 201.

27. Tang Wenbiao offers a long list of those *shuici* poems quoting from works by such celebrated playwrights as Wang Shifu 王實甫 , Guan Hanqing and Qiao Ji 喬吉 . Ibid., pp. 191–207.

28. Zhou Yibai, *Zhongguo xiqu fazhan shi gangyao* 中國戲曲發展史綱要(Shanghai: Guji chubanshe, 1979), pp. 228–229.

29. "Snakes running through nostrils" as a sign for the future emperor is a common legend, which might have its origin in the biography of Wang Tingcou 王廷湊 in *Xin Tang shu* 新唐書. In *Wudai shi pinghua* 五代史平話, for instance, Zhu Wen 朱溫, the first emperor of Liang, is seen to have snakes running through his nostrils when he was sleeping.

30. Wang Jisi 王季思 holds that the white rabbit legend is borrowed from Guan Hanqing's *zaju* play *Liu Furen qingshang wu hou yan* 劉夫人慶賞五侯宴. See "Liu Zhiyuan gushi de yanhua" 劉智遠故事的演化, *Song Yuan Ming juqu yanjiu luncong* 宋元明劇曲研究論叢(Taipei: Dadong tushu gongsi, 1979), pp. 4–9. Actually this magic white rabbit appears frequently in Chinese popular literature. In chapter 43 of *Shuihu zhuan* 水滸傳, Li Kui is led by a white rabbit to his lost mother. In chapter 37 of *Xiyou ji* 西遊記, a prince is led by a white rabbit to the ghost of his father. In *Wudai shi pinghua*, when Zhu Wen is giving a banquet, a white rabbit runs in and turns into a piece of paper bearing the prediction for his future; Shi Jingtang catches a white fox on a hunt which tells him about his future in human language.

31. Zhou Yibai, p. 224.

32. The best known example is found in the Yuan Southern Opera *Zhangxie zhuangyuan* in which two actors improvise as the two doors of a temple, and a clown turns himself into a banquet table, and, as can be expected, steals the fine food on his back, since he could change back into his other role at will.

33. Ye Kaiyuan 葉開沅, after comparing an "selected act" play of Wu opera with Act 34 of the Fuchun Tang version, finds that though the two are similar, the Wu opera act is nearer to the selected act preserved in *Qiuye yue* 秋夜月, an anthology of "selected acts". He concludes, "the Fuchun Tang version must be a recension from a still earlier version, part of which is preserved in the

present Wu opera version". See his *"Baitu ji* de banben wenti — Fuben xitong" 白兔記的版本問題—富本系統 , *Lanzhou daxue xuebao* 蘭州大學學報 No. 1, 1983, pp. 81–92; *"Baitu ji* de banben wenti — Jiben xitong" 白兔記的版本問題—汲本系統 , *Lanzhou daxue xuebao*, No. 2, 1983, pp. 76–84.

34. Sun Chongtao also concludes that the *Liushi zhong qu* version must be based on a version possibly earlier than the Chenghua version. He arrives at this conclusion by textual criticism of the arias, not by comparing the clowning scenes. Sun, p. 58. His method is of course more exact, but mine, I hope, may shed light on the structure of popular plays.

35. To name just a few: Among *zaju* plays *Yuhu chun* 玉壺春 (Spring in the Jade Pot); *Xiaoxiang yu* 瀟湘雨 (Rain on the Xiang River); *Hong lihua* 紅梨花 (Red Peach Flower); *Yuanyang bei* 鴛鴦被 (Mandarine Duck Quilt); *Bi taohua* 碧桃花 (The Green Peach Flower); among early *nanxi* plays *Jinchai ji* 荊釵記 (The Thorn Hairpin); *Fenxiang ji* 焚香記 (Burning the Incense). When *chuanqi* opera was at the height of its popularity, plays of this type became more abundant. Wang Jisi holds that the play *Fen he wan* 汾河灣 (The Fen River Bend) is a redressing of the Liu-Li story in the White Rabbit (Wang, p. 4). This inference is not necessary as the formula is so frequently used that it is only another application of the same pattern.

36. Both are of course manifestations of women's dependency. Colette Dowling defines what she calls the Cinderella Complex in her militant book *The Cinderella Complex, Women's Hidden Fear of Independence* (London: Fontana, 1982, p. 29) as "a network of largely repressed attitudes and fears that keeps women in a kind of half-light ... waiting for something external to transform their lives".

37. To borrow Walter Scott's term for the British power-structure — open-aristocracy.

38. See Plato, *Socrate's Defense*, pp. 30e–32, and also Sallustius, *Bellum Catilinae*, p. iii.

39. Zhou Yibai, the well-known Chinese scholar of traditional drama, declares, after summarizing plays of this type:

    ...Why does this theme seem to be so welcomed in *nanxi* by the end of Yuan? Here lies an important social problem of the time.... The literati at the time, after their success in the civil examination, discarded their old friends, changed their wives, some even stamped the former wife to death or forced her to commit suicide.... Thus a class conflict arises from their betrayal of their former class (Zhou Yibai, pp. 228–229).

    As if to support Zhou's argument, the Taiwan critic Tang Wenbiao quotes from a number of documents that there were actual cases of families splitting after the scholars' success in the civil examination, and he even called such plays "current affairs plays" (Tang Wenbiao, pp. 90–92).

40. Yang Weizhen, "Song Zhu nüshi Guiying yanshi xu" 送朱女士桂英演史序,

Dongweizi wenji 東維子文集 Sibu congkan 四部叢刊 (Shanghai: Hanfeng lou, 1929), Vol. 6, p. 12. Similar statements can be found in his other two essays "Zhu Ming youxi xu" 朱明優戲序 and "Youxi lu xu" 優戲錄序 , Ibid., Vol. 11, pp. 14–16.

41. Michael R. Booth, Introduction, *English Plays of the Nineteenth Century* (Oxford: Clarendon, 1969), Vol. 1, p. 7.

42. Ibid, p. 8. M. Janowitz, in his study of mass communication in modern society, "The Application of Social Knowledge to Mass Communication", *World Congress of Sociology* (London: Sage Publications, 1959), p. 142, also concludes:

> The vast majority of mass communications appear to have little content directed toward challenging existing normative patterns, encouraging critical thoughts, or stimulating individual or collective actions disruptive of the more or less orderly flow of existent social progress.

J.S.R. Goodlad, when examining modern Western drama in *A Sociology of Popular Drama* (London: Heinemann, 1971, p. 60) argues:

> ... popular drama, as opposed to drama favoured by social revolutionaries, innovators, and intellectuals, is likely to be conservative in orientation. If it is concerned with crime, it is likely to show who is to be excluded from the conventional society and why.

A. H. Cooke, ("Human Values in Drama", *Journal of Human Relations*, Spring Issue, 1958, p. 75) concludes after investigating the audience of different types of plays that the most morally disturbing plays are bound to be unpopular because in popular plays, "the morality discussed, and by and large upheld, is straight-forward, conventional, and simple, even if slightly crude".

J. T. Klapper, too, finds that modern mass communication "serves more often as an agent of reinforcement than of conversion".

43. Zheng Zhenduo, *Zhongguo su wenxue shi* (Beijing: Zuojia chubanshe, 1954), Vol. 1, p. 21.

44. Ibid., Vol. 2, p. 377.

45. Hu Feng (Zhang Guangren 張光人), *Lun mingzu xingshi* 論民族形式 (On National Form) (Shanghai: Haiyan shudian, 1949), p. 51.

46. It seems that most critics since Aristotle are for this theory. Its modern apologists include critics of diverse tendencies such as Coleridge, Emerson, Hegel, Croce, Dewey, Wimsatt, Lukacs and others. It is no coincidence that both Wimsatt's defense of organicism, "The concrete universal", and Lukacs's "The dialectical totality" are avowedly Hegelian. But the most powerful defenders of organicism are none other than the structuralists. Frank Kermode in "The Use of Codes", *Essays on Fiction 1971–1982* (London: Routledge and Kegan Paul, 1983), p. 75, hit the nail on the head when he commented on Roland Barthes:

One reason why Barthes gave up the Formalist attempt to establish a narrative *langue* of which every *recit* is a *parole* was precisely his fear that success in this operation would revive the old organicist myth of a structure peculiar to a particular work.

47. John Crowe Ransom, "Criticism as Pure Speculation", *The Intent of Critic*, edited by Donald A. Stauffer (Princeton: Princeton University Press, 1941), p. 109.

48. Tang Xianzu 湯顯祖 , "Ji Daguan" 寄達觀 , *Tang Xianzu shiwen ji* 湯顯祖詩 文集 , edited by Xu Shuofang 徐朔方 (Shanghai: Shanghai guji chubanshe, 1982), p. 1268.

49. T. S. Eliot, *The Use of Poetry and the Use of Criticism* (London: Faber and Faber, 1933), p. 151.

50. Xue Juzheng 薛居正 *et al*, *Jiu Wudai shi* 舊五代史 (Beijing: Zhonghua shuju, 1978), Vol. 5, p. 1341.

51. Piet van der Loon, "Les Origines rituelles de theatre chinois", *Journal Asiatique*, cclxv (1977), p. 87.

52. J. I. Crump, p. 160.

53. The term "undercoding" was first suggested by Umberto Eco in his *A Theory of Semiotics* (Bloomington: Indiana University Press, 1979), pp. 135–136. His definition runs as follows:

Undercoding may be defined as the operation by means of which in the absence of reliable pre-established rules, certain macroscopic portions of certain texts are provisionally assumed to be pertinent units of a code in formation, even though the combinational rules governing the more basic compositional items of the expressions, along with the corresponding content-units, remain unknown.

Eco's definition and his explanation in his book clearly indicate that his notion of undercoding is actually under-decoding, a way of interpretation with a rough coding when adequate coding is unavailable or unnecessary. What I mean by undercoding in this paper, however, is under-encoding which, I venture to suggest, occurs when some parts of a text are less sufficiently encoded by a particular set of codes than other parts of the same text, to the extent that they are semantically less functional. I shall refrain from going too deep into this rather abstract discussion, but I have to point out that the idea of under-encoding (and over-encoding too) in the production of the text is necessary if we want to understand the complicated control of texts by the ideological metalanguage.

54. When comparing traditional Chinese drama with Greek drama, Tang Wenbiao's words are interesting:

Traditional Chinese drama is basically for entertainment ... for the leisure and pleasure of the audience. Even when there is some moral admonition or satire, it is only in the habitual sense of social mission.

The Chinese never entertain or throw themselves into the sorrow of life whole-heartedly (Tang Wenbiao, p. 2).

I do not agree with Tang that this dualism is a habit of Chinese literati. This "piecing-together" of two extremes is more visible in popular drama.

55. Dick Hebdige, *The Subculture: The Meaning of Style* (London: Methuen 1980), p. 56.

56. The following is a list of the anthologies that included acts of the White Rabbit play. The list is only roughly chronologically arranged, since in many cases we are not very sure of the publishing date. Many of the anthologies have been carefully described by Luo Jintang 羅錦堂 , *Zhongguo xiqu zongmu huibian* 中國戲曲總目匯編 (Hong Kong: Wanyou tushu gongsi, 1966), or reprinted by Wang Qiugui 王秋桂 in his *Shanben xiqu congkan* 善本戲曲叢刊(Taipei: Xuesheng Shudian, 1984).

   (1) *Gelin shicui* 歌林拾翠, compiled by anonymous, printed by Kuibi Zhai 奎壁齋. Eight acts of the White Rabbit Play.

   (2) *Qiuye yue* 秋夜月 , compiled by Yin Qisheng 殷啟聖 , printed in Wanli period by Yanshi Ju 燕石居. Three acts of the White Rabbit Play.

   (3) *Qingyang diao cilin* 青陽調詞林, compiled by Huang Wenhua 黃文華, printed in Wanli period. One act of the White Rabbit Play.

   (4) *Kunchi xindiao* 崑池新調 , compiled by Huang Wenhua, printed by Airi Tang 愛日堂 in Wanli period. One act of the White Rabbit Play.

   (5) *Yugu diaohuang* 玉谷調簧, printed in 1610. Three acts of the White Rabbit Play.

   (6) *Zhaijin qiyin* 摘錦奇音 , compiled by Gong Zhengwo 龔正我 , printed 1611. Three acts of the White Rabbit Play.

   (7) *Chantou bailian* 纏頭百練 , printed in 1630. Two acts of the White Rabbit Play.

   (8) *Xuanxue pu* 玄雪譜 , compiled by Chulan Renren 鋤蘭忍人 , printed around the end of Ming. One act of the White Rabbit Play.

   (9) *Zui yiqing* 醉怡情 , compiled by Gulu Diaosou 菰蘆釣叟, printed by Zhihe Tang 致和堂 around the beginning of Qing Dynasty. Four acts of the White Rabbit Play.

There is stored in the Escorial, Spain, an anthology with a few acts of the White Rabbit Play printed in 1553 by Jinxian Tang 進賢堂.

5

The Problem of Incest in *Jin Ping Mei* and *Honglou meng*

Andrew H. Plaks

In this article I wish to consider the "paradox of virtue" in traditional Chinese literature from the perspective of what may be the most extreme possible affront to the foundations of moral order: the violation of the primary boundaries of sexual sanction.[1] Instances of incest or near-incest are not at all uncommon in world literature, despite the fact that this area of experience lies somewhere beyond the ken of most authors and readers. This is not to ignore the troubling incidence of this form of social pathology in the contemporary world, perhaps greater in the United States than elsewhere, as a number of recent studies have revealed.[2] But even if reported cases of incest represent just the tip of an iceberg, what this generally refers to is the plague of child abuse, or in some cases mindless experimentation on the part of siblings — things quite different from the sort of mad sweeping passion at issue in literary manifestations. This leaves the prominence of incest as a literary phenomenon somewhat out of proportion to its significance as an empirical problem in actual society.

The incest theme has exercised a continuing fascination on the Western literary imagination. The elemental power of tales of taboo unions quickens a number of passages in the Old Testament and in classical mythology, often laying bare unresolvable contradictions between raw life force and the containing forms of culture, or tensions between consanguinity and community within patterns of social order.[3] In the later narrative fiction of Christian Europe this magnetic pull continues to be felt, though it is most often displaced into more equivocal relationships, such as those involving in-laws (Dante's Paolo and Francesca), adopted children (Boccaccio), or quasi-siblings (*Wuthering Heights*), to name a few examples.[4] In the meantime, classic Western drama, from Sophocles to

Shakespeare, continues to exploit cases of potential incest due to confused sexual identity, leading to climactic recognition scenes in fulfilment of either comic or tragic design.[5] With the steady removal of censorial restraints on fictional representation, the incest pattern has re-emerged as a major focus of the novel in recent times. Beginning with Poe and Melville, and on through D. H. Lawrence and Nabokov, a number of writers — especially in the English-speaking world — have turned to this dark subject in order to probe some of the deepest layers of the human psyche.[6] In the writings of such masters as Faulkner and García-Márquez, the incest theme becomes an almost obligatory element in multi-generational novels of family decay, one in which a lingering sense of the grotesque, or the pre-ordained, throws us back to the mythical origins of this literary phenomenon.[7] Even where literal examples of incest may not be presented, in a good many modern novels we feel something vaguely incestuous about various types of surrogate relationships and metaphoric acts of possession.[8]

In some of these Western examples, we can observe a special affinity shown by the novel form to this particular subject. Given the general lack of reticence in the novel in matters of forbidden fruit, this preoccupation cannot be attributed entirely to a psychological need to voice the unspeakable. Nor does it seem to me to be simply a matter of contriving piquant twists of plot by introducing a less common variant of adultery (in fact, tales of incest may provide even less plot interest than conventional sexual transgression, since in such cases the narrative complications of getting the two lovers alone together in the same room may be dispensed with). Rather, I believe this has more to do with the special *project* of the novel: its commitment to exploring the essential boundaries of the self. Within the context of the novel's tendency to chronicle a process of self-realization, the stubborn recurrence of this theme can be understood as the logical conclusion of its characteristic "inward turn" — its frequent focus on problematic individuals caught up in attempts to define and validate the self, not as much through engagement with the outside world as by pulling in to the inner core of a reflected self-image.

This abiding fascination with incestuous relations is by no means endemic to Western literature alone; it turns up in a variety of other traditions as well. This is to be expected, of course, in texts of a mythological nature. For example, in the Japanese *Kojiki* 古事記 , the sibling-marriage of the divine progenitors Izanagi and Izanami may perhaps be dismissed as an aetiological folktale, but the violent imagery of the bizarre encounters between Susa-no-o and his sister Amaterasu clearly takes us into deeper layers of consciousness.[9] Similar examples can be found in the Indian tradition, in the rejected incest of Yama and Yami, and in certain myths of Indra and Agni, in the *Rig Veda*; and the theme recurs in a subtle form in the classical Indian epics: in the marriage of Draupadi to the five Pandava brothers in the *Mahabharata*, and in the suspicion of an incestuous lapse that provides the fatal flaw in the perfection of Rama's wife Sita in the *Ramayana*.[10] In later fictional works, the incest theme continues to present a model of destabilizing passion in a variety of examples, notably the *Thousand and One Nights*, which gives us a number of scenes where the flames of self-consuming desire are conceived in terms of incestuous unions.[11] The most relentless pursuit of the implications of incest, however, is surely that found in the *Genji Monogatari* 源氏物語 (Tale of Genji). Here the awesome gravity of the elemental act is multiplied: by conflating the violation of the sexual taboo with the pollution of the sacred imperial line, and later by replaying the fatal error over and over with a succession of figurally-linked lovers, and by visiting the karmic consequences of the crime over three generations, as Genji's original brilliance is gradually refracted and finally extinguished.[12]

At first glance, the Chinese literary tradition would appear to be relatively free of this blight on moral propriety. Given the predominance in Chinese fiction and drama of didactic modes of discourse rooted in Confucian social values or Buddhist schemes of karmic retribution, open narrative treatment of the theme of incest is rather hard to come by. To be sure, instances of intramural sexual transgression are occasionally brought up in certain early narrative texts, such as the *Zuo zhuan* 左傳 , in order to be roundly denounced as anathema to both political and moral order.[13] And at the other extreme, a few works of the "subversive" fiction of the seventeenth century take perverse pleasure in staging grotesque exaggerations of incestuous behaviour, as illustrations of the total breakdown of human values in an age of chaos.[14] In one startling example in *Xingshi yinyuan zhuan* 醒世姻緣傳, an utterly unprincipled wretch dresses up as a fox spirit and carries out a mock-rape of his mother in order to strip her of her meagre life savings.[15] More often, however, the issue is raised in more palatable form in certain second-degree relationships of special relevance to traditional Chinese society.[16] These include stories about incestuous attachments involving sworn brothers and sisters,[17] or entanglements arising out of the overlapping of polygamy and concubinage, among others.[18] Of particular interest here is the ambivalent status of cousin-marriage in traditional China, which prepares the ground for a number of problematic unions, not the least of which we will return to shortly.[19]

In view of the relative paucity of direct treatment of the problem of incest in Chinese literature, it is all the more striking that two of the greatest works of the colloquial narrative tradition — in fact, the two un-paralleled models of the so-called *renqing xiaoshuo* 人情小説 (novels of human experience) — give a rather prominent place to intimations of in-cestuous behaviour that are just too palpable to ignore. In both of these novels the examples of incest brought before us manage to steer clear of textbook cases of violation of brother-sister or parent-child blood taboos, giving us instead what I would call "pseudo-incestuous" entanglements based on ties by marriage and adoption, figural substitutions, and retroac-tive changes of status. In terms of literary symbolism, however, the im-plications are very much the same. In a sense, the treatment of incest in these two works parallels the use of the theme of sexual involution to probe the issue of Self and Other in recent Western fiction (this is one point on which the critical analysis of *Jin Ping Mei* 金瓶梅 and *Honglou meng* 紅樓夢 as "novels" is fully justified). In other ways, however, we may observe here a reflection of what is a strictly Confucian conception of the paradox of self: the dilemma whereby the pursuit of the ideal of self-cultivation, when pressed to its logical conclusion, leads to an an-tithetical state of self-containment, one that threatens the foundations of social order and calls forth extreme forms of purgation. In the following pages, I will attempt to trace the outlines of this issue by briefly reviewing the textual evidence regarding instances of incest in each of these two novels, and then suggesting some possible interpretations of the sig-nificance of the theme.

The idea of self-enclosure underlying the incest theme in *Jin Ping Mei* and *Honglou meng* takes on a special force within the formal structural design of the "classic" Chinese novels. It is no accident that these two texts are among the most intricately structured — to a degree we would today call "self-referential" or "overdetermined" — of the Ming-Qing master-works; and the many points of common form they share betray the immen-sity of the debt of the later book to its earlier model.[20] In both we observe a narrative design based on a nesting of inner and outer worlds, centring around an enclosed garden within a private compound, in the recesses of which the principal lines of the stories are played out. In each, despite periodic reminders of the impingement of forces from the outside world, the narrative eventually telescopes down to a central figure at the heart of the garden, one who is, in one way or another, uniquely equipped to pursue the fulfilment of individual desire in defiance of the normal rules of the game. Ximen Qing 西門慶 and Jia Baoyu 賈寶玉 could scarcely be more different as fictional heroes, but they also have certain things in common. For both, the attempt to grasp and hold an illusion of self-containment — whether in sensual, emotional, or aesthetic terms — is riddled with irony. And the world eventually catches up with both of them, bursting in upon their vaguely incestuous gardens of the self.

In *Jin Ping Mei*, the depiction of acts of incest may not at first seem particularly striking within the smorgasbord of sexual excess set before our eyes. It hardly needs repeating here, however, that the common misconception of this novel as a work of pornographic intent fails to account for both the quality and the quantity of its passages of erotic description — unless, of course, as Zhang Zhupo 張竹坡 cuttingly quipped, one takes the time only to read the obscene parts.[21] Thus, we cannot dismiss the instances of incest in this novel as simply one additional offering on the sexual menu served up for the titillation of the jaded reader.

In order to appreciate the degree to which the incest theme is worked into the structural framework of this book, we should note a few points about its overall design. Despite the obvious fact that *Jin Ping Mei* is deeply indebted to pre-existing source materials and is marred by inconsistencies of detail — leading a number of recent critics in China to conclude that it must have been a product of "collective composition" (*jiti chuangzuo* 集體創作), the text exhibits a remarkable degree of intricate structural patterning.[22] Three aspects of this patterning will be particularly relevant to my discussion of the treatment of the incest theme in the novel. First, the text is divided into one hundred roughly equal *hui*-units grouped into a well-articulated sequence of ten-chapter sections, a pattern loosely paralleled in the arrangement of chapters in the full recension (*fanben* 繁本) of *Shuihu zhuan* 水滸傳 and in *Xiyou ji* 西遊記. Within this numerical grid, the author sets up symmetrical contrasts between the first and the second halves of the book, while setting off the central 60-chapter body of the narrative from the structurally discrete sections of the first and last twenty chapters. At the same time, he pays considerable attention to the placing and serial ordering of individual chapters within his overall scheme. Second, the structure of the novel is governed by a vertical cross-reflection between the microcosm of Ximen Qing's garden world and the macrocosm of the Empire at large. These two narrative levels are tied together by threads of plot that periodically move from one world to the

other. Third, the myriad characters that pass on and off the stage tend to
fall into overlapping types, linked according to a compositional principle I
have called "figural recurrence", and often they merge with one another to
form composite images.

We are now ready to consider the functioning of the incest theme
within the overall design of the *Jin Ping Mei*. My insistence on pointing
out instances of sexual involution in this novel may seem a bit exaggerated
at first sight. After all, Ximen Qing is, if anything, *outgoing* in his range of
sexual activity. He casts his net widely to pull in six wives, high and
low-born paramours, cheap and elegant courtesans, numerous maids, and
even a few boys. In the course of the narrative, however, these far-flung
conquests are gradually pulled together into a tight snarl of relations,
among which quasi- or pseudo-incestuous links account for a considerable
number.

The most obtrusive example of incest in the novel does not directly
concern Ximen Qing at all, but rather involves his sixth wife Pan Jinlian
潘金蓮 and his son-in-law Chen Jingji 陳敬濟. This infatuation is initiated
when the two meet in Ximen Qing's newly inaugurated garden in chapter
18, and reaches its ultimate consummation, symmetrically enough, right
after Ximen Qing's death in chapter 82, thus neatly embracing the entire
inner structural core of the garden world.[23] What begins as casual flirtation
goes through a long chain of less and less innocent encounters, and a series
of farcical near-misses, until it reaches its logical conclusion immediately
upon the death of Ximen Qing in chapter 80.[24] This lowers the curtain on
the central phase of the novel's structure, and ushers in the final 20-chapter
phase of karmic retribution, in which swift justice is visited on Jinlian at
the hands of her erstwhile brother-in-law Wu Song 武松, and Chen Jingji
is sent off on a path of self-destruction that occupies the bulk of the
remainder of the book. One of the crucial moments in this chain of
development occurs in the suggestively-numbered chapter 33.[25] This major
textual node brings the by-now dangerous erotic link between secondary
wife and son-in-law into glaring conjunction with several other elements
of related symbolic import: Yueniang's 月娘 miscarriage of an heir and
Ximen Qing's miscarriage of yamen justice, Ximen Qing's blatant dalliance with his shopkeeper's wife Wang Liu'er 王六兒 (whose num-
ber/name "6" marks her as an icon of female sexuality), and the
well-founded rumours of Wang Liu'er's scandalous affair with her own
brother-in-law Han Er (Han Daogui 韓搗鬼).[26] Toward the very end of the
book — in chapter 99 — the author pulls some of these tangled threads

together one more time by having Chen Jingji fall in love with Han Aijie 韓愛姐, the daughter of his "father"'s old lover Wang Liu'er, and then adding the apparently sarcastic touch of having the unlikely couple Wang Liu'er and Han Daogui survive the fall of the Empire and go off to the countryside to live a life of happy simplicity.[27]

One may object at this point that Chen Jingji is not Ximen Qing's son by blood, so that his sexual misadventures should be read not as foul incest, but as a "cleaner" form of adultery — and it is just pleasingly symmetrical for the master seducer of other men's wives to be betrayed and cuckolded by his own protégé. Yet, Ximen Qing does call Chen Jingji his "son" in chapter 18, and again on his death-bed in chapter 79; and in many ways Chen really is a chip off the old block.[28] One could even go further and say that the linkage between the two is one of a shared identity. This, at least, is the sense we get in chapter 53, when Ximen Qing's unexpected return home interrupts one of the pathetic/comic attempts of the furtive lovers to consummate their passion, and the "father" slips into bed to finish the act his son-in-law has started — all this amidst increasing signs that his own flesh-and-blood son, the baby Guan'ge 官哥, is on the verge of extinction.[29] After chapter 80, it is Chen Jingji who takes over where Ximen Qing leaves off, an impression immediately reinforced when Pan Jinlian inaugurates their new sexual freedom by turning over to him the late master's emblematic set of erotic paraphernalia. In the meantime, Pan Jinlian herself is more and more insistently identified as her lover's mother-in-law: first jokingly (in chapter 53), and later more ominously (in chapter 76), until in chapter 82 the truth is put up in neon lights in the verse: "On the false presumption of the close affection of a son-in-law, he repeatedly engaged in topsy-turvy acts of seduction with his mother-in-law" (假認做女婿親厚, 往來和丈母歪偷).[30]

It could be repeated here that Ximen Qing is not responsible for this illicit union, even if he does allow it to germinate in his household, and it is his own principal wife, Yueniang, who first "invites the wolf into the chamber" (引狼入室), as the commentators are fond of putting it.[31] On the other hand, Ximen Qing himself is also enmeshed in a tangle of parallel relations of a quasi- or pseduo-incestuous nature. This is where the fun starts. To begin with, the initial affair of adultery and murder borrowed from *Shuihu zhuan* takes off, we recall, on the rebound from Pan Jinlian's abortive seduction of her brother-in-law Wu Song. In the following 10-chapter section of the text (the first original line of the narrative), the author contrives to turn simple adultery into pseudo-incest by making Li

Ping'er 李瓶兒 the wife of Ximen Qing's sworn brother Hua Zixu 花子虛
(the utter falsity of this brotherly tie does little to diminish its symbolic
significance).[32] As if to strengthen the point, the author indulges in one
more flagrant distortion of his sources by identifying Ping'er as a former
concubine of Liang "Zhongshu" 梁中書, a son-in-law of the infamous
court minister Cai Jing 蔡京 who is later to become (yet another abandonment of the pretense of plausibility) the adopted father of Ximen Qing
himself. This gives Ping'er, retroactively, a degree of relationship to
Ximen Qing distant enough to be technically unimpeachable, but close
enough to provide ominous resonance with the other, more troubling,
whiffs of incest in the book.

Granted these ties are a bit tenuous, to say the least, but a similar skein
of incestuous threads binds Ximen Qing to Li Guijie 李桂姐, a rather
cheap courtesan who happens to be the niece of his second wife Li Jiao'er
李嬌兒, a former courtesan of abiding cheapness.[33] When Guijie somehow
manages to get herself admitted to the family as an adopted daughter of
Yueniang after chapter 32, her past relations with Ximen Qing in the
brothel are retroactively turned into a kind of second- or third-degree incest
(the situation is paralleled when Wu Yin'er 吳銀兒, a former mistress of
Hua Zixu, signs on as an adopted daughter of Ping'er in chapter 42). This
thread is pulled again in chapter 69, on the threshold of the final "decade"
of Ximen Qing's life, when he pulls off the seduction of his highest-rank-
ing conquest, the widow Madame Lin 林太太, on the pretext of using his
influence to help her son Wang Sanguan 王三官 out of his entanglements
in the *demi-monde*. With Ximen's solution of adopting Wang Sanguan
under his own family aegis, we arrive at an almost comical situation in
which it is now somehow incestuous for him to be sleeping with the
mother of his "son".[34] And this point is hammered home when we discover
that Wang Sanguan's troubles stem from his involvement with none other
than Li Guijie, the adopted daughter of his adopted father. Toward the end
of Ximen Qing's final 10-chapter swing, his soaring sexual ambitions and
flagging physical powers lead him into links that never pass beyond
voyeuristic desire: with Wang Sanguan's official wife Lady Huang 黃氏,
and with another figurally-related beauty Lady Lan 藍氏 (whose name also
happens to be a colour-word). In the penetrating interpretation of Zhang
Zhupo, it is precisely these emptiest of metaphoric acts of possession that
bring about the final depletion of Ximen Qing's over-spent life force.[35]

With the passing of the baton to Chen Jingji in the final 20-chapter
section of the novel, the incest theme continues to form the nexus of the

author's design. In the course of his wandering in search of refuge, Chen's attempt to pass himself off as a brother of Meng Yulou 孟玉樓 in chapter 92 is firmly rejected, but the same trick finally works at the mansion of Chunmei, now the wife of a man of great wealth and noble standing. As they proceed to resume their sexual relations begun many years ago when she was Pan Jinlian's maid, the false siblings create a certain measure of incestuous truth, and Chen Jingji pays for this simultaneous violation of family purity, civic duty, and personal honour with a violent end. Even at this point, the author is not yet ready to drop his central theme. He brings Chunmei to her inevitable self-destruction in the throes of an intramural liaison with the son of a trusted family retainer who bears the same sur-name as her husband (not to mention a transparently symbolic given name: Zhou Yi 周義), and has her expire in precisely the same vampire pose that launched the fatal career of her mistress in chapter 5.[36] With this the author closes the circle, by having all three of the female characters for whom the book is named, as well as the two principal male figures, meet their just retribution through a web of actually or symbolically incestuous relations. Admittedly, most of the examples of incest cited here are tenuous taken alone, but read together I believe they indicate the centrality of this theme to the structure of ideas presented in the book, a question I will return to at the end of this essay.

Turning now to *Honglou meng*, I expect that there may be even more resistance to the idea of incorporating the notion of incest into my inter-pretation of the work. As soon as I apply the inelegant term "incest" to this most elegant of books, it is obvious that what I have in mind is the vaguely incestuous quality of Jia Baoyu's overly intimate relations with his "sisters" in the enclosed garden of the Daguan Yuan 大觀園 . But there is no denying that both Lin Daiyu 林黛玉 and Xue Baochai 薛寶釵 represent legitimate, perhaps even ideal, marriage partners for the young hero, just as the various maids in the garden are, for that matter, also fair game within the limits of sexual license tolerated by this particular social stratum. How, then, can we speak of incest at all in this context?

My primary justification for pursuing this topic is the fact that the text itself, true to its model in *Jin Ping Mei*, confronts us with the spectre of incest practically from the beginning, and then goes on to integrate the incest theme into its overall structural design. To say that the appearance of the goddess Nüwa in the opening pages of the novel carries a shadow of the mythical sibling-marriage of Nüwa and Fuxi would be stretching the point, but by the time the narrative returns to the supramundane plane in the prophetic dream-vision in chapter 5, as we shall see, intimations of incest are already very much in evidence.[37] By chapter 7 the unnamable sin is named, if only in the slightly obscure vulgar expressions in the curse of Jiao Da 焦大 : "The ones who feel like 'crawling in the ashes' go right ahead and do it; the ones who want to take up with 'little uncles' let nothing stop them" (爬灰的爬灰，養小叔子的養小叔子).[38] The first half of this drunken curse is understood by all readers as referring to the incestuous dalliance of Jia Zhen 賈珍 with his daughter-in-law Qin Keqing 秦可卿. Even without the benefit of the information provided in the Zhiyan Zhai commentary about a missing autobiographically-based chapter depicting Qin Keqing's suicide out of shame for licentious behaviour, "Death by Lust in the Tower of Heavenly Fragrance" (淫喪天香樓), we would have sufficient clues in the subsequent narrative — Jia Zhen's excessive grief, the unduly elaborate funeral — to reconstruct the hidden turn of events.[39] In the uproar surrounding Qin Keqing's demise, however, we may easily lose sight of the parallel accusation in the second half of Jiao Da's curse. Usually this is taken as a hint of the only barely hidden flirtation between Wang Xifeng 王熙鳳 and Qin Keqing's husband, Jia Rong 賈蓉, which seems to bespeak an intimacy greater than a simple breach of propriety (although the line remains ambiguous, and may have another possible interpretation I will suggest below).[40] In any event, the figural link between Qin Keqing and Wang Xifeng suggested in the double curse of Jiao Da is strengthened by a number of ties more substantial than may at first meet the eye. Not only do the two share a crime; they also share a punishment, as we see in the common imagery of their debilitating illnesses, marked by profuse bleeding that is as much symbolic as it is pathological.[41] In both cases, moreover, their individual errors are explicitly linked to the fate of the entire family.

Once the narrative settles into the slow-paced rhythm of life in the garden, these literal cases of incest fade to just vague hints of unease about the impropriety of Baoyu's situation. Much later, the issue comes to the surface one more time when the maid Yuanyang 鴛鴦 stumbles upon a tryst between two lovers in a secluded spot in the garden, and soon thereafter the discovery of an incense-bag embroidered with an erotic scene brings to light the illicit affair between the maid Siqi 司棋 and her cousin Pan Youan 潘又安.[42] Since Pan is Siqi's maternal cousin (*gubiao xiongdi* 姑表兄弟) their match is legitimate — if premature, but all of the symbolism surrounding the incident: the conventional associations of Taihu rockery, the role of the half-wit maid Sha-dajie 傻大姐 , the incense-bag itself (as well as a possible erotic allusion in Pan's name), make of this something more than just a comic interlude.[43] As in the case of Qin Keqing, this loss of innocence on the part of an otherwise peripheral character is strongly linked to the downfall of the family as a whole, here by virtue of the miniature search of the garden that foreshadows the final search and confiscation of the Jia clan's enclosed domain. If one is willing to entertain the possibility that the 80-chapter length of the early manuscripts that have come down to us may have a greater structural integrity than is normally assumed (as I am, but that is another story), then the numerical symmetry of the incidents in chapters 7 and 73 might bear more serious consideration.[44]

Even if it is accepted that the irruptions of incest at these two significant points somehow bracket the main body of the novel, the question still remains as to what this means for our understanding of the characters and events in the space in between. For one thing, the aura of incestuousness hanging over the enclosed world of the Daguan Yuan thickens occasionally to yield fairly explicit statements about what is wrong in the garden. For example, in chapter 23 we are told that "most of those in the garden were young girls living in a world of blissful ignorance, a time of innocent heedlessness; they sat and slept together without inhibitions, laughed and joked without self-consciousness" (園中那些人多半是女孩兒, 正在混沌世界, 天真爛熳之時, 坐臥不避, 嬉笑無心), and in chapter 37 we read: "Every day in the garden he would run free, roaming at will wherever his spirit would lead him; he truly passed his time in vain, idly piling up the months and years" (每日在園中任意縱性的曠蕩, 真把光陰虛度, 歲月空添).[45] And if these passages may sound too neutral, it is important to add that at a significant number of points Baoyu's innocent joys — the common romanticized reading notwithstanding — take on a decidedly erotic flavour. This is true not only of his bathing, rouge-licking, and general disporting with the maids, or of his playful quoting of suggestive passages from *Xixiang ji* 西廂記 and *Mudan ting* 牡丹亭, but also of several scenes in which the shared experience of Baoyu and his cousins borders on sexual intimacy. Some of the Qing commentators read into such moments as his bedroom visits to Daiyu in chapters 19 and 26 among others, or Baochai sitting at his bedside during his afternoon nap in chapter 36, examples of the literal crossing of those borders.[46]

Of course Baoyu, Daiyu, and Baochai are not technically siblings, despite the loose use of the words "brother" and "sister" in Chinese honorific kinship terms and the rhetoric of affection. (Interestingly,

Baoyu's only common-womb sister is Yuanchun 元春 , a point I will return to shortly.) And so even when they may engage in physical intimacies that contradict their assumed innocence, the most we can say is that this is impropriety or indiscretion, hardly incest.

This brings us to the difficult issue of cousin-marriage as it bears upon the interpretation of the novel. As in most traditional societies, Confucian practice not only did not prohibit, but in fact idealized the matching of cognate (表) children, outlawing only the marriage of partners with a common surname, in accordance with the dictates of clan exogamy. Yet, we can find warnings against this practice in a variety of Chinese texts, ranging from classical sources such as the *Bohu tong* 白虎通 to fictional works such as *Liaozhai zhiyi* 聊齋誌異 .[47] And so, when the elders of the Jia clan invoke the principle of "adding a marriage-relation to an existing blood-relation" (*qinshang zuo qin* 親上做親) in considering a match for the principal heir of the family (a practice specifically discouraged, by the way, in at least one Song guide to family morality), this ideal is not without a certain subtle taint.[48] Coming within the context of a narrative structure that gets underway and reaches its climax amidst parables of quasi-incestuous relations linked to the inevitable destruction of both the individuals involved and the family as a whole, the notion of this kind of intramural marriage can no longer be taken in an entirely positive light. At the very least, it is symptomatic of the excessive pursuit of gratification (*yin* 淫) — in this case an excess of family intimacy (*qin* 親) — about which Baoyu is warned and instructed as early as the prophetic dream-vision of chapter 5.[49]

In terms of their precise kinship ties, Baoyu's relations to each of his two most likely mates are quite symmetrical, both being his non-agnate cousins (*biao jiemei* 表姐妹), — with the slight distinction that Daiyu is his father's sister's daughter (*gubiao mei* 姑表妹), while Baochai is his mother's sister's daughter and a year older (*yibiao jie* 姨表姐). In the other direction, Baoyu is a maternal cousin to both (*biao xiongdi* 表兄弟), Chinese kinship terminology not normally distinguishing between mother's brother's son (*jiubiao xiong* 舅表兄) and mother's sister's son (*yibiao di* 姨表弟).[50] This makes the relations between Baoyu and the two girls, especially Daiyu, nearly parallel to the relation of Pan Youan and Siqi, as the author takes care to remind us through Wang Xifeng's very pointed questioning of Wang Shanbao's 王善保 wife in chapter 74.[51] And so the possible marriage of Baoyu to either of his closest confidantes represents a match that is legally permitted, perhaps poetically ideal, but still frequently discouraged in various sources.[52]

Once again, what we are dealing with here is a literary rather than a sociological phenomenon. And within the context of the symbolic structure of the novel, the union of Baoyu with either of the two girls remains at best problematical. This becomes clear from very early on in the book. I will resist, for once, the temptation to over-read here the myth of Nüwa and the little parable of the Stone and the Crimson-Pearl flower in chapter 1. But by chapter 5 the issue of excessive intimacy is set directly before us in the conjoining of the two maidens into the double figure of "Combined Virtues" (Jianmei 兼美) in the "Red Chamber Dream" sequence. (Hawkes' translation of this name as "Two-in-one", otherwise a bit misleading, is perfect in this context.) Here, by the way, we have a good example of the common Chinese fictional pattern of two quasi-siblings sharing a lover, a situation often idealized but not without its own pseudo-incestuous overtones in some instances.[53]

In any event, the author carefully frames his presentation of the Combined Virtues figure to pull together several layers of meaning. Even before the onset of the dream vision, we are given a glimpse at the beginning of the chapter of the unnaturally close relationship between Baoyu and his "sisters": "He viewed all his brothers and sisters as springing from an undivided entity, without the slightest distinction of intimacy and distance" (親姊妹弟兄皆出一體，並無親疏遠近之別).[54] It is therefore no idle touch when the author has the dream-encounter with Combined Virtues take place while Baoyu is sleeping in the bed of Qin Keqing. The idea of taking a nap in the boudoir of his nephew's wife had already raised a few eyebrows, and to make sure we do not miss the point, the setting is depicted with highly-charged erotic imagery carrying conventional associations of dangerous liaisons.[55] In the dream itself, the figure of Combined Virtues is not only a conflation of Daiyu and Baochai, but also a shadow of her older sister the "Goddess of Disillusion" (Jinghuan Xiangu 警幻仙姑), who uses her as the instrument of Baoyu's sexual initiation both inside and outside the dream. And this image is compounded when Combined Virtues is further identified with Qin Keqing, whose name she also bears. This erotic link between Baoyu and Qin Keqing does not have to be taken literally to be of crucial symbolic significance (although I suppose Baoyu could also be called Keqing's "*xiaoshu*" 小叔 , in the literal sense of "little uncle" since he is technically one generation above her in the clan order).[56] Instead, the symbolic import of Baoyu's connection to Qin Keqing is brought out through his parallel relation to her own brother Qin Zhong 秦鍾 . Not only is Qin Zhong's rather transparent name synonymous with that of his sister (universally glossed by commentators as *qing* 情),[57] but they both go the way of all flesh through passionate attachments in the same part of the book, as Baoyu stands by in the role of a not quite innocent spectator.

Beyond this, Baoyu's intimacy with Qin Keqing takes on its full force as part of a whole chain of older, sexually-mature initiatrix figures that touch his life. One link in this chain is Wang Xifeng (herself figurally linked to Qin Keqing, as we have seen). Of course, there is no hint of any erotic tie between these two, but they are significantly connected in a number of other ways. Baoyu and Xifeng, his cousin's wife, hear Jiao Da's curse together in chapter 7; they enjoy an unspoken alliance at the Mantou Nunnery (饅頭菴) in chapter 15; and they share the near-fatal effects of another curse in chapter 25. One might also say that Baoyu is in some ways a figural equivalent of Xifeng's own putative lover Jia Rong.

Finally, the chain of "older sister" figures in the novel also includes Baoyu's only full sister Yuanchun, to whom he has a special emotional bond despite the fact that she is absent for most of the book. Yuanchun is very much an *être de fuite*, not much more than a warm memory, but she still effects a deep influence on Baoyu's destiny. It is she who first taught him to write poetry, it is she who occasions the construction of Baoyu's enclosed garden and makes it possible for him to live there with his "sisters", and it is her illness and death in the continuation that in large measure seal his tearful fate.[58]

At this point I would like to suggest, as promised, a few possible interpretations of the significance of these examples of incest in the two books. I believe that the thrust of the incest theme in both novels lies in the exploration of the gratification of desire in what might be called an enclosed garden of the self. But this obviously takes quite different forms in the respective works.

In *Jin Ping Mei*, the gravity of the crime of incest takes on its full conceptual weight within the novel's well-articulated scheme of cross-reflection between the microcosm of the family and the macrocosm of the Empire. One need not necessarily make of this a specific allegory of the breakdown of the Ming political order, however, because it conforms neatly enough to a more generalized Confucian understanding of the way of the world, and the role of individual moral responsibility within that framework. One easy way to paraphrase this conception is to cite the seminal passage in the *Daxue* 大學 canon linking disarray in family life (不齊其家) to various manifestations of individual imperfection (不修其身，不正其心，不誠其意) and political chaos (不治其國，不平天下),

wisdom that finds frequent expression in the text itself.[59] What we observe in the course of the novel is an almost systematic violation of every phase of this canonical paradigm: loss of self-control (亂心), corruption of personal values (亂身), breakup of the family (亂家), and finally national ruin (亂國). All of this adds up to a general state of disorder (*luan* 亂) in human relations that we can subsume under the term *luanlun* 亂倫 , whose more focused usage refers specifically to incest.[60] Given the abject violation of the foundations of moral order in the novel, the final invocation of a fairly conventional scheme of karmic retribution takes on new force as a more convincing demonstration of the law of actions and consequences than it is usually given credit for.

At the same time, the tangle of incestuous relations depicted in the *Jin Ping Mei* also illustrates another cardinal principle of Confucian moral consciousness: the horror of excess. One of the classic formulations of this idea, the notion of the "four vices of excess" (*sitan* 四貪), as I like to call it, is featured prominently at the head of both of the earliest recensions, it finds expression in a number of poems and authorial asides in the text, and it may have even provided the original inspiration for the composition of the work.[61] Although all four of these areas of immoderate gratification come up for systematic exposition in the book, the second in the usual listing: lust (*se* 色) provides the most memorable examples. Whether or not the *Jin Ping Mei* deserves to be labelled a *yinshu* 淫書 , it is very clearly a book about *yin* in its basic meaning of an unchecked effusion.[62] In the course of the narrative we witness an accelerating outpouring of libidinous energy, particularly in the last 10-chapter phase of Ximen Qing's mortal existence. It is here that the theme of incest takes on a special meaning, as an abandonment of the last barrier to the fulfilment of desire. In his treatment of this issue, the author shows his fine grasp of the principle that the unbounded pursuit of an illusion of plenitude tends to yield only depletion and emptiness, the exact conceptual opposite of the Chinese ideal of self-containment.[63] In our novel, Ximen Qing ends up empty in more ways than one. His worldly career comes to naught, he dies effectively childless and friendless, and he plays out his last days in a state of existential loneliness, surrounded by chilling images of pale moonlight, melting slush, and finally, a cold puff of air.[64] In this light, the web of incestuous entanglements in the novel comes to express not so much the evil of sexual licence, as the sterility and inconsequentiality of unbounded desire.

In *Honglou meng* the implicit parallel between the breakup of the family and the breakdown of the world is never far from view. This is presented most concretely, of course, in the miniature invasion of the garden in chapter 74 that presages the violent intrusion of state power in the continuation, as well as in the subtle repercussions of the deaths of various court ladies on life within the Jia compound.[65] Though this is obviously not the main focus of this author's vision, still he does pay considerable attention to the creeping process of disintegration that is slowly tearing the family apart. We become aware of the advancing disorder of this enclosed world through the economic imbalances addressed after chapter 56, in the increasingly unseemly relations between masters and servants, and, in general, in the glaring improprieties of Baoyu's garden of delights. In one of the most penetrating insights in an otherwise erratic commentary, the nineteenth-century critic Zhang Xinzhi 張新之 relates the process of moral dissolution in the Daguan Yuan to a passage in the *Yi jing* 易經 . "When a minister murders his lord or a son murders his father, the causes are not simply the matter of a single day or evening; what leads up to this is the course of gradual development" (臣弒其君，子弒其父，非一朝一夕之故，其所由來者漸矣）[66] As he goes on to spell out, what Zhang has in mind is not any specific cases of regicide or parricide, but rather their frequent literary companion: acts of incest, such as those obliquely or metaphorically presented in the novel.[67]

The idea of incest as sheer excess is also well represented in *Honglou meng*. This is treated most explicitly in the famous disquisition on *qing* and *yin* in the dream-vision in chapter 5 — and more generally in the pursuit of perfect individual fulfilment (*qiuquan* 求全) on the part of many of the residents of the Jia compound: the illusory attempt to have it all, to embrace both the joys of innocence and the delights of experience within a single undiluted self. As in the case of *Jin Ping Mei*, this grasping for plenitude, whether of a physical or an aesthetic nature, tends to yield its conceptual opposite, a sense of emptiness hounded by unfulfilled longings and lost posterity.[68]

The treatment of the incest theme in *Honglou meng*, however, takes it apart from *Jin Ping Mei* and closer to the writings of Faulkner and García-Márquez by virtue of its inescapable sense of the taint of inbreeding, spilling over into such things as Oedipal fears and monosexual longings. The logical conclusion of this kind of involution is the pursuit of completion within the bounds of one's own self-image. Nearly every critic of the novel from Zhiyan Zhai to the present day has pointed out that the double object of Baoyu's desire — the Combined Virtues of his dreams — is composed of the two girls in his garden whose names represent the two halves of his own self.[69] It is in this sense of self-containment that Baoyu's story, from the stone's original state of questionable completeness to its final escape from the self by withdrawing from the world, can be most meaningfully described as "incestuous".[70]

Before concluding, I would like to bring this discussion back to the question of the "paradox of virtue" for a final word. Although the preoccupation with the philosophical implications of incest sounds like a fixation of Western literature and criticism, I believe that it is also of special relevance to the problematics of Neo-Confucian thought. What we see here is the contradictory conceptual core of the central Confucian notion of self-cultivation: on the one hand passionately enjoining the outward-directed integration of self and world, yet at the same time placing a premium on the ideal of unruffled self-containment. The author of *Honglou meng* puts his finger on this nerve — playfully, perhaps — when in chapter 19 he has Xiren 襲人 beg Baoyu to modify his exclusive focus on the idea of "illuminating one's bright virtue" (*mingmingde* 明明德) highlighted in the opening catechism of the *Daxue*.[71] At first sight Baoyu's special interest in this classic text seems out of character, until we realize that it is the subversive unorthodox interpretation of this line, in the sense of polishing one's own inner mirror at the expense of social responsibility, that Xiren — mindful of her own future — finds so dangerous. In *Jin Ping Mei* the treatment of this paradox of self-cultivation does not go much beyond its vicious parody of the proper ordering of self at every level of the *Daxue* paradigm. But by the Qianlong 乾隆 period two hundred years later, the bitter-sweet musings on this issue on the part of one sensitive scholar whose own process of self-cultivation had largely failed, plumb the very depths of the paradox.

Notes

1. Many of the ideas in this paper have been presented in several lectures under the title "Paths of Involution in *Jin Ping Mei, Genji Monogatari*, and *Honglou meng*". My thinking on this topic gained much from discussions related to the dissertation work of my former student Wai-wah Chin.
2. See, for example, Robert E. Masters, *Patterns of Incest* (New York: Julian Press, 1963), plus many journalistic treatments of the subject.
3. As examples in the Old Testament, I am thinking of the story of Judah and

Tamar (Genesis: 38), that of Amnon and Tamar (2 Samuel: 13), etc. Cf. also the story of Lot and his daughters (Genesis: 19). In Greek mythology, I am thinking of the opening passages of Hesiod's *Theogony*, for example.

4. *Divina Commedia*, Inferno, Vol. V, pp. 115–138; Boccaccio, *Decameron*, 5:7, 7:3, 7:10.

5. e.g.,*All's Well That End's Well, The Twelfth Night*. Cf. hints of incestuousness in Chekhov, Ibsen, Strindberg, not to mention various works of recent cinema.

6. I am thinking of Poe's *Fall of the House of Usher*, Melville's *Pierre*, D. H. Lawrence's *Sons and Lovers*, Nabokov's *Ada*, etc.

7. See especially Faulkner's *Sound and Fury*, and García-Márquez's *Hundred Years of Solitude*.

8. For example, Thomas Mann's *Buddenbrooks*, Proust's *Recherche*, etc. For discussions of the importance of the incest theme in the modern Western novel, see such works as Réne Girard, *Deceit, Desire, and the Novel* (Baltimore: Johns Hopkins University Press, 1965); Patricia Tobin, *Time and the Novel* (Princeton: Princeton University Press, 1978); Leslie Fiedler, *Love and Death in the American Novel* (New York: Criterion Books, 1960); etc.

9. *Kojiki*, Book I, chapters 4–5, 9–10, and 14–16. The violent encounter in chapter 16 in the *Kojiki* involves a different female deity, the "heavenly weaving-maiden", but in the *Nihon shoki* 日本書紀 version of the myth, it is Amaterasu herself. See Donald Philippi, *Kojiki* (Princeton: Princeton University Press, 1968), p. 80, note 9.

10. See the *Rig Veda*, translated by Wendy Doniger O'Flaherty (Penguin, 1981), pp. 139ff., 247ff.

11. See, for example, *Thousand and One Nights*, translated by N. J. Dawood (Penguin, 1973), pp. 26lff ("The Porter and the Three Ladies of Baghdad").

12. For an excellent discussion of this aspect of *Genji Monogatari*, see Norma Field, *The Splendor of Longing in the Tale of Genji* (Princeton: Princeton University Press, 1987).

13. See, for example, *Zuo zhuan*: Huan: 16:5 (see James Legge, *The Ch'un Ts'ew with the Tso Chuen* (1872), various repts., Vol. 5, p. 66), Zhuang 28:2 (Legge, p. 114), Xi 15:13 (Legge, p. 167), Cheng 4:9 (Legge, p. 355), and Cheng 11:2 (Legge, p. 376). In most of these cases, the term used is *zheng* 烝 .

14. e.g.,the mother-in-law who makes a practice of seducing her sons-in-law in the collection *Yipian qing* 一片情 , No. 6 (see Keith McMahon, *Causality and Containment in Seventeenth-century Chinese Fiction*, Leiden: Brill, 1988, p. 96). For that matter, the tangled interaction of sworn sisters and sworn brothers in works such as *Yesou puyan* 野叟曝言 , while intended no doubt to be an ideal situation, results in relations that would be problematic in other works.

15. *Xingshi yinyuan zhuan*, chapter 92.

16. For a good discussion of the range of problematic marriages in Chinese practice, see Chen Guyuan 陳顧遠 , *Zhongguo hunyin shi* 中國婚姻史 (Taipei: Shangwu yinshuguan, 1966), pp. 131–141.

17. For example, *Paian jingqi* 拍案驚奇 I:23, II:38; *Rou putuan* 肉蒲團 , chapter 5, etc. See also McMahon, p. 100.

18. Of course, the rhetoric of kinship among "sister" wives and concubines should not be taken literally, except in those cases where the symbolic implications are developed in a given text.

19. On the other side, we see the perfect ideal of cousin-marriage in *Fusheng liuji* 浮生六記.

20. For a review of scholarship and discussion of the question of *Honglou meng*'s debt to *Jin Ping Mei*, see Mary E. Scott, *Azure from Indigo* (Princeton University dissertation, 1989); and Sun Xun 孫遜 , *Honglou meng yu Jin Ping Mei* 紅樓夢與金瓶梅 (Ningxia: Ningxia renmin chubanshe, 1982).

21. For reference, see my *Four Masterworks of Ming Fiction* (Princeton: Princeton University Press, 1987), p. 137, plus following discussion of this aspect of the text (pp. 137–151). The expression *feiyinshu* 非淫書 used by Zhang Zhupo follows a comment in the Chongzhen recension; see my article "The Chongzhen Commentary on the *Jin Ping Mei*: Gems amidst the Dross", in *Chinese Literature: Essays, Articles, Reviews*, 8 (1986), p. 28.

22. See, for example, Xu Shuofang 徐朔方 , "*Jin Ping Mei* chengshu xintan 金瓶梅成書新探", in *Zhonghua wenshi luncong* 中華文史論叢, 3(1984); and "Zailun *Shuihu* he *Jin Ping Mei* bushi geren chuangzuo"再論水滸和金瓶梅不是個人創作, in *Xuzhou shifan xueyuan xuebao* 徐州師範學院學報 1986: 1; and Liu Hui 劉輝 , "Cong cihuaben dao shuosanben 從詞話本到説散本 ", in *Zhongguo gudian wenxue luncong* 中國古典文學論叢, 3(1985): I disagree with this theory in *Four Masterworks*, p. 69. For a review of the intricate structural patterns in the novel, see Ibid., pp. 72–85, plus such critical works as Sun Shuyu 孫述宇 , *Jin Ping Mei de yishu* 金瓶梅的藝術 (Taipei: Shibao wenhua, 1978); Katherine Carlitz, *Rhetoric of the Jin Ping Mei* (Bloomington: Indiana University Press, 1986); etc.

23. i.e., the structural core from chapter 20 to 80.

24. I count instances of sexual or pseudo-sexual interaction between the two in chapters 18, 19, 20, 24, 25, 29, 33, 52, 54, 55, 72, 80, 82, 83 and 85. See Paul V. Martinson, *Pao, Order, and Redemption in the Jin Ping Mei* (University of Chicago dissertation, 1973), pp. 172ff. The notion of incest is brought up explicitly in the novel as early as chapter 22 (5a) (all quotations are from the *Jin Ping Mei cihua* edition, various reprints available). On the question of whether or not Jinlian and Chen Jingji had actually consummated their relation before chapter 80, see *Four Masterworks*, p. 174.

25. See comment by Zhang Zhupo, chapter 33 (chapter-comments), discussed in *Four Masterworks*, p. 175.

26. Later, yet another strand is added to the tangle when Ximen Qing sleeps with Wang Liu'er's brother Wang Jing 王經 in chapter 71 (see *Four Masterworks*, pp. 143, 148).

27. A similar pattern, probably with very different implications, is followed in the "salvation" of Qiaojie 巧姐 and Liu Laolao 劉姥姥 in *Honglou meng*.

28. See *Four Masterworks*, p. 175.

29. Significantly, the near-consummation in chapter 53 is interrupted by the barking of dogs, an image endowed with special negative associations in the novel. See *Four Masterworks*, pp. 100, 175.

30. *Jin Ping Mei*, chapter 82; also see chapters 53, 76 and 82 for reference.

31. See *Four Masterworks*, p. 170, and "Chongzhen Commentary", p. 26.

32. Various details lend support to the theory that the relationship between Ximen Qing and Li Ping'er is intended to reflect the infatuation of the Wanli emperor for the Imperial Concubine Zheng. See *Four Masterworks*, pp. 60, 64, for references.

33. Cf. the parallel development of Ximen Qing's relations with Li Ping'er and those with Li Guijie, beginning in chapter 12.

34. See *Four Masterworks*, p. 176, and Sun Shuyu, p. 98. Zhang Zhupo is quite explicit about the incestuous nature of these relations in his chapter-commentary to chapter 69.

35. See *Four Masterworks*, p. 150.

36. See *Four Masterworks*, p. 144. Zhou Yi's father Zhou Zhong 周忠 is apparently meant to stand for Zhou Shoubei 周守備.

37. For discussion, see my *Archetype and Allegory in the Dream of the Red Chamber* (Princeton: Princeton University Press, 1976), p. 78.

38. *Honglou meng bashihui jiaoben* 紅樓夢八十回校本, edited by Yu Pingbo 俞平伯 (Peking: Renmin wenxue chubanshe, 1958), p. 80. See note 56.

39. See Yu Pingbo, *Honglou meng bian* 紅樓夢辨 (Shanghai: Yadong tushuguan, 1973), pp. 159–178; Wu Shih-ch'ang, *On the Red Chamber Dream* (Oxford: Clarendon Press, 1961), pp. 216ff.; and Susanna Li, *Rhetoric of Fantasy and Rhetoric of Irony* (Princeton University dissertation, 1987), chapter 5. In the mid-nineteenth century, the *Jinyu yuan* 金玉緣 commentator shows he is fully aware of these implications, probably without the help of Zhiyan Zhai. See *Pingzhu Jinyu yuan* 評註金玉緣 (Taipei: Feng huang, 1974), 5 (16b), 6 (24a), etc. For discussion, see my paper "Late-Qing Confucian Interpretations of *Honglou meng*: The Zhang Xinzhi Commentary", Harbin International Conference on Dream of Red Mansions, 1986, pp. 7ff. (Published in Chinese in *Honglou meng yanjiu jikan*, 紅樓夢研究集刊, No. 14 (October, 1989), pp. 393–482.)

40. Zhang Xinzhi picks up on this implication in his chapter-commentary on chapter 5.

41. See comments by Zhang Xinzhi cited in "Late-Qing Interpretations", note 25.

42. See *Archetype and Allegory in the Dream of the Red Chamber*, p. 160.

43. I suspect that Pan Youan's name may contain a joking reference to the proverbial lover Pan Yue 潘岳 (Pan Anren 潘安仁).

44. To give away my theory, I believe that the original design of *Honglou meng* follows the 100-chapter pattern of its models, especially *Jin Ping Mei*, in accordance with which a watershed structural break at chapter 80 is also mandated. Some of Zhou Ruchang's arguments for a 108-chapter length would also support this possibility, as could a freer interpretation of Zhiyan Zhai's reference to "the last thirty chapters" (後三十回). I hope to work out this argument in the near future.

45. See chapter 23, *Honglou meng bashihui jiaoben*, Vol. I, p. 233, and chapter 37, Vol. I, p. 383.

46. The *Jinyu yuan* commentator gives a shockingly blunt reading of this scene in chapter 36, p. 19a, *et al.*

47. Tjan Tjoe Som, *Po-hu t'ung* (Leiden: Brill, 1949–1952), pp. 253, 255. The *Li ji* is silent on this question, evidently permitting it. In the story "Jisheng" 寄生 in *Liaozhai* 聊齋, a cousin-marriage is vigorously opposed on moral grounds.

48. I am thinking of Yuan Cai 袁采, *Shifan* 世範; see Patricia B. Ebrey, *Family and Property in Sung China* (Princeton: Princeton University Press, 1984), pp. 98, 223. The original term is 因親及親. See Chen Guyuan, pp. 135ff.

49 The point is, *qinshang zuo qin* is simply too much *qin*.

50. The Chinese terms *tang* 堂 and *biao* 表 do not quite match the use of "agnate" and "cognate" in anthropological studies, with respect to the categorization of a father's sister's children. I am using "agnate" to refer to the direct paternal line, and stretching "cognate" to cover more than maternal kin.

51. We can compare these relationships in the following simple charts:

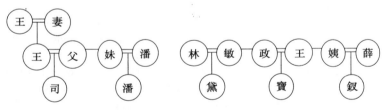

52. See above, notes 16 and 48.

53. For example, Zhao Feiyan and Zhaoyi in various versions of *Zhao Feiyan biezhuan* 趙飛燕別傳.

54. The line reads as quoted in the Jiaxu manuscript, but it is emended to … (弟兄皆出一意) … in *Honglou meng bashihui jiaoben*, p. 45. Cf. the *Jinyu yuan* commentator's strange notion of the "marriage" of Daiyu and Baochai; see "Late-Qing Interpretations", p. 8.

55. See *Honglou meng baishihui jiaoben*, pp. 46–47.

56. Of course, as a term of endearment *xiaoshu* does not normally mean literally "little uncle", referring more loosely to brother-in-law relations.

57. Thus Qin Zhong's name is an unmistakable allusion to the Six Dynasties expression:情之所鍾正在我輩, cited at the start of the *Jin Ping Mei cihua*, itself borrowed from the short story *Wenjing yuanyang hui* 刎頸駕鴦會. See *Four Masterworks*, pp. 153ff., for translation and discussion.

58. The *Jinyu yuan* commentator goes as far as to blame Yuanchun for Baoyu's ultimate fate. See chapter 109 (23b).

59. For discussion, see *Four Masterworks*, pp. 158ff. Zhang Zhupo emphasizes this connection in chapter-comments in chapters 33 and 69.

60. Cf. the earlier use of the term *luanlun* in a more general sense of moral disorder in *Shishuo xinyu* 世説新語, "Fangzheng" (方正) chapter (5:24). See discussion of *Jinyu yuan* comments on this aspect of the text in "Late-Qing Interpretations", pp. 9ff.

61. For discussion of the "Four Vices", see *Four Masterworks*, pp. 154ff. The possible reflection of the "Four Vices" incident in Wanli politics and its connection to the authorship of the novel is explored in David T. Roy, "The Case for T'ang Hsien-tsu's Authorship of the Chin P'ing Mei", *Chinese Literature Essays, Articles, Reviews*, 8: No. 1–2 (1986), pp. 31–62.

62. See my *Archetype and Allegory in the Dream of the Red Chamber*, pp. 28, 75f.

63. For an excellent discussion of this issue, see Keith McMahon, *Causality and Containment, passim*. See also *Four Masterworks*, pp. 147ff.

64. See *Four Masterworks*, pp. 179ff.

65. e.g. chapters 58 and 95.

66. Zhang Xinzhi expounds on this idea at length in the following comment: "Baoyu and Jia Rong are undeniably an uncle and a nephew, so what is this dream of Keqing if not incest? What deep resentment does the *Honglou meng* have in its treatment of human feeling that forces it to open its treatment of this theme with a case of incest? ... The author clearly finds himself necessarily deprived of middle ground in expounding the subtle ties of heaven and man and the ultimate conclusions of reason and desire according to the *Daxue* and *Zhongyong* 中庸. 'A minister murders his lord, a son murders his father.' Can such things happen just spontaneously?" (寶玉賈蓉明明叔姪，則可卿此夢非亂倫而何？一部紅樓談情有何大恨 而必以亂倫開談情之首？……作者固自演大學中庸天人之微理欲乏極，必無中立之處也，臣弒其君，子弒其父，豈生而然哉).

The *Yi jing* passage is from the *wenyan* commentary on the hexagram *kun*. See *Zhouyi zhezhong* 周易折中, compiled by Li Guangdi 李光地 (reprinted, Taipei: Zhen Shan Mei, 1971), Vol. 2, p. 1135; and H. Wihelm, *The I Ching* (Princeton: Princeton University Press, 1950), p. 393.

67. The symbolic connection between incest and parricide is well established in

Freud's *Totem and Taboo*, among many other places. For discussion, see René Girard, *Violence and the Sacred* (Baltimore: Johns Hopkins, 1977).

68. Hence the strong emphasis on childlessness and short-lived offspring in the novel. See *Four Masterworks*, pp. 172ff.

69. In this light, Miaoyu 妙玉 and Jiang Yuhan 蔣玉函 also share in aspects of Baoyu's selfhood, by virtue of their common half-names.

70. For discussion of the implications of Baoyu's "enlightenment", see *Archetype and Allegory in the Dream of the Red Chamber*, chapters 8 and 9. These implications are already well adumbrated in the first 80 chapters, especially the final "decade", and do not depend on the authenticity of the final 40 chapters. The problem of "self-enclosure" in the novel, of course, applies as well to the introverted self-indulgence of Jia Jing 賈敬, Jia She 賈赦, and most of the other figures in the compound.

71. Similar implications come out in the final "debate" between Baoyu and Baochai on the ideal of child-like self-containment. See my *Archetype and Allegory in the Dream of the Red Chamber*, p. 209.

6

Unpredictability and Meaning in Ming-Qing Literati Novels

Robert E. Hegel

To the extent that Ming and Qing novelists were at best marginal members of the official, hence nominally morally superior, stratum of society, their situation might be better understood as parallel to that of marginalized writers of other times and places. Concerning twentieth-century women writers in America and Western Europe, Rachel Blau DuPlessis explores the implications of their subverting the narrative conventions endorsed by writers from the socially dominant — male — group: "... breaking the sequence can mean delegitimating the specific narrative and cultural orders of nineteenth-century fiction...." By "sequence" she means conventional plot patterns that exemplify dominant male values.[1] Similarly, when Chinese novelists of the late Ming and Qing periods self-consciously modified the narrative structures of popular fiction conventional at their time in the name of greater historicity or clearer presentation of moral truth, perhaps their innovations should be considered challenges not only to received literary practice but to the popular Confucian sense of moral order as well. I believe that a particularly interesting paradox is visible in Chinese fiction of the late Ming and Qing periods when one considers the implications of these challenges. Specifically, certain writers simultaneously reaffirmed popular morality as commonly expressed in vernacular fiction while by implication questioning the validity of the whole Confucian enterprise. Unconventional structural and thematic elements may very well have significance far beyond the development of the literary form in which they wrote.

It is well known that the rhetorical stance of the narrator conventional in Ming-Qing vernacular fiction — and that expressed in the prefaces as well — involved confirming dominant social values, those of Confucianism understood at an unsophisticated level. However, certain Ming and Qing writers used their novels to explore the "paradoxes" of virtue unrewarded or of ostensibly moral action that provokes serious social disruption; at least one seems to exemplify the exhaustion of such rational explanations by regularly undercutting all predictability of the consequences of human behaviour when using conventional moral standards as the basis for anticipating social success or failure, much less of any sort of divine justice.

The present essay is an exploration of ways in which traditional Chinese novels conveyed meaning to their readers. It is based on several assumptions that should be made clear at the outset. First, I see at least the literati novels (*wenren xiaoshuo* 文人小説) of late Ming and Qing as generally serious attempts at self-expression in narrative form. Many students of Chinese popular literature conclude that a spirit of playfulness pervades most of these novels, an observation that I do not dispute. However, the writing of a novel took months, years, even decades to complete. Many novelists were deeply engaged with the political concerns of their time and revealed their personal opinions in their writings; others addressed current moral and philosophical questions. One major characteristic of literati fiction is most certainly the intellectual and artistic seriousness demonstrated at least sporadically throughout their works.[2]

Secondly, while I am aware of the tremendous intellectual upheavals occasioned in part by the Manchu conquest and by the disaffection with Song period Neo-Confucianism growing among segments of society's educated elite during the late Ming,[3] the world-view most commonly expressed and structurally embodied in Ming-Qing novels is that of "popular" Confucianism, an unsophisticated version of Confucian cosmology (overlain with a sense of "karmic justice" incorporated later from Buddhism) that began in the Han and that is still visible in morality books for the masses produced in Taiwan and Hong Kong even at the present time. This view assumes that the universe is structured and that structures have moral value, that virtue will be rewarded and wrong-doing will be punished, and that the universe is ultimately comprehensible in moral terms. In fact, this feature of Chinese narratives is visible even in the earliest examples. John Wang has identified it in the *Zuo zhuan* 左傳, one of the earliest collections of historical materials compiled perhaps in the fourth century before the Common Era:

> Put very simply, the pattern is this: just as the evil, the stupid, and the haughty will usually bring disaster upon themselves, the good, the wise, and the

humble tend to meet their just rewards…. The pattern is not preconceived, but rather is something the author simply detected in the events he recounted. In other words, it represents his own interpretation of the significance of the events that had transpired.[4]

Finally, the question I focus on here, the expectation of reward or punishment appropriate to morally significant action, allows speculation concerning the deliberately subversive attitude taken in certain novels toward dominant morality. There are numerous other features one might examine in understanding the relationships between events narrated in fiction; I choose the question of reward and retribution as a way to demonstrate another level of paradox in Chinese literature: that between surface meaning and deeper significance in sophisticated fictional texts produced in late imperial China. I hope in this way to reveal facets previously overlooked in certain historical novels and to elucidate elements heretofore not readily explained in other works.

Self expression in moral terms to Ming-Qing literati generally involved furthering social harmony by act or by example, self being that central element in the famous dictum from the Confucian canonical text *Daxue* 大學 (The Great Learning):

> The ancients who wished to manifest their clear character to the world would first bring order to their states. Those who wished to bring order to their states would first regulate their families. Those who wished to regulate their families would first cultivate their personal lives. Those who wished to cultivate their personal lives would first rectify their minds. Those who wished to rectify their minds would first make their wills sincere. Those who wished to make their wills sincere would first extend their knowledge. The extension of knowledge consists in the investigation of things. When things are investigated, knowledge is extended; when knowledge is extended, the will becomes sincere; when the will is sincere, the mind is rectified; when the mind is rectified, the personal life is cultivated; when the personal life is cultivated, the family will be regulated; when the family is regulated, the state will be in order; and when the state is in order, there will be peace throughout the world. From the Son of Heaven down to the common people, all must regard cultivation of the personal life as the root or foundation.[5]

The essential message of Mencius, that human nature is fundamentally good, further informs the traditional image of self, especially as developed by Wang Yangming's 王陽明 (1472–1529) Neo-Confucian *Xinxue* 心學 : spontaneous, genuine action is good, i.e., naturally in harmony with the moral structure of the universe. If society were orderly, as in the *Daxue* situation, one could contribute thereto by spontaneous and morally proper behaviour. And yet the Master himself cautioned, "Show yourself when the Way prevails in the Empire, but hide yourself when it does not."[6] This assertion problematizes both "missionary" activity and political endeavours: one might choose not to demonstrate his own moral worth, hence not attempt to effect greater social harmony in the Empire in a time of rampant political and social immorality. There seems little reason to conclude, given the testimony of Ming-Qing vernacular fiction, that these writers perceived that the Confucian way — in its original sense of moral order and social harmony — "prevailed" at any time either in the past narrated in their historical fiction or in their own day. Confucius's comment suggests that an intellectual might thereby be excused from moral action in the public arena.

It is worth considering in this regard the fictional career of Qin Shubao 秦叔寶 in *Sui shi yiwen* 隋史遺文 (Forgotten Tales of the Sui, 1633).[7] A popular figure in legend, theatre history, and even folk religion — where he appears as the fairer of the two gods painted on double-leaved temple doors and gates — Qin starts out with what might be considered a "natural goodness" in the Mencian sense;[8] he is unfettered by any formal teaching in the Confucian school. The motivations behind his actions are initially pure, uncoloured by selfish interests. His generosity is thus spontaneous and natural, but he becomes influenced by the kind of altruism to be found among *Shuihu zhuan* 水滸傳 heroes — the sort that encourages the breaking of heads and the squandering of personal wealth in order to right injustices and to play host to anyone who seems to acknowledge one's worth (often measured in physical prowess).[9] Such rowdy activity in the name of personal integrity leads to his mother's insistent demands that he heed her words of guidance. In opposition to the paradigm of personal altruism that her son nominally exemplifies, she urges him to choose the conventional Confucian alternative of selfless service to family and State.

As a consequence, he begins to demonstrate his filial piety; Qin learns to curb his impulses and to come home when she calls him, thereby avoiding altercations with common bullies and ruffians. In this way his actions promote greater harmony within the family and, presumably, in local society as a whole. By inference we see this youthful hero following the *Daxue* path to moral perfection and self-expression. But this is accomplished through the external pressure of his mother's urging; it is not as a result of any "investigation" of society's needs on Qin Shubao's part that he becomes "good", i.e., obedient, filial, and law-abiding. Again following the advice of others he joins the local peace-keeping establishment as a constable, which is, of course, his initial undoing.

Sui shi yiwen demonstrates through comic exaggeration that superficial "morality" (accommodating oneself to conventions of socially accepted behaviour — as defined by his mother — and to dominant political institutions in society — from which he is frequently excluded) does not necessarily equate with any kind of practical common sense on the one hand, much less with any wisdom into the way the universe works on the other. Similarly, neither participation in the supposedly moral political hierarchy nor action intended to promote social harmony automatically produces any knowledge of the real structure of power in a work-a-day society or of how to get along with one's social equals. Competing moral paradigms simply compound this character's confusion, as the dramatized narrator elicits the readers' amusement.

Specifically, the erstwhile local hero Qin Shubao is easily manipulated by a calculating city inn-keeper; indecision over how to respond to poverty and alienation leaves him utterly disoriented. In the end Qin suffers such disgrace that he falls ill. When he throws himself on the mercy of a local "benefactor", the latter demonstrates his personal altruism much as Qin himself had before learning more acceptably conventional "morality". This selfless hero, Shan Xiongxin 單雄信, generously provides for the needs of passersby and victims of official abuse; Qin is just one of many so welcomed. While one should not blindly equate untrammeled knight-errant altruism with the spontaneous goodness explored by the philosopher Mencius, the moral authority attributed to such martial heroes by China's storytellers and writers surely derives from this Confucian conception, even though knight-errantry came to be parodied by some Ming and Qing novelists.[10] For my purposes here it is sufficient to see the altruism of the warrior developed in *Sui shi yiwen* as a set of values consistent in general outline with Confucianism and only slightly in opposition to those espoused by the state — and ostensibly by society as well.[11]

Conventionally "moral" service to family and State does not equip Qin Shubao to handle money efficiently, to cope with the normal "bad luck" that afflicts everyone at times, or to deal with isolation from his usual social support system. The implications of this section of *Sui shi yiwen*, the *Bildungsroman* of Qin Shubao, are two-fold: as novelist Yuan Yuling 袁于令 (1599–1674) says in his preface to the novel, he intends that his narrative will supplement orthodox (i.e., Confucian) historiography; in fact, Yuan parodies the seriousness of the formal histories through the bathos of his historical fiction. Likewise, by extension one might see the novelist questioning the rightness of the State-supported dominant morality, of the political/social structures supposedly founded on proper moral relationships, or even of the Confucian system of values as a whole. Nor does he necessarily endorse knight-errantry as an alternative. Yuan Yuling begins his narrative with mock-serious introduction by his narrator in the guise of author:

> People in situations of greatest wealth, of greatest honour, and of greatest luxury — it has always been so that to speak of them delights the heart, to hear of them delights the ear, and to read of them delights the eye. Yet sorrow and destruction are ever inherent in such situations; if these persons do not provoke everlasting vituperation, then, worse yet, they become the laughing-stock of the ages.... But the hero in the wilds who will not make a name for himself, will not take pleasure in wine or in women, instead must suffer ignominy and loneliness in fullest measure. Still it is he who can capitalize on the downfall of others from their lives of ease; regardless of whether he aids in the recovery of an imperial house or founds a dynasty on his own, his name will last throughout eternity. Though his reputation may shine in later ages, the man himself becomes no different in attributes through his success. Like the sun and the moon he has always shone of himself; skiffs of cloud or wisps of fog may obscure him, but he will always shine through whether or not his contemporaries recognize his greatness. And later when people begin to eulogize him, what they record with paper and pen will be nothing more than the circumstances immediately surrounding his successes; they will say noth-ing of his life in obscurity. Who can foresee in a tiny seed the pine or cypress reaching to the heavens, or that a cub tiger or leopard will someday be able to devour a whole cow? Still, to speak of such matters [as the early life of a hero] strikes people as being new and different. I will not introduce this person until I have outlined something of the events which he encountered at that time...[12]

The tenor of this section is familiar, as if the narrator were sharing a joke with the reader: we all know that Qin Shubao was a great hero, but even heroes take their lumps, etc. Thus by claiming continuity in this hero when in fact he undergoes a radical transformation in character from youth to maturity, *Sui shi yiwen* deliberately parodies the historiographical tradi-tion it ostensibly "supplements", as did *Sanguo yanyi* and *Shuihu zhuan*.[13] By introducing the protagonist as a realized hero, the novel is structured somewhat like the classical Western epic and as many Western novels: it starts in the middle, moves back to the beginning through flashback, and then finishes the story (an observation made by Gérard Genette).[14] By referring in this introduction first to the extratextual historical record concerning Qin Shubao, the novelist draws the reader's attention to the story as it is generally known, of the adventures of a mature, self-assured and competent military hero. Yuan Yuling's narrative then refers backward in time to Qin's glorious ancestors, his auspicious birth, and his impoverished childhood before detailing his protagonist's painful maturation process. One might say that the novel in this way creates an obvious ironic distance between itself and the historiographical tradition by developing the concern for biographical details characteristic of the folk, oral tradition.[15] The last half of the novel is more conventionally devoted to rapid-paced narration of historical or pseudo-historical battles and intrigues; there Qin Shubao becomes merely one of a welter of military protagonists.

One must not overlook the significance of the moral orthodoxy implicit in the standard histories and in the formal historiographical tradition. From the beginning of self-conscious historiography in China, not only was the invariable structure of chronological sequence imposed upon historical data; the social/political functions and the exemplary acts of outstanding individuals were used as the basis for grouping them in paradigmatic categories.[16] Early historical fiction in the vernacular, the Yuan period proto-novels known as *pinghua* 平話 and even early versions of the *Sanguo yanyi* and other historical novels dating from the middle Ming period, follow rather closely the chronicle format (*piannianti* 篇年體) of traditional historiography. In the more complex of these historical novels the action narrated generally confirms the basic Confucian sense of order in explicit terms: social disorder is condemned as are those who disrupt social harmony, peace ultimately reigns, and good acts are rewarded while evil is punished. In short, the outcomes due moral and immoral acts are predictable, as logically they should be in an orderly, moral universe — although the testimony of narrators and other characters may be introduced to affirm how events *should* have evolved, when the historical fact to which the fiction is hinged provides less than morally ideal consequences. Such novels thus seemingly confirmed their Confucian readers' notions about the nature and significance of reality.[17]

The novelist Yuan Yuling's decision to invest most of his artistic energy in *Sui shi yiwen* in the creation of a *Bildungsroman* of comic proportions demonstrates his innovative use of the narrative form conventional for historical fiction; this in itself establishes a double-sided problematique in his attitude toward traditional historiography. First, his hero must necessarily confront competing value systems if he is to mature to the point that he can choose as his own the "correct" moral path. That initially Qin suffers by following both of these value systems by implication throws open to question the legitimacy of Confucianism's monopoly on moral authority. Furthermore, his hero can be both morally good and socially correct in the mundane Confucian sense and yet still suffer mentally and physically; Qin Shubao is the same person, his narrator explains, in youth and in maturity despite wildly differing fortunes during those two periods of his life. That this assertion is subverted by the narrative itself — Qin's youthful ineptitude contrasts sharply with his success in maturity — provokes questions of no small magnitude in understanding the text and its original meaning: How can fool become hero? Can a person lauded by the historians ever be less than exemplary? Is it appropriate to find moral dilemmas humorous? Can there be any validity to the idea that spontaneous self-expression will be widely recognized as good? Alternatively, does socialization in the Confucian sense involve stifling all spontaneous self-expression or just certain types? More to the point, do the histories tell the truth? (Czech novelist Milan Kundera: "Historiography writes the history of society, not of man."[18]) All of these questions seem clearly implicit in the narrator's introduction and events subsequently narrated in *Sui shi yiwen*. One should notice, too, the challenge to traditional assumptions about appropriate and morally charged structure implicit in Yuan's radical revision of the orthodox narrative format: his starting in the "middle" of Qin Shubao's tale before moving back to its beginning highlights the discontinuity between youth and age, between the "reality" behind the verisimilitude with which Qin's youthful misadventures are narrated and the historian's conventional paradigm visible in the mature protagonist's predictable battlefield victories.

It is not surprising that novelists like Yuan Yuling should question — albeit playfully in *Sui shi yiwen* — the moral supremacy of Confucianism, given his marginal political, hence social, status in Confucian society.[19] He and other novelists were educationally prepared for the civil service examination system and emotionally ready for the high status and wealth that an official position would bring. Being selected for the civil service in Ming and Qing China ostensibly confirmed the moral education and high moral stature of these Confucian scholars. Failure in the civil service examinations, as so graphically demonstrated in chapter 4 of Dong Yue's 董説 *Xiyou bu* 西遊補 (Tower of Myriad Mirrors, 1641),[20] for example, could bring on serious doubts — in oneself or among others — about one's moral viability as a human being in addition to the more obvious concerns over one's diligence as a student and one's appropriate social status as a consequence.

Ming-Qing novelists generally criticized society from a conservative Confucian moral perspective, demanding reform and attacking dereliction of moral duty on the part of men in positions of power — positions which, by inference, the novelists themselves might have filled more appropriately and more ethically. That is, the concerns of moral self-assertion (demonstration of one's own moral discrimination through acts that encourage social harmony) may well have been served by strenuous affirmation of those ideals of Confucian education they were debarred from practising — as they were trained to do — in the political arena. One might pursue this line of thought farther to conclude that, as Marxist and Marxist-influenced critics have always said, certain novelists expressed their personal frustrations and anxieties by attacking the very structure of power in Chinese society at the time, e.g., the Confucian moral order nominally, *but in their minds not actually*, practised. Numerous novels such as *Shuihu zhuan* demonstrate the moral bankruptcy of extant political structures by cataloging the immoral acts of those who hold power; *Sui shi yiwen* does exactly the same thing in a more imaginative manner by outlining a structure of local social control that can neither accommodate nor even tolerate the naïve Confucian moral sensibility of an immature Qin Shubao. At the grassroots of society money and influence determine all real power, this novel reveals; morality of the dominant Confucian sort is simply irrelevant: it is visible neither in the moral outcomes of spontaneous acts of the innocent individual nor exemplified by the distribution of power in society.

The correlation between the subversion of the conventional narrative sequence and the delegitimation of received moral teachings, hence the social structures they nominally define, can be seen most clearly in the eighteenth-century masterpiece *Honglou meng* 紅樓夢 (*The Story of the Stone* in the translation by David Hawkes and John Minford). The narrative is, in essence, the extensive biography of a single protagonist, the stone; in this regard it too can be considered a *Bildungsroman*, an exploration of the process by which Jia Baoyu 賈寶玉 receives his painful education in the real world before he returns again to his stony state in the celestial realm. In contrast to the structure implicit in *Sui shi yiwen* — starting the "story" in the middle — and to the historiographical sequential narrative structure conventionalized for the novel by that time, *Honglou meng* both begins and ends in chapter 1; the rest of the novel in effect is flashback from which we actual readers are to derive an enlightening lesson. To this end, we are shown how to read the novel in chapter 1 by the character Kongkong Daoren空空道人.This conclusion is suggested by the fact that the entire story is merely an inscription on that stone read by Kongkong Daoren. In format, *Honglou meng* is thus a more radical departure from traditional historical chronicle than is *Sui shi yiwen*. This fiction, deliberately and explicitly neither a history nor a pseudo-historical text, is meant to provoke a catharsis in the mind of the reader, greater in degree than any of the Buddhist or Taoist classics with which the implied reader characterized as Kongkong Daoren must already be familiar, to judge from his religious name. The dramatic effect of this reading suggests the vitality of the fiction and, alternatively, the moribundity of more formal — hence less profound — writings; by implication it also subverts the conventional moral views of society and history contained in other writings, if we consider Kongkong Daoren's experience seriously.

The complaints of successive generations of *Honglou meng* critics that the last forty chapters are at least partially spurious reflect conventional limitations of both Qing fictional narrative and of the Confucian mindset: both expect predictable structures and clear linkages between cause and effect; both demand greater narrative attention to the morally/socially more prominent figures. (In the now venerable words of Edmund Wilson, "… all our intellectual activity, in whatever field it takes place [including fiction], is an attempt to give a meaning to our existence … [to make it] something orderly, symmetrical and pleasing …".)[21] Chinese readers have always expected that the events predicted in the dream of chapter 5 and elsewhere should be realized by the end of the novel, that Yinglian 英蓮 should be killed by Xue Pan's 薛蟠 wife, that Tanchun 探春 should end up far from home, that Wang Xifeng 王熙鳳 should be dispossessed by the Jia family, that Daiyu 黛玉 and Baochai 寶釵 should each have a song and an image to herself in the celestial registers, etc. (Hawkes calls this last unexpected element "special treatment for which there must have been a special reason".)[22] The dissonance between these expectations on the part of the actual reader and the resolution of conflicts and crises as narrated in the novel produces an unprecedented degree of realism for the Chinese literary tradition. This is not to say that action in the novel corresponded closely with events in historical reality, necessarily; I mean only that there exists far more contingency and less predictability between events narrated in the novel than was desirable for the Confucian mindset and than was conventional in the Ming-Qing novel, to judge from early examples such as *Xiyou ji* 西遊記 and *Jin Ping Mei* 金瓶梅 and seventeenth-century works such as *Sui Tang yanyi* 隋唐演義. (Consider George Levine's insightful comments on "realism": that it is based on a notion of reality shared by writer and reader, that each new conception parodies the view it replaces, and that there is moral value in representing "reality" accurately;[23] in this regard consider again the importance of "the investigation of things" (格物) in the *Daxue* passage above. It is in Levine's sense that I perceive intellectual seriousness and moral relevance in the verisimilitude with which the early life of Qin Shubao is narrated in *Sui shi yiwen*; the new visions of reality there and in *Honglou meng* do parody more conventional views.)

Certain among the crises predicted early in the *Honglou meng* narrative ultimately are fulfilled (as in the fates of Lin Daiyu and Xue Baochai); others are mitigated (Wang Xifeng's punishment), and some avoided (the total financial and social ruin of the Jia family on the model of the experience of the author) or reinterpreted/rewritten (the death of Qin Keqing 秦可卿). The causal linkages between fictional events in *Honglou meng* thus differ considerably from the moral predictability expected in literature and in life during the Ming and Qing — and even now, by certain Chinese critics. In contrast to Confucian conceptions of ideal order — the cosmic harmony that should be reflected in social hierarchy and moral retribution in this mundane world — the causality at work in *Honglou meng* is rarely "neat", to use Frank Kermode's term.[24] The extreme contingency of all elements of narrative art in *Honglou meng* is visible from the very beginning of the novel: there characters are introduced as they are viewed through the eyes of other, fallible, fictional observers, none of whom is equatable with the "ideal reader" as is Kongkong Daoren — ironically a mere featureless fiction — in chapter 1.

Furthermore, no one moral evaluation can ever be sufficient for many characters and situations in *Honglou meng*; each must depend on the particular perspective dictated by specific circumstances. This fact in itself contradicts traditional historiographical categorizations. Take Qin Keqing, for example. Readers learn, for the most part indirectly, that this sensuous young woman has had an adulterous affair of the worst kind, incest with her father-in-law. She dies early, a seemingly appropriate end for a woman of such loose morals (comparisons with the adulteresses in *Shuihu zhuan* and *Jin Ping Mei* immediately spring to mind). One might anticipate that her partner in sin, Jia Zhen 賈珍 , would try to hide his indiscretions in silence or at least try to balance his self-indulgent behaviour through a belated show of moral rectitude. But instead Jia Zhen makes a public

spectacle of himself through inappropriate levels and intensity of mourning — while heedlessly contributing to the family's financial decline.
More surprising still is the reappearance of the adulteress in Wang
Xifeng's dream early in chapter 13; there she urges sound economic
measures to protect the Jia family to whose moral dissolution she so
strongly contributed! (Appropriately, in Confucian terms, she suggests
investment in schools, care of family graves, etc.) Her comments are not
merely ironic; the implications of the seeming moral paradox Qin Keqing presents are noteworthy, even far-reaching: When miscreants are
rewarded, when in fiction what society condemns as sin only masks virtue
(or is it that Confucian platitudes are only the stuff of whores and house-
wreckers?), the standards for moral judgment, even the moral structure of
the family and society in general, are necessarily thrown into question. By
generally destabilizing the predictive potential of certain major elements of
his narrative, the novelist signals the implied reader about the appropriate
way to read and how to regard *reality* at the same time: in this text the
usual "rules" simply do not apply with any exactness; similar "rules" may
mean no more in the reader's own life.[25]

   In earlier novels such as *Sui Yangdi yanshi* 隋煬帝艷史 (The Merry
Adventures of Emperor Yang, 1631) the plot may also alternate between
the mundane and the celestial realms of existence, but these earlier works
confirm traditional morality: the "fates" of characters — that is, the retribution for their acts — vary predictably with their corporal motivations; their
destinies are generally not already worked out in advance of their appearance in the world of men. In earlier novels characters typically have a
kind of "free will" to the extent that they are morally responsible for their
actions. Even the dissolute Emperor Yang of the Sui could have *changed*
his fate by genuine moral reform and proper behaviour, both narrator and
characters in *Sui Yangdi yanshi* suggest. By contrast, the stone Baoyu
innocently and altruistically waters the celestial flower; this nurturing act
parallels the generous distribution of food and money by the youthful Qin
Shubao. But in *Honglou meng* this naïveté engenders a fateful, ultimately
fatal, attachment between flower and stone that informs the tragedy of the
entire work; in tone this later novel contrasts markedly with the comedy of
incongruity between Qin Shubao as bumbling youth and the competent
military hero supplied to the reader by the historiographical tradition and
copied into *Sui shi yiwen's* later chapters. Yet in neither work is cause —
action bearing moral significance — related to effect — in terms of reward
and punishment — logically and with moral appropriateness.

The alternation between realms of existence in *Honglou meng* simultaneously parodies earlier fictional references to the other world and heightens the sense of contingency concerning events of this world. Baoyu finds himself in a place of beauty and of mystery during his initial dream; presumably this realm is related to that of the Taoist and Buddhist from the novel's frame-story who punctuate with their appearances the rest of the narrative. These curious figures may also be beautiful in the upper realm; the text does not detail their appearance there. Yet in the world of the Jia family they are deformed, dirty, perhaps even demented. Are their looks deceiving? Certainly their actions and their words are unpredictable, even enigmatic. Compare these figures with other-worldly actors in ideologically more conventional novels such as *Sui Tang yanyi* or even *Xiyou ji*: the gods and their hangers-on may be comic in the latter, but in both novels it is just such superior beings who represent order, rectitude, predictability. In novels such as *Sui Yangdi yanshi* they maintain the "account books" (*zhangbu* 賬簿) of right and wrong to ensure that moral justice is meted out in due course.[26] One might argue that these denizens of the beyond maintain a kind of order in *Honglou meng*: they punish Baoyu for his attachment by "sentencing" him to a life in the Red Dust of mortal existence. Yet since his initial attachment is conceived in innocence and is essentially selfless, this result seems unjust, as inappropriate for its sorrowful consequences as the comic sufferings of the fledgling warrior Qin Shubao. That the Buddhist and the Taoist figures of *Honglou meng's* celestial realm are only agents of inscrutable destiny and not acting in their own right further problematizes the moral uprightness of that higher order.

Thus the actual reader might well sympathize with *Honglou meng's* more "realistic" characters, rejecting this frame story and the fate thereby imposed on Baoyu and Daiyu. One must conclude that the novel parodies earlier literary conventions of how to represent divine justice in narrative. Moreover, a reading of this sort is founded on the proposition that the novel rejects, through this parody, all earlier assertions that divine justice or cosmic moral order exists in any meaningful way. Conversely, reading the frame story as "true", and considering the "enlightening" effect that reading the Stone's inscription had on Kongkong Daoren as a representation of how we actual readers are to apprehend the text still involves nearly the same conclusions. That is, if we see, through the magnificent welter of detail in this work, an endorsement of the basic Buddhist truth that all human attachments lead ultimately to suffering, we must accept the implications of the radical departure of the text from commonplace Confucianism to another philosophical paradigm: earlier novels are thus parodied (they were pedestrian and mechanical in their application of "fate" and the supernatural) and their conventions are subverted. This is despite the observation at the end of the novel by a character given the novelist's name that the work has no value other than as mere diversion, an element to be considered the last in a lengthy series, each of which seems to mean the opposite of what it says.[27]

Furthermore, for a Qing period intellectual trained in the Confucian canon for government service (the goal toward which all education was directed) to reject all Confucian definitions of moral self-expression through moral action in society and thus to deny the ability to make one's own fate through that action — the course followed by Jia Baoyu in *Honglou meng* — is a powerful subversion of the entire Confucian mindset. But one should also observe that even detachment from worldly ties, in the basic Mahayana Buddhist sense, is also of dubious value: it necessitates that all "enlightened" characters (Zhen Shiyin 甄士隱, Jia Yucun 賈雨村, Jia Baoyu) abandon their families and turn away from human society altogether. Zhen Shiyin achieves some degree of tranquility, but the celestial stone Baoyu feels remorse and loss while Jia Yucun ultimately lapses into a state of lethargy and incomprehensibility — rather like Baoyu when his jade, his *tongling* 通靈 or "spiritual understanding" — is lost. In *Honglou meng* the emotional and spiritual release brought by Buddhist enlightenment is presented as a distinctly unattractive alternative to suffering in the "real" world. Only Zhen Shiyin achieves any lasting contentment. By the end of chapter 120 when the character named Cao Xueqin 曹雪芹 chides him, even Kongkong Daoren appears a gullible fool to have been so "enlightened" by this philosophically thin tale; he thereby becomes a parody of the wise Buddhists in chapter 19 of *Xiyou ji* and in other works, and problematic as an "ideal reader" of this text. Through him and other Buddhist figures in *Honglou meng*, the novel exposes the shortcomings of the conventional Buddhist values they seemingly represent. Earlier novelists regularly used prefaces to argue for the moral efficacy of didactic fiction; here the "novelist" appears at the end of his novel to deny all moral seriousness therein, declaring the work mere light entertainment. Consequently, *Honglou meng* intertextually parodies other writers' ostensible concern for the edifying effect of reading fiction while simultaneously subverting the reliability of the characters presented as reader and author of the text. Such an extremely self-conscious manipulation of the text "from within" can only alert the actual reader to read carefully, looking either for meaning expressed unconventionally or for unconventional realms of meaning.

While the events in the Jia family household that produce unexpected results are too numerous to mention, the abiding sense of tragic irony that pervades the work is of central importance to its interpretation. "Prophecy" often is misleading; other incongruities abound. The Daguan Yuan 大觀園 (the "Grand View Garden"), for all its supposed purity, is built on the site where the men of the family frequently had engaged in debauchery. The "nun" in residence there, Miaoyu 妙玉, has never formally taken the tonsure; furthermore, she is ultimately undone by lusty thoughts which may or may not produce a prophetic dream — the text is unclear about her physical fate. Excesses go unpunished and goodness is poorly rewarded — the youthful widowhood visited upon Shi Xiangyun and Li Wan 李紈 (despite the limited success of the latter's son in the civil service examinations) are examples. If *Sanguo yanyi, Sui Tang yanyi*, and other historical novels project order and balance in a moral universe, *Honglou meng* does just the opposite: there is no dependable order in society; moral balance is infrequently, if ever, effected by the higher powers. The novel is not structured to simulate moral balance; by implication, the fictional world of the novel has no final, overarching moral structure. The bulk of its chapters narrate the daily activities of its youthful protagonists; they are filled with details of social life of the author's time. However, since the cosmic framework behind them is neither predictable nor moral, as a mirror of quotidian reality *Honglou meng* approaches subversion of the sense of moral order dominating the social context in which the novel appeared.

In this regard it is worth repeating the well-known fact that the novelist Cao Xueqin spent years rewriting his masterpiece. Biographical references scattered throughout the commentaries have been painstakingly pieced together; they reveal a process of textual production that was neither linear nor continuous. Cao wrote back and forth, writing and rewriting, removing some — but not all — vestiges of events from early versions that were modified in later recensions. His aim and style of work might become more comprehensible if viewed from this perspective: it is likely that Cao Xueqin did not intend that all details of his novel would fit "neatly" together. Without burying oneself in the morass of the intentional fallacy, a few speculations seem justified by the direction of the novel's development in China.

In view of the increasing degree of individual self-expression in Qing period novels,[28] it is not unreasonable to expect unorthodox or unconventional sentiments in *Honglou meng*, the undisputed masterpiece of the period. Biographical details enforce the testimony of "reader" (Kongkong Daoren) and "author" (Cao Xueqin) in the first and final chapters; they suggest strongly that Cao strived throughout the last years of his life to *de*stabilize his text — to create *more* logical inconsistencies, *more* moral paradoxes, as his way of revealing his fundamental skepticism about the moral validity of didactic elements in popular fiction and even in conventional world-views of his time. His work ultimately, then, reflects the dicta with which I began this exploration: when his family was cashiered in 1728, Cao Xueqin was deprived of any place in the political realm that bore the mantle of Confucian moral superiority; assertion of his own moral sense might necessarily involve subverting that system which had found his family wanting. His dilemma was profound: to perform as a good Confucian when the Way did not prevail necessitated either complete withdrawal from society (which to some Cao seems to have done, subsisting meagerly on income from his painting) or social engagement of an influential sort. Other writers previous to *Honglou meng* had condemned the shortcomings of the system as practised in their time (in fact, this became the conventional novelistic stance for literati writers and seemingly constituted, in their minds, engagement with political issues); instead Cao questioned that system at its logical core, by destabilizing all predictability of rewards and punishments on the basis of moral action. By choosing the latter alternative, it might be said that Cao Xueqin realized most fully the tendency in the developing novel to subvert literary conventions on the surface while, by implication, expressing a radical lack of faith in the Confucian moral order as a whole.

In sum, by focusing on elements of ideology related to the core conception of a moral universe, a survey of selected Ming and Qing novels reveals an increasing degree of destabilization of moral order through the unpredictable consequences of the protagonists' moral actions. In this way, paradoxical rewards for vice and punishment for virtue serve to break the mold of earlier narratives, both historical and fictional. Such paradoxes also threaten the very basis of the traditional Chinese world-view when, in the hands of a consummate novelist, the lives of fictional characters reach a level of contingency that is commensurate with later western European realism — and that is no longer compatible with traditional beliefs that goodness and order can or will triumph in human society.

Notes

1. Rachel Blau DuPlessis, *Writing Beyond the Ending* (Bloomington: Indiana University Press, 1985), p. 34.
2. See Robert E. Hegel, *The Novel in Seventeenth-Century China* (New York: Columbia University Press, 1981), especially chapters 3 and 4; Ellen Widmer, *Margins of Utopia* (Cambridge: Harvard University Press, 1987), especially chapter 3; Paul Ropp, *Dissent in Early Modern China* (Ann Arbor: University of Michigan Press, 1981), etc. Comments by Professors Wang Ch'iu-kuei, Andrew H. Plaks, and Leo O. Lee have been especially important in helping me to clarify my thinking on these points.
3. See, for example, John B. Henderson, *The Development and Decline of Chinese Cosmology* (New York: Columbia University Press, 1984), especially chapter 7; Benjamin A. Elman, *From Philosophy to Philology: Intellectual and Social Aspects of Change in Late Imperial China* (Cambridge: Harvard University Press, 1984), etc.
4. John C. Y. Wang, "Early Chinese Narrative: The *Tso-chuan* as Example", *Chinese Narrative: Critical and Theoretical Essays*, edited by Andrew H. Plaks (Princeton: Princeton University Press, 1977), pp. 14–16. For observations on the moral nature of the universe in traditional Chinese ideology, see Frederick W. Mote, *Intellectual Foundations of China* (New York: Knopf, 1989), 2nd ed., chapter 3, especially pp. 39–40; Daniel L. Overmeyer, *Religions of China* (New York: Harper & Row, 1986), especially pp. 83–85; Laurence G. Thompson, *Chinese Religion: An Introduction* (4th ed., Belmont, California: Wadsworth, 1989), pp. 12, 77–83, 105–111. Especially given the involvement of various novelists in political and social movements of their time, I would dispute this assertion made by Andrew H. Plaks in his "Towards a Critical Theory of Chinese Narrative", *Chinese Narrative*, p. 349: "... it may be said that the presence in Chinese narrative of patterns of order and balance, reward and retribution, the general confiction of an inherent moral order in the workings of the universe, function more often as formal aesthetic features than as thematic points of doctrine". That is, while such moralistic patterns are in fact conventional in Chinese narrative, they nonetheless reflect values that have persisted in Chinese society for millenia, specifically the hope — if not the conviction — that theirs is a moral universe in which justice ultimately reigns.
5. Wing-tsit Chan (trans. & comp.), *A Source Book in Chinese Philosophy* (Princeton: Princeton University Press, 1963), pp. 86–87.
6. *Lun yu* 論語 , 8:13; Confucius, *The Analects*, translated by D. C. Lau (Hong Kong: The Chinese University Press, 1983), p. 73.
7. Several of my earlier studies focus on this and other novels in which Qin Shubao figures as an important character; see especially my *Novel*. The

present essay should be considered as a supplement to them; my reading through the years has placed the seventeenth-century novels in ever broader contexts, hence the development of my understanding of their significance.

8. On Mencius' conception of the basic goodness of human nature, see Chan, pp. 49–51; Mote, pp. 49–53; Donald J. Munro, *The Concept of Man in Early China* (Stanford: Stanford University Press, 1969), discusses the relationship between man and nature in Confucian thought on pp. 26–48.

9. Andrew H. Plaks discusses *yi* 義 as personal honour in his *Four Masterworks of the Ming Novel* (Princeton: Princeton University Press, 1987), see pp. 344ff, 413ff. Notice that *yi* has positive associations in *Shuihu zhuan* and negative ones in *Sanguo yanyi* 三國演義.

10. This equation happens at the verbal level: *yi* denotes both the sense of personal honour or altruism of the knight-errant and a general moral sense to Mencius. See Munro, chapter 3, especially pp. 75–80; see pp. 72–73 for Munro's discussion of Mencius' conception of human nature.

11. Andrew H. Plaks, *Four Masterworks*, p. 489, notes the seriousness with which *Sanguo yanyi* commentators, especially Mao Zonggang 毛宗崗 (b. ca. 1630), have treated moral dilemmas created by conflicting standards or mutually exclusive claims, such as those of family and of the state. The significance of Qin Shubao's plight lies not in his experience of conflicting moral paradigms but in the misfortunes he suffers when he makes the "right" moral choice, to serve the state ostensibly for the greater harmony within society.

12. Yuan Yuling, *Sui shi yiwen* (Taipei: Youshi wenhua shiye gongsi, 1975), p. 1.

13. See Andrew H. Plaks, *Four Masterworks*, pp. 384–386, 392–393, 398–399; see also my review of this book in *Harvard Journal of Asiatic Studies*, Vol. 50, No. 1 (1990), especially pp. 349–351.

14. "Time and Narrative in *A la recherche du temps perdu*", *Aspects of Narrative*, edited by J. Hillis Miller (1971), reprinted in *Essentials of the Theory of Fiction*, edited by Michael Hoffman and Patrick Murphy (Durham: Duke University Press, 1988), p. 278.

15. Pei-yi Wu observes a similar fascination with events "too trivial or too improbable" for the historians in seventeenth-century autobiographical writing; see *The Confucian's Progress* (Princeton: Princeton University Press, 1990), p. 164.

16. For a discussion of Confucian didacticism and the values implicit in historiographical texts, see E. G. Pulleyblank, "The Historiographical Tradition", *The Legacy of China*, edited by Raymond Dawson (Oxford: Clarendon Press, 1964), pp. 144–146, 150, 153, 160–161.

17. See prefaces to such works, of which those attached to the earliest extant edition of *Sanguo yanyi* are typical. There Jiang Daqi 蔣大器 using the pen-name Yongyuzi 庸愚子 writes:

The loyalty of Chu-ko Liang 諸葛亮 [Zhuge Liang] shone like the sun and the stars ... then there is the righteousness of Kuan Yu 關羽 [Guan Yu] and Chang Fei 張飛 [Zhang Fei] which was also superlative. As for other examples of success and failure, they are all exhibited clearly [in this text], both the fragrant and the foul, the worthy and the unworthy. "Sanguo zhi tongsu yanyi xu" 三國志通俗演義序, *Sanguo yanyi ziliao hui bian* 三國演義資料匯編, edited by Zhu Yixuan 朱一玄 and Liu Yuzhen 劉毓枕 (Tianjin: Baihua wenyi, 1983), p. 270; translated by Anne E. McLaren in her "Chantefables and the Textual Evolution of the *San-kuo chih yen-i*", *T'oung Pao* 通報 71, 4–5(1985), p. 67, note 96.

18. *The Art of the Novel* (New York: Grove, 1988), p. 37.

19. For the social status of novelists in general, see Hegel, *Novel*, chapter 1, and Plaks, *Four Masterworks*, chapter 1.

20. Hegel, *Novel*, pp. 151–152. The most accessible description of the examination system is Ichisada Miyazaki, *China's Examination Hall: The Civil Service Examinations of Imperial China*, translated by Conrad Schirokauer (1963; New Haven: Yale University Press, 1981).

21. "The Historical Interpretation of Literature" (1938), quoted in Hoffman and Murphy, p. 83.

22. Cao Xueqin, *The Story of the Stone*, Vol. 1 (New York: Penguin, 1973), p. 529.

23. See George Levine, "Realism Reconsidered", *The Theory of the Novel: New Essays*, edited by John Halperin (New York: Oxford University Press, 1974), pp. 236–237.

24. See Kermode, "Literary Fiction and Reality", *The Sense of an Ending: Studies in the Theory of Fiction* (New York: Oxford University Press, 1967), pp. 127–152; he uses this term on p. 130.

25. This point is central to the cosmological criticism that developed among late Ming and early Qing period intellectuals, according to Henderson, pp. 137–173. Henderson notes, p. 170, an exchange between Shi Xiangyun 史湘雲 and her maid in which the maid ridicules the whole notion of correlative cosmology, the *yin/yang* duality in particular. See Cao Xueqin, *The Story of the Stone*, Vol. 2 (New York: Penguin, 1977), pp. 121–124, from chapter 31.

26. See Hegel, *Novel*, chapter 4, especially pp. 107–111.

27. No commentator has ever failed to be affected by the couplet on the entry to Taixu Huanjing (The Land of Illusion) in chapter 1: "Truth becomes fiction when the fiction's true; Real becomes not-real where the unreal's real" (假作真時真亦假，無爲有處有還無), Cao Xueqin, *The Story of the Stone*, Vol. 1, p. 55.

28. See Andrew H. Plaks, "Full-length *hsiao-shuo* and the Western Novel: A Generic Reappraisal", *New Asia Academic Bulletin*, 1(1978), pp. 163–176; and Hegel, *Novel*, pp. 43–51. In his *Four Masterworks*, Plaks takes great pains to demonstrate the elaborate structures that appear in ten chapter

segments of the works he discusses, structures particularly visible when he reads those texts in reverse chronological order. While admittedly *Honglou meng* parallels to some extent the structure of *Jin Ping Mei*, such structuring seems to have more meaning *within* the text, as a means to exemplify the self-consciousness with which the novelist has written. Such structuring, to my mind, reflects conventions of literati novel writing rather than projecting any predictability, even comprehensibility, about events in the novel's human realm that can be abstracted as referring to the world *outside* the text, to its social context.

7

Tragedy or Travesty? Perspectives on Langxian's "The Siege of Yangzhou"

Ellen Widmer

"Jiangdu shi xiaofu tushen" 江都市孝婦屠身(hereafter "The Siege of Yangzhou"), eleventh in the fourteen-story collection *Shi dian tou* 石點頭 (The Rocks Nod Their Heads) strikes the modern reader as a travesty of morality. The plot revolves around a couple engaged in business who have travelled from their home town of Hongzhou 洪州 (near Nanchang 南昌) to a Yangzhou under seige in the Bi Shiduo 畢師鐸 uprising, just after the An Lushan 安祿山 (?–757) Rebellion. War has caused the husband, Zhou Di 周廸, to fail at business, which he normally carries out in Xiangyang 襄陽, some distance from his home town. He and his wife, Second Sister Zong 宗二娘, are both in their late thirties. They are still childless. Because of this, his mother suggests that the husband and wife travel together on business. The mother herself had been quite elderly when she gave birth to Zhou Di, and she feels the couple ought not to stay apart, although she has relied on her daughter-in-law to take care of her for years. The couple strenuously object to the mother-in-law's suggestion, whereupon she threatens suicide. She then finds an unattached female relative to live with her, obviating the need for the daughter-in-law to stay home. She also brings up the daughter-in-law's fine education, suggesting that it might be useful for Zhou Di to have a clerk and assistant on the road. Finally, she gives them her coffin money to support them on their journey back to Xiangyang.

In Xiangyang, their money is stolen by the son of Zhou Di's former landlady, a man who has many gambling debts. They are forced to take jobs as assistants to a Huizhou 徽州 salt merchant, who happens to be in the Xiangyang area, but who has a shop in Yangzhou, to which they soon move with the merchant. The merchant eventually leaves town as the city of Yangzhou is closed off in a skirmish between competing armies. Normal sources of food become unavailable in the city, and butchers begin to sell human flesh instead. In the course of these events, Zhou Di and his wife run out of money and supplies. Their only recourse is to leave town once conditions improve, but even that will be a problem because of their total lack of funds. While her husband blubbers helplessly, Zhou Di's wife works out a plan of selling herself to the butcher, so her husband can return home alone to his mother. Their interaction at this moment goes as follows:

> Zhou Di said, " All mother wanted was that the two of us would do business for a year or two, make a small profit, and have a child. Who would have thought that today we'd be on the brink of death in this place. It's almost as though she has done both of us in." When he finished talking he burst into tears. Second Sister Zong for her part sneered and said, "You can cry until tomorrow or the next day, it still won't bring both of us home. Remember the story of Zuo Botao and Yang Jiaoai.[1] They were freezing and starving, but in the end only one died and the other was rescued. Now they are killing people and selling them for meat in the market. One can earn a few strings of cash this way. Either you sell me and use the money to go home and care for your mother, or I'll sell you and use the money to go home and care for my mother-in-law. Think about it carefully. I'll do whatever you say."[2]

As her husband is terrified by the idea of self-sacrifice, Second Sister Zong goes to negotiate with the butcher. She conceals her decision from her husband by pretending she has arranged to sell him, not herself. Zhou Di cries and equivocates at what she tells him, but after securing a high price from the butcher, she marches bravely off to meet her fate. Her last hours are described in some detail:

> Dear Reader, when Zhou Di mentions death he is filled with fear. When Second Sister Zong speaks of being killed she hardly bats an eye. You can see that a woman of virtuous nature is actually superior to a weak male.
>
> Second Sister Zong thereupon went to the door of [their landlord's] shop and spoke to the owner: "My husband and I are from Hongzhou. We want to go home but we have absolutely no money. I would like to sell myself on the market, so my husband will have travel money, also so we can clear the rent with you. May I trouble you to go to the market with me and help negotiate a price?" By this time, the practice of selling people for food was commonplace, and no one thought anything of it. The shop owner agreed, saying, "I'd be glad to." So he went with Second Sister Zong to the [Yangzhou] market. They walked into the shop of a butcher with whom he

was acquainted. The shop had just that day sold everything out and had nothing more to sell. Seeing that Second Sister Zong, though not plump, was not thin, the butcher agreed at once to pay three strings of cash. Second Sister Zong thought this was too little, and bargained the price up to four strings. The butcher took out the money and gave it to the shop owner, then asked Second Sister Zong to come inside with him. Second Sister Zong said, "The truth is that my husband could not bear to come here with me and is waiting in the house. Let me go give him this money; I'll come right back. If you don't trust me, you can have someone accompany me." The butcher was unwilling but the shop owner gave his guarantee, and the butcher finally agreed. Second Sister Zong took the four strings of cash home and put them on the table, saying, "This is the money your mother will get for selling her son. Please go to the market, and I will use this as travel money to return home and see my mother-in-law." Zhou Di was completely disconcerted. His face turned ashen. He wanted to answer, but his voice caught in his throat. He arched his neck forward three or four times, but he could not spit out a single word. Tears the size of beans poured out. Second Sister Zong took one look at him, smiled again and said, "This will never do. I will cancel the deal." She turned and walked speedily over to the butcher's house and said to him, "I will die in a moment, but first give me some water so that I can clean myself. I also need to pay my respects to my mother and father and my in-laws. After that I shall be ready to die." The butcher thought her a real pedant. He laughed and said, "So, a stickler for cleanliness!" He led her inside. She filled a tub with water, took a bath, put her clothes back on, then went outside. She asked for a piece of white paper, picked up the pen with which accounts were kept, and wrote a formal eulogy for herself. When she was finished, she went out on the street and faced in the direction of Hongzhou. She bowed four times and knelt on the ground. Unrolling the paper, she read the eulogy. The butcher, the neighbours, and some passersby gathered around to watch. She recited unhurridly in a strong voice:

"Heaven has not favoured me, for I was born under an unlucky star. At an early age I married into the Zhou family. My father-in-law died first, and I looked to my mother-in-law for guidance. I was deeply afraid of neglecting my wifely duties and worked from dawn to dusk. Unfortunately, the times were bad, and there was constant war. I was distressed at the country's predicament and at our family's collapse. My mother-in-law ordered us to go into business, which proved to be entirely profitless. I lived temporarily in Yangzhou where bandit soldiers surrounded the city. Battle followed upon battle, and crops failed. Sparrows and rats were hunted for food, and grain and firewood became as precious as jade and cinnabar. As death is imminent, I have no regrets at giving up my life. The money I get will enable my husband to travel a thousand *li* so he can see his family. If he could see his mother, as her daughter-in-law I would die without regret. I pray to glorious Heaven: May my mother-in-law live on indefinitely, and I wish my husband a prosperous life. May he marry again happily and have a lovely child. Alas, alas, to have such a fate, but I meet it calmly, as Heaven is my witness. When the war is over, may all who died in battle be spared the pain of reincarnation."

When she had finished reading, she again bowed four times then turned to leave. Because she spoke a local dialect, no one understood her. Second Sister Zong went into the shop and gave the piece of paper to the butcher, saying: "My husband will certainly come by to ask about me. Please be so good as to give this to him. Ask him to go home at once, and tell him not to miss me." The butcher said, "I will do as you say." He took the piece of paper and put it aside. When the crowd heard this they said, "Oh, her husband sold her to be killed." Then they dispersed. Second Sister Zong thereupon removed her clothes and went into the slaughter room. Her face did not change colour. The butcher, though he felt sympathetic, had paid out four strings of cash and wanted to get his money's worth. He controlled his emotion and resolutely gave her a death blow with his hand, then opened the chest cavity and eviscerated her as one would slaughter a pig or a sheep. In a moment's time the virtuous and filial Second Sister Zong had been rendered into meat on the counter. As a poem attests:

> The couple's business activities were designed to support their mother.
> What were they to do when they encountered disaster?
> Unfortunately a jade was destroyed in a Yangzhou market.
> Will her spirit make it back to Hongzhou?

The populace of Yangzhou had meanwhile been warned by a matching, Heaven-sent poem against consuming this flesh, and those who did so promptly died. The area was beset with thunder and other unusual weather, and the grass and trees withered. In the end, the husband was spirited home on a magic horse, supplied to him by a descendant of Qu Yuan 屈原 (340?–278 B.C.); Second Sister Zong bid her mother-in-law farewell in a dream; and the two remaining family members lived very long lives, Zhou Di until age 110 and his mother until age 130.[3] Second Sister Zong, meanwhile, became an immortal, specializing in deciding whether daughters-in-law would go to Heaven or Hell, the choice depending on how well they had served their parents-in-law.

The rhetoric of "The Siege of Yangzhou" gives the strong impression that Second Sister Zong's self-sacrifice should be regarded as praiseworthy. Although the story raises doubts about the decision which led her to accompany her husband on his business travels, it does not blame her for this decision, which she had argued against most strenuously. As later developments reveal, her proposed solution to the problem of the couple's childlessness — that the husband find a second wife in the vicinity of his business while she stay at home with her mother-in-law — is shown to have been the correct course of action. For a variety of reasons, her mother-in-law had resisted this suggestion, and her husband, who was not a strong person, had agreed with his mother. Second Sister Zong's self-sacrifice, then, is all the more regretable because if her good judgment had been properly recognized, it would have averted the need for heroic self-sacrifice.

In contrast to the author's approval for Second Sister Zong's desperate action, readers today may view the story as a good example of what Lu Xun 魯迅 (1881–1936) had in mind in "A Madman's Diary" (狂人日記) when he talked of Confucianism "eating people". So alienated have Chinese editors been by the story's manifest ethic that "The Siege of Yangzhou" is omitted from most twentieth-century editions of *Shi dian tou*.[4]

My reasons for taking it more seriously are, first, that it offers a good opportunity to understand the "mentality"[5] through which such an act of self-sacrifice could be regarded as virtuous. Second, Patrick Hanan's work now provides a basis on which to connect this story to a specific author, Langxian 浪仙. To set this story in the context of Langxian's other fiction gives us deeper insight into Second Sister Zong's patterns of thinking.[6] Third, modern deconstructive criticism helps alert us to certain ways in which this work of literature may have subverted its own manifest purposes,[7] for example, in the apparent tension between Second Sister Zong's powerful heroism, which accentuates her husband's weakness, and the paradigm of shrewish wife/henpecked husband which Langxian uses in other connections and which seems to hover in the background here.[8] A still more disturbing chink in the story's moral armour is found in the form of the gaze and knife of the butcher, which address the heroine's physical qualities. Thus, to the butcher, she is a body, neither fat nor thin, and eventually a naked body, despite all the fuss about keeping that body clean. At this point the close analogy between selling flesh as meat and in prostitution threatens to rise to the surface, though it never overtly crosses the narrator's or the heroine's mind. The heroine's utter unawareness of this possibility contributes to her heroic stature, but in so doing it raises yet another interpretative problem, that her learning may have made her pedantic rather than heroic. Lying at the heart of this inquiry is the question of whether these subversive overtones were intended by the author, and if so what they mean.

The Thinking behind the Story

Two major patterns of thinking in seventeenth-century China are important as background to "The Siege of Yangzhou". One concerns fleshly sacrifice; the other has to do with new developments in women's literacy and reading.

The first subject is usefully introduced via Jonathan Chaves' 1986 article "Moral Action in the Poetry of Wu Chia-chi (1618–1684)".[9] There Chaves discusses the practice of flesh slicing (*ge rou* 割肉 or *ge gu* 割股), by which filial children presented ailing parents with portions of their flesh as a means of curing their illnesses. Unlike works which inveigh against this practice, Chaves' article illuminates the state of mind under which filial children might undertake such a sacrifice and shows why a moralist might support it. According to Chaves, Wu Jiaji 吳嘉紀 was distressed at the decline of familiar Confucian virtues and blamed this decline for the collapse of the Ming. His remedy was to look for examples of loyalty, filial piety and similar virtues among the common people, both to show that such virtues were still alive and to use them to admonish less principled people of high status. Among the cases of virtue he celebrated in his poetry were several involving flesh slicing. According to Chaves, Wu's support for this kind of sacrifice was received quite ambivalently by his contemporaries, even those who were close to him. In Chaves' opinion, mainstream views from at least the Tang dynasty on were that such sacrifices were wrong. This was because they went against the Confucian injunction to keep one's body whole for the sake of one's parents. Any sacrifice of flesh on behalf of one's parents could only be regarded as a misguided kind of piety, or *bi xiao* 鄙孝, in the words of Pi Rixiu 皮日休 (833–883).[10]

Wu's poems are only one of many sources that depict flesh slicing in a positive light. Others include local histories and didactic literature for women and children.[11] All make it clear that flesh slicing is approved of only when it follows certain rules: First, the direction of sacrifice is always from the person of lower status to the person of higher status. Almost always the person who sacrifices flesh is a son, daughter, or daughter-in-law of the person on whose behalf the sacrifice is made. There are examples of faithful servants who perform this act for their masters, but the vast majority of cases involve blood relatives or relatives by marriage. Second, the person receiving the sacrifice must be seriously ill. Occasionally, a doctor informs the would-be sacrificer that thigh slicing is the only remedy for the sick parent. At other times, the news that sacrifice is the only remedy is conveyed through dreams and other means.[12] Whichever the case, the reader is left with the impression that no other method will save the parent. Third, the parent receiving the sacrifice must not know what is going on. In one of Wu Jiaji's most memorable examples, the filial daughter who performs the sacrifice uses a blunt knife because she is afraid that her father might suspect what was about to happen if he heard a knife being sharpened. (Usually the fleshly sacrifice is cooked in a broth and fed to the parent, but it can also be made into a salve and applied to a wound.) Fourth, the sacrifice must be of something the sacrificer could, in theory, survive without. One can find examples of seemingly vital organs like hearts, brains and livers being sacrificed,[13] but even so, the assumption is that the person making the sacrifice will survive. Fifth, secrecy about what has happened is preserved until someone happens to notice a scar on the sacrificer's body. The sacrificer herself must make no attempt to advertise what has been done. Sixth, Heaven is said to be moved by the sacrifice, and it rewards both donor and recipient with long life, as well as with miraculous absence of pain.

In attempting to fathom the reason that made such deeds seem noble, one must conceive of such acts not in terms of cannibalism but as something more saintly, like self-immolation, for in literature celebrating these practices the sacrifice is voluntary and the recipient does not know what he or she has received.

The exact mechanism by which flesh slicing helps the sick or injured parent is not entirely clear in Wu Jiaji's work and in other literature. In some cases, the flesh is said to have medicinal value. At other times, recovery appears to take place through a more indirect process: Heaven is so moved by the child's sacrifice that it decides to restore the parent's health. This is especially true in popular narratives. There even if a child pleads to have his or her allotted span of years shortened so they can be added to the parent's, in practice both usually enjoy long lives. In this case, the Confucian injunction about keeping one's body intact for one's parents' sake becomes quite irrelevant. According to the logic of this literature, as long as such sacrifice is the only way to cure the parent, the path of virtue is quite clear.

This is not to say that one cannot find violations of Wu Jiaji's implicit rules in much of the literature on the subject. Less idealized accounts of fleshly sacrifice, such as those in local histories, often mention the deaths of one or another or both parties, and it is quite clear that donors of flesh were sometimes pressed into performing a sacrifice by the person who received it.[14] Yet when this practice is presented at its most idealized, it can probably stand comparison with accepted medical practices of today, like the organ transplant. Setting aside the question of efficacy, one could argue that except for the direction of the donation — necessarily from child to parent — which offers a contrast with modern medicine, there are at least three similarities: the rule that such a step be taken only when no other recourse is available; that it be of a part of the body which the donor could survive without; and the preference for a close physical kinship between donor and recipient. Yet however one might strain to put a good face on this practice, a number of Chinese emperors considered fleshly sacrifice barbaric. Ming Taizu 明太祖 (朱元璋, 1328–1398) spoke out against it early in his reign and the Qing code refused to grant such acts any special merit from 1729 on.[15] The great sixteenth century medical writer Li Shizhen 李時珍 (1518–1593) also spoke out against flesh-slicing, not so much on medical grounds but because of its violation of other Confucian norms.[16] However, the practice, like certain other forms of self-destruction, appears to have been on the increase toward the end of the Ming.[17]

"The Siege of Yangzhou" begins to make somewhat more sense when considered against this background. Although flesh *slicing* is not specifically at issue in this story, and although inadvertent flesh-eating was actually severely punished, the ethos of sacrificing one's body to help a parent or parent-in-law makes one good way to account for this story's approval of Second Sister Zong's virtuous deed. Second Sister Zong's effort to conceal her sacrifice from her husband is also consistent with the rules previously described. The fact that she cannot survive her act of self-immolation would have moved it beyond the boundaries of what Wu Jiaji found praiseworthy. Nevertheless, her appearance in her mother-in-law's dream, her commemoration in a monument, and the miracles which take place after she dies belong to the literary tradition in which Heaven rewards sacrifices of this kind.[18]

The other major pattern of thinking to be brought in as background relates to female readership. This subject may be encapsulated with the help of Joanna Handlin-Smith's article "Lü Kun's New Audience: The Influence of Women's Literacy on Sixteenth-Century Thought".[19] Here Handlin-Smith looks at a thinker who predates Wu Jiaji by about one hundred years, which also means that he wrote before the change of dynasty, not after it. Lü Kun 呂坤 (1536–1618) is thus unconcerned with what caused the Ming to fall, though he is similarly obsessed with finding virtue in unlikely places as a way of shoring up a degenerate age. One of Lü's preoccupations is to defend against threats posed by increasing commercialization.[20] Lü writes in the face of commerce's seductions, hoping to cultivate female readers in whom the appeal of virtue is stronger still. His *Gui fan* 閨範 (preface 1590; hereafter *Regulations for the Women's Quarters*) is interesting in this connection, for it is addressed to a female readership not only from wealthy households, but also including women from humbler classes.[21]

Recent research on upper class women and courtesans can be brought in to broaden this picture, for it fills in some details about the highly educated woman whose ranks were increasing by the end of the Ming.[22] The world of courtesans was directly affected by late-Ming prosperity, which probably also augmented their literacy, in that it led to advances in publishing. In the case of gentry woman, their numbers may not have been increased by commercial expansion, but they too must have benefited from the greater availability of reading matter. Among the gentry, reading matter for women could include "frivolous" literature, as well as moral exempla; and poetry reading and writing might be undertaken partly for pleasure as well as for edification. However, it is edifying reading that concerns us here.

Like the classic *Lienü zhuan* 烈女傳 (Biographies of Virtuous Women), Lü's *Regulations for the Women's Quarters* presents examples of female moral paragons, most of whom display their virtues on behalf of husbands, parents, and parents-in-law. In contrast to that classic, *Regulations for the Woman's Quarters* tries to reduce idealized moral standards to more manageable form. Handlin-Smith cites one example in which Lü counsels women not to stay in a burning house as a way of demonstrating one's modesty — under such circumstances, the sensible thing would be to step outside.[23]

Lü's work is motivated partly by anxiety about the growing idleness of women, and his rules were often suggestions about how women might turn their minds to something more edifying than jewellery and clothing. One of his most persistent messages is that literate women need education, both to improve their minds in a general sense and to develop self-reliance.[24] More explicitly than Wu Jiaji, Lü seems willing to assert that in certain cases, women's behaviour could be superior to men's.[25] For Lü Kun, as for Wu Jiaji, female virtue did not have to depend on high social status, and he gives examples of beggars who acquitted themselves especially well. Alternatively, he did not believe that all highly literate women were paragons of good behaviour. On the whole, however, he believed that properly guided reading could improve a woman's mind.

As with Wu Jiaji, Lü Kun's work had its detractors, though in somewhat different quarters. Where Wu's emphasis on flesh slicers struck many as a perversion of Confucianism, Lü's virtuous women readers provoked fears that literate women might threaten existing hierarchies. Handlin-Smith mentions in this connection that Feng Menglong 馮夢龍 (1574–1646) was ambivalent about women's literary, moral, and other qualities. Though he believed that "only the virtuous man is talented; only the untalented woman is virtuous",[26] his collections of vernacular stories often revolve around interesting and resourceful women, and in some of them the heroines can read.

Lü Kun's *Regulations for the Women's Quarters* offers points of overlap and of contrast with the ethical assumptions of "The Siege of Yangzhou". We have already observed that Second Sister Zong's moral superiority to her husband is consonant with Lü Kun's views on the way virtuous women could prop up less virtuous male counterparts. Lü's views also come to mind in connection with an introductory comment to "The Siege of Yangzhou", which reads as follows:

> As for [illiterate] women, their natures are petty, their knowledge is small. They sit stupidly at home, spending most of their time with female relatives, talking over what clothes they are making, what jewellery they are wearing, where to go to visit relatives, call on family, burn incense or honour the dead, all the while thinking themselves most virtuous and intelligent. Yet they might as well be talking about firewood, rice, oil, salt, soy, vinegar and tea, so little do they know of Ti Ying 緹縈 saving her father or Fifth Daughter Zhao 趙五娘 practising filial piety.[27]

These comments are not noticeably different in tone from certain remarks of Lü's, about high- and low-class women who think only about jewellery and food.[28] Indeed, Lü's remarks could well have been one source from which the opening generalities of "The Siege of Yangzhou" were drawn. In addition, Second Sister Zong is literate, virtuous and of good family — exactly the kind of woman whom Lü Kun hoped to cultivate with his writings. Although she lived in the ninth, not the sixteenth century, and although her sharp commercial instincts might not have pleased him, her general outlines are more or less those of the female reader he had in mind. We will soon have occasion to compare the portrait of Second

Sister Zong in "The Siege of Yangzhou" with that in earlier versions of this story. Suffice it now to mention that the heroine is never said to be a reader in these versions, nor is any mention made of her Confucian upbringing. This is certainly not to say that Lü Kun would have approved of Second Sister Zong's ultimate sacrifice. If it could be called a resourceful response to desperate circumstances, it was hardly the kind of life-affirming manoeuverability that Lü Kun was trying to inspire. Lü's common sense would probably have prevented him from turning to such an example in any case, even if Second Sister Zong did have certain qualities that he admired. The extreme nature of the central episode aside, however, the story's emphasis on piety and female self-sacrifice, as well as its demonstration of quick, decisive action under trying circumstances seem more comprehensible in the light of Lü Kun's views.

In the final analysis, the issues of fleshly sacrifice and female reading turn out to be surprisingly closely intertwined. Lü Kun, for all the moderation of his appeal to female readers, was not totally opposed to flesh-slicing and other acts of filial devotion, as long as they were truly called for by parental illness and not undertaken for show. In his commentary on one biography featuring such practices, he explains that the sages would not have advocated them but that he included this example in his household rules because of its fine example of daughterly solicitude.[29] Conversely, in other literature such as local histories, discussions of widow suicide commonly assume either that the "accomplishment" was the result of "classical learning" or that it was wonderful to find a woman who lacked such learning proving her mettle in this way.[30]

"The Siege of Yangzhou" in the Light of Langxian's Other Writing

Broad cultural discussions give one kind of insight into Second Sister Zong's behaviour, but the most immediate context for this story lies in other vernacular stories of the time. Among these are twelve of the thirteen others in *Shi dian tou*, from the second quarter of the seventeenth century and twenty-two others from Feng Menglong's third collection of vernacular stories, *Xingshi hengyan* 醒世恒言 (Constant Words to Awaken the World, preface 1627). Though many of these stories are the product of earlier decades and centuries, Patrick Hanan's *The Chinese Short Story* of l973 hypothesizes on the basis of linguistic evidence that "The Siege of Yangzhou" and the thirty-four related stories were written by a single author who was probably active in the early seventeenth century.[31] Hanan regards this hypothesis as less than fully proven, but it is secure enough to provide a useful means of pursuing the question at hand. As far as this author's name is concerned, I follow Hanan in referring to him as Langxian, a name which Feng Menglong once called him, though it is otherwise unclear who Langxian is.

The distinction between these stories and the others in Feng's celebrated collections is not only linguistic. Other bases allow a contrast between them and those Feng wrote or rewrote in his own style, as well those by still other authors in the *San yan* 三言 collections. To note a few points other than language which Hanan finds to be characteristic of Langxian's writing, there are the heavy use of introspection, dialogue, and dreams to reveal inner mental patterns; the interest in Confucian moral exempla of a certain kind; and the tendency to draw material from one or more pre-existing stories, often dealing with the Tang Dynasty in general and the An Lushan Rebellion in particular. All of these points characterize "The Siege of Yangzhou".[32]

When we compare "The Siege of Yangzhou" with its literary antecedents, we discover that many of these features of Langxian's stories were not present in earlier versions. One antecedent appears in the Song compendium *Taiping guangji* 太平廣記 (Taiping Compendium). It is short enough to present in its entirety:

> Zhou Di had a wife of uncertain surname. Di was good at business, for which he travelled around the Guangling [Yangzhou] area. He encountered the uprising led by Bi Shido. People were plotting to sell each other for food. Di was dying of hunger. His wife said, "We would like to go home, but we cannot both survive.... Your mother is still alive, so we must not both die. I would like to be sold so that I can help you leave. Di could not stand it, but his wife went out to the market place and sold herself for several thousand cash which she left to Di. He went to the city gate. The guard asked him who he was and what was going on and did not believe that the money had been left to him. He went with him to the market to check. They saw the wife's head already on the counter. Di gathered up the remains, went home, and buried them.[33]

A second version, with scarcely any more detail, appears in the collection *Qingshi Leilüe*, with which Feng had some connection.[34]

In *Shi dian tou*, the same fragment is considerably expanded, from only a few lines in these versions to twenty-six pages in modern reprint. In addition to adding an inner view of the heroine, dialogue, and a dream, much of the rest of the expansion concerns the background through which the couple ended up in Yangzhou. The classical sources do not show Zhou Di to be a weak character, they do not name his wife, they do not develop the mother-in-law as a character, they do not raise the issue of childbirth, and they say nothing about the failures at business which led him to work for the salt merchant and then move on to Yangzhou. This expansion is characteristic of others of Langxian's expansions, particularly in its close attention to the details of the business trade.[35]

Rather than prove this last point systematically, I shall turn instead to a more relevant embellishment, the transformation of Zhou Di's wife from an unnamed to a named character and the sketching in of characteristics which classical versions did not supply. It is particularly here that Second Sister Zong can be linked to certain others among Langxian's heroines who are both well educated and capable of unusual acts of self-sacrifice in pursuit of Confucian goals.

Second Sister Zong as a Langxian Heroine

The first point to note in this connection are the terms in which Second Sister Zong enters the scene:

> This Miss Zong came from a Confucian family. From an early age she could read and knew Confucian principles. She was one year younger than [her husband]. Because she was second among the children in her family, she was called Second Sister Zong.[36]

This description is typical of the way Langxian introduces his highly virtuous female characters — as literate women who are knowlegable about Confucian principles and (inevitably, although it will not concern us here) as younger than their present or prospective husbands. Often these virtuous women are adept at skills other than reading, such as painting or embroidery, and they are sometimes said to be physically attractive. The reader is often told how the girl received her education. In one unusual story, "Brother or Bride?" (劉小官雌雄兄弟) (*Xingshi hengyan*, Juan 10) the girl's adopted father mistakenly thought she was a boy and taught her himself. A more common pattern is for female talent to show itself early and for a formal tutor to be engaged. In two cases (see below), the girl is said to be so intelligent she could have come out first in the imperial examinations were she allowed to take them. In these two cases and in "Love in a Junk" (吳衙内鄰舟赴約) (*Xingshi hengyan*, Juan 28), it is obvious that to Langxian, as to Lü Kun, women's intelligence was potentially the equal of men's. Beauty, skill at painting or embroidery and unusual genius do not happen to enter into Second Sister Zong's characterization, but the fact that she turns out to be of firmer moral fibre than her husband, and that there is a link between her learning and sense of duty, are not exceptional in Langxian's fictional world.

In addition to "The Siege of Yangzhou", Langxian has eight stories featuring well educated, virtuous females. Not every one of these women could be considered a paragon, but all are capable of impressive feats of sexual self-denial or of stoic resistance to evil. Their stories, in brief, are as follows.

In "Brother or Bride?", as we have seen, a woman is thought to be a man throughout most of the story and is educated accordingly. She sleeps in the same bed with her adoptive brother for several years without revealing her sexual identity. When she finally does reveal it — in a poem — she becomes the brother's bride and helps to carries out proper mourning rites for their adoptive parents.

In "Master Dugu"(獨孤生歸途鬧夢) (*Xingshi hengyan*, Juan 25), the heroine puts up with a two-year absence on the part of her husband, who was expected to return from his trip after a year. She is one of the two women Langxian says were intelligent enough to have come first in the imperial examinations. When two years have gone by, she prays that she might dream of him but instead dreams of exchanging flirtatious lyrics with a bunch of hooligans who later try to accost her. It turns out the husband has the same dream at the same time, and he comes home to awaken her from her nightmare just in time.

In "Li Yuying" (李玉英獄中訟冤) (*Xingshi hengyan*, Juan 27), Yuying's intelligence becomes evident at an early age, and her father decides to hire a tutor and educate her with her brother. This is one of many acts that arouse the jealousy of his second wife, who subjects sister and brother to many trials. Eventually the brother dies from maltreatment, and Yuying is sent to jail, under the false accusation of wantonness. There she resists the attentions of an amorous jailor and manages to write a petition about her predicament which reaches official hands. At this point the tables are turned on the jealous second wife, and Yuying goes on to marry happily and well.

"Love in a Junk" introduces a young woman whose parents have no son. They decide, therefore, to educate their daughter by summoning a tutor to their house.[37] This daughter is the least virtuous of the women we will consider, for most of the story shows her performing the role of "beauty" to a young "scholar" whose family happens to have moored their boat in Jingzhou harbour, just next to her family's boat. This story is a comedy of budding romance, in which the relationship is initiated and furthered by the girl's skill at poetry. The comedy revolves around the large quantity of food which the young man regularly consumes and which makes his presence difficult to conceal once the girl decides to hide him on the family boat. Eventually, the two marry, for they turn out to be socially appropriate partners. After their marriage, she behaves according to proper Confucian rules.

"Rainbow Cai" (蔡瑞紅忍辱報仇) (*Xingshi hengyan*, Juan 36) is about an intelligent young woman whose parents love to drink. We are not told how she acquired her education, only that it comes in handy, since she has to run the family because her parents are usually inebriated. When the father foolishly attempts to take his wife and daughter on a business trip, everyone but the daughter are killed by bandits. The daughter is abducted and goes through a number of partners and humiliations before finally ending up with a kind husband as his second wife. She adopts a child with her parents' surname, Cai, then kills herself, to her husband's enormous grief. As she explains in a suicide letter, now that she has found a way to carry on her family name and because she knows she can rely on her husband's first wife to take care of her adopted son, she is free to clear the moral stain of numerous sexual partners by taking her own life.

In "Lu Mengxian Seeks a Wife" (盧夢仙尋妻) (*Shi dian tou*, Juan 2) the juvenile heroine is the daughter of a Confucian tutor. She is educated by her father. The father later opens a school, where the daughter meets Lu Mengxian and is engaged to him. Later, Lu's fortunes decline and he leaves on a long trip. The future groom's family, with whom she has been living, decide to marry her to a rich businessman. She tries to hang herself in protest, but is talked out of it. She moves to the businessman's house, and is again on the verge of suicide. Thanks to the kindness of one of the businessman's subordinate wives, she is allowed not to consummate the marriage and instead pays for her keep by serving as an accountant. Eventually, she is able to annul her marriage to the merchant and marry Lu Mengxian, whose fortunes have taken a turn for the better.

"Mistress Wang" (王孺人離合團魚夢)(*Shi dian tou*, Juan 10) begins with a happily married woman who is abducted by criminals. Eventually, one of the criminals sells her to a man who has almost the same name as her first husband. She thinks of killing herself but decides to live and take revenge. At this point we are informed that she is educated. Her second husband is a good man, who at age forty-nine, still has no child and has married her in the hope of having one. Eventually the second husband finds out about the first one, and agrees to return the wife to him. As a reward for this act of virtue, he is eventually blessed with a child, quite miraculously, since both he and his first wife are over fifty by the time the child is born.

"The Martyr" (侯官縣烈女殲仇) (*Shi dian tou*, Juan 12) is the other story in which the heroine is said to have enough intelligence to come out first in the examinations. She is also an excellent swordswoman. She is married to a worthy husband, and is soon blessed with a son. Husband and wife become entangled in a property struggle with the evil second wife of the husband's father. The evil second wife conspires with several others to get rid of the husband and marry the wife off to a notorious pirate. After depositing her son with kind relatives, she agrees to the marriage, then uses the opportunity to butcher the pirate and several of his accomplices, including the evil second wife. All this takes place on her (second) wedding night. She hangs the pirate's head on her first husband's grave and commits suicide after writing a letter explaining the need for revenge. Her son eventually goes on to a successful political career.

What stands out in this listing is the close correlation between female education and Confucian virtue in almost every case. At times, the main application of this virtue lies in protecting family property or seeing to the continuation of the family line. Often, it is specifically chastity that is at issue. In either case, female virtue is defined in terms of patriarchal family values, yet specific males and families are often wrong about the correct path of action. When this happens, the educated female calls on her inner sense of virtue and lives to see the wisdom of her decision. Second Sister Zong is clearly not alone in her ability to sense out truths that her masculine partner fails to apprehend. Rainbow Cai is another heroine who understands morality better than the man in her family, in this case her father. Interestingly, in this story too the subject of disagreement is a journey. Rainbow's correct analysis of why her family's trip should not be undertaken is reminiscent of Second Sister Zong's conviction that a wife should not leave home. In these two and other examples, Langxian seems to echo Lü Kun's conviction that education creates women who may act more virtuously than men.

The direct relevance of reading and writing as solutions to the problems posed in these stories is often rather minimal, although heroines sometimes quote from the classics when making up their minds to do heroic deeds. Li Yuying is one case in which the woman's heroism is expressed through writing — in her case a petition to the authorities, but actual reading and writing often enter the picture more obliquely, or not at all. Rather, emphasis seems to lie on the way in which the teaching of reading and writing conditions the female mind to unravel complicated evidence and arrive unerringly at the right conclusion. Interestingly, this seems to be true even when the female mind has been educated as if it were male — the case in "Brother or Bride?".

Like any generalization, this one is made in the face of exceptions which prove the rule. Langxian's writings make it clear that he does not think female literacy is *always* a guarantee of virtue. In one of his stories literate nuns turn out to be positively evil, for example, but here lack of virtue is associated with the religious way of life, which Langxian often satirizes, not with education *per se*. It is also not the case that all of Langxian's virtuous women are literate. In "Zhang Tingxiu" (張廷秀逃生 救父) (*Xingshi hengyan*, Juan 20), for example, the wife is consistently more correct than her husband in her moral instincts, but the question of whether she is literate never comes up at all. This evidence suggests that Confucian education is a sufficient, but not a necessary, condition of female virtue in Langxian's mind.

Langxian's descriptions of virtuous, literate women from these stories have something in common with his description of virtuous, literate men. Given the large number of rapacious officials who cross his pages, it is far from impossible that educated male characters will turn out to be evil in Langxian's writing, but it is once again the case that if a male is described as intelligent and well educated at the beginning of a story, he will eventually turn out well. However, the means through which the good individual demonstrates virtuousness is vastly different for females than for males, with chastity being the main means through which female virtue is portrayed. Thus, Rainbow Cai, a woman who through no fault of her own has been abducted and forced into several sexual relationships, is praised for taking her own life, even though her husband is devastated by this action. In a rather similar example, a woman (Mistress Wang) who has had two husbands, again through no fault of her own, insists that she not be buried in the family tomb and maintains fifteen years of chaste widowhood after her second husband dies. Perhaps the most spectacular demonstration of chastity is that in "The Martyr", where the heroine's second marriage, to her husband's enemy, a pirate, is never consummated. The denouement, with the pirate's murder and her suicide on their wedding night, again wins the narrator's praise. Predictably enough, chastity is not at issue when male virtue is described.

Even when a story's focus lies elsewhere, chastity seems to come up for comment in most of the other stories we have considered. "Master Dugu", for example, concentrates on the astonishing coincidence of a shared dream, but that dream comes about because the husband has been away from home for two years. Its alarmingly sexual content raises questions about what the wife must have been feeling (and presumably suppressing) during her husband's time away. "Brother or Bride?" is manifestly about mistaken sexual identity, but it demonstrates the heroine's extreme sexual self-discipline as she lies nightly for several years in the same bed with her future husband, who thinks she is a man. Even "Love in a Junk", which is willing to show the heroine as mildly flirtatious, ends on the reassuring note that the young man she flirts with turns out to be a socially appropriate husband, despite his large appetite, and the story ends with the further assurance that the woman behaved virtuously from the moment of her "engagement" on. Whether or not issues of chastity are foregrounded in a particular Langxian's story, the group as a whole leave the impression that Confucian training drives all thought of unchaste behaviour out of a woman's mind.

This is not necessarily to say that Langxian is always a hard-line Confucian moralist, although one could draw that conclusion about some of his attitudes toward women. In fact even Langxian is capable of leniency toward uneducated women who behave immorally, in the sense that he does not kill them off, though he may call their behaviour animalistic;[38] and he does not automatically favour suicide for widows or betrothed maidens — two of the most common forms of righteous female suicide during the late-Ming.[39] The point, rather, is that when he includes educational background in his description of a woman, unless it be to set up a scholar-beauty scenario, the woman is sure to demonstrate extraordinary powers of sexual self-denial and an intolerant stance toward anyone other than her husband (future, present, or deceased) who makes overtures toward her. Should her strictness toward would-be second partners lead her to suicide, even murder, Langxian's narrator may express vague regret at the loss of life, but the overall tone is admiring.

Because Langxian's plotting and characterization frequently follow antecedents, it is worth noting that in these other eight stories, too, the interrelation between chastity and education is developed more elaborately than in earlier versions. No source of any of these eight stories that I know of ever talks about females coming in first in the examinations, and the prototype for the lead character in "Mistress Wang" was not literate. Though reading women do figure in earlier versions of "Brother or Bride?", "Li Yuying", "Lu Mengxian Seeks a Wife", and "The Martyr", their high level of virtue is merely noted, not described in detail.[40]

Just as Langxian's equation of chastity and Confucian education is his own elaboration on the antecedents from which he borrowed, so they are not an inevitable consequence of the vernacular story as a genre. It is well known that a few other stories in the *San yan* collections take a flexible attitude toward chastity, most notably "The Pearl-Sewn Shirt" (蔣興哥重會珍珠衫) (*Gujin xiaoshuo* 古今小説, Juan 1), "The Dead Infant" (況太守斷死孩兒) (*Jingshi tongyan* 警世通言, Juan 35), and "Censor Chen's Ingenious Solution of the Case of Gold Hairpins and Brooches" (陳御史巧勘金釵鈿) (*Gujin xiaoshuo*, Juan 2) — all of which feature women who are or have been respectably married. "The Pearl-Sewn Shirt" invites comparison with several Langxian stories, at least one of which seems to echo it deliberately. This is "Mistress Wang", which invokes the figure of the benevolent second husband who gives up his wife so she can return to her first husband, whom she still loves. This generous act recalls Fortune's second husband, the magistrate, who returns her to her first husband, Jiang Xingge 蔣興哥. In contrast to Fortune, however, "Mistress Wang" feels the need to punish her own lack of chastity by depriving herself of the right to be buried in her husband's tomb. Another contrast to "The Pearl-Sewn Shirt" is brought to mind by Langxian's "Master Dugu". There the heroine waits one year beyond the deadline that her husband has set for returning — altogether two years — before experiencing the sexual nightmare that he shares. In contrast, Fortune's long wait for her first husband lasted only a year and a half — half a year beyond the promised return date — before she succumbs to Chen Dalang. "The Dead Infant" offers another contrast to Langxian's moral rhetoric, for its main point is that young widows are better off remarrying, since it is too hard for them to endure sexual deprivation for years on end. In contrast, Langxian's "Qu Fengnu" satirizes a widow who gives in to her sexual needs. "Censor Chen's Ingenious Solution of the Case of Gold Hairpins and Brooches" makes a particularly interesting contrast to Langxian's writing, for it is the only one of these three stories to feature an educated woman. She is a highly resourceful female who leaves one husband when he proves immoral then marries an appropriate one (after many intricate manoeuvres), without incurring the narrator's blame. Langxian's more rigid association of female literacy with chastity thus stands out as a distinctive feature of his writing, not as a general parameter of his day.

In view of Langxian's attitudes toward chastity and the educated woman, it seems almost superfluous to ask why Second Sister Zong did not sell herself sexually rather than as food when she needed to raise money for her husband in Yangzhou. From what we know of her way of thinking, it is quite in character that the discomfort of death for money should have been greatly preferred to the dishonour of sex for money, a calculus that would also have made sense to other Langxian characters who were forced to abandon chastity. Rainbow Cai's suicide letter to her husband makes this logic abundantly clear, as in the following line: "A woman's virtue lies in chastity. If she is not chaste, how is she different from an animal?" A similar sentiment can be found in the suicide note at the end of "The Martyr": "I have devoted myself to [keeping] my valuable purity. The occasion of my second marriage thus becomes the night of my death".[41]

Since Second Sister Zong was not *forced* to abandon chastity, one might argue, the thought of doing so never entered her mind. On the other hand, when she talks of selling her body on the market, it is difficult to avoid the impression that some kind of sexual selling is implied as a hidden subtext, simply because of the wording.[42] In an alternative scenario, Second Sister Zong might have chosen something like what Rainbow Cai was eventually forced into — first that she sell herself sexually and raise travel money for her husband; second that she see to his marrying again or otherwise finding an heir; third that she dispose of herself by suicide. Such a plan would have meant that Second Sister Zong could die in a less ghastly fashion. Further, Zhou Di might sooner or later have produced a child, for his decision not to remarry has a great deal to do with his horror at his wife's demise. However, this alternative is never raised.[43]

Though Second Sister Zong's final oration betrays regret at her situation, doubt or hesitation are nowhere in evidence, nor is there any evidence that she even *considered* the alternative of sex for money, if only to reject it out of hand.[44] Langxian is often quite sophisticated in his depiction of human thought processes, so that the absence of complicated cogitation prior to Second Sister Zong's demise is striking, and it calls into question similar instances of resoluteness on the part of other virtuous heroines — women such as Rainbow Cai, who had a number of other alternatives before her when she chose to die. If the final thoughts of these women are sincerely meant as interiority, they reveal minds so firmly made up that no alternatives were, are, or ever could have been contemplated — an odd result of their education, it might seem.

Another peculiarity of these women's high-minded cogitations is the allusions which inspire them to die. In Second Sister Zong's case, her inspiration comes from the story of Zuo Botao and Yang Jiaoai, from the *Lieshi zhuan*, while Rainbow Cai's telling example concerns Li Ling 李陵 and comes from the *Hou Han shu* 後漢書 (History of the Later Han). Our knowledge today of texts which women studied in Ming Dynasty China is not wholly reliable, and it is possible that either or both of these stories were available in popular anthologies. However, dramas such as *Mudan ting* 牡丹亭 (The Peony Pavilion) lead one to expect that female learning was different from male learning, and that history was not heavily emphasized; Lü Kun's writing further suggests that when historical allusions did come to the attention of females, they did so via the *Lienü* tradition, not the *Lieshi zhuan* or the *Hou Han shu*.[45]

As previously noted, Langxian's stories are a rich store of accurate description of late-Ming business practices, and it might be sensible, by analogy, to use his heroic women's citations to supplement our shallow understanding of the texts from which women learned. However, judging from what can only be regarded as the highly idealized interior expressions of Second Sister Zong, Rainbow Cai and others, it seems safer to regard their final declamations as set pieces, whose use of sources may have more to do with masculine educational experience than with what contemporary educated women actually knew. By the same token, the firmness of these women's minds prior to suicide may have more to do with conventional depictions of heroic women than with the sort of "realism" found elsewhere in Langxian's writings. For whatever reasons, the supposed interior monologues of his heroic females are noticeably more stilted and less complicated than those of his negative women characters and of his good (though all too human) males.[46]

A final oddity about Langxian's ultra-virtuous women is their tendency to be paired with very weak male counterparts. This situation is particularly acute in "The Siege of Yangzhou", though it can also be illustrated in his other stories about highly heroic females, namely "The Martyr" and "Rainbow Cai". It is not only that Second Sister Zong is far braver than her husband, she also has a far better sense of how to conduct business, so that she can anticipate the consequences of his poor judgment before they actually materialize — as when they lead to the theft of their money in Xiang-yang.[47] Moreover, Langxian's efforts to highlight her resoluteness seem to be undertaken at the expense of her husband, Zhou Di, who is very often shown weeping — eleven times in twenty-five pages — and whose negative comments about his mother (for sending the couple off together) prompt admonitory lectures and sneers from the wife with whom he supposedly got along so well. Zhou Di's weakness is especially noticeable in connection with Second Sister Zong's white lie about selling her husband rather than herself to the butcher, noted above. Although it is the wife who actually dies, the decision making process is entirely in her hands. It seems that Langxian has gone out of his way here to emphasize Zhou Di's lack of "normal" masculinity, the subject upon which his wife feels called to lecture him from time to time. Both in his use of historical allusions and in his juxtaposition of male and female characters, Langxian seems now to hint at another hidden subtext, that this couple's source of authority, if not its actual masculinity, has been transferred to the female from the male.

Feng Menglong's story "Censor Chen's Ingenious Solution of the Case of the Gold Hairpins and Brooches" is again instructive, for it demonstrates that competent, educated women could be found in vernacular short stories alongside more confident males. Just as Langxian's heroic women take chastity more seriously than they had to within their genre and period, so their unimpressive male counterparts are Langxian's own elaboration on the educated/virtuous women paradigm, not an unbreakable convention of his day.

Tragedy or Travesty?

These hints of hidden subtexts in "The Siege of Yangzhou" encourage us to pursue a still more outlandish possibility, that the story was intended as a comic inversion of the values for which it seems to stand. In support of this reading, we can point to the presence of deliberate comedy in at least two other Langxian stories. Like "The Siege of Yangzhou", both of these have to do with food. We have already seen how the story "Love in a Junk" creates a humorous ambience by concealing a very heavy eater in a virginal young woman's quarters on her family boat. When her orders for food suddenly go from dainty to gargantuan proportions, the family rushes to consult a doctor, with predictably farcical results. There is no question here that Langxian intended humour, though the narrator gives no indication that the scene is humorously conceived.[48]

Humour is also obvious in a second Langxian story, "Metamorphosis into a Fish" (薛錄事魚服證仙) (*Xingshi hengyan*, Juan 26). This story is much closer in structure to "The Siege of Yangzhou" than "Love in a Junk" is. Based on a Tang original, it tells of a man who turned into a fish and confronts the prospect of being eaten by his friends. Like "Love in a Junk", "Metamorphosis into a Fish" is often straightforwardly comic, as when it shows the hero screaming to be understood by the company at a party, who look forward to consuming this hefty specimen for dinner. The sputtering pompousness of this hero intensifies the comic mood. Here, however, the dominant tone is one of terror. The fish/hero's prospect of being eaten alive in this story is quite similar to what Second Sister Zong faces, and the fish's inability to make himself heard by those who would eat him is further reminiscent of the moment when Second Sister Zong's self-commendation falls on incomprehending ears.[49] Alongside the fish/hero's failure of communication, Second Sister Zong's resoluteness seems less formidable and more touching precisely because she utters it in a dialect which no one can understand.

On the other hand, what this example also helps to establish is the freshness with which Langxian approaches literary stereotypes and the unpredictablity with which he draws in alternatives to the main action. In "Metamorphosis into a Fish" the unpursued alternative — that the fish is eaten — merely serves to heighten narrative tension. It does nothing to subvert the apparent story line. In "The Siege of Yangzhou", on the other hand, alternatives of sexual inversion and wantonness hover in the background, enlivening clichés of fleshly sacrifice and virtuous womanhood even as they threaten to undermine the main story line. For example, as against the traditional image of the self-sacrificing daughter-in-law, Langxian invokes Second Sister Zong's white lie about selling her husband rather than herself, which in context is mildly plausible, even reasonable, given her far greater competence at business affairs. In this vaguely hilarious though completely unexplored course of action, Langxian adds to what he has already been stating indirectly, that the take-command stance of the typical virtuous female is emasculating for her partner, who must stand helplessly by as she assumes moral control. Embedded in scenes in which Second Sister Zong admonishes her husband — about filial piety, masculinity, and business practice — lie authorial hints of her coldness, which come close to invoking the paradigm of shrew versus henpecked male.

It is along such lines of analysis that the silence about prostitution seems to speak more loudly than if Langxian had put it into words. The commercial aspect to Second Sister Zong's fateful transaction makes it easy for the reader to think of other kinds of selling to which she might have committed herself, even as her mind works its way to the chaste, if barbaric, demise. Moreover, the hidden alternative is accentuated by the contrast between Second Sister Zong's utterly idealistic way of thinking and the butcher's more pragmatic vision, which seizes on her physical size as ideal for butchering and leads to a mildly sarcastic joke about her love of keeping clean. Her dressing and undressing in this latter connection, play against the butcher's disrespectful laugh, his concern for getting his money's worth, his distress at having to butcher this woman, and other evidence of his feelings. In context, they accentuate the inevitability that she must stand naked before her executioner, whether or not she is only merchandise to him. Horrible though they would have been in reality, these events threaten to become mildly comic as the adventures of a bluestocking whose education has made her oblivious to nuances of this kind. And against the suppleness of the butcher's reactions, Second Sister Zong comes across as particularly single-minded, thinking nonstop about right and wrong throughout these highly trying moments, failing even to notice that she had "given" herself to a strange man. Only when the butcher is visibly moved by her predicament does her earnest concern for virtue supersede the hidden sexual question that the selling motif has raised.

As is already obvious from "Love in a Junk" and "Metamorphosis into a Fish", Langxian's alternative scenarios are not inevitably hilarious. The best example of a horrific variant in "The Siege of Yangzhou" comes almost at the end of the story, when Second Sister's Zong's ghost appears to her mother-in-law — one day before Zhou Di actually returns home. There the daughter makes the following announcement: "Mother, I am back. Your son has married a second wife — not too tall, not too short, not coarse, not fine, with broken bones and body, in other words myself. Your son now has produced a grandson — not large, not small, not true, not false, with disheveled hair and dirty face, none other than your old son Zhou Di".[50] Depending on whether one emphasizes the news of marriage and birth in this announcement or the vertigo provoked by their retraction, it will be viewed either as cruelly encouraging of the mother's wish for a grandson or as a sarcastic recapitulation of all that has just occurred. Second Sister Zong's ghost's intention may be partly to blame the mother-in-law for her incorrect decision or simply to give vent to her own distress at what she has been through. In any event, this vignette is of a piece with the story's other alternative scenarios in that it raises startling possibilities without acknowledgment from the narrator that something startling is going on.

Partly because of the plethora of alternative scenarios in this story, it is difficult to read any one of them as pre-eminent, and since they do not subvert the manifest rhetoric in the same direction, that manifest rhetoric seems, in the end, to stand. Though the image of pedant and wanton both undercut the heroine's positive portrayal, for example, they undercut it from opposite points of view. Second Sister Zong's points in common with other educated Langxian heroines would further caution against reading too much satirical crossfire into "The Siege of Yangzhou".[51] Like her counterparts in "Rainbow Cai" and "The Martyr", Second Sister Zong has her one, brief moment of self-expression, which shows her as Langxian most wants her to be seen. However stilted her thoughts may have been up to this occasion, in this fleeting but memorable burst of self-expression, she dispels all hints of the coldness, sarcasm, and impatience that come out at other times. And because this manifestation of her own point of view follows, rather than precedes, the interaction with the butcher, since even he had felt sorry to have to kill her, it tends to recoup the dignity that was almost lost when she came before the reader through his eyes. In conjunction with her apparition to the mother-in-law several pages later, this interior portrait just before her death accentuates the dreadfulness of her demise. Without this final disquisition, it might be easier to dismiss the story as a subtle attack on heroic women. With it the heroine's vulnerabiliy commands attention and anchors the narrative on its heroic side.

Nevertheless, the question still remains as to why this author raised so many alternative possibilities if his intention was not to poke fun at his subject. One possibility which might occur to readers far removed from Langxian's time and culture is that he is unconsciously hostile toward his heroine, whom he wished to deflate by invoking irreverent paradigms, such as those of pedant and shrew. However, though hostility may account for some of this story's complications, Langxian does not seem to have been unconscious of many of the negative undertones that arise. Indeed his use of dreams, jokes, *double entendre*, and other devices suggest a subtle sense of everyday psychopathology, through which combinations of contradictory emotions are presented unresolved.[52] Particularly in the case of Zhou Di's tears and incompetence, one has to conclude that Langxian saw the henpecked husband paradigm in the background, all the more because he goes out of his way to negate it by repeated examples of how much the wife wanted her husband to marry a second time. As for the subplot of sexual selling, it is somewhat harder to read. The *double entendre* contained in the words "selling myself on the market" may really have been unconscious, though it is more likely that Langxian was again aware of the hidden theme. And again the joke is silenced when the butcher is won over to the heroine's side.

If unconscious motivations fail to account for the imbalances in this story, then other possibilities must be reviewed. Langxian's other writings encourage the interpretation that he meant his subplots as enlivening filigree, for vividness is one of the hallmarks of his writerly skill. In this case, however, the adding of realistic detail to such an implausible story may have been partly responsible for some of the interpretative problems that arise. In particular, Langxian's habit of situating the action in the context of late-Ming commercial practice may have served him badly on this occasion, for the detailed elaboration of how flesh could be sold for money is one major reason that the theme of prostitution comes into view. Likewise his attention to unspoken thought processes, which normally makes his characters so lively, may have worked less well with a larger-than-life character like Second Sister Zong, who loses as much as she gains when her acts are cast in ordinary human terms. Especially when Langxian probes the "miscalculations" that sent the couple off to Yangzhou in the first place, her husband comes across as deficient — whether because he is too deeply influenced by his mother, loves his wife too much, or has failed at business several times. Implicitly, then, the background on how the couple got to Yangzhou exposes the weakness of the husband and inverts the normal balance between females and males. Here again the kind of development which Langxian employs so successfully on most occasions tends to work against the story's manifest themes. These points create a basis on which to argue that "The Siege of Yangzhou" does not succeed completely as a story, that its rhetoric and elaboration work at cross-purposes, creating comic nuances which the author could not control. In this, "The Siege of Yangzhou" could be seen as typical of *Shi dian tou* as a collection, many of whose other stories fail to work out perfectly in artistic terms.

At the same time, the contests between different readings of this story add artistically interesting tensions, which improve it over the spare, flat narratives from which the story is derived. Moreover, as in much better

Langxian stories,[53] the latent scenarios lend telling insight into how virtuous, literate womanhood was received in Langxian's day. Particularly when wives and daughters are more virtuous or prescient than the men around them, but also in other circumstances, these scenarios betray ambivalences to which newly articulate female talent must have given rise. Langxian's overall purpose was, on balance, to celebrate his heroine, just as it seems to be. At the same time, hints of pedant, wanton and shrew embedded in his story reveal a considerable measure of disquiet at Second Sister Zong's formidable qualities, which could vanquish even a butcher's gaze.[54] No less than the wars of words between Lü Kun and his detractors, Langxian's multifaceted depiction reveals complex patterns of reaction toward the late-Ming women of proud background who were just then gaining access to the written word.

Notes

1. Figures from the Warring States Period. The two of them were in perilous straits and realized both would not survive. Zuo Botao 左伯桃 gave his clothing to Yang Jiaoai 羊角哀 , with the thought that Yang was more learned than he. Yang made it to safety and Zuo Botao perished. The story is found in the *Lieshi zhuan* 烈士傳 (Biographies of Eminent Gentlemen).

2. Citations are based on the Zhongguo wenxue zhenben congshu edition (Shanghai: Juye shanfang, 1935), pp. 279–305, in this case p. 295.

3. The implication seems to be that they die at the same time. If so, Langxian has miscalculated, since Zhou Di's mother is thirty years older than he.

4. See for example the Shanghai guji chubanshe edition of 1984.

5. For an elaboration of this term, see Robert Darnton, *The Great Cat Massacre* (New York: Vintage, 1984), pp. 3–7.

6. On Hanan's theory, see below.

7. As for example in Barbara Johnson, *A World of Difference* (Baltimore and London: John's Hopkins University Press, 1987), pp. 68–85 especially.

8. On this paradigm, see Yenna Wu, "The Inversion of Marital Hierarchy: Shrewish Wives and Henpecked Husbands in Seventeenth-Century Chinese Literature", *Harvard Journal of Asiatic Studies*, Vol. 48, No. 2 (December 1988), pp. 363–382.

9. *Harvard Journal of Asiatic Studies*, Vol. 46, No. 2 (December 1986), pp. 387–469.

10. Ibid., p. 411.

11. See for example *Nüzi ershisi xiao tushuo* 女子二十四孝圖説 (Illustrated

narratives of twenty-four filial women), citation in Chaves, p. 421, original in Library of Congress; also Wang Tingna 汪廷訥 , *Quanyi daoren shu* 全一道 人書 (The book of Taoist Quanyi), reprinted in *Researches on Zen'ichi dōjin*, compiled by Hoshu Amenomori (Kyoto: Kyoto University, 1964). This book was first published some time after 1607. See p. 9 on sacrifice.

12. Ibid., p. 417.
13. See note 11 above for citations from *Quanyi daoren shu*.
14. See note 16 below.
15. On Ming Taizu, see Zhao Jishi 趙吉士 and Ding Tingjian 丁廷楗 , *Huizhou fuzhi* 徽州府志 (Gazeteer of Huizhou Prefecture, 1699), 15:37b. On Qing policy, see J. J. M. De Groot, *The Religious System of China* (Taipei: Litera-ture House, 1964), Book 1, Vol. 2, p. 751.
16. See De Groot, book 2, Vol. 4, p. 384. One of Li's principal objections was that such sacrifices were not always voluntary.
17. T'ien Ju-k'ang 田汝康 , *Male Anxiety and Female Chastity* (Leiden: E. J. Brill, 1988), pp. 47, 161. I completed most of the work on this paper before reading T'ien's book, which is certainly the best source of information on female suicide in China available in English.
18. Or as found elsewhere in literature, such as in stories by Pu Songling 蒲松齡 . Other types of fleshly sacrifice could also be mentioned in this connection, such as the tradition of widow suicide, which also seems to have become more widespread toward the end of the Ming. Though Second Sister Zong's sacrifice seems unrelated to questions of widowhood or chastity, and though it is not exactly a suicide, it brings to mind certain features of this custom which was quite prevalent among the upper classes in certain parts of China at around the time "The Siege of Yangzhou" was written. Specifically, one learns from both legend and literature that the deaths of righteous women caused disturbances in the weather, among them drought, conditions which follow upon the death of Second Sister Zong. Such details in "The Siege of Yangzhou" may mean that literature or folklore on the subject of widow suicide exerted an influence on its composition, even though the story never mentions the subject in so many words. A third kind of fleshly sacrifice might also bear on this picture. Tanaka Issei cites one example of a woman, celebrated in Huizhou drama, who was posthumously honoured for feeding her flesh to hungry soldiers during the An Lushan rebellion. (See note 44 below.) Of course there are obvious contrasts to Second Sister Zong's case, in that the soldiers actually ate the woman's flesh, as is not the case with Second Sister Zong. Also, the drama says nothing about the woman becoming an immortal, only that she was posthumously honoured with an official title, along with her much more famous husband, Zhang Xun.
19. Margery Wolf and Roxane Witke, *Women in Chinese Society* (Stanford: Stanford University Press), 1975, pp. 13–38. See also Joanna F. Handlin,

Action in Late Ming Thought (Berkeley: University of California Press, 1983), pp. 143–160 especially.

20. Ibid., p. 18.

21. i.e., *minjian funü* 民間婦女, Ibid., p. 17. Lü kun, *Guifan* (Jiangning weishi yingyin mingkeben, 1927).

22. See, for example, Dorothy Yin-yee Ko, "Toward a Social History of Women in Seventeenth-Century China", Doctoral Dissertation, Stanford University, July 1989 (quoted with permission), passim, and Ellen Widmer, "The Epistolary World of Female Talent in Seventeenth-Century China", *Late Imperial China*, December 1989, pp. 1–43.

23. Handlin-Smith, p. 19.

24. Ibid., pp. 19–23.

25. Ibid., p. 24.

26. Ibid., p. 29.

27. *Shi dian tou*, p. 279.

28. Handlin-Smith, p. 17.

29. Lü kun, 3:27 a–b.

30. T'ien, p. 65.

31. *The Chinese Short Story* (Massachusettes: Harvard University Press 1973), pp. 66–74. See also Hanan, *The Chinese Vernacular Story* (Cambridge: Harvard University Press, 1981), pp. 120–139.

32. We have already seen that this story presents an inner view of Zhou Di's wife, in the form of the speech just prior to her death; and the story is rich in dialogue, especially when the mother-in-law is trying to persuade the daughter-in-law to leave home. Dreams enter the picture after Zhou Di's wife has died, for they are the means by which she is reunited with her mother-in-law. As for moral examples, this is one of several stories by Langxian on the subject of filial piety. The story is based on one in the *Taiping guangji* and another in Feng Menglong's *Qingshi leilüe* 情史類略 (Anatomy of Love). And it takes place during the Tang Dynasty, just after the An Lushan Rebellion. Zhou Di's first failure at business, before the story begins, is the result of this rebellion.

33. Section 270; translation based on Taipei: Wenshizhe chubanshe edition, 1981, pp. 2117–2118.

34. On Feng's connection to *Qingshi leilüe*, see Hanan, 1981, p. 95. My translation is based on the Changsha Yuelu shushe edition of 1984, p. 453. It runs as follows: A person from Yuzhang (Nanchang) became bankrupt in Guangling (Yangzhou). There he encountered the [Bi] Shiduo disturbance and could not leave. People were eating one another in the city. Di was on the brink of starvation. His wife said, "With the military situation so bad, we certainly cannot be saved. Your old mother is far away. It is wrong for you and me both to die. I would rather sell myself to a butcher, then you could go home

safely". Di was forced to agree. With half of what she got [for selling herself], he bribed a guard to let him go. The guard was suspicious, but Di insisted he was telling the truth. No one believed him, so they went with Di to the scene of the event to check. When they got there, they saw her head already on the counter. All who witnessed this gasped with amazement and competed to give him gold and precious cloth. Di was thus able to retrieve the rest of her corpse and carry it home on his back. Feng Menglong comments: For a wife to accompany her husband on business must mean the couple could not bear to be parted. But who would have known this meant their eternal separation? The point is not so much that his wife could stand to be killed, it is that she wanted to send her husband on his way. It is not so much that Di minded his wife's death, it is that he valued her righteous wifehood.

35. See for example the story of A Ji (*Xingshi hengyan*, Juan 35) in contrast to the original version by Tian Rucheng 田汝成. Tian's version is cited in Hanan, 1973, p. 244. Compared to the original, Langxian's version gives many more details about how and where the servant traded goods in order to get rich. Ray Huang makes the point that the *San yan* stories as a group are a rich store of information on late-Ming business practice. Many of the ones he cites to prove the point were written by Langxian. See his "Merchants of the Late-Ming as Presented in the *San-Yen* Stories", *The Journal of the Institute of Chinese Studies of the Chinese University of Hong Kong*, Vol. VII, No. 1 (December 1974), pp. 133–154.

36. *Shi dian tou*, p. 282.

37. This story, with its emphasis on courtship assisted by dreams, female educa-tion, and daughters who are the only child, suggests some relationship to Tang Xianzu's 湯顯祖 *Mudan ting*.

38. See "Qu Fengnu" 瞿鳳奴情愆死蓋 (*Shi dian tou*, Juan 4).

39. He presents not a single widow suicide, and he thinks of a way out for one of two betrothed maidens among his characters who contemplate self-destruc-tion when she is asked to marry someone other than her fiancé. The one he does allow to die is Qu Fengnu, who is a good maiden from a bad family. The other one, who survives, is from "Lu Mengxian Seeks a Wife". It is only when a wife is not altogether chaste that he metes out severe punishment. On the frequency of widow and maiden suicide, see T'ien, p. 46 and passim.

40. The sources of *Shi dian tou* stories are noted in Ye Dejun 葉德均, "*Shi dian tou* de zuozhe he laiyuan" 石點頭的作者和來源, *Tiandi* 天地 No. 6 (March, 1944). Those of Langxian's other stories are found in Hanan, *The Chinese Short Story*, pp. 233–235.

41. *Xingshi hengyan*, p. 781 and *Shi dian tou*, p. 339.

42. *Wo qingyuan maishen shishang* 我情願賣身市上, p. 296.

43. The main reason seems to be that Langxian wants to emphasize the error that allowed the wife to accompany her husband in the first place. See below.

44. Such inability to imagine the obvious seems to have played a part in heroic female thinking in higher class versions of *Pipa ji* 琵琶記 (The Lute), a drama which Langxian may have parodied elsewhere in his writing. See Tanaka Issei 田中一成, "A Study on *P'i-p'a chi* in Huichou Drama", *Acta Asiatica* No. 32 (March 1977), pp. 34–72. See p. 50 especially. On the question of Langxian's parody, see *Xingshi hengyan* 17, which takes place in Chenliu, the site of much of the action in *Pipa ji*.

45. See note 19 above.

46. Good examples of more complex ruminations can be found in *Xingshi hengyan*, Juan 18 and *Shi dian tou*, Juan 4.

47. The business manual *Shishang yaolan* 士商要覽 (Essentials for the Gentleman-Merchant at a Glance), original in the Naikaku bunko, edited by Wang Qi 汪淇 sometime in the seventeenth century, makes a special point of telling merchants not to get involved in drinking and gambling when they travel. It was becasue Zhou Di did not heed this rule that he fell victim to robbery in Xiangyang. His wife had warned him to be more careful before the trouble arose. *Shishang yaolan* is discussed in Timothy Brook, *Geographical Sources of Ming-Qing History* (Ann Arbor: Michigan, 1988), p. 41.

48. See Zhao Jingchen 趙景琛, *Zhongguo xiaoshuo congkao* 中國小說叢考 (Collected Studies of Chinese Fiction) (Jixun: Shandong renmin chubanshe, 1980), pp. 352–353.

49. See translation in Hanan, 1981, pp. 130–131.

50. *Shi dian tou*, pp. 302–303.

51. Another point is her eventual promotion to sagehood. Unless one is prepared to believe that Langxian is satirizing Qu Yuan as well as Second Sister Zong, it seems safer to take the story's rhetoric at face value.

52. Coincidentally, the four methods with which Langxian's text gives rise to ambiguity — dreams, jokes, *double entendres*, and (white) lies — all figure in Freud's pathbreaking *The Psychopathology of Everyday Life* (New York: Norton, 1966), first published in 1901.

53. "Master Dugu" is a particularly successful and interesting depiction of the relationship between female literacy and wantonness. The dream which the heroine shares with her husband evokes contemporary fears that the literary abilities of the woman of good family make it difficult to distinguish her from the courtesan, who is expected to use her poetry flirtatiously.

54. It is interesting to compare Langxian's story with a Japanese adaptation by Takizawa Bakin 滝沢馬琴. To begin with, Bakin situates the heroine's heroic sacrifice in a far less threatening context from a masculine Confucian point of view. It is merely one of several adventures experienced by a male adventurer, who is never shown to be weak or morally incompetent as Second Sister Zong's husband was. Moreover, the woman does not die from her sacrifice. Rather, she is rescued by the Buddha once her husband returns to the butcher

shop after hearing what she has done. Her written eulogy is shredded, as the woman pops out of the coffin completely unharmed. Bakin's interest in this episode appears to be partly sadomasochistic, in that he gives a loving description of the woman's eviscerated organs which the butcher sets out on his counter "like autumn flowers on a plain". In any event, the heroine of this adventure is not portrayed as morally overwhelming, and because she returns to life only when her husband comes to find her, it is he, not she, who is given superhuman powers. The name of the work in which Langxian's episode is used is entitled "Fukushuu kidan wakae no hato" (復讐奇談稚枝九得) (The Steadfast Dove, A Strange Tale of Revenge). It was first published in 1804. See Tokuda Takeshi 徳田武 "Bakin to Chuugoku shosetsu"馬琴と中国小説 (Bakin and the Chinese Novel) in *Kyokutei Bakin* (Nihon no koten 19) 曲亭馬琴 (日本の古典) (Tokyo: Shuueisha, 1980), pp. 130–140. I have also consulted the full text of Bakin's novel in *Zoku Bakin kesaku shuu* 続馬琴傑作集 (Sequel to Bakin's Masterpieces) (Tokyo: Hakubunkan, 1960), pp. 1–96. The quotation about autumn flowers is from p. 78. I am indebted to Haruko Iwasaki for help with Japanese translation. Eva Hung gave valuable assistance with Chinese translation. I am further indebted to Lydia Liu for a number of suggestions on the content of this article.

8

Projection, Displacement, Introjection: The Strangeness of *Liaozhai zhiyi*

Karl S.Y. Kao

After a lengthy eclipse at the end of the Song Dynasty, the classical-language tale in China experienced a resurgence in the early Qing, primarily as a result of Pu Songling's 蒲松齡 (1640–1715) *Liaozhai zhiyi* 聊齋誌異. Heralded by a few writers in the early- and mid-Ming such as Qu You 瞿佑 (1341–1427) and his imitators, Pu Songling's anthology inspired a host of followers who put out many collections of a similar nature. One may notice that this revival of the classical-language tale seemed to have been effectuated by nothing more than a continuation of the established generic track of the Six Dynasties *zhiguai* 志怪 and the Tang *chuanqi* 傳奇. As signalled by its title, *Liaozhai zhiyi* ostensibly keeps to the aesthetic tradition based on the notions of *qi* 奇, *guai* 怪, and *yi* 異, i.e., "the unusual", "the anomalous", and "the strange". It falls into the context of the literature of the supernatural and the fantastic that is the mainstay of early classical-language fiction.

Critics have been quick to point out that Pu's anthology is not merely an outgrowth of *zhiguai* (or the more inclusive genre of *biji* 筆記) and *chuanqi*. They have noticed the author's lively style, his social consciousness, and his progressive ideological proclivities that make the anthology different from the earlier genres.[1] Apposite as these observations are, they fail to take into account the central literary issue of how the *yi* in *Liaozhai* is different from "the strange" of the earlier fiction. An anthology that continues the tradition of the strange, *Liaozhai* distinguishes itself from its precursors by a fundamental change in the conception of the *yi* itself. Even as the collection uses the same raw material of the supernatural and the fantastic that appeals to the sense of wonder to attract attention and sustain interest, it transforms the strange items into a new mode of fantasy, which might be called *zhiyi* fantasy, by creating a new kind of strangeness aesthetics.

Identifying this *zhiyi* fantasy is part of the subject of this article and will be more fully dealt with later. It may be pointed out here that the aesthetics of the strange in *Liaozhai*, particularly that which concerns the supernatural, is accompanied or in fact brought about by an epistemological change in comparison with the earlier conceptions of *qi*, *yi*, and *guai*. Three perspectives can be posited regarding the "source" of the strange, each representing the dominant view of three periods in the history of Chinese fiction. The conception of the *guai* in Six Dynasties fiction, generally speaking, has a "factuality" orientation; i.e., the "supernatural occurrences out there" are taken to be the source of the strange.[2] Exceptions notwithstanding, events of the *zhiguai* tales usually purport to record "something real", referentially pointing to some external supernatural phenomena as part of nature. To most Tang literati who engaged in the writing of anomalous tales, whether the supernatural is real or not has become a bracketed question, or was only of marginal literary concern. Even as they habitually tag a claim at the end of the text asserting the "documentary" nature of the story, the primary interest of the writers has turned to giving literary representation to the subject, while the subject itself is to a great extent the bequest of the Six Dynasties anthologies or adaptations of folklore and legends.[3] The *Liaozhai* continued the tradition of the collection of legends and hearsay, but the author adds to the anthology something distinctly his own. In contrast to the referential assumption of the early *zhiguai*, Pu's anthology shares with the *chuanqi* an interest in representation, but it differs from the latter in the way it generates the strange in a text. A sizable amount of strangeness in *Liaozhai* may be seen to have its origin in linguistic and rhetorical associations. There is an epistemological, perceptual shift from the strange as the transcription of reality to the strange as mental associations. In terms of reading, recognition of the reported marvel does not direct one's attention to nature but to the working of human imagination or the rhetorical process. This new conception of the strange seems to reflect a general Ming-Qing intellectual concern usually posed in terms of the relations between self and society or the personal aspirations and changing values of the time.

The decline of the classical-language tale also had to do with the issue of orthodoxy in literary history.[4] As if to compensate for its non-orthodox status as a *xiaoshuo*小說 genre, *Liaozhai* asserts with over-determination its legitimacy and orthodoxy as a literary form. In his preface to the collection, the author indicates the seriousness of the intent of the anthology by comparing it with the orthodox poetic works of Qu Yuan 屈原 (340?–278 B.C.) and Li He 李賀 (790–816) and associating his taste for the strange with that of Su Shi 蘇軾 (1036–1011).[5] He claims that his tales are the expression of his *gu-fen* 孤憤 ("isolation and indignation" or "solitary indignation"), a term taken from *Hanfeizi* 韓非子 where it is used as a chapter title to signal the rhetorician-philosopher's frustration for lack of recognition. And finally the seriousness of the intent of *Liaozhai* is marked by a format of meta-textual comments modelled directly on the *Shi ji* 史記 (the authorial comment attached to a text is introduced by the phrase *Yishishi yue* 異史氏曰, coined after Sima Qian's 司馬遷 (145–86 B.C.) *Taishigong yue* 太史公曰). References to Hanfei 韓非 (280?–233 B.C.), Qu Yuan, and Sima Qian imply a connection with a sanctimonious view of literary creation — extreme personal tribulations and misfortune are a pre-condition for an author to create works of enduring value, as Mencius has eloquently stated and the Grand Historian and many others before Pu have forcefully exemplified.

Such claims of the author's intent have no doubt helped the text's acceptance by the author's contemporary and later readers. Modern critics have also emphasized this aspect in their evaluation of this anthology. The late Professor Jaroslav Průšek in his articles devoted to the study of *Liaozhai zhiyi*, for instance, emphasized the "personal feelings and experiences" of the author as the animating, motivating force behind the creation of the tales and pointed to the fact that there is "[a] strong note of indignant social criticism running through his [Pu's] writing".[6] Chun-shu Chang and Hsüeh-lun Chang's recent study has described even more systematically the heavy social implications of the tales,[7] while a good number of critical articles, and chapters in books, published in China in the last decade are devoted to the same topic.[8]

A member of a disfranchised gentry family, Pu Songling failed repeatedly to pass the provincial examination for the civil service[9] and had to spend much of his time (over thirty years) away from home as a private tutor to earn a living.[10] Living at a time of dynastic transition, Pu no doubt also witnessed much social instability, abuses of power by the ruling class and corrupt officials, the savagery of the rebellion, the hardships of the farmers caused by natural calamities as well as harsh government policies.[11] The combination of such social conditions and personal fate would make many feel indignant, and it may well be expected that Pu would vent his feelings in some of the entries in a collection that contains well over four hundred pieces.

The use of non-orthodox fiction to convey the orthodox values of social concerns and personal feeling constitutes an interesting phenomenon in the *Liaozhai*. This alliance — the employment of a literary form disapproved of by Confucius for the purpose of what is essentially a Confucian function of literature — had long been a dilemma for the literati who indulged in writing fiction with *guai* and *yi* subjects.[12] By the late-Ming and early-Qing, writers often treated the subjects self-reflexively, sometimes making parodic references to the Master's dictum on them. Yuan Mei's 袁枚 (1716–1797) *Zi buyu* 子不語 (What the Master Did Not Speak of), a collection of tales similar to *Liaozhai* in nature, directly confronted the issue with its title. Pu's use of fantasy in *Liaozhai* for the "serious" purpose of literature was but a continuation of this consciousness, but this practice is not without its inherent problems. For *Liaozhai* as a whole has a strong "frivolous" side to it; a good number of its tales give the impression of a flaunting of literary wit and the display of male fantasies. Often a tale starts out dealing with a social issue in a grim realist vein, then suddenly changes to the mode of fantasy and concludes on a happy note.

In order to enquire into these issues — the nature of the *zhiyi* fantasy and the claim of serious intention — this paper will examine roughly three groups of tales dealing with different subject matters: "ghosts and foxes", civil service examination, and social concerns. It will analyze the rhetorical operations that produce the different kinds of fantasy by relating them to the expressions of human desires, personal aspirations, and anxiety over changing social values. The generation of the strange and its imaginative propensity in the different kinds of tales will occupy the foreground of the discussion.

The Nature of the Anthology

Before referring to the individual texts, some general observations might be made regarding the nature of *Liaozhai* as a whole, so as to qualify the arguments to be presented later. Even a casual reader will notice that, although the anthology has a predominant subject of "ghosts and foxes", it is rather heterogeneous in content and in its mode of representation. It blends the familiar with the unfamiliar, and while it astonishes the reader with descriptive and narrative novelties, it does not shun old motifs adapted from past literature. The collection lures the reader with stories about supernatural beings but may also present him with pieces of perfect realism. Tales of high-sounding moralism are placed next to those featuring banter and occasional bawdiness. Well-structured tales of complicated plot are mixed with short items of an anecdotal nature included primarily for their curiosity or marvel appeal (the conception of *yi* here does not differ too greatly from that of the Six Dynasties), while the mimetic art of vivid description that sustains the narrative is often doctored with argumentation and even lyricism.

The heterogeneous nature of the style and subject matter is partly due to the origins of most of the items collected in the anthology. From the author's own preface and from internal evidence, many of the stories are shown to have originated in legends, folklore, hearsay, "eyewitness accounts", etc.; they were given to Pu orally or in writing, which he sometimes barely elaborated as he edited and wrote them down for inclusion in his anthology. Many are layered texts resulting from the rewriting of old texts and superpositioning, grafting, and juxtaposing of texts (or motifs). The significance of an old text is often left visible, not entirely "erased", as it is interconnected to other texts by expansion, intersection or accretion. Such origins and the fact that Pu Songling probably worked on the anthology for over twenty years seem to account for the great diversity in style, mode, and subject matter. The examples singled out for analysis and discussion here will not cover all varieties, and generalizations derived from these examples have limited applicability. Nevertheless the discovered features are typical and dominant, and it is these features that seem to make *Liaozhai* distinct.

Because of this manner of origin and their layered structure, the texts require a reading attentive to the complexity of creation by the mixed mode of adaptation. However, an adequate reading, or even just the attempt to sort out the "author's intent" from that of the adapted text, for example, would complicate the paper beyond management. It may be simply explained here that these are often texts with heterogeneous motifs and thematic charges that exert centrifugal pulls in several directions and usually resist a centripetal reading. In this connection, the Yishishi's Authorial Comment is a meta-text that attempts to provide a kind of centripetal control, but it often shows itself as an incomplete reading; it tends to impose a moralistic, didactic view on the text by allegorizing. By the device of the Authorial Comment, the text in fact makes a clear distinction between the "textual intent" and "authorial intent" (the voice of

Yishishi may be considered to coincide with that of the "author" and is clearly distinguishable from that of the "narrator" of the main text). Our reading, by the dictate of the article's topic, will be largely centripetal and eclectic; it will attend to overall textual elements (mostly related to the plot) by relating them to the dominant theme (explicit or implicit). But it will occasionally take into account some heterogeneous and seemingly inexplicable motifs, and to that extent attends to the latent meaning of the text as well. This would necessarily neglect centrifugal pulls of many other heterogeneous elements, just as the Authorial Comment often does. The Yishishi's comment indeed will serve as a useful reference — it often gives a moralistic reading and suppresses, or overlooks, other "intentions" of the text, which this article will occasionally try to bring out.

Fantasy and Rhetorical Operations: Transformation by Metonymic Association

I shall begin the discussion of the generation of strangeness in *Liaozhai* fantasy by referring to a linguistic phenomenon in Chinese. A most colourful type of expression in the Chinese language is the so-called *chengyu* 成語, which are often metaphoric, their presence serving as a noticeable reminder of the general figurative nature of the language. As we know, many of the *chengyu* are derived from *yuyan* 寓言, the short narratives used often in early Chinese philosophical writings to illustrate or make concrete abstract ideas and arguments. Normally composed of four characters, these adage-like expressions capture the main point of the original narratives in a nutshell and become set expressions in the language by the principle of condensation. They in turn are often applied figuratively to describe comparable situations or ideas.

Liaozhai zhiyi has been considered as *yuyan*, or "imputed words" which work like fables in that they often carry a symbolic, non-literal level of meaning, more or less as allegory does. This allegoric mode of *Liaozhai* will be relevant to our discussion later. For the present the term is mentioned here to explain a process of narrative generation used in *Liaozhai* which reverses the condensation process from *yuyan* to *chengyu*. This opposite mode might be called *matrix expansion* which works by amplifying a common, set expression (a short verbal text) into a full narrative structure. A tale entitled "The Dream of Wolves" (夢狼)[13] may be cited for illustration. Constructed by superposition and juxtaposition of different "worlds", the first part of this tale tells of a father's visit to his son's office in a dream. Informed of his son's new appointment to an official position, he visits him and finds, to his amazement and horror, that the son's office is filled with wolves that feed on human flesh as regular fare; white human bones are piled up outside the hallway. At one point his son turns, right in front of his eyes, into a tiger. This scene is later explained in the Authorial Comment as exemplifying the expression *guan hu li lang* 官虎吏狼 ("the official a tiger, his subordinates wolves"), an expression derived from a remark made by Confucius that cruel government policies were worse than ferocious tigers (苛政猛於虎).[14] It is not difficult to see that this story is generated from the matrix of a metaphoric saying: it makes "real" or literalizes the metaphor, albeit in a dream. Although this matrix is not a *chengyu per se*, the reverse process of generating a full narrative from a short verbal text is evident.

To continue with the story: the son in real life (i.e., in the diegetic world) turns out indeed to be a corrupt, avaricious official and is in time decapitated by some avenging peasant-bandits. Subsequently restored to life by a deity, his head however is grafted sideways so that the chin is made to rest on the shoulder, a way of marking his inhumanity (because of his ferocity towards the people). Also the head is so postured as to make him always "look at his own back" (自顧其背) — the expression being a metaphoric way of saying that one should consider ahead of time the evil *consequences* of one's actions (i.e., what follows in one's back). This portion of the tale thus is similarly a literalization of a metaphoric expression. In such a narrative operation the entities and relationships in a linguistic expression are animated and expanded analogically to become an *occurrence* in the diegetic world of the narrative. The Authorial Comment appended at the end gives a clear indication that the entire story is a creation based on a linguistic cue — the metaphor is the source of the narrative imagination.

Such a linguistic basis or the "matrix" provides the structural relations of elements and the basic tone (or thematic overview), but normally does not contain all the "genetic information" for the actual shape and features of the narrative, making superposition of other texts and variations in tone possible. That Pu Songling sometimes uses this mode of generation playfully is shown in the tale called "The Fool for Books" (書癡).[15] The matrixes in this tale are the sayings that through the study of books one may earn an income of "a thousand bushels of grain" (千鍾粟) and find the beauty with "countenance like jade" (顏如玉) — exhortations to students promising rewards for their diligence. So one day a book blown out of the "fool's" hand by the wind leads him to discover a cellar full of grains, but already *rotten*; and then in time a cut-out of a girl placed between the pages of his book comes alive and jumps out of it, only to enjoin him *not* to study anymore.

Narratives generated by literalization of verbal expressions, however, are but a particular form of a general mode of transformation between two systems of signification frequently seen in *Liaozhai*. Further examples will help illustrate the general principle behind such transformation. The tales "The Taoist of Lao Mountain" (勞山道士), "The Mural" (畫壁), and "The Picture Horse" (畫馬)[16] all show a generation of the strange based on the iconic relationship of signs and things. In the first, a Taoist master amazes a novice with the magic of transforming a paper-cut moon into a "real" moon and a chopstick into a slip of a lady who sings and dances to entertain guests. Even more iconic in the relationship between the matrix and the narrative text is the transformation in "The Mural" and "The Picture Horse". The first story tells how a scholar is transported into a wall painting in a Buddhist temple that represents a scene from the *Vimalakīrti Sūtra*: "The Heavenly Maiden Scatters Flowers". The scholar's attraction to one of the maidens in the painting — he gazed at her, entranced — seems to be the cause of the strange occurrence. As he enters the painting, the painted world turns "real" in that the represented figures take on life, and soon he finds himself engaged in an affair with the girl who attracted him in the first place. Similarly the marvelous horse that gallops a hundred *li* in a blinking of the eye in the second tale turns out to be one that has escaped from a hanging scroll, said to be by Zhao Mengfu 趙孟頫 (1254–1322), the famous painter of horses.

These examples display a distinct process involved in the generation of the "supernatural": a matrix system of the signifier (verbal or visual representation), which is static or constitutes an abbreviated text, is animated and expanded by narrativization within a framework suggested by the matrix. All of the examples given above reveal an imagination that may be characterized as metonymic in nature — metonymy being metaphoric substitution by the relation of cause and effect, the sign and the thing, and by contiguity. The *Liaozhai* tales transform the "sign" to "the thing" it signifies.

The example of "The Mural" points furthermore to another feature of the strangeness in the *Liaozhai* transformations. In time the scholar comes out of the painting and returns to the human world, and amazingly he finds that his affair with the girl has left an effect on the painted world — the maiden now wears her hair style like a married woman, as she was made to do by her companions after they discovered her affair with the scholar. This extra dimension of strangeness may be described as a "transmutability effect" that characterizes many of the trans-world interactions of the *Liaozhai* tales. In retrospect, this trans-world effect also marks the fantasy in "The Dream of Wolves" and "The Fool for Books". The girl in the latter tale proceeds to teach the "fool" the "facts of life" and bears him a son. In "The Dream of Wolves", not only does the father dream of something unknown to him which then comes true (the son made an official), but the dream records a telepathic event: the father sees his human-turned-tiger son getting his teeth knocked out, an incident which has a "real life" correspondence in his son losing all his teeth from a fall from horseback that occurs at exactly the same time.

Thus an initial characterization of the strangeness of *Liaozhai* may be described as follows. There are two aspects to a transformation: first is the animation or narrativization of a static (verbal or visual) text. When the transformation involves interaction between two worlds (one of them usually the human world), there tends to be a cross-world effect of transmutation in the non-human (the other) world. Certain human properties (or attributes of the "real world") normally denied the "represented" other world are acquired by it through animation or narrativization — the papercut girl becomes pregnant and bears a human baby; the painted girl changes (grows) from a maiden to a woman. There is a projection of human, temporal attributes, such as growth and change, to the static representation in which time is frozen. The transmutation thus contains an oxymoron: A static situation (spatial) with dynamic properties (temporal) — change is combined with changelessness. Projections of human world qualities to the non-human world — often accompanied by a blending of contradictory properties — seem to be the propensity of the mode of transformation in *Liaozhai* fantasy in general. Such propensities are also seen to underlie the central subject of the book — "ghosts and foxes".

Tales of Ghosts and Foxes: Fantasy as Projection of Oxymoronic Desires

It is primarily the subject of "ghosts and foxes" that makes *Liaozhai* a continuation of the *zhiyi* tradition, and the centrality of this subject in the book is indicated by its original title of *Guihu zhuan* 鬼狐傳 (Accounts of

Ghosts and Foxes).[17] Interactions of fox spirits, ghosts, and other super-natural beings with humans are motifs that have been part of the literary tradition since the Six Dynasties *zhiguai* and Tang *chuanqi*, and even earlier in historiographies. But *Liaozhai* engenders the sense of unusual-ness by modifying the generic conventions of how these motifs work. It is the wont of the writers of Tang tales, as we know, to claim at the end of a story that the reported supernatural occurrence is based on an eyewitness account. This is also the case with many of the tales in *Liaozhai*, but by now the pretense has lost its innocence and is made an element of literary play in the moment of self-reflexivity. The tale "Dreaming of the Fox" (狐夢)[18] is generated in such a moment.

The hero of this tale, named Bi Yian 畢怡安, is said to have been reading the story of the fox-fairy in "Qingfeng" 青鳳[19] from Pu Song-ling's *Liaozhai zhiyi* (Yes! it is so stated in the fictional text) and has been so charmed and fascinated by her that he longs for a meeting with a fox-spirit like her. The realization of his wish (or "dream") forms the narrative of this new story: one night he dreams of a visit by a fox-lady who, after he wakes up, miraculously appears at his side. The dream image is transmuted into reality. The transmutability between dream and reality is high-lighted again in a scene where the hero dreams of attending a drink-ing party with the "sisters" of his bride (the fox he originally dreamed of was there to act as a matchmaker to introduce him to a younger fox girl). He awakens from the dream of the party to find that his mouth still tastes of wine, about which his fox bride assures him that even though the party took place in his dream, it "in fact was no dream" (實非夢也).

The generation of a "real" fox out of a "dream" induced by a previous text is another strange case of "dream come true", but it points to a non-referential, self-reflexive, and self-generative process. Leaving aside the issue of self-reflexivity for now, the text here pushes the notion of cross-world relations to the foreground and sets a playful tone from the outset by telling the reader that the hero is Pu's own friend, a member of the clan with whom Pu is employed as a family tutor — a fact his contem-porary coterie readers no doubt recognized. The same mechanism of cross-world interactions is applied twice here: one transmutation exists between "fiction" and "reality" in the diegetic world, and another between the *Liaozhai* fictional world and the author/reader's actual world, making the fantasy world a part of the real world (or vice versa). Bi is said to have told the author-narrator about his marvelous experience because the fox-fairy he met requested that he ask his friend, the author of the famous stories of fox fairies, to write and circulate a story about herself. Transmutability points back to textuality for its origin.

As has often been noted, one of the basic features that differentiates Pu's imagination from the strangeness of traditional *zhiguai* is the change of the mode of existence of the ghosts and foxes that populate the world of *Liaozhai*. According to the traditional generic code of *zhiguai*, ghosts and animal spirits may traffic with humans and have sexual relations with them, but the relationships are as a rule temporary: "the ways of the living and the dead are separate" (*you ming yilu* 幽明異路) and must be kept so. With Pu Songling, the prevailing situation is that such unions would become permanent. Here ghosts and fox spirits may become fully human, assimilating into the real world to lead a normal human life; they may marry a human and give birth to healthy human babies (who are often submitted to, and successfully pass, the "shadow test" — ghosts are said to cast no shadows under the sun). New ground rules are introduced: a ghost may die again, and may also bleed; a "bleeding ghost" is not an oxymoron in this fantasy world.[20]

This fantasy of transformation used for the generation of the imaginary coincides with a modification of a traditional rule of the fantastic in the use of the dream motif. Dreams in Chinese narrative traditionally perform two functions: either they are allegorical, as is the case in the well-known Tang tale "Zhenzhong ji" 枕中記 ("The World Inside the Pillow"), or they form a "twilight zone" where the living and the dead or other beings may communicate with each other (as often seen in the Six Dynasties *zhiguai* and early historiographies). Both "Dreaming of the Fox" and "The Dream of Wolves" add to the dream motif a further dimension by making the dream world interact with reality through transmutation.[21]

In terms of human relevance, literalization and animation of representational systems seem to consist of a semiotic *projection* of attributes of the human world, including human desires, onto the *other* worlds, be it the world of the spirits of fauna, flora, and even mineral, or of ghosts and fairies. Images from the other world acquire the status as duplicates of the human world and furthermore become the manifestations of idealized, most desirable beings. Indeed, some of the most endearing and memorable stories in *Liaozhai* are the stories of fox-fairies and female ghosts, who embody certain human qualities and virtues that are not only admirable, pleasing and desirable, but would also be beneficial to the maintenance of order in human society.

The heroine in "Qingfeng"[22] that so charms Pu's friend Bi Yian is just such a creature. Moderate and mindful of the code of chastity, Qingfeng is not unresponsive to the hero's appeal to her tender feelings. And when her uncle, who brought her up, is in need of help, she is observant of the principle of *bao* 報 ("requital") and does not forget her debt of kindness to him. "Yingning" 嬰寧[23] features one of the most appealing heroines for the mirthful mood that characterizes her existence. The description of her innocent, impulsive laughter in various situations forms a small literary *tour de force* in the anthology — the sound of Yingning's laughter must have lingered in the ears of many a reader even after they put down the story. But she is also marked by her filial concern for the ghost mother who raised her. In "Xiaocui" 小翠 ,[24] we have a fox-girl who comes to pay a human family a debt of gratitude incurred by her mother (*bao* being one of the most compelling ethical codes in Chinese society, a distinct trait of man as a social being). A veritable "god-send", she marries the son and cures his mental retardation; her harmless play- acting with her young husband brightens the mood of the entire family and serves as a device to save her father-in-law from the evil schemes of his rival at court. But most endearing of all her acts, to the male reader at least, must be the last thing she does before she takes her final leave of her husband to return to her own world. Hoping to ease his pain of losing her and to make it easy for him to transfer his affection to his new wife, she gradually changes her own looks and voice to becomes those of his future bride. As for ghost stories, the vivid description of Yingning is matched perhaps only by the endearing mischievousness of the two young female ghosts in "Xiaoxie" 小謝[25] (who are also caring, even chivalric, when the hero runs into trouble and is imprisoned), or the ghost girl in "Nieh Xiaoqian" 聶小倩 [26] who, once removed from the dominance of her demon master, becomes gentle, industrious, and compliant to her human companion and benefactor. Coupled with her dazzling looks, these traits make Xiaoqian very much an "ideal female" in the author's cultural tradition.

Liaozhai may be understood in one sense as a kind of fantasy that portrays human desire; it betrays particularly the desires of Chinese males. The appealing portrayals of foxes and ghosts and other transformed spirits in this vein are the transference of what men want from their wives to the creatures of another world. The transference is necessary because of the separation of love (libidinal desire) from marriage (which is oriented to the continuation of the family line) in traditional Chinese culture. This image of desire and conflict is probably most nakedly revealed in the piece entitled "Hengniang" 恒娘 ,[27] which also provides a key to the real meaning of the *guihu* 鬼狐 image in *Liaozhai* in general.

Mainly a story about how a wife learns to secure the love of her husband by following the step-by-step instructions of a lady friend, the text describes this process as that of "making the wife a concubine", or *yi qi wei qie* 以妻爲妾 (in this marriage system the wife has the official, legal status, whereas the concubine often is the object of the husband's real affection and sexual desire). The instructions are based on the psychological principle that "it's human nature to be bored with the old and to crave the new, to value what's difficult to get and slight what's easily available".[28] To complete the lesson of how to put the husband under her total sway, the wife finally must learn to make her demeanour sexy — that is, to act like a concubine. Hengniang, the lady who shows such an understanding of man's desires, is revealed at the end to be a fox-fairy. This most clearly reveals the true implication of the fox metaphor in the book.[29]

The Authorial Comment indicates an ambivalence towards this story which is consistent with the ambivalent value served by foxes and other animal transformations in Chinese tradition. As the tale revels in the expression of a desire (a public secret), the use of the metaphor (animal spirit) also carries with it a warning. And the Authorial Comment adds another gesture of censorship. It expresses disapproval of the husband's psychology by characterizing it as *huo* 惑 ("delusion" or "folly") and comparing it to the *Hanfeizi* story of *maidu huanzhu* 買櫝還珠 — "buying the box; returning the pearl" — a parable describing the human folly of being taken in by the showy and neglecting the substance. It further compares a concubine's enchantment with the manipulation of the emperor by obsequious, self-serving eunuchs. Evidently there is a conflict between the "textual meaning" and the "authorial intention": the display of desire in the narrative must be explicitly countered by a moralistic reading. Foxy qualities are desirable but can also constitute a real danger; their supplantation of the wifely qualities of being "dignified and virtuous" 端莊賢淑 would undermine the entire social and familial order. Yet the image of desire is ultimately allowed expression.

Glen Dudbridge in his illuminating study of Tang tales has identified the group of ideas associated with the theme of "beautiful creatures" (*youwu* 尤物) in the context of that literature.[30] Pu Songling is apparently dealing with the same issue here. But his fox-fairies are not simple duplicates of the virtuous alien creature of "Renshi zhuan" 任氏傳. His *guihu* stories develop the canonical problem of "beautiful creatures as beguiling and dangerous" that confronted Zhangsheng 張生 of *Yingying zhuan* 鶯鶯傳 by putting the problem in the new context of conflicting desires. What is at issue here is not simply the desire for the sexual qualities of women, for this could easily be met by the institution of the concubine or the courtesan.[31] The ghost-and-fox is thus not a metaphoric displacement for prohibited desires either. The conflict arises from the desire of the *combination* of wifely virtues with the seductive qualities of the concubine/courtesan in the same person, which is unattainable or not permitted in the familial structure and the marriage institution. The image of the fox (or ghost) portrayed in *Liaozhai* is an oxymoron — the combination is impossible as it is impermissible. In this light most of the ghost-and-fox stories are semiotic projections where the "other world" is a metonymic representation of the "human world" in the diegetic context. Metonymy furthermore serves as an oxymoronic solution to a social complex in the conflict between personal desire and familial institutions.

This type of fantasy and use of metaphor in *Liaozhai* is pervasive but not exclusive. We now turn to look at tales that focus on the examination system with which Pu Songling had a close personal experience; they may be seen to work in a different mode of narrative imagination.

Examination Candidates: Fantasy as Reflection of Displaced Aspirations

There are enough tales dealing with the civil service examinations in *Liaozhai* to give a cumulative impression of a frequent, recurrent theme.[32] Many of these tales have been taken as the author's expression of frustration and indignation arising from his failure in the civil service recruitment system. A tale like "Wang Zian" 王子安,[33] which describes the neurotic anxiety of a candidate awaiting the results of the examinations, no doubt testifies to Pu's own emotional involvement and the distress and agony the examinations could inflict on an individual. This piece is more a sketch than a fully developed story; for the study of narrative imagination we will consider some others. But a few constant factors in these tales may be summarized first.

The civil service recruitment system used the examinations as a device for the selection of candidates to take government posts. In this selection, two factors were of crucial importance: the candidate's ability in essay writing and the examiner's recognition of that ability. It takes more than one's own talent and efforts to succeed in this enterprise — ultimately the selection hinges on the assessment by an examiner. Examiners therefore become the object of either sincere gratitude (considered both as a "master", *shi* 師 , and a *zhiyin* 知音) or heart-felt resentment and spite. For a failed candidate, the qualifications of the examiners apparently could be a point of contention. As there existed no official channel for protest against suspected or real incompetence or corruption, fictional tales may have served as a channel for such gripes.[34] Another important feature of these tales is the rival candidates in the competition who could become good friends or *zhiji* 知己 . A government position not only enabled the successful individual to contribute to the administration of public affairs and the welfare of the common people, it also meant social status, wealth and power. The motivations of the candidates may vary; success in the selection process, for some, may lead to corruption and loss of personal integrity. A candidate's moral character then also becomes a prominent theme in these tales.

"Yu Qu'e" 于去惡 [35] is a tale that shows the fate of examination candidates to be heavily dependent upon which examiners were assigned to read the papers. Made up again of various motifs as subtexts, the story tells of how a human scholar named Tao makes friends with the ghost scholar Yu Qu'e (the new kind of strangeness described here is Yu's "memorizing" texts by burning and swallowing the ashes of written pages — again a metonymic imagination.) He learns of the outrage of incompetent examiners in the underworld institution of examination, which is said to exist in the parallel system of the human world also. The text registers a strong protest against the incompetence and avarice of the examiners when Yu Qu'e scoffs that the *blind* musician Shi Kuang 師曠 and *treasurer* He Chiao 和嶠 are among regular readers for the underworld examination papers. Yu Qu'e is confident in passing the selection process, but the situation changes when the original examiner (the God of Literature) is replaced. The story however ends on a happy note for the ghost scholar Yu whose rejection is reversed when his compositions are re-read by the Marquis of Huan (桓侯) (i.e., Zhang Fei 張飛 , ?–221) and as a result he receives an appointment to a position as he had hoped. It is Tao's *fate*, however, to be kept back from an official career: although chosen as a senior licentiate, he goes no further in advancement (like Pu Songling himself). The tale has an accreted portion that deals with the incarnation of another of Tao's ghost friends as his baby brother. He takes consolation in tutoring his new sibling.

The tale "Overseer of Literature" (司文郎)[36] again has a good scholar failing the examination due to the dubious qualification of the assessors, who are the direct object of satire in this tale. Three scholars are involved here. Wang (from whose perspective the narrative is presented) is an intelligent student but lacking in social savvy. He meets a "student from Yuhang" 餘杭生 who has come to sit for the same examination and is staying in the same Buddhist hostel. Mediocre in talent but arrogant, he snubs Wang's overtures to make his acquaintance. Then comes along a witty scholar named Song, who is not an aspirant (he turns out to be a ghost); he befriends Wang and exposes Yuhang's shallowness by his witticism. The three scholars meet a blind fortune-teller (also a ghost) who makes perceptive evaluations of the quality of essays by sniffing on the writings put to fire (based on the metaphor that bad writing "stinks"). When sniffing the essays written by the examiner who has passed Yuhang and failed Wang, he is so offended by the smell that he "retches violently" and "breaks wind like thunder". Later on the ghost scholar Song is selected to be the Overseer of Literature at a certain locality. Before taking leave of Wang he has found out that Wang's path to officialdom is blocked because of a misdeed in his previous life (killing a maid), again using fate to explain the failure of a good scholar.

The two stories both point to the role of the examiners; we also see that both use the device of dual or multiple roles (contrasting types of candidates — the arrogant candidate is a recurrent character-type). The ghost scholar is friendly to the sympathetic human candidate, who always fails to obtain a position. In both stories, the ghost scholars are vindicated by their selection to an office that will enable them to help with the condition of literature in the underworld, a good fortune not shared by their human counterparts.

Rather than the projection of desire seen in the ghost-and-fox stories, tales of examination candidates are concerned with social status and self-image, and may be understood through the model of discourse related to aspiration and self-esteem. To attain an official position was a goal in life prescribed for most members of Chinese intelligentsia. Earning the desired degree brought with it, besides prestige, power and wealth, an affirmation of one's worth. Failing to attain the aspired status could result in guilt, remorse (a disappointment for the family) and dejection. Guilt may be expiated by attributing the failure to the external factors on which success ultimately depends — the examiner or fate, or both. Hence the derision of the assessors — which at the same time vents the feeling of frustration. Fate as a cause lies beyond the purview of human intelligence — maybe this is why a ghost scholar must be brought into play, for an otherworldly being may have access to information on the workings of fate. But why are the ghost scholars, despite temporary setbacks in their effort to contribute to the justice of the underworld system, always vindicated? It may be because the world beyond is understood to abide always and ultimately by the supra-conception of universal justice (Heavenly Law). These considerations may quiet the sense of guilt or remorse, but would not uplift the spirit depressed by the inability to attain the goal of higher social status. The only alternative is some other kind of recognition, by a *zhiji*, for example, or re-investment of energy and hope in some other goal. We notice the motif of tutor-student relationship in "Yu Qu'e"; other kinds of substitution are highlighted in other tales of examinations.

"Yesheng" 葉生 [37] is a story often considered to offer the closest counterpart to Pu's own career (and state of mind) since it features a failed scholar-turned-tutor as hero. The titular character Ye is a talented scholar who meets with no luck in the examinations until a new magistrate arrives in his district. The magistrate, named Ting, takes very much to Ye's writings; his influence helps Ye pass the prefectural examination in first place. Cherishing high hopes for himself, Ye fails however in the subsequent provincial examination (see note 9) (just as Pu Songling did). Devastated, he falls sick and dies, but his ghost takes on a bodily form and accompanies Ting home to become the tutor of his son. A brilliant student, the son passes both the provincial and metropolitan examinations (*xiangshi* and *huishi* 會試) and is duly appointed to a position. Through Ting's assistance, Ye eventually also passes the *xiangshi*, which makes him eligible for appointment to minor offices. Without knowing that it is his own ghost that has obtained the degree, Ye goes home feeling satisfied. Upon arriving, he is confronted by a desolate household; his impoverished wife tells him that he has been dead for three years and asks him "not to use his apparition to frighten the living". As he enters the house, he sees his own coffin; thereupon his body fades away, leaving a heap of clothes on the ground.

Ye's ghost goes with Ting to become his son's tutor so as to pay back his appreciation of him — for being a *zhiji*, as explained both in the text and in the Authorial Comment. The Authorial Comment compares the strangeness of this with that of Qianniang's 倩娘 disembodied soul following her lover to live away from her family described in Chen Xuanyou's 陳玄祐 (fl. 779) Tang tale. The libidinal energy that animates the ghost of Chen's tale is re-invested in the object of a *zhiji*, which in this cultural tradition is indeed one of the most deeply felt and forceful needs for a member of the intelligentsia. The external agent, originally in the form of the examiner or fate who would not recognize one's worth, is replaced by "the one who knows me". This tale in fact describes an intertwined complex of substitution: Ye's hope for recognition by the examiner is replaced by the recognition by a *zhiji*; his aspiration to an official post is realized in his student's career; the gratification of holding office is replaced by the gratification of seeing one's student receive appointments; and a life-long dream for obtaining a crucial degree is realized only when the hero is in his changed state as a ghost. The *zhiji* here lacks the power to confer status (just as the ghostly friend, also a *zhiji*, may explain the working of fate but is powerless to alter it).[38] This *zhiji* may affirm one's worth and self-esteem to an extent, but is always a lesser substitute for the other "real agent". The obtaining of a degree in ghostly form again brings no real benefits — rather it is an ironic reflection of failure in life. But the tone of the tale is pathetic rather than ironic. There is an inability or unwillingness to transcend the condition or fully re-invest one's energy in an alternative goal.

The cultural tradition itself in fact provides an alternative to the career in officialdom and the "examination hell". In literature this alternative is put in terms of the Taoist pursuit, best represented in fiction by the Tang tale "Zhenzhong ji". There are several tales in *Liaozhai* that deal with this theme which ostensibly embraces a Taoist outlook, but which contain motifs that do strange things to the overt message. In fact one of the best known stories in the anthology is "A Sequel to the *Yellow Millet Dream*" 續黃粱,[39] a story modelled on the Tang prototype (and Tang Xianzu's 湯顯祖 (1550–1617) adaptation of it in the Ming drama form). But instead of a simple "travelling young man"(as in "Zhenzhong ji"), the hero here is a student who has just passed the highest *jinshi* 進士 (doctorate) degree and, full of smugness and self-complacence, is looking forward to an eminent appointment. The dream that begins with the realization of the appointment is heavily slanted to the description of the appointee's abuse of power and neglect of duties. The Taoist enlightenment theme about the vicissitudes of fortune and ephemerality of life, although present, is largely overtaken by the Buddhist concept of retribution — the corrupt official is punished in life, in hell, and again in reincarnation. The excessiveness of the most horrendous tortures applied to the hero makes the tale read very much as a tirade against the corrupt official rather than an allegory of Taoist-Buddhist enlightenment (this is corroborated by Yishishi's own reading). The scholar in awaking is presented as being thoroughly chastised of his smugness.

Two other tales, "Jia Fengzhi" 賈奉雉 and "The Island of Immortals" (仙人島),[40] are frequently cited for their presentation of a similar Taoist alternative; we will take a quick look at the former. It describes the scholar Jia's repeated failure at the examinations, not because his essays are no good but because they are too good and too profound for the understanding of the examiners. Only through the magic trick of a Taoist adept is he able to write *below* his usual standard and thereupon pass the test. But the scholar is so ashamed of these essays that he renounces his degree to retreat to the mountains in search of spiritual freedom. However, because his desire for his wife has not been fully cleansed, he is sent back to the human world. There he inexplicably turns to the pursuit of a career in the bureaucracy again and has a stint of rise and fall before his friend (the Taoist adept) comes to take him and his wife away. The Yishishi in his comment refers to an actual case of a scholar who obtained his degree by composing essays inferior to his usual non-examination writings. It ends the comment with a remark on the fictional hero's career: "The fact that Jia felt ashamed and left the world suggests that he had in him the making of an immortal. Yet he returned to the human world and degraded himself for the need of sustenance. To what extent indeed could poverty reduce a person!"

There is no drama of Freudian psychic compensation in these tales, for the human factor here is not the repressed desire in want of expression and the need for reconciliation with the fact of repression. It is the deprivation of an aspiration, for which the energy may be (has been) re-invested in some subjected goal, which however will never be like the "original" one. In human terms, the subject matter concerns a material condition that cannot be amended by literary sublimation. Taoist tales of aspiration to immortality could be made a metaphor for a mental transcendency of the dejection induced by the impossible aspiration to success in officialdom. But strangely these tales on Taoist themes are made to serve again the purpose of satire and derision against examiners and impudent candidates. Yishishi's remarks on Jia's "poverty" and "need of sustenance" perhaps betrays part of the reason of Pu's own continuous attempts to take the examination until an advanced age — provided, in place of these words, we read "the aspiration to honour, glory and wealth". Maybe there is some truth in the mainland critics' view that there is a deep "feudalistic" streak in Pu's outlook of life.[41]

Social Themes: Fantasy as Introjection of New Values

Tales that imply a criticism of social injustice, misguided government policies and corruption of the bureaucracy are generally more impersonal and detached, although some of the public issues (e.g., unjust taxation) could have a bearing on the author as a lower-echelon member of the gentry class. A large number of the *Liaozhai* entries touch on social evils and bureaucratic corruption, making this theme a prominent one in the anthology.

The topic of social criticism involves the question of censorship and the author's personal safety, and thus becomes a much more complicated issue for the writer and the reader alike. Fantasy may serve as a convenient form to deflect censorship and thus make veiled criticism easier with its device of reference to the other world. Metaphoric modes of representation may also provide the assumption for an allegoric reading that injects a social import to fantasy. The validity and force of criticism of public affairs however could only come from an objective ground and realistic representation. The question then shifts to the reader's "allegoric" reading (taking the tales as *yuyan*) and the application of a perceived import on either the general condition of society or some particular aspect of reality. Many of the tales with a social theme are obvious in their intent and the Authorial Comment often further persuades or guides the reader toward such allegoric applications. "The Dream of Wolves" mentioned earlier, for example, uses fantasy to describe the reality of corrupt officials (without pointing to any actual individuals); its didactic intention is made clear from the punishment meted out to the evil official at the end, while the Authorial Comment strengthens the point by seeing in it "a lesson from gods and spirits". Some of these tales, however, contain heterogeneous elements and motifs which contradict the obvious meaning of the text. We will be confined in this section to looking at a few such stories.

A tale often cited by critics to show the "serious" side of *Liaozhai* is "The Cricket" (促織).[42] The usual reading sees in it a clear manifestation of Pu Songling's concerns with the social conditions of the time, his indignation regarding how government policy could cause, or had actually caused, extreme misery for the people. Based on history, the story begins as a daring socio-political exposé, pointing the finger directly at the emperor himself (even though it is a Ming emperor Xuan Zong 宣宗 —

who reigned in 1426–1435, about three hundred years before the author's time). But it ends strangely on a happy note for all concerned.

The story starts out by recounting how an honest but inarticulate man by the name of Cheng Ming 成名 is made chief of a village by the local bailiffs and becomes responsible for collecting crickets to present to the imperial court, a job made very costly because of the Emperor's indulgence in cricket fighting. Cheng Ming exhausts his limited resources without finding a good fighting insect, is whipped and flogged, but not relieved of his job. Despairing of ever fulfilling the duty, he suffers great anguish and contemplates suicide. Only with the aid of a soothsayer does he finally manage to catch a presentable cricket, which, however, is killed accidentally by his nine-year-old son before he has the chance to present it to the official in charge. In fear of his father's wrath, the son jumps into a well and drowns himself. By this, the tale reaches the height of its tragic pathos in a convincing tone of realism; but then fantasy sets in and puts into motion a reversal of fortune for Cheng's family. The spirit of the son turns into a cricket and after many victories in test matches the insect is presented to the Emperor: it wins rewards for both the officials involved as well as for Cheng's family. The soul of the son later returns to the body, restoring the boy to life to tell the story of his miraculous transformation.

Blending a realistic social picture with marvelous occurrences, the story produces an overall effect not quite congruent with the sombre tone of social criticism set forth in the first part. The tragic crescendo built up by the death of the son is annulled by the plot's flight into the world of fantasy: tragedy is replaced by a gratifying victory of the puny-looking cricket over vicious adversaries. The Yishishi Comment offers a frank remonstration against the Emperor, while laying the blame of Cheng Ming's suffering also on the ruthless magistrate and bailiffs — the admonition is daring. However, the force of this counsel is diminished, even neutralized at the end. The Comment sees the good ending, the transformation, as a reward for Cheng Ming's honesty, thus absorbing the shock of the criticism into a rhetoric of "the good is rewarded after all his tribulations".[43]

Here we see a pattern observable in more than one tale of social criticism: an unpleasant, disturbing state of affairs is transformed into, with the turn of the narrative, a state more satisfactory, more acceptable to human wishes. Another frequently cited tale for its exposure of corruption, "Xi Fangping" 席方平,[44] for example, shows a similar pattern. The titular hero, in seeking justice for his recently diseased father who is being unjustly persecuted in the underworld, goes into hell himself and lays complaints at the various courts of the underworld hierarchy. At each court he is either ignored, coaxed to give up, or intimidated by being put through unendurable tortures (normally meant for use on the sinful dead). He finally takes his grievance to the god Erlang who redresses the wrong by having the corrupt officials punished. In the end both father and son are restored to life and amply compensated with longevity and wealth, while the family of their evil enemy suffer a decline in fortune.

As opposed to the change of status of the examination candidate, tales of a social theme tend to be concerned with the change of external reality. That is, a social injustice may be said to arise from a perception of an external condition going awry, measured against an ideal or a traditional "normative" practice accepted by the individual who perceives the injustice. The two sets of values (internal and external or the individual's and society's) are at odds with each other. When the individual affected by the changing values and ways refuses to adjust to the new reality, injustice is felt. The question is a matter of perspective and the enigmatic transformations and the turns of events in these tales may have to do with the difficulties of such adjustments.

An examination of the story called "The Kingdom of Rakshasas and the Ocean Bazaar" (羅刹海市)[45] may throw some light on this. Usually seen as a social satire, the tale relates the adventures of Ma Ji 馬驥 in two places which have opposite values systems — values relating specifically to the criterion of how to judge a person's worth. In the first place, the Rakshasas Kingdom, Ma Ji encounters a situation that puts the Chinese ideal (the "norm") on its head; there official positions are assigned not according to a person's talents or literary abilities but according to his looks. The standard of the beautiful and the ugly is also of a topsy-turvy order: what is ugly to Ma Ji, and presumably the reader, is considered beautiful by the local inhabitants, and vice versa. However, after painting his face black like that of Zhang Fei and applying his abilities of operatic singing to entertain the King, he receives great favour and rewards. The second place where Ma Ji found himself, i.e., the Ocean Bazaar (and is eventually the Dragon King's underwater palace), is a place where literary talent is respected; Ma Ji receives the greatest of honours for his skills at composition and is eventually given the hand of the Dragon King's daughter in marriage. But significantly the marriage ends in separation, as Ma Ji longs for the human world and decides to return to it. A son and a daughter are later sent to live with him but the wife comes to the human world only for a couple of rare visits. Although the son may go to the water region to see the mother whenever he desires, the father and the daughter are confined to the human world.[46]

We can see that the two parts of the tale are apparently intended as the opposites of each other that could be read allegorically like the mirror images of a distopia and a utopia relative to the reality of China. One serves as a satiric representation of the "actual world" (where high positions are accorded the hideous and the untalented — a double misplacement), the other an ideal place which mocks the "actual world" for falling short of the model conceptualized by its own ancient sages. Two sets of comparisons are implied in the construction of this narrative. The two are juxtaposed with an implicit, third term, the actual world of Pu's China.

The Authorial Comment rants at the behaviour of those who paint their face to curry favour, likening it to the way of the hobgoblin (世情如鬼). The image of the hideous looking Rakshasas has also been considered as a veiled satire on the Manchus.[47] If it is indeed so intended, is the tale then an unwitting irony on Pu himself who spent a great part of his life seeking service under Manchu rule? Or is there an ambivalence that will not be settled easily? In the tale Ma Ji's adaptabilities do not go unrewarded; whereas his marriage with the Dragon King's daughter, unlike that of Liu Yi 柳毅, gives him not immortality but a family that is forever broken and incomplete. The Authorial Comment ends its remark on the second part in a lamentation that real talent is rarely recognized and therefore glory and wealth for a scholar are but a mirage.

The two parts of the text present two worlds embodying the "ideal" and "corrupt" values, and also two conditions in which the hero's fate are to be manifested. There is an equivocation lurking in both: the obvious satiric intention seems to be contradicted by added motifs. The tale, on the one hand, reaffirms traditional values or a certain mode of conduct (this affirmation is made explicit by the Authorial Comment): the ideal social condition should be that natural endowment (talent and good looks) is properly rewarded and the correct principle of conduct is to hold fast to one's "true self". On the other hand, this conformist view is tempered. Flexibility and adaptation are debasing only because the traditional view values permanence over flux. Yet this belief in the accepted values, as suggested by one of the metaphors in the title, is nothing but an "ocean bazaar", an *haishi* 海市 (a Chinese term for "mirage"), an illusion.

Two manners of transference of qualities are seen in this tale. The Dragon King's esteem for literary talent can be understood as a *projection* of human values (or idealized values);[48] whereas Ma Ji's "debased" transformation by painting his own face is an *introjection* of the qualities of the alien world, the Rakshasas' value system (the other), to the human. Projection affirms human values (accepted ideals) and hence is perceived as positive; introjection assimilates alien qualities (or values) — it dehumanizes, and therefore must be resisted. In this light, the transformation of Cheng Ming's son in "The Cricket" may also be seen as an introjective transformation. A new social reality may be a violation of the expected norm, although it could be a new opportunity. But to change one's old stance is not right; flexibility in conduct means lack of principle. The miraculous transformation becomes a displaced form for the introjection of alien properties; it serves as a solution to the accommodation of new precepts in the face of opposition from tradition.[49] The reversal of family fortune, as it undermines the intent of social criticism, gives a nod to such an attempt at change. Similarly Xi Fangping's realization of justice through the adventures and the nightmarish transformations in the other realm may be seen as the realization of a state through the incorporation of alien properties before a new order may be allowed to emerge. The underworld, as said before, has the contradictory association of being a realm of "hellish" tortures and a realm where justice ultimately prevails despite its temporary corruption by the bad bureaucrats at some levels of its hierarchy.

In this sense, the fantasy of transformation may be taken to embody the tension in a changing society where individuals are required to adjust their values and adapt. Adjustment and adaptation are a necessity, but changes, assimilation of external values and properties, are "inherently" evil, or so perceived by society, and must be rejected. For some individuals caught in a transitional period of dynastic change, the necessity of making choices and re-adjusting ethical principles may become an acute problem. Many of the tales with a social theme, though not necessarily subversive, can be seen to contain such a problem. As a last example, I will refer to "Zhang Hongjian" 張鴻漸 [50] as a case of an individual caught in the predicament of making choices.

The tale again mixes the realistic subject matter (social injustice) with fantasy. A rapacious, violent magistrate has beaten a student to death. The student's friends plan to seek justice for him by taking the case to a higher authority and enlisting Zhang to join them and draft the petition. Having agreed to participate, Zhang is subsequently persuaded by his wife of the danger of the enterprise and, after drafting the petition, decides to withdraw and take flight. In the course of fleeing, he seeks overnight accommodation in a village and becomes involved with a fox-lady, who proposes "marriage" to him. After three years, Zhang misses his wife and asks for the fox-fairy's help to take him home. The fox-fairy first plays a trick on him (taking him "home" to see his "wife" who is in fact her own transformation), but finally complies with his wish. The night he is home Zhang kills a blackguard who has an interest in his wife and who threatens to expose him. Refusing to take his wife's advice to run again, Zhang turns himself in and is sent, under guard, to the capital for trial. On the way, the party run into the fox-fairy who rescues Zhang. After another ten years of exile, Zhang secretly makes his way home again. That night there is a commotion outside the house and, frightened, he slips out of the back door and runs away once more. It turns out that messengers have come to report the news of his son's passing the provincial examination, but Zhang is already gone. A third time on the run, he stops at the house of a retired official living in a village on the way to the capital. There he meets his son coming home from the examination and the family is finally reunited, the case against him dropped by the plaintiff because of his son's newly acquired status.

Two conflicting propositions are set forth in the initial scene of the story. It is a moral obligation to counteract social injustice — when a fellow townsman (here a member of one's own intelligentsia class) suffers an unjust death, one must demand justice even when the case involves a person who has power over one's safety. On the other hand, it is also necessary to consider self-preservation — at a time when evil prevails, as Zhang's wife puts it, it is pointless to fight against it and camaraderie may prove false. Caught in this dilemma, Zhang makes a compromise — he participates in the cause for justice by drafting the petition but abandons the group to run for his own life. This is unsatisfactory conduct under Confucian ethics, according to which one should value principle over life. There is no compromise between right and wrong. The rest of the tale seeks a resolution to the moral uneasiness by finding a new code of ethics.

This is where the supernatural element comes into play. The romantic involvement with the fox provides a model for reconciling the contradiction. In emotional matters, jealousy precludes one from keeping faith with two loves at the same time. It is the accepted principle that one should be faithful to a relationship to the end of one's days. However, when the circumstances are such — when a benefactor professes her love, for instance — one may be forced to form a new relationship. But even then to forget the old relationship would be wrong — as Zhang says in reply to the fox-lady's jealous nagging against his wish to see his first wife: "I'll be thinking of you in the future as I'm thinking of her now; were I to forget the old [love] because of the new, would you think me worthy as a person?" And that is indeed the case — he retains his love for his fox wife when he returns to his human wife (actually the fox in disguise). As he says in response to his "human wife", although he desires her as much as before, he "could not cut off my feelings for her [the fox-lady] because of her love and kindness". Here we have a mental paradigm of combining conflicting interests with moral and emotional justification. The fox-fairy gives the narrative the advantage of bringing her on and off the scene at its own convenience, but the guilt feeling for abandoning one's comrades must be worked out on the level of realistic experience; therefore Zhang himself becomes entangled with the law. The lengthy exile serves as an atonement and a cleansing. However, at the end, with his son's success in the establishment, Zhang's relationship with the system (and its values) may have changed, perhaps leading to the need for another adjustment, which would be another story that we cannot pursue here.[51]

Conclusion

This study has pointed to some rhetorical operations as well as a recurrent tendency of the author's imagination in the *Liaozhai*. With a semiotic bent of mind, we might see the rhetorical and intertextual generation as the manifestation of a literary imagination often characteristic of the cumulative period of a literary history. Consciousness of linguistic properties, including its rhetoricity, becomes the source of inspiration. Such a generation of text has also been seen as symbolic, metaphoric operations in a projectional or introjective manner. By these operations the supernatural elements (the factor that generates the strange) become a tool for the expression of contradictory desires and the resolution of tension caused by changing values. Stories of examination seem to reflect a personal condition without literary sublimation. As a reflection of the aspiration and the fate of an individual unable to transcend social conditioning, these tales nonetheless record a ponderous cultural phenomenon relating to some "perpetual" values of the Chinese intelligentsia.

Notes

1. The following is a concise and fair evaluation: "In many respects, *Liao-chai chih-i* can be seen as having created a tradition of its own, such as the incorporations of minor historical facts through painstaking research, affirmation of the value of love and personal freedom beyond the extent to which most traditional story writers would like to or dare to go, and systematic but subtle criticism of the social ills and political problems of the day." See *Traditional Chinese Stories: Themes and Variations*, edited by Y. W. Ma and Joseph S. M. Lau (New York: Columbia University Press, 1978), p. 580.

2. Gan Bao's 干寶 statement in his preface to *Soushen ji* 搜神記 is typical. Without claiming that all items in the collection are verifiable, he does say unequivocally that his purpose of compiling the book is to "show that the way of spirits is not false" (以明神道之不誣也). See *Soushen ji*, edited by Wang Shaoying 汪紹楹 (Beijing: Zhonghua shuju, 1979), p. 2.

3. Cf. Glen Dudbridge's anthropological approach in his essay in "The Tale of Liu Yi and Its Analogues" in this volume; also his *The Tale of Li Wa* (London: Ithaca Press for the Board of the Faculty of Oriental Studies, Oxford University, 1983). His approach may seem to contradict the view presented here, but not necessarily. My focus in this article is on the "strangeness" as a literary phenomenon.

4. The classical language tale is an unorthodox form of literature in comparison with historiography, poetry, and prose essay, mainly because of its association with *xiaoshuo* ("small subjects"). Confucius' reticence on the matters that involve "anomalies, feats of strength, disorders and spirits" has been taken as his disapproval for engagement in fictional discourse, which adds a dimension of conceptual bias against the genre.

5. See Pu's preface to *Liaozhai*. For a complete translation of the preface, see Chun-shu Chang and Hsüeh-lun Chang, "The World of P'u Sung-ling's *Liao-chai chih-i*: Literature and the Intelligentsia during the Ming-Ch'ing Dynastic Transition", *Journal of the Institute of Chinese Studies of The Chinese University of Hong Kong*, Vol. 6, No. 6 (1973), pp. 418–419.

6. See Jaroslav Průšek, "*Liao-chai chih-i* by P'u Sung-ling" and "P'u Sung-ling and His Work", in his *Chinese History and Literature: Collection of Studies* (Dordrecht, Holland: D. Reidel Publishing Co., 1970), pp. 92–108, 109–128, respectively; also "Two Documents Relating to the Life of P'u Sung-ling", pp. 84–91.

7. See Chang and Chang, which classifies P'u's tales into four groups by theme. One of them is related to criticism of social injustice; see, especially, pp. 401–421.

8. See, for instance, articles in the journal *Pu Songling yanjiu jikan* 蒲松齡研究

集刊 (Jinan); and chapters in Li Houji 李厚基 and Han Haiming 韓海明, *Ren gui hu yao de yishu shijie* 人鬼狐妖的藝術世界 (Tianjin: Renmin wenxue chubanshe, 1982); Wu Zuxiang 吳組緗, *et al*, *Liaozhai zhiyi xinshang* 聊齋誌異欣賞 (Beijing: Peking University Press, 1986); Liao Biguang 廖苾光, *Liaohua Liaozhai* 聊話聊齋 (Guangdong: Guangdong gaodeng jiaoyu chubanshe, 1987).

9. He passed his *xiucai* 秀才 (licentiate) exam in 1658 when he was nineteen (Chinese count) and obtained the status of Stipend Student (廩生) in 1683, which allowed him to take the provincial exam (*xiangshi* 鄉試) held every three years. Lu Dahuang 路大荒 gives the year 1690 (when Pu is fifty-one) as his last attempt at the examination. See "Pu Liuquan xiansheng nianpu" (蒲柳泉先生年譜) in *Pu Songling ji* 蒲松齡集, edited by Lu Dahuang (Shanghai: Guji chubanshe, 1986), pp. 1755–1811. But there is evidence that he may have kept at it until he was sixty-six years old (1705). See Gao Ming'ge 高明閣, "Pu Songling de yisheng" (蒲松齡的一生) in *Pu Songling xueshu taolunhui zhuankan* 蒲松齡學術討論會專刊 (Jinan: Qi-Lu shushe, 1981), pp. 207–246; See also Chang and Chang, pp. 402–406; and Prušek's two articles in *Chinese History and Literature*, pp. 92–108 and 109–128, for information of Pu's life and its relation to his creative work in general.

10. He worked as private tutor to an eniment Bi 畢 family in Wangcun 王村 of Zichuan 淄川 County from 1672 to 1710.

11. Many of his poems and *liqu* 俚曲 (popular dramatic song-suites) attested to his concern with the plight of the farmers, which might have a direct impact on the Pus' livelihood. His family belonged to the small "landed gentry" class which had to pay tax in grains; inability to pay on time could be the cause for flogging. One of Pu's sons in his *muzhi* 墓誌 talks about their efforts to meet the taxation deadlines as a consolation to their father when he was alive.

For a narrative of the hardships of the people in the Shandong area around this time, see Jonathan D. Spence, *The Death of Woman Wang* (Penguin, 1978) and Tsing Yuan, "Urban Riots and Disturbances", in *From Ming to Ching: Conquest and Continuity in Seventeen-Century China*, edited by Jonathan D. Spence and John E. Wills, Jr. (New Haven and London: Yale University Press, 1979), pp. 279–320, especially, 298–311.

12. The Tang writer Huangfu Mei 皇甫枚 (fl. 873–910) in a tale with a *zhiguai* motif, "Wang Zhigu" 王知古, for instance, claims at the end of the text that, although it is "talks of anomalies", the story is "based on fact", and therefore may be permissible as a literary subject, showing the consciousness of a need to justify the anomalous matter. See *Taiping guangji* 太平廣記 (Beijing: Zhonghua shuju, 1981), Juan 455, p. 1.

Both Gao Heng's 高珩 and Tang Menglai's 唐夢賚 prefaces to *Liaozhai* make a point to justify the book's use of the materials that "the Master did not

speak of". See Pu Songling, *Liaozhai zhiyi: huijiao huizhu huiping ben* 聊齋
誌異會校會注會評本, compiled by Zhang Youhe 張友鶴 (Shanghai: Guji
chubanse, 1978), pp. 1–2, 4 (of the 序跋題辭 section).

13. See *Liaozhai zhiyi: huijiao, huizhu, huiping ben*, pp. 1052–1056. Page references for the original tales cited are all to this edition. Two commonly
available anthologies of English translations of selected *Liaozhai* tales are:
Denis C. and Victor Mair (tr.), *Strange Tales from Make-do Studio* (Beijing:
Foreign Languages Press, 1989) and Herbert A. Giles (tr.), *Strange Stories
from a Chinese Studio* (New York: Dover Publication, 1969). The latter often
abridges the texts. For this tale, see the Mairs (hereafter "Mair"), pp. 292–
298.

14. See *Liji zhengyi* 禮記正義, *Sibu beiyao* (ed.), Juan 10, pp. 9b–10a.

15. *Liaozhai*, pp. 1453–1458; Mair, pp. 389–397.

16. *Liaozhai*, pp. 14–17, 38–41, 1027–1028, respectively; Mair, pp. 5–9, 19–24,
283–284, respectively.

17. See Zhao Qigao's 趙起杲 preface to the Qingketing 青柯亭 edition of *Liaozhai*, included in *Huijiao huizhu huiping ben*, p. 27.

18. *Liaozhai*, pp. 618–622.

19. *Liaozhai*, pp.112–118; Mair, pp. 43–52.

20. In the story "Xiangqun" 湘裙 (pp. 1322–1329), a young female ghost eagerly
tests whether she is qualified to live with humans by cutting herself on the
arm: the rule being that she would be only if she bleeds.

 It might be mentioned that the fox spirit's crossing from the "other world"
to this world through the "dream zone" is a phenomenon shared by ghosts. In
"Wu Qiuyue" 伍秋月 (pp. 668–672), for instance, the hero dreams of repeated
visits by a female ghost, and finally, as he wakes up from one of these dreams,
the girl is in front of him. (Cf., Tang Xianchu's *Mudan ting* 牡丹亭 [The
Peony Pavilion], in which the heroine also returns to life from death, but the
mode of transformation there is different.)

 For a comprehensive coverage of the types of ghost stories in Chinese
fiction, see Anthony C. Yu, "Rest, Rest, Perturbed Spirit! Ghosts in Traditional Chinese Fiction", *Harvard Journal of Asiatic Studies*, Vol. 47, No. 2
(December 1987), pp. 397–434. A discussion of the story "Nie Xiaoqian"
from *Liaozhai* is given on pp. 426–429.

21. Besides these a third possibility is also suggested by a Tang dynasty story in
which the dream world could interact with the actual world and affect the
latter in a physical way. Bai Xingjian's 白行簡 *Sanmeng ji* 三夢記 includes a
story about a man who on his way home saw his wife drinking with strangers
and threw a stone at her. When he reached home he was greeted by his wife
who had just awaken from a dream. She dreamt of taking part in a drinking
party and was hit by a stone thrown from outside, her forehead now still
smarting from the hit. This story however is not typical (its attribution to Bai

has been disputed). See *Shuofu* 説郛 (edited by Hanfenlou, reprinted by Taipei: Commercial Press, 1972), Juan 4, pp. 23b–24b.

22. *Liaozhai*, pp. 112–118; Mair, pp. 43–52.
23. *Liaozhai*, pp. 147–159; Mair, pp. 73–89.
24. *Liaozhai*, pp. 1000–1008.
25. *Liaozhai*, pp. 772–779; Mair, pp. 212–225.
26. *Liaozhai*, pp. 160–168; Mair, pp. 90–102.
27. *Liaozhai*, pp. 1431–1435.
28. 人情厭故而喜新，重難而輕易(p. 1434).
29. A variation of the process may be seen in a "realist" tale called "Da'nan" 大男 (*Liaozhai*, pp. 1564–1570; Giles, pp. 183–188). The story is essentially about how the status of two wives, i.e., the official wife and the concubine, are exchanged. The wife is shrewish, jealous, and evil, and the concubine chaste, kind, and upright. Through a series of extraordinary coincidences, an exchange of the positions of the two is effectuated, resulting in a transformation of relationship and a reversal of status: the wife becomes concubine, the concubine official wife (the connotation of "concubine" here is overtly social, but it is not without a sexual overtone).

    Cited by Allan Barr as an example of advance narrative control and complex plot formation in the matured tales of *Liaozhai*, the plot of this tale is characterized by him as consisting of a complication with the "device of dual female roles". See his "A Comparative Study of Early and Late Tales in *Liaozhai zhiyi*", *Harvard Journal of Asiatic Studies*, Vol. 45, No. 1 (1985), pp. 157–202.
30. See Glen Dudbridge, *The Tale of Li Wa*, pp. 61–80.
31. The tale "Yatou" 鴉頭 (pp. 600–606) features fox-spirits as prostitutes and tells of an *evil* madam's persecution of a *virtuous* young prostitute. The Authorial Comment at the end remarks that "all prostitutes are 'foxes'; but never was it heard that foxes could take up the profession to become prostitutes! Then for a fox to act as a procuress, the animal had indeed turned into a beast" (妓盡狐也，不謂有狐而妓者，至狐而鴇，則獸而禽矣) (p. 606).
32. Chang and Chang discuss this theme on pp. 412–414.
33. *Liaozhai*, pp. 1238–1240.
34. Although mechanisms to ensure objectivity and qualification of the examiners were in place, they were not always properly administered. For examples of punishment of corrupt examiners, see Ichisada Miyazaki, *China's Examination Hell*, translated by Conrad Schirokauer (New Haven: Yale University Press, 1963), pp. 64–65, 72.
35. *Liaozhai*, pp. 1166–1173; Mair, pp. 299–309. Incidentally, the clause: 簾官之考遂罷, rendered in Mair as "the examination for examiners has been cancelled" (p. 302) should be amended to read something like: "[the God of Literature's] appointment to supervise this examination for examiners has

been cancelled" — it is the appointment, not the examination, that is cancelled.

36. *Liaozhai*, pp. 1098–1106; Giles, pp. 347–348.

37. *Liaozhai*, pp. 81–85.

38. Cf. "Judge Lu" 陸判 (*Liaozhai*, pp. 139–146; Mair, pp. 61–72), in which an underworld judge befriends a human scholar and gives him a new heart to make him a better essay writer — the heart being considered the seat of intelligence — but Lu is unable to change his friend's lot so that he may obtain an office.

39. *Liaozhai*, pp. 518–527; Mair, pp. 172–185.

40. *Liaozhai*, pp. 1359–1366 (Giles, pp. 316–319) and 946–956, respectively.

41. These critics often cite Pu's *liqu* "The Banquet of Penglai" (蓬萊宴) and "The Tribulations Song-Suite" (磨難曲) to show Pu's unregenerated hope for worldly success within the system (see, for example, Kao Ming'ge, "Pu Songling de yisheng", pp. 234–237). Some of the scenes in these plays revel in the description of the glory and gratification brought about by the appointment to an official position.

42. *Liaozhai*, pp. 484–490; Mair, pp. 156–164.

43. Li Houji and Han Haiming in *Ren gui hu yao de yishu shijie*, pp. 106–109, give a similar reading of the incongruity of the views given in this Authorial Comment. They believe that Pu's criticism is weakened by his contradictory attenuation for the ruling class, which shows that he was "backward in his outlook".

44. *Liaozhai*, pp. 1341–1348; Giles, pp. 322–326; see also Chang and Chang, pp. 409–411, for their discussion of other examples.

45. *Liaozhai*, pp. 454–465; Mair, pp. 139–155.

46. This portion is an adaptation of a Six Dynasties motif; see, for instance, "Lu Chong" 盧充 in *Soushen ji*, Juan 16, p. 397.

47. See Chang and Chang, pp. 414–415.

48. The concept of "projection" should be revised then to concern, not human desire or qualities, but idealized qualities.

49. Cf. the relatively rare cases of man-into-beast transformations in *Liaozhai*. In "Xiang Gao" 向杲 (pp. 831–833), for example, the hero is transformed into a tiger (introjection) for the explicit purpose of carrying out revenge on a vicious enemy. In Tang stories of such transformations the reason for the transformation is usually vague.

50. *Liaozhai*, pp. 1227–1234.

51. The tale is made the subject of a *liqu* by Pu himself entitled "The Tribulations Song-Suite" (cf. note 41 above). There all the episodes are greatly expanded; the ending especially shows Zhang's family interest coinciding entirely with that of the government, not only because of his own success as a martial official but also his sons' and grandsons' prominent careers in the officialdom.

9

Edifying Depravity: Three Late-Qing Courtesan Novels

David D. W. Wang

Novels dealing with courtesan life constitute an important part of late-Qing fiction. In his *A Brief History of Chinese Fiction* 中國小說史略, Lu Xun 魯迅 calls these novels "depravity fiction" (*xiaxie xiaoshuo* 狹邪小説),[1] a term indicating not only the decadent subject matter but also the air of prurience and even self-congratulation that pervades their narratorial discourse. Critics have usually complained that late-Qing courtesan novels are crudely written and rife with sentimental clichés, stock figures, and formulaic action. But these are conventional observations; more salient issues remain: How and why can writers of courtesan novels render their "immoral" desire in moralistic terms? Does the vogue of the courtesan novel imply changes in the late-Qing code of sexuality? How did they assimilate debauchery to the romantic repertoires of traditional Chinese literature? And, if they had done so, had they really redefined cultural and ethical verisimilitude for late-Qing fiction?

With these questions in mind, I will discuss three late-Qing courtesan novels, *Pinhua baojian* 品花寶鑑 (Precious Mirror for Judging "Flowers", 1852), *Haishang hua liezhuan* 海上花列傳 (Singsong Girls of Shanghai, 1892), and *Niehai hua* 孽海花 (A Flower in the Sea of Sins, 1907). Each of the three novels presents a distinctive picture of late-Qing courtesan life, introducing morals and manners that either celebrate or parody established norms of virtue and propriety. Put side by side, they further call into question one another's ethical, sexual, and even rhetorical assumptions. Of course, within the limits of this article, I cannot fully answer the questions I raised. I can, however, suggest: (1) that *Pinhua baojian*, the first full-length courtesan novel of the late-Qing period, romanticizes the liaisons of male Beijing opera singers by situating them in a "feminine" discourse, thereby raising serious questions as to the "sexual orientation" of textual and ethical law; (2) that *Haishang hua liezhuan* attains a more "realistic" portrait of courtesan life, because it subverts romantic conventions endorsed not merely by its implied readers but also by its characters; and finally (3) that *Niehai hua* mockingly assesses late-Qing history in terms of a sexual adventuress, making her an index of contemporary moral commerce.

Pinhua baojian

Pinhua baojian by Chen Sen 陳森 (1796?–1870?) has generally been regarded as the first full-length courtesan novel of the late-Qing period.[2] Chronicling, in sixty chapters, the romances of a group of Beijing opera singers and their patrons, the novel is heavily indebted to two romantic traditions from classical Chinese literature. In terms of plotting and characterization, it is nurtured on the tradition of the idealized scholar-courtesan love story, a tradition which can be traced back to the Tang *chuanqi* 傳奇 stories, such as *Li Wa zhuan* 李娃傳 (The Story of Li Wa). In terms of rhetoric and narration, its love-ridden sentimentality and lyrical extravagance place it in the grand "sentimental-erotic tradition", a tradition that, in C. T. Hsia's words, includes "such poets as Li Shangyin 李商隱, Tu Mu 杜牧, and Li Houchu 李後主, and such works of drama and fiction as *Hsi-hsiang chi* 西廂記, *Mu-dan t'ing* 牡丹亭, *T'ao-hua shan* 桃花扇, *Ch'ang-sheng tien* 長生殿, and *Hung-lou meng* 紅樓夢".[3]

Passing from erotic daydreams to high-strung sentiment, Chen Sen too often decorates *Pinhua baojian* with stale allusions, turgid description, and unimaginative hyperbole, signs of a bad romantic tale. Indeed, the novel would have been quite negligible had it set out to retell the romances of ordinary courtesans and scholars. But Chen Sen's teenage courtesans are all opera singers and Beijing opera singers are male. The novel's old theme of "talented men and beautiful girls" (*caizi jiaren* 才子佳人) actually enacts a double parody. First, *Pinhua baojian* does not depict talent and beauty in their own right; rather it depicts these courtesans and clients as if they were talented men and beautiful girls. Second, the girls under discussion are not really girls, but boys treated like girls. We get "talented men and beautiful boys". Even as the novel departs from the textual/sexual norm, the textual/sexual norm reimposes itself.

Given the novel's seemingly sensational subject, a cautious reader will not be lured to take it only at face value. Social historians who looked into *Pinhua baojian* for evidence on pederasty or sodomy in late-Qing society have found very little. And as mentioned above, the novel's artistic defects are apparent — a wooden narrative, flat characters, tedious descriptions of parties and wine games, predictable melodramatic sequences, etc. No wonder that, in frustration, a critic like Stephen Cheng should have complained, "If *Pinhua baojian* proves anything at all, it is that a homosexual love story written by an incompetent novelist, is as corny, teary, and lugubrious as a conventional heterosexual love story, and equally unbelievable. Mediocre writers produce mediocre novels, whatever their sexual or affectional preference."[4]

I will suggest an approach to *Pinhua baojian* not as a novel lobbying for deviant sexual activities but as a fantasy that titillates and reinforces in a roundabout way a society's set discourse on sexuality. Mediocre as it may be, *Pinhua baojian* addresses the transgression and legitimization of sexual norms in a given social context, and the ethical pretexts for writing and reading them as such. Moreover, as its hidden theme of sexual transvestism surfaces on the rhetorical level, the novel disturbs the "gender" boundaries of narrative conventions, and sheds light, however unexpected, on women's position in the formation of romantic conventions. For that reason, the novel is about women just as much as about men. As I will argue later, the absence of women serves as the secret motivation of the novel, and it is the search for the lost ideal "woman" in man that drives home the novel's sexual and ethical ambiguities.

Pinhua baojian centres on two lover couples, through whose romantic adventures and vicissitudes the true meaning of virtues like love, faithfulness, perseverance, chastity, and integrity is to be made clear. Our leading hero(ine) is Du Qinyan 杜琴言, a female impersonator who repels the advances of many admirers and remains faithful to his lover, Mei Ziyu 梅子玉, a handsome, talented young scholar of the best kind. Next to Du Qinyan is Su Huifang 蘇蕙芳, a more resourceful opera singer who picks a poor but talented scholar, Tian Chunhang 田春航, for his lover and grooms him for eventual success in the civil service exam. Both romances undergo many tests, amid longing, tears and love-sick groans, to say nothing of endless exchanges of love poems and letters. Lu Xun and other scholars have suggested that Du Qinyan and Mei Ziyu are fictitious creatures, as parts of their names, yu 玉 and yan 言, are homonym with *yuyan* 寓言 or fable;[5] Su Huifang and Tian Chunhang, on the other hand, are based on real historical figures: Bi Qiufan 畢秋凡, onetime Governor of Hunan 湖南

and Hubei 湖北 in the Qianlong 乾隆 reign, and Li Guiguan 李桂官 , Bi Qiufan's life-long friend.[6]

The two couples' love affairs conspicuously demonstrate Chen Sen's indebtedness to the two romantic traditions of Chinese literature mentioned above. Su Huifang and Tian Chunhang act out the stereotypical situation that a generous courtesan falls in love with a down-trodden scholar and helps him attain fame, at the cost of her own future welfare. As for Du Qinyan and Mei Ziyu, who else can better serve as their models than Lin Daiyu 林黛玉 and Jia Baoyu 賈寶玉 , the archetypes of Chinese erotic-sentimental fiction since the early-Qing period? Du Qinyan and Mei Ziyu "competently" carry out the three virtues without which "no one can be called a lover: *qing* 情 (capacity for love or feeling), *cai* 才 (literary talent), and *chou* 愁 (capacity for sorrow)",[7] in a way suggesting not so much mutual admiration as mutual competition. Meanwhile, tentative break-ups, misunderstandings, and external adversities seem to take place only to testify to their unconditional willingness to suffer and love. As if human passion were not strong enough to justify our lovers' romance, we are also told at one point (chapter 55) that Du Qinyan is actually the reincarnation of some divinity, sent to the red dust to realize a predestined romance with Mei Ziyu. For their love and mutual dedication, both couples are rewarded with reunion at the end of the novel, yet on an odd condition, that our heroes first have to get themselves legal wives. Conveniently, the two ladies not only look just like the two female impersonators but also welcome the *menage à trois*! The three's-companies live happily thereafter.

Note how Chen Sen exploits both the high and low forms of traditional romantic clichés for his own purposes. Also note how he takes pains to cover up the ethical and even legal gaps between his version of a love story and its antecedents. Of all the literary sources he might have drawn upon, Chen Sen clearly made the *Honglou meng* his primary model. One can easily find in *Pinhua baojian* counterparts for the Grand View Garden (chapter 1 and following), the gallery of twelve "golden pins" (chapter 60), the carnal test in a magical mirror (chapter 10), the pseudo-philosophical discussion of love (*qing*) vs. lust (*yin* 淫) (chapter 12), the predestined love relations, the concept of double beauty (*jianmei* 兼美), the comic interludes staged by licentious clowns (chapters 19, 23, 58) and many other episodes and themes. But the irony is that even the romantic vision projected by the *Honglou meng* seems not "pure" enough for Chen Sen. His male opera singers and patrons might drift around the quarters of ill fame, but they are twice as noble-minded and hygiene-conscious as Lin Daiyu and Jia Baoyu. Du Qinyan and Mei Ziyu do not even "see" each other often throughout the novel, let alone engage in any improper thoughts: that would be too devastating to their Platonic relationship.

But for all their admirable virtues, Du Qinyan and Mei Ziyu are male lovers. Whatever laudable deeds they carry out, their relationship is itself laughable, if not condemnable, as one critic puts it.[8] The confusion of gender simply deconstructs all the romantic formulas which *Pinhua baojian* "appears" to abide by. It also forces us to rethink those romantic formulas in terms of the ethical prerequisites behind them. I am not saying Chen Sen consciously writes his novel as a critique or parody of romantic conventions. I am just saying precisely because he tries hard, probably too hard, to identify boys with girls, to treat courtesans and their customers like Confucian stoics, and to deal with depravity in strict, virtuous terms, Chen Sen ironically highlights the contradiction between the means and end of his novel, and betrays his anxiety to bridge the dialectic between ethical imperatives and erotic temptations. This contradiction (together with its implied anxiety) is not exclusive to a novel like *Pinhua baojian*; rather it points to an ethical and rhetorical inconsistency underlying most late-Qing "straight" courtesan novels and the old scholar/beauty romantic tradition they set out to imitate in the first place. The displacement of sexual identity in Chen Sen's novel lays bare the clichés one could otherwise have taken as natural to Chinese romantic literature.

Chen Sen was after all neither radical nor competent enough to go further and probe into the intricate moral tensions suggested by his given subject. Compare the two romances in *Pinhua baojian* with a story like, say, "Nan mengmu jiaohe san qian" 男孟母教合三遷 (A Male Mencius's Mother Educates His Son and Moves House Three Times) by Li Yu 李漁 (1611–1680?), and one finds how "conservative" Chen Sen really is. Li Yu's story also describes a romance between two males, in which our hero(ine) is so driven by his passion for his lover that he castrates himself to show his unconditional devotion. After the death of his lover, our hero(ine) raises and educates his lover's son (from a previous legitimate marriage), and eventually makes the boy pass the civil service examination. For his feminine virtues and maternal dedication, our hero(ine) earns himself the title of a male "Mencius's Mother".

Li Yu's imagination let him play with the rules of romantic literature in such a relentless way as to turn all Confucian morals against themselves, thereby "carnivalizing", in Bakhtinian terminology, the sexual and ethical codes of his fictional world. In his study of Li Yu, Patrick Hanan points out that the story pokes endless fun at such prominent themes of Chinese fiction as "heterosexual love, heterosexual marriage, chaste widowhood, and strict motherhood".[9] Pushing Hanan's observation one step further, we could say Li Yu ridicules not only the moral/sexual prudery of a "normal" society but also the self-deception and hypocrisy of those who are oppressed by that society yet choose nonetheless to obey the strictest of its laws. Thus, by pushing ribald imagination to its limits, "Nan mengmu jiaohe san qian" ironically attains a more comprehensive sense of the ambiguity of ethical/sexual relations.

Putting aside the problem of anachronism, one finds *Pinhua baojian* could best have served as a target of Li Yu's ridicule. Chen Sen endeavoured to write a romance that transgresses the boundaries of both social hierarchy and sexual normalcy, but he only ended up squarely reinforcing those boundaries. He lacks the kind of cynicism that makes Li Yu a playful social critic, and the wisdom of a Cao Xueqin 曹雪芹 who sees in life a vertiginous interplay of love and lust, illusion and reality. The "virtue" of *Pinhua baojian* has to be found somewhere else. While the novel makes an impotent apology for depraved love, it nevertheless presents a dramatic agenda, showing how a nonconformist theme can be "naturalized" by a writer who secretly obeys the established discourse of sexuality. I suggest that this fact brings about the ultimate paradox of the novel, namely, that Chen Sen is writing about men with women in mind, and that he is writing about women (in their absence) only in terms of an image prefigured by men and for men, an image from which women were always absent.

One of the common charges against *Pinhua baojian* is that its narrative sounds too much like an ordinary romance of straight couples. Though the female impersonators do not appear like drag queens in real life, they are first judged by the roles they play on stage, and treated and talked about by their patrons (and their narrator) like women. Chen Sen lavishes names, idioms, imagery, and the general vocabulary normally reserved for women characters on his effeminate hero(ine)s, so much so that a careless reader might completely miss the gender peculiarity of the romance. Women are denied any important roles in *Pinhua baojian*, but through dialogues, poetic works, literary allusions, puns, jokes, and descriptive passages, they have a continued "presence" in the novel, to the point that "they" become the dominant offstage voice of the narrative. "No one surpasses this singer in beauty; even a painter cannot draw a woman as perfect as him. His surname is Du, couldn't he be the reincarnation of Du Liniang?" In this way is Mei Ziyu first told by his friend about the beauty of Du Qinyan, in chapter 2 of *Pinhua baojian*. Du Liniang 杜麗娘, the famous heroine from Tang Xianzu's 湯顯祖 drama *Mudan ting*, takes exactly the form of a magical incantation, whose purpose is to conjure up in imagination the presence of the absent loved one.

As their profession indicates, the female impersonators are but "spokesmen", on and off stage, for the absent "women" they and their patrons conjure up. Du Qinyan is cast as a figure (Du Liniang, or Lin Daiyu) in a time-honoured romantic tradition, adored not so much for what he is (whatever that might be) as for what he resembles. Throughout the novel, he is never regarded as an immediate, fully present object of desire, because within the dialectic of desire he is himself a substitute. Woman, not man, is the invisible motivation of the novel. And only when this invisible woman figures in the narrative, do the ethical bearings of the novel from fidelity to chastity make sense to us.

Chen Sen's appropriation of a feminine discourse to define his male courtesan romance also has an obvious historical cause. The sudden prosperity of male courtesan troupes in the late-Ming and Qing Dynasties was due not to a capricious change of Chinese men's sexual preference but to the reinforcement of a governmental law forbidding bureaucrats and the gentry class to frequent women prostitute houses.[10] It was in response to the "man"-made denunciation of women in pleasure quarters that male courtesans were introduced as substitutes — an alternative that should have been considered twice depraved and yet was ironically tolerated by the law.

Whereas this fact easily invites a Foucauldian interpretation on the eternal struggle between sexual discourse and social/legal/political surveillance,[11] it concerns me more as a direct cause that gives rise to the linguistic transvestism of Chen Sen's novel. Writing about men like women, about licentious rendezvous as virtuous encounters, *Pinhua baojian* works well either as a disguised confession or as a self-serving alibi. Chen Sen may be hypocritical on both accounts, but he writes faithfully for and about a society that sees only what it wants to see, a society that turns sexual prohibition into a transvestite masquerade. Accordingly, Chen Sen's failure in distinguishing his "male" romance from traditional ones can even be credited, in that it does demonstrate how he manages to talk about women "under erasure", and how his homo-erotic fantasy reinscribes an original man/woman dichotomy.

Nevertheless, to say that Chen Sen wittingly or unwittingly subjects his writing to a feminine discourse reveals only part of our story. Under a closer reading, the paradox of gender and gender-related ethics implied in *Pinhua baojian* takes yet another turn. There must be a contradiction, when one comes to think of it, that Chen Sen should make woman the secret ideal object of his desire on the one hand, yet easily usurp the feminine discourse for men's use on the other. If woman stands for the supreme vision of beauty and virtue in the novel, how can the female impersonators be so readily appreciated in a substitute form? In what sense can a man in the guise of woman be described as even better than the "original"? Who, after all, prescribes the virtues of woman and the terms of a feminine discourse?

As early as chapter 1 of the novel, all patron characters are summoned together to discuss the etymological origins of euphemisms ascribed to women. They come to a conclusion that words like *jiaren* 佳人 (good person) and *meiren* 美人 (beautiful person) refer to both men and women in classical texts like the *Shi jing* 詩經 and *Chu ci* 楚辭, and, accordingly, that it is never indecent to chase after the good and beautiful among men. They further develop a "philosophical" outlook on the necessary superiority of *yang* over *yin*, male over female, in both human and natural worlds. This pseudo-academic talk is crucial because it blurs and problematizes the gender difference from the start. Following the logic of the talk, woman is just an object inscribed with "womanly" features by man, a "role" that is created and can be perfected by man. From here onwards, the innocent Mei Ziyu launches his long search for the supreme (male) beauty, and his final reunion with Du Qinyan proves that the quest is a worthy one. Even Mei's newly-wed wife, who looks exactly like Du, has to concede that she is "not quite" as perfect as her male sister.

The tripartite marriage sounds silly, yet it must have mattered a lot to Chen Sen, as it is also the means through which the romance between Su Huifang and Tian Chunhang is brought to a satisfactory conclusion. With it, one might certainly talk of androgynous relations, but a different reading will suggest that the happy ending is no better than a male-centred fantasy. *Pinhua baojian* sets out to describe a quest for the ideal feminine beauty as the premise of its male lovers' romance, only to reveal that the factors constituting the "ideal" woman are predetermined by men. What is at stake here is no longer just gender by birth but sexual "qualifications" endorsed by a society like the one described and participated in by Chen Sen.

It is these basically derivative and substitutive guises that lead us to face the most outrageous kind of fantasy about women in the novel — that women can be played by men, in theatre and in reality, to satisfy the ultimate standard of "double" beauty. I have argued previously that Du Qinyan acts as a substitute for a female beauty like Du Liniang or Lin Daiyu. I will now further argue that, since both Du Liniang and Lin Daiyu are only fictional characters, Du Qinyan represents the image of what is already an image, a face which belongs to no one but the literary discourse called romance. When woman is reduced only to a label, a sign without substantial referent, the ethical rules that make "woman" what she is reveal their arbitrary essence. The sexual disorientation of the text of *Pinhua baojian* foregrounds what is normally backgrounded in the surrounding linguistic culture; it "makes strange", defamiliarizes what in conventional romantic literature is taken for granted.

One can take yet another viewpoint to see how the discourse of sexuality conceived by *Pinhua baojian* works in favour of men's desire. Somewhere beyond the happy depiction of Mei Ziyu and Du Qinyan and the rest, there lurks the chilly fact that almost all the male courtesans come from impoverished families and that they are sold into theatres to "learn" to become "beautiful" and "good" creatures. The society Chen Sen describes is one which not only observes man-made sexual and ethical standards for women but, when necessary, also "makes" men of lower social or economic status into women on order. Literally and symbolically, the boy singers are "feminized" so as to survive.

Back to where I started, I would therefore conclude that *Pinhua baojian* is a novel written about and for men, not because of the homo-erotic subject it claims to deal with, but because of the intricate sexual and ethical terms it tries to dissemble or legitimize. Ironically, its cliché-ridden language was only the first sign of its layered voices speaking the sexual and ethical contradictions of its age.

Haishang hua liezhuan

The second courtesan novel I will discuss is *Haishang hua liezhuan* by Han Bangqing 韓邦慶 (1856–1894). A panoramic survey of life in the Shanghai pleasure quarters at the turn of the century, the novel casts more than two dozens of courtesans and their patrons as major characters, detailing the ups and downs of their intrigues, and inquiring into the moral and psychological consequences of their affairs. The novel has never been popular among readers, then or now, while critics from Lu Xun, Hu Shi 胡適 , Liu Dajie 劉大杰 , Zhao Jingchen 趙景琛 , A Ying 阿英 , Meng Yao 孟瑤 , to Stephen Cheng have never hesitated to applaud its artistic achievement.[12] People usually attribute the unpopularity of *Haishang hua liezhuan* to the fact that it was written in the Wu dialect and is therefore unreadable for readers from other parts of China. Actually, the novel should not be all that unintelligible to Chinese readers, because only the dialogue was in the Wu dialect. Moreover, the language problem has now been overcome, so to speak, thanks to the acclaimed novelist Eileen Chang 張愛玲, who translated the whole book into Mandarin Chinese in 1983.[13]

The real reason for the novel's unpopularity might be that it does not read *like* the courtesan novel we generally know of. And this will be the starting point of my discussion. Compared with *Pinhua baojian*, *Haishang hua liezhuan* is just what the pioneering courtesan novel is not. I am of course not referring only to the gender difference in the courtesans. What I am indicating is Han Bangqing's rewriting of the laws of verisimilitude that prefigure the characterization, plotting, rhetoric, and general moral/cultural assumptions of a fictional genre known as the courtesan novel. Gone are the stereotypes of scholars and beauties. The girls and customers of Shanghai prostitute houses appear as a group of amazingly plain women and men. They meet, fall in love, quarrel, break up, or get reunited just like ordinary couples, but on the other hand, they do *know* they are only playing roles commensurable with those of husband and wife. While they could not care less about composing love letters and poems to each other, they are not obsessed with the business in bed either. Eileen Chang is right in pointing out that "there is no sensuous quality [in the novel], though the novel's topic is the pleasure quarters of Shanghai eighty years ago".[14] The demarcation lines between love and lust, decency and depravity, which are so conveniently drawn in most courtesan novels, can no longer be identified with ease. It suffices to say that critics consider *Haishang hua liezhuan* to have excelled most Chinese fiction since the *Honglou meng* in its stark realism.[15]

For all the critical praise, the realism of *Haishang hua liezhuan* should not be taken merely as a meticulous account of the manners and morals of a given social stratum. One should also see the novel's life-like atmosphere as an "effect of the real", an effect that arises as the novel pits itself against the narrative conventions of the courtesan novel. The realism of the novel thus brings into question not only the life style of courtesans as perceived or imagined by society, but also the cultural and aesthetic motivations of reading and writing the courtesan romance as such. At his best, Han Bangqing achieves in his novel fascinating and contradictory goals: he writes to upset the romantic myth of courtesan life; yet his realistic endeavour works also to ensure the continued existence of that myth, which, however questionable, is part of our cultural reality.

It is Han Bangqing's refusal to let either one of his goals be subservient to the other that makes his novel swing back and forth between the poles of fantasy and arguable "reality", romance and realism, tests of desire and tests of virtue. From this viewpoint, we can say the most compelling part of *Haishang hua liezhuan* lies not so much in courtesans being allowed to act and talk in a realistic way, as in that the supposed "realistic way" they talk and act turns out to be partially drawn from the unbelievable romances the novel seemed to deny at the outset. Insofar as being a courtesan is a profession, or an art, of faking virtues and indulging desires, the sing-song girls' life does not just imitate art; rather their life is art. Engaging drama often happens, nevertheless, when the girls spoil the delicate balance between romantic illusion and realistic necessity by consuming one at the expense of the other. In particular, when our Chinese sirens are enchanted by their own devastating songs, they become the parodies of their bitter profession.

Haishang hua liezhuan thus describes a group of courtesans who are not paragons of virtue but players upon desire in the name of virtue. By desire, I mean one's attempt to obtain what one does not have, or one's yearning for being what one is not, while by virtue, I mean a sanctioned system of behavioural and intellectual norms that constraints desire within a given social/cultural closure. Paradoxically, when they fail to carry out their professional arts, the sing-song girls show, either in personality or in action, a magnanimity that would have been endorsed by the romances they first set out to fake. But even more interesting are cases which confuse the conditions of virtue and desire. When a girl is determined to carry out a "genuine" virtue against all odds, she may do so in such a fervent way as to cultivate a new kind of desire. An excess of virtue often verges on a transgression of virtue; a fanatic passion to be virtuous tends to place itself ambiguously in the courtyard of desire. Contrary to most late-Qing courtesan novels, which mouth crude moral pretensions as an excuse for debauchery, *Haishang hua liezhuan* ventures to mix virtues with temptations in a truly dialogical way.

Three examples will help us explore the facets of the sing-song girls' romantic adventures we have talked about. The affair between the courtesan Li Shufang 李淑芳 and the scholar Tao Yufu 陶玉甫 can be picked out as one of the most romantic cases in the novel. Theirs is love at first sight. As their affair progresses, Tao proposes to marry Li as his wife, not concubine, a proposal which naturally caused vehement opposition from his family. Although Li is at first willing to settle for the position of a concubine, her lover will not change his mind. In the meantime, Li contracts tuberculosis. As there is no hope to a solution to the dilemma of marriage, Li slowly withers away and dies a pitiful death.

While the love affair may first look like a Chinese version of *La Dame aux camélias*, which was yet to be translated into Chinese in 1892, or a vulgarized remake of the romance between Jia Baoyu and Lin Daiyu, it contains interesting twists with regard to moral terms as conceived in courtesan circles. Li Shufang, from the start, is quite aware of her position and does not really expect to marry her lover as his wife. But for a reluctant pragmatist like her, it is too hard not to be tempted by the dream of becoming a wife in a scholarly family — just like what might happen in the wish-fulfilment moment of a courtesan romance. Ironically, after the marriage plan is denied by Tao's family, Li turns out to be a person much tougher than expected: if she cannot be a wife worthy of a scholar's family, she can be a courtesan proud of her profession.

It is now Li Shufang's turn to take the initiative. Thus even when she is dying, she turns down time and again Tao Yufu's suggestion to move out of her boudoir to rest in a quieter place; she does not want to die the "kept person" of her lover. One may well imagine that, if Tao Yufu had not proposed the fatal "formal" marriage, the lovers would have ended up living together happily as husband and concubine. But the aborted proposal brings out Li's hidden self-esteem, driving her to achieve a kind of virtue people often take for self-abandonment. However quixotic it may appear, her death amid the hustle and bustle of Shanghai prostitution houses becomes a sign of moral triumph, not only over the hypocrisy of the genteel social class but also over the humble alternative she originally would have taken in compliance with social expectation. Still, we wonder if her virtue is immune to a hidden wish to achieve the romantic "martyrdom" of a spectacularly sad death; to bid farewell to the world in the (vulgarized) dramatic context of Lin Daiyu's death scene.

In sharp contrast to the above love story is the triangle relationship between Wang Liansheng 王蓮生, Shen Xiaohong 沈小紅, and Zhang Huizhen 張蕙貞. Wang Liansheng is a middle-ranking official temporarily staying in Shanghai. At the beginning of their story, he has been going steady with his favourite courtesan Shen Xiaohong for a while. This relationship, however, neither keeps Wang from frequenting other girls' houses nor prevents Shen from entertaining other customers. There is an unwritten deal between courtesans and their customers: no matter how much affection they may have for each other, business has to go on. But the delicate situation is endangered when Wang Liansheng discovers that Shen is secretly developing a liaison with an opera singer — behaviour despised by both customers and other courtesans because of social bias and the notoriety of opera singers' lifestyle in general. Out of revenge, he starts a closer relationship with Zhang Huizhen, a more understanding and amiable courtesan.

In a world where love and treachery are part of the masquerade, neither Shen's nor Wang's new affair should have led to any trouble. But in the case under discussion, Shen Xiaohong is simply outraged by her old patron's betrayal. In chapter 9 of the novel, Shen storms into Zhang Huizhen's place when Wang is giving a banquet there, ruins all the furniture, and, what is more, engages in a fight on the floor with her rival. Throughout the whole scene and afterwards, Wang may feel embarrassed, but he never really loses his temper. He eventually goes back to Shen to apologize. Could it be love that makes both Wang and Shen behave so "improperly"? Or could it be just a risky romantic game of which each party is a willing player? If Shen is put out by Wang's new affair, what excuse does she have for her secret romance? Whereas Shen seems to play the contradictory roles of both an adulterous mistress and a jealous wife, Wang, in his turn, has unwittingly allowed himself to assume the double part of a cuckold and an unfaithful husband.

The sound and fury of the story thus partakes of a strange domestic quality one rarely comes across in courtesan novels. Domestic, in the sense that Shen and Wang are conscious of the ethical tie that links them together, whatever happens, and because they act out their emotional capacities, including violence and guilty conscience, in terms of codes otherwise applied to husband and wife. But Wang and Shen are staging their domestic interludes in an environment that salutes the transgression of family-oriented sexual relations. As a matter of fact, it is this environment that first allows the couple to meet and try out their desires and fantasies, domestic or not. Yet they are now trapped in the continuous shift of the roles they are playing.

The character of Shen Xiaohong particularly merits attention. She values her relationship with Wang Liansheng (of course partially for financial reasons), but she feels just as strongly about her new lover. The desperate passion that drives her to destroy Zhang Huizhen's chamber, thus declaring in public her possessive love for Wang Liansheng, simultaneously motivates her to carry on with her own intrigue at the expense of Wang's love (and money). The environment where she lives and thrives teaches her no domestic scruples; her professional promiscuity means that she has to undergo a double share of the trial of desire and passion. Her jealousy and volatility certainly remind us of someone like Pan Jinlian 潘金蓮 from the *Jin Ping Mei* 金瓶梅 (Golden Lotus), a rare thing in a fictional tradition which derives its imagination ironically from the *Honglou meng*, but she is capable of love and self-sacrifice. She sticks to her unreliable new lover towards the end of the novel, at the cost of losing most of her customers. And one of the highest prices she pays is to let Zhang Huizhen marry Wang Liansheng as concubine, an ideal domestic role most courtesans are supposed to take after they leave their profession.

The romance between Shen and Wang does not end here. Shen Xiaohong is no doubt greatly humiliated by Wang Liansheng's "betrayal" through his taking Zhang Huizhen as his concubine, but a similar humiliation falls on Wang only too soon, when the newly-wed Zhang Huizhen is caught committing adultery with her husband's cousin. It is Zhang's misconduct that truly ridicules Wang Liansheng and other like-minded people who attempt to "domesticate" a courtesan. However, the problems involved here are no longer just infidelity or moral retribution, nor just different ethical assumptions held by (ex-)courtesans and their customers, but the endless self-delusion and desire to grab what is unavailable or forbidden, that spare nobody. If even a marital relationship cannot always check the overflow of passion and desire, why should one be serious about infidelity outside the wedding bond? Or, just the other way around, shouldn't one cherish more a romance with a courtesan like Shen Xiaohong, because it demonstrates an emotional intensity, however short-lived, under impossible conditions?

Thus, possibly with these thoughts in mind, Wang Liansheng visits Shen Xiaohong again in chapter 54 of the novel, after being told that her business has hit the bottom. He does not meet Xiaohong, but through her servants, he learns how she has been rejected by almost all customers. He reluctantly accepts a pipe prepared by the servants, and, "without good reason, two drops of tears fell from his eyes". It is at this moment that Wang Liansheng seems to come to an awareness that he and Xiaohong are in the same boat after all, continuously drifting in and out of a series of roles and paying a high price for willingly believing in these roles. His residual passion for her has transcended to a compassionate understanding.

The third example I will draw from *Haishang hua liezhuan* is the sad case of Zhao Erbao 趙二寶. By all signs, her case is used by the author as the underlying plot line that links other discrete stories into a coherent narrative. The novel opens with Erbao's brother Puzhai's 樸齋 visit to his uncle in Shanghai, followed by his visits to prostitute houses and his total degradation, financially and morally. Erbao is lured by her brother to Shanghai in the middle of the novel, and she is soon fascinated by the glittering night life of the city and the advances of playboys. As she uses up her money and feels embarrassed to go home, she and her mother, who has been with her all the time, decide to start their own business as courtesans.

One can hardly miss the naturalist quality of Erbao's story. She comes from a poor family in the countryside, and is yearning for a better life with fun and pleasure. Given her beauty and vanity, her downfall seems inevitable from the beginning. Yet throughout the story, neither she nor our narrator feels sorry for what she has become. Erbao adapts herself to the new life with no trouble; actually, in a short time, she has made herself one of the most popular figures in the courtesan world.

Nevertheless, precisely because her "success" comes too easily, Erbao is twice as susceptible as her fellow sisters to the spell of the fantastic scholar/courtesan romance. A wealthy young man from an aristocratic family, Shi Tianran 史天然, is enchanted by Erbao. He books her for the whole summer season and installs her in his villa. What follows is not difficult to guess. Before leaving for home, Shi proposes to marry Erbao as his legitimate wife, and thereafter, she closes up her business and tries to learn to become a decent lady of a noble family. Shi, of course, never comes back. Meanwhile, Erbao finds herself heavily in debt for the dowry she prepared for herself.

Erbao is described as too vain and too naïve to see her possible fate. But this does not mean that Han intends to criticize the stupidity of his heroine. Han's apathetic narratorial stance seems to indicate that the courtesans are all too human when they are deluded by the impossible dreams and virtues they of all people should have shunned, and that clichéd stories are happening and made to happen repeatedly in reality simply because they are part of the human condition.

For this reason, it is extremely suggestive that the novel ends with Zhao Erbao's awakening from a dream. In the dream, Erbao is first told

that a Mr. Lai, who has earlier destroyed her house due to her cold reception of him, is coming back to stir up more trouble. But as she hurries to
the door, she meets only messengers sent by Shi Tianran bearing tidings of
the overdue wedding. Immersed in ecstasy, she doesn't forget to caution
her mother not to mention the embarrassments and pains they have been
through. But then Erbao is reminded that Shi Tianran is actually long dead,
and with this warning, the messengers suddenly turn into monsters,
threatening to grab her and take her away.

It is at this moment of crisis that Erbao wakes up, and the novel comes
to a sudden end. The dream/nightmare lays bare the desires and fears of
Erbao, which are nevertheless motivated by and directed to the myth of the
courtesan romance both she and her readers are familiar with. An interesting dialectic can be discerned here. In the dream, Erbao has shown us her
capacity to love, suffer, and forgive — virtues celebrated by all great
romances. But in the novel's realistic context, these are virtues more
"dreamed of" than adhered to by courtesans and their patrons. Here Han
Bangqing lays bare his scheme of realism on two levels: first by letting his
girls indulge their "dreams", and then by making them take reality as a
dream. Awakening from the dream, would Erbao "come to an understanding" that dreams vaporize and vanish as fast as nightmares, and that
she might have been deceived not only by her desires but also by her
self-imposed virtues, virtues which might be vanity for her?

Both Eileen Chang and Hu Shi have high praise for Erbao's generosity
and selfless love.[16] In so doing, they have ignored the "dream"-like quality
of Erbao's virtues and therefore exposed themselves as wishful consumers
rather than critics of romantic idealization. Whereas Erbao has "wakened
up" from her dream, Chang and Hu still think that the dream should come
"true", and that a courtesan is "desirable" because she acts out "virtues"
that would have jeopardized her profession. The last paradox of *Haishang
hua liezhuan* thus is its secret, anticipatory retort to even its most sympathetic defenders, showing how easily the grounds of realism and fantasy
can be confused at every level of the courtesan romance.

Neihai hua

The third novel I am going to deal with is *Niehai hua* by Zeng Pu 曾樸
(1872–1935). We normally associate *Niehai hua* not with the courtesan
novel but with the exposé fiction or the *roman à clef*.[17] But insofar as the

novel is based on the romance at the turn of the century between the famous scholar Hong Jun 洪鈞 (1840–1893) and two courtesans, Li Airu 李靄如 and Sai Jinhua 賽金花 (1874–1936), one may look at it from the vantage point of the tradition of the courtesan novel. As a matter of fact, the "mixed" generic quality of the novel should serve as a clue, directing us to look for a dialogical tendency in its discourse.

Zeng Pu was a writer committed to revolutionary thought. He originally meant to write *Niehai hua* as a historical novel, presenting a panorama of China's political turmoils from 1870 to the eve of the Republican revolution. Instead of adopting the classical Chinese historical discourse, he consciously tried to imitate such French masterpieces as Hugo's *Les Misérables* and (selected works of) Balzac's *La Comédie humaine*. The reason for Zeng Pu's preference for foreign works is not difficult to see, since of all late-Qing novelists, he is probably the only one who knew a foreign language — in his case, French — and therefore had direct access to European literature without depending on distorted translations.[18]

Echoing the discourse of the nineteenth century European historical novel, Zeng Pu intends to relate history not as an expanded biography of princes, politicians, and generals but as an account of both important and petty events as experienced by ordinary individuals living through a certain period of time. Accordingly, in his preface to *Niehai hua*, he announces that he wants to "portray the phenomena [of late-Qing social-political dynamics], together with their profiles, backgrounds, and correlated trivial events in a photographic manner, so they will unfold vividly one scene after another, and give the readers an impression as if they were watching a live panorama of all the great events".[19]

Ironically, when Zeng Pu comes to write his ideal historical novel, his imagination is indebted to the Chinese narrative modes he wanted to denounce. How he "rewrites" conventional genres, in this case, the courtesan novel, for his own purpose will be interesting to observe. The plotline Zeng Pu uses to reflect his historical vision is the highly mythologized romance of Hong Jun and Sai Jinhua, as previously mentioned. Hong Jun (named Jin Jun 金洵 in the novel) was appointed special emissary to Russia, Germany, Holland, and Austria from 1887 to 1890. He was later dismissed because he had once allegedly bought twelve Sino-Russian maps to help him settle border disputes, but they turned out to be faulty and thus caused China to lose land to Czarist Russia. Sai Jinhua, on the other hand, acquired an international reputation — even notoriety — during the Boxer Rebellion of 1900 when she was associated with the German field marshal Count Waldersee (1832–1904), who was in command of the allied occupying forces in Beijing.

Although long denied by historians,[20] legend has it that Sai Jinhua first started an affair with Count Waldersee when she was living with Hong Jun in Europe, and that she met the Count again in 1900, and persuaded him (in bed?) to stop the allied troops' looting and other atrocities in Beijing. Taking up the legend in a manner of willing suspension of disbelief, Zeng Pu creates the courtesan Fu Caiyun 傅彩雲 as a highly dynamic character, who starts in a parlour of courtesans and ends up a national heroine. Under his pen, Fu Caiyun is never a pure, virtuous woman. Her protean social status in *Niehai hua*, including courtesan, concubine, "official" wife of Jin Jun during their stay abroad, socialite, and mistress, is deliberately parallelled in her moral resilience. Totally unscrupulous, she keeps liaisons with other men throughout her "marriage" with Jin Jun, and after his death, she manages to run away from Jin's family. An unfinished project, the novel never reaches the part of the legend where Fu Caiyun (or Sai Jinhua) and Count Waldersee are reunited; we last see her engaged in an affair with a Beijing opera singer.

Fu Caiyun, of course, does not make herself famous just by committing adultery. As Zeng Pu's narrative tells us, while in Europe, she is a woman capable of winning the favour of the German Empress Victoria and other European royal families. What is more, she even develops a friendship with the Russian Nihilist revolutionary Sara Aizenson, spending nights listening to her talk about the ideals of revolution. Compared with Jin Jun, a model (or a caricature) of the late-Qing politician, Fu Caiyun is much more resourceful in every aspect of life. Jin is an old-fashioned scholar in the guise of an "enlightened" reformer, fumbling about in the fast-changing historical course to secure his position. His mission to Europe marks the climax of his career. But because of his rigidity and incompetence in coping with foreign affairs, the mission is destined to fail. Zeng Pu obviously indicates that Jin Jun is as much a cuckold in the bedroom as he is a dupe in the office. The bedroom comedy Jin Jun and his concubine Fu Caiyun stage may well be read as a political satire, pointing to the impotence and corruption of the late-Qing court in general.

Our question is simple and clear here: can a "bad" woman like Fu Caiyun (or Sai Jinhua) be adopted as a pivot of a grand novel to which all late-Qing socio-political events are related, constituting an overall historical fresco? In response to such a question , Zeng Pu might have enjoyed playing with a moral paradox that was already embedded in the legend his novel is based on. Sai Jinhua is a decadent, promiscuous woman. But who else is better qualified for ushering us into a world in which corruption and decadence prevail as normalcy, in which people meet and part, in a promiscuous mingling of groups, trades, professions, classes? Promiscuity provides the metaphorical matrix in *Niehai hua*, linking the different worlds of politics, commerce, revolution, and foreign affairs. Sai Jinhua is the *femme fatale* who "flirts" her way through the moral and political downfall of the Qing empire, but, on the other hand, isn't she also the woman of destiny who changed the country's fate at the last minute? As China is helplessly ravished by foreign powers, it is Sai Jinhua who ventures to save her from further humiliation; and what enables Sai to win her cause is not her moral prudery but her Machiavellian tactics and her "virtue" of promiscuity.

Niehai hua thus brings to the fore one of the most controversial mythic discourses in recent Chinese (cultural) history. Rarely have we seen in classical Chinese fiction a woman character like Fu Caiyun who shuttles vigorously back and forth between the public and private spheres of a society, and demonstrates in her action a fascinating mixture of political, ethical, and sexual powers. While patriotism does not have to presuppose marital chastity, sexual transgression may work to the benefit of a country in crisis in a roundabout way! The romantic adventure of Fu Caiyun ridicules the holistic mode of Confucian teachings Chinese intellectuals held on to, and practically turns the "ultimate cause" of all sins — promiscuity or licentiousness (*yin* 淫), as the Chinese would have it — into a magical cure for national suffering. One might have fun trying to figure out whether (the fictional version of) Sai Jinhua represents the forerunner of modern Chinese feminism or just another invention of men's fantasy. Even more interesting, her characterization indicates the clash of two ideologies in Zeng Pu: the cynicism and self-mockery of an enlightened late-Qing intellectual, and the carnivalesque nonconformism of a revolutionary advocate.

A few more observations can be made as to how Zeng Pu simultaneously celebrates and parodies the conventions of the courtesan novel. He pushes to the extreme the image of a high-minded courtesan who sacrifices herself for a noble cause, but immediately deflates it by revealing the moral ambiguity of her personality and action. Zeng Pu must have cherished a secret fascination with this woman character, who ironically acts out a "liberal" spirit in the late-Qing period. Even so, there are moments of uneasiness in Zeng Pu's toying with the discourse of the courtesan novel in a new political and historical context. With her mercurial adaptability and inexhaustible energy, Fu Caiyun could appear to be a formidable character, threatening to laugh away not only the old moral/political canons but also the new, "revolutionary" ones yet to be established. She releases forces which run beyond the author's presumably omnipotent control. Though entertaining a secret preference for the character, Zeng Pu must have felt obliged to either rectify or justify her ruthless potential, and, not without good reason, he turns to the convention of the courtesan romance for inspiration.

Therefore Zeng Pu takes pains to indicate that, beneath the story of Fu Caiyun, there lies another courtesan romance long ignored. We are told in the novel's beginning that the affair between Fu Caiyun and Jin Jun does not happen by chance but is pre-ordained in terms of karmic retribution and redemption.[21] Jin Jun had an affair with another courtesan, Liang Xinyan 梁新燕 (reportedly named Li Airu in reality), in his student days. Liang supported Jin and in return, he promised to marry her if he passed the civil service exam. When Jin did pass the exam but failed to keep his promise, the disappointed girl hanged herself. Fifteen years later, when Jin first meets Fu Caiyun, there is at once a strange mutual attraction between the two, and when he notices a red mark around her neck which Fu Caiyun tells him she has had since birth, Jin Jun realizes that she is the reincarnation of his former love.

The romance between Jin Jun and Liang Xinyan sounds admittedly clichéd, but as a pretext for the legend of Fu Caiyun (or Sai Jinhua), it takes on another dimension. The character of Fu Caiyun can now be seen not only as a licentious coquette but also as a moral agent, sent by Fate to take vengeance on Jin Jun for his unfaithfulness. Her promiscuity is her weapon of punishment. Zeng Pu never seems bothered by this double vision that he applies to Fu Caiyun. The most striking example is the death scene of Jin Jun. In chapter 24 of the novel, we learn that Jin Jun's illness is mainly caused by his shame at being cheated in settling the long dispute over the delineation of the Sino-Russian border. But when he is dying, to his greatest horror, he sees the ghost of the betrayed courtesan waiting to take him away. Jin Jun's death is thus shown as caused both by his incompetence in dealing with foreign affairs, in which he is only tangentially involved, and by his infidelity, for which he must be punished.

By introducing the romance of Liang Xinyan, Zeng Pu may satisfy those readers who are bothered by the fact that Fu Caiyun, unlike other

femme fatales of classical Chinese fiction, is never condemned throughout
the novel. But because of this, he makes Fu Caiyun even more complicated
a character, in that she and her previous incarnation Liang Xinyan embody
old and new morals and values which are contradictory, and in that they
are intertwined with each other in such a way as to cast doubt on the
fundamental historical scheme of the novel.

Deeply influenced by nineteenth century European historiography,
Zeng Pu is inclined to see history as a linear, progressive development, full
of changes and struggles. Individuals are hurled into the tremendous flux
of changing trends and their fates are forged by it. No one can go untouched by external influences, for good or for bad. Correspondingly, a
new moral standard is expected of our judgments of success or failure. In
this sense, Fu Caiyun deserves to be the "flower" of her time, as indicated
by the novel's title, since she thrives at a historical moment when all order
is disintegrating in anticipation of impending changes.

But the insertion of the romance of Jin Jun and Liang Xinyan invokes
a contradictory historiography. Insofar as the character Fu Caiyun is made
as she is to punish Jin Yun's heartlessness, one can say that Zeng Pu is
writing to bracket history within a pre-determined moral mechanism. We
can infer this tendency even from the novel's title, *Niehai hua*, because in
its Chinese original the word "sin" (*nie* 孽) has a strong Buddhist implication of samsara, or spiritual transmigration, pointing not only to the "sin"
itself but also to its predetermined cause and inevitable punishment. Thus
Zeng Pu's progressive, revolutionary vision is strangely qualified by a
non-progressive, almost cyclical mode of moral retribution. Fu Caiyun is a
free spirit who transcends contemporary moral and sexual bondage; yet
she is also not a free-willed individual, as her personality and deeds are
conditioned by the sins and debts of her previous life.

The late Průšek once complained that "the main weakness of *Niehai
hua* is the great disparity we feel between two unharmonized elements.
The romantic story of an exceptional couple ... goes ill with descriptions
of patriotic Japanese Gangsters and fanatic Annamese 'black flags' ".[22] Hu
Shi holds a similar view.[23] But this structural disparity may well also open
up a new horizon for writers on history and politics. As I see it, Zeng Pu's
most important achievement lies exactly in that he rewrites the two courtesan romances and interweaves them with ongoing historical issues, thus
mingling national and personal concerns, and equating the moral system
of politics with that of romance. He makes Fu Caiyun one of the most
unforgetable courtesan characters in classical Chinese fiction. It is her

movement up and down social levels that tentatively focalizes and gives meaning to the scattered socio-political events of the late-Qing period; and it is her changeable character that makes her swim within and over the streams of her time, to the point that she seems even to outdistance her creator.

Conclusion

In my reading of the three courtesan novels, I have tried to show that the "paradox" of virtue does not just stem from clashes between moral and ethical codes which characters enact in a mimetic situation; I have tried to demonstrate how paradox arises as the novels are situated in the intertextual network of sentimental-erotic discourse. In other words, I intended to problematize the conventions developed by the courtesan romance, the rhetoric codes that lead one to appreciate or reject a courtesan romance, and the general cultural motivations for the reading and writing of the courtesan novel.

Accordingly, I find that *Pinhua baojian* establishes itself as the pioneer of late-Qing courtesan novel only in the most ironic manner. Borrowing romantic clichés to describe the virtues of love and fidelity among male courtesans and their patrons, the novel is nevertheless just as much about men as about women. The displacement of gender and gender-oriented rhetoric paradoxically calls attention to the absence of woman: it exposes how "woman" has been treated as an idealized object of a male-centred fantasy on the one hand, and as a subordinate social "position" which can be filled even by man on the other.

Haishang hua liezhuan reverses the image of the conventional courtesan romance not so much by denying wishful readers formulaic characters and themes as by exposing courtesan life itself as a complicated mixture of "romance" and reality. Moreover, in contrast to most courtesan novels which embellish their stories with noble causes, *Haishang hua liezhuan* offers not a simplified agenda of virtue but a dialectic of virtue. Due to its writer's persistent inquiry into the twists and turns of the sport of love, the novel manages to locate virtues in the most impossible situations and, at its most sophisticated moments, reveal the interchangeable relation between virtue and desire, dream and reality.

Niehai hua proposes to evaluate national vicissitudes in terms of the ups and downs of a courtesan's life. Writing a courtesan romance as if it were a historical novel or vice versa, Zeng Pu's is an ambitious task that turns upside down the familiar moral and ethical bearings of the fictional. In addition, thanks to Zeng Pu's elaboration, the legend of Sai Jinhua has become one of the most peculiar turn-of-the-century cultural myths, embodying the sexual and political fantasies (and fears?) of a generation of Chinese people.

Thus, the three novels approach the questionable definition of virtue from three different angles: the clash between male and female sexual roles, the dialogue between realism and romance, virtue and desire, and the confrontation (and confusion) of public and private domains. The courtesan novel has been regarded as a weaker part of late-Qing fiction. But as my discussion of the three courtesan romances has shown, "depravity fiction" may contain hidden "virtues".

Notes

1. Yang Xianyi and Gladys Yang translate the term "*xiaxie xiaoshuo*" as "novels about prostitution". See Lu Xun, *A Brief History of Chinese Fiction*, translated by Yang Xianyi and Gladys Yang (Beijing: Foreign Language Press, 1976), p. 319.

2. Ibid.

3. C. T. Hsia, "Hsu Chen-ya's *Yu-li hun*: An Essay in Literary History and Criticism", in *Chinese Middlebrow Fiction: From the Ch'ing and Early Republican Eras*, edited by Liu Ts'un-yan (Hong Kong: The Chinese University Press, 1984), p. 201.

4. Stephen Cheng, "*Flowers of Shanghai* and the Late Ch'ing Courtesan Novel", unpublished dissertation, Harvard University, 1979, pp. 14–15.

5. Lu Xun, p. 323; Cheng, p. 10.

6. Zhao Jingchen, "*Pinhua baojian* kaozheng 品花寶鑑考證, in *Pinhua baojian* by Chen Sen (Taipei: Guangya shuju, 1984), pp. 762–764.

7. Hsia, p. 214.

8. Cheng, p. 10.

9. Patrick Hanan, *The Chinese Vernacular Story* (Cambridge: Harvard University Press, 1981), p. 175; also see Hanan, *The Invention of Li Yu* (Cambridge: Harvard University Press, 1988), pp. 97–98.

10. For the activities of male courtesans and prostitutes in the late-Ming and Qing Dynasties, see, for example, Jonathan D. Spence, *The Memory Palace of Matteo Ricci* (New York: Viking, 1984), pp. 201–231; Kong Lingjing 孔另境, "*Pinhua baojian* shiliao" 品花寶鑑史料, in *Pinhua baojian*, pp. 769–774, Chai

Sang 柴桑, "Jingshi ouji京師偶集", in *Beijing lishi fengtu congshu*北京歷史風土叢書(Taipei: Guanwen, 1969), pp. 30–32.

11. See, for example, Michel Foucault, *The History of Sexuality*, I, translated by Robert Hurley (New York: Vintage, 1980).

12. Lu Xun, *Zhongguo xiaoshuo shilüe*, pp. 279–283; Hu Shi, preface to the Yadong edition of *Haishang hua liezhuan*, reprinted in *Haishang hua* (Taipei: Guangya shuju, 1984), pp. 1–22; Liu Dajie, *Zhongguo xiaoshuo fadashi* 中國小說發達史 (Hong Kong: Guwen shuju, 1974), pp. 256–258; Zhao Jingchen, *Xiaoshuo xiqu xin kao* 小説戲曲新考 (Shanghai: Shijie shuju, 1943), pp. 81–84; A Ying, *Wan Qing xiaoshuo shi* 晚清小説史(Hong Kong: Zhonghua shuju, 1973), p. 172; Meng Yao, *Zhongguo xiaoshuo shi* 中國小説史 (Taipei: Zhuanji wenxue, 1980), pp. 666–670; Stephen Cheng, "*Flowers of Shanghai* and the Late-Ch'ing Courtesan Novel"; Zhang Ailing (Eileen Chang), *Zhangkan* 張看 (Taipei: Crown Press, 1979), pp. 177–178.

13. Eileen Chang's annotated translation of *Haishang hua* is published by Crown Press (Taipei, 1983).

14. Eileen Chang, *Zhangkan*, ibid.

15. Hu Shi, preface to the Yadong edition of *Haishang hua liezhuan*, p. 8. Zhang Ailing (Eileen Chang), *Honglou mengyan* 紅樓夢魘 (Taipei: Crown Press, 1977), p. 9, and her afterword to the Mandarin version of *Haishang hua*, pp. 591–608.

16. See Hu Shi's introduction to *Haishang hua*, p. 8; Eileen Chang's afterword to the Mandarin version of *Haishang hua*, p. 599.

17. For example, in his *A Brief History of Chinese Fiction*, Lu Xun classifies *Niehai hua* as an exposé, p. 326.

18. See Zeng Pu's letter to Hu Shi, appendix II, *Niehai hua* (Taipei: Shijie shuju, 1960), pp. 18–19. It has been noted, however, that the comparison between Zeng Pu's novel and his French models cannot be pushed too far, since he basically writes within the discursive framework of classical Chinese fiction. See Peter Li, "The Dramatic Structure of *Niehai hua*", in *The Chinese Novel at the Turn of the Century*, edited by Milena Dolezelova-Velingerova (Toronto: University of Toronto Press, 1980), p. 150.

19. Zeng Pu's preface to the revised edition of *Niehai hua*, p. 5.

20. See, for example, Luo Jialun's 羅家倫 discussion of the legend, app. *Niehai hua*, p. 4; also see Zhao Shuxia 趙淑俠, "Sai Jinhua yu Wadexi"賽金花與瓦德西, *Zhuanji wenxue* 傳記文學, Vol. 51, No. 6 (1987), pp. 102–106. Wei Shaochang 魏紹昌, "Guanyu Wa-Sai gongan de zhenxiang"關於瓦賽公案的真相, reprinted in *Zhuanji wenxue*, Vol. 52, No. 3 (1988), pp. 58–64.

21. Also see Peter Li's discussion, in "Tseng P'u: The Literary Journey of a Chinese Writer", unpublished dissertation, University of Chicago, 1972, pp. 169–171.

22. Jaroslav Průšek, "The Changing Role of Narrator in the Chinese Novel in the

Beginning of the Twentieth Century", in his *The Lyrical and the Epic*, edited by Leo Ou-fan Lee (Bloomington: Indiana University Press, 1980), p. 117.

23. See Zeng Pu's answer to Hu Shi's charges in his preface to *Niehai hua*, p. 2.

Index